Social Justice Education for Teachers
Paulo Freire and the Possible Dream

Edited by

Carlos Alberto Torres
Paulo Freire Institute, University of California, Los Angeles, USA

and

Pedro Noguera
New York University, USA

SENSE PUBLISHERS
ROTTERDAM / TAIPEI

A C.I.P. record for this book is available from the Library of Congress.

ISBN 978-90-7787-269-8 (paperback)
ISBN 978-90-7787-270-4 (hardback)

Published by: Sense Publishers,
P.O. Box 21858, 3001 AW Rotterdam, The Netherlands
http://www.sensepublishers.com

Printed on acid-free paper

Cover picture: 'Open minds' Oil and temple on linen by Mora Ninci. Santa Monica, Sierras de Cordoba, Argentina.

SOCIAL JUSTICE EDUCATION FOR TEACHERS

TABLE OF CONTENTS

1. Paulo Freire and Social Justice Education: An Introduction   1
Carlos Alberto Torres

2. Paulo Freire and Ivan Illich: Technology, Politics, and the
Reconstruction of Education   13
Richard Kahn and Douglas Kellner

3. Bringing Freire to the Hood: The Relevance and Potential of Freire's
Work and Ideas to Inner-City Youth   35
Pedro Antonio Noguera

4. Antonio Gramsci and Paulo Freire: Some Connections and Contrasts   51
Peter Mayo

5. The Utopian Legacy: Rousseau and Freire   69
Danilo R. Streck

6. Paulo Freire, Indigenous Knowledge and Eurocentric Critiques of
Development: Three Perspectives   81
Raymond A. Morrow

7. Reason, Emotion and Politics in the Work of Paulo Freire   101
Peter Roberts

8. Civilization of the Oppressed   119
José Eustaquio Romão

9. Freire, Apathy and the Decline of the American Left: The Future of
Utopia in the Age of Cynicism   129
Richard Van Heertum

10. Paulo Freire and the Culture of Justice and Peace: The
Perspective of Washington vs. the Perspective of Angicos   147
Moacir Gadotti

TABLE OF CONTENTS

11. Paulo Freire and the New Latin American Pedagogical Imaginings   161
Adriana Puiggrós

12. Untested Feasibility in Paulo Freire: Behind the Profile of a Dream   177
Isabel Bohorquez

13. New Ways of Transnational Regulation of Educational Policies:
Evidences and Possibilities   191
Antonio Teodoro

14. Travels in Troy with Freire: Technology as an Agent of Emancipation   205
Paulo Blikstein

CARLOS ALBERTO TORRES

PAULO FREIRE AND SOCIAL JUSTICE EDUCATION: AN INTRODUCTION

Social Justice Education: Paulo Freire and the Latin American Heritage iof Critical Pedagogy.

Paulo Freire's notions of radical change were based on a complex set of theories and philosophical, political, sociological, as well as theological orientations, which were, then in vogue and typified the spirit of the age, in Latin America; a daring, libertarian and creative spirit.

It was Herbert Marcuse[i] who suggested that the use of the term volksgeist in Hegel refers to the spirit of a nation, its history, its religion, and the level of political participation it has attained. The Latin American volksgeist in the 1960s was closely linked to the revolution and the transgression of established norms as well as creativity in critical thinking, innovation in science and technology, and political utopia.

This Latin American volksgeist was the product of rich and ancient traditions, such as many of the millenary cultures inhabiting this surly continent which make it at the same time indigenous, mestizo and European, but it also received different academic contributions from theories that sought to explain and also transform social reality.

Among these was dependency theory, established in Chilean academic circles in the 1960s with the publication of the now-classic book by Fernando Henrique Cardoso and Henzo Faletto, Dependency and Development in Latin America[ii] which spread like wildfire through the continent, articulating one of the most systematic critiques of the traditional models of economic and social development, of underdeveloped capitalism itself and, to a lesser extent, of the theories of democracy. If Dependency and Development was a seminal book, many other authors deserve mention, among them André Gunder Frank,[iii] Theotonio dos Santos,[iv] the critical work of CEPAL,[v] Pablo González Casanova,[vi] or Rodolfo Stavenhagen[vii] to name only a few of the academics of note who helped to explain Latin America's underdevelopment, exploitation and internal colonialism.

But we must not leave out the figure of the revolutionary who as much in his life as in his death symbolized the revolutionary spirit of the age, Ernesto "Ché" Guevara, whose speech in Punta del Este on August 16, 1961, in the plenary session of the Interamerican Economic and Social Council, represented a complete rejection of the North American development model exemplified by the Alliance for Progress.

As Atilio Borón recently said in an introduction to the Havana Declarations: "…who could forget the olympic stature of the delegate the island

C.A. Torres & P. Noguera (Eds.), Social Justice Education for Teachers, 1–11.

sent before that assembly, no one other than Ernesto "Ché" Guevara, a universal-historical personage, as Hegel would say, whose speech was a true masterpiece of Latin American political literature."[viii]

Along with the critiques of the models of development, a new philosophical perspective –Liberation Philosophy– was articulated in continental academies by mostly European-trained Latin American philosophers. A standout among these was the Argentinean theologian, philosopher and historian Enrique Dussel.[ix]

This philosophical model, hinging on certain phenomenological and existential analyses but incorporating Marxist perspectives, questioned notions of 'otherness' in Western rationality and sought to incorporate notions of traditional Latin American cultures as options for the articulation of a more rational and generous civilizing model than that of the ethnocentric, racist, and self-congratulatory European civilization. Without the perspective of the philosophy of liberation, and as we will see presently, of liberation education, the question of multiculturalism would be unthinkable in Latin America. Rather, it was one of the great themes that emerged at the time in a practical way as part of an eminently postcolonial way of thinking in the style of Frantz Fanon[x] and Albert Memmi,[xi] two highly influential European postcolonial thinkers of the time.

The themes of authenticity and truth as well as the debate about the proper ethos of the Latin American people, articulated many of the principles of liberation philosophy, respectful of the disciplinary tradition but seeking rupture beginning with the emotions, the traditions of struggle, social practices and cultures of the peoples of the region. This theological model centered its liturgical, canonical, theological and moral idea of 'the preferential option for the poor,' as the true zenith and origins of the religious effort of churches like the popular church or base communities. This theological option was clearly counter to the model of civilizing institutions that had existed since the Spanish and Portuguese conquests; a religious model where the churches were intimately allied to those in power, especially the armed forces and socially dominant sectors.[xii]

Finally, Paulo Freire is a representative of popular education, a model sprung from Spanish socialist and anarchist roots, propelled by the vision of mass education for the working class, transferred to Latin America as a model for the education of the downtrodden with a radical orientation and explicit, well-defined political objectives, although the term 'popular education' had been appropriated by Domingo Faustino Sarmiento at the end of the nineteenth century for public education in its infancy.[xiii]

But Latin America was not an exception. In the 1960s, in many places in the world, accepting the logic of possibility at any cost, revolutions were conceived, unimaginable inventions were created, sexual ethics were revolutionized in search of free love and peace through the emotions. Originating in the utopian and revolutionary songs of the Beatles, and especially the legacy of John Lennon with his anarchist manifesto "Imagine," education, the last bastion of conservative culture, succumbed to the utopian attacks, the social movements, the practices of the political parties and the ideas of the revolutionary thinkers.

The aforementioned four great social and/or intellectual movements that sheltered Paulo Freire's work (dependency theory, liberation philosophy, liberation theology and popular education) have Latin American roots and it is no surprise that they served as a platform for Freire, a man very sensitive to the cultural particularities which make up our identities, to articulate his ideas. He says as much in language which, although poetic, is no less incisive in Letters to Guinea-Bissau:

My Recificity explains my Pernambucality, my Pernambucality explains my Northeasterness, my Northeasterness explains my Brazilianity, my Brazilianity explains my Latin Americanism, my Latin Americanism makes me a citizen of the world. Recife is the context and origin, which has marked me, marks me and will mark me. That is why I say that you cannot understand me if you do not understand Recife, and you do not love me if you do not love Recife.[xiv]

Freire was born in Recife, capital of the State of Pernambuco and cultural capital of the Brazilian northeast, on the 19th of September 1921. After working as a teacher of Portuguese in secondary schools and as a private tutor, he is hired by SESI, a training service for workers in Pernambucan industries, as Director of Literacy, between 1947 and 1954 and then as Superintendent, until 1957. Soon after, his reputation spread and he was named Director of Culture and Recreation in the Department of Documentation and Culture of the Recife Municipality. In 1959, he competes for a professorship at the University of Recife, and the title of Doctor in Philosophy and History of Education is conferred upon him as the result of his thesis entitled "Educação e Atualidade Brasileira (Education and Today's Brazil)," recently published post-mortem.[xv] After the successes of his literacy model, especially the experience in Angicos, Rio Grande do Norte, Freire is named Director of the Commission of Popular Culture by the João Goulart government and serves less than a year, 1963-64, when the government is deposed by a military coup d'état. Freire is accused of being a subversive and imprisoned for 70 days in Recife and Olinda, he is exiled to Bolivia and leaves, soon after, for Chile where he has contacts in the Christian Democratic government of Eduardo Frei. In Chile, he finds work as an adviser for ICIRA[xvi], one of the most important projects of Frei's democratic government.

Working in Santiago, Chile, he publishes his first two books which receive enormous acceptance: Educação como a prática da liberdade (Education as the Practice of Freedom, 1967) which becomes almost mandatory reading for the continent's Catholic educators, and Pedagogia do Oprimido (Pedagogy of the Oppressed, 1968), a truly revolutionary manifesto on education which, as time goes by, is reprinted in English and sells more than half a million copies, is translated into more than thirty languages and has to be considered, along with John Dewey's Democracy and Education, one of the two most influential books of educational philosophy in the twentieth century.

In 1969, he travels to Harvard as an invited professor and, while he is there, receives information that his contract with ICIRA will not be renewed so he accepts the position of educational counselor in the World Council of Churches, whose headquarters are in Geneva, Switzerland where he lives from 1970 until his return to Brazil in 1980, when his Brazilian passport is reinstated. In 1971, he founds IDAC, the Institute for Cultural Action, together with other Brazilian exiles in Geneva, from where he becomes involved with revolutionary experiences, especially in the newly post-colonial nations of Africa.

During the time when he is working at the World Council of Churches, he becomes involved as an educational counselor with revolutionary movements in Guinea-Bissau, São Tomé e Príncipe, and Cabo Verde, writing different texts of which the most important is Cartas à Guinea-Bissau (Letters to Guinea-Bissau, 1975), perhaps, of all his books of analysis, the one most linked to Marxist thought.[xvii]

In Europe, he reinitiates the dialogue, which results in a book between Freire and Illich.[xviii] He returns to Brazil in March 1980, and is employed as a professor at the University of Campinas and, later, at the Pontifical Catholic University of São Paulo (PUC-SP) where, curiously, it takes many years to grant him a full professorship.

Paulo Freire was a founding member of the Workers Party (PT), along with Inácio "Lula" da Silva, the current President of the Republic and Moacir Gadotti, another of the founders of the PT who represented Paulo Freire in the act of signing the constitutional papers of the new party as part of a group of labor leaders and leftist intellectuals. When the PT won the São Paulo Municipal election, the mayor elect, Luiza Erundina, asked Freire to serve as Secretary of Education for the City of São Paulo.[xix] Freire accepted and remained in that position for three of the four years of his term (1989-1991), stepping down to resume his writing and world-wide conferences.

Recognized as one of the founders of critical pedagogy, Freire received more than 50 honorary PhDs and different awards. He died in São Paulo of a heart attack on May 2, 1997, not without first having left a final intellectual legacy, a small book that includes a series of meditations about ethics and the politics of teaching, *Pedagogia da autonomía,* [xx] a book that is central for the constitution of a social justice education.

THIS BOOK

This book, the result of a number of workshops held at the Paulo Freire Institute at UCLA during 2002 and 2003, traces with great detail and erudiction, by distinguished cadre of Freirean pedagogues and theoreticians, the origins and evolution of Freire's work, and its reverberation in international arenas. Some of the ethical and political connections of the work of Freire with classical pedagogues such as J. J. Rousseau are aptly analyzed by Brazilian sociologist Danilo Streck. Similarly, the connections between Freire and more contemporary theorists such as the Italian Marxist Antonio Gramsci are critically analyzed by Maltese educator Peter Mayo. In addition to key connections of Freire with thinkers in Critical Pedagogy, this book also describes in detail some of the main influences of Freire in his journey as an intellectual and adult educator in Latin America. In this regard, the chapter by Argentinean historian of education Adriana Puiggrós offers a rich contribution to understand the ways in which Freire challenged the hegemony of dominant educational positivist thought in the region. From the perspective of a teacher and psychologist working in the trenches, the poor barrios of the interior of Argentina, Isabel Bohorquez explores one of the most complex concepts of Freire, the notion of 'untested feasibility.' This concept is truly a manifest for an utopian education. However, Bohorquez works not from the lofty perspective of an academic calmly seated at her desk in the university, manipulating data or narratives, but from the trenches, in that place on Earth that to imagine a future seems to be the only recourse against nihilism.

The political implications of Freire's work for a social justice education model are highlighted in the work of Brazilian scholars, and founders of the Paulo Freire Institute in São Paulo,[xxi] Moacir Gadotti and José Eustaquio Romão. Gadotti offers a most insightful contrast between what he calls the Angicos's perspective, the place where Freire began his experiments on literacy training with peasants, and the ethics that animated the model, with the Washington's perspective, the ideal of the U.S. government of achieving worldwide hegemony, as a neo-imperial superpower. Gadotti's discussions of the international analysis of the attacks on the 11th of September, 2001 are so constrasting with most of what he have heard in this country justifying the Patriotic Act, or the seemingly continuous path to war set by the U.S. government in Washington that deserve to be seriously considered. Romão, however, takes a different approach asking if the pedagogy of the oppressed, created by Freire with a book of similar title, was referring to a civilization of the oppressed, with all the ethical, political and epistemological implications of such project. There is, however, a most serious challenge to the implications of Freire's work to social justice education in the work of Richard Van Heertum, a graduate student, Program Officer and research associate at the UCLA's Paulo Freire Institute. Van Heertum traces the decline of the American Left, and wonders about the future of utopia in an age of cynicism as well as the possibilities and limitations of Freire's analysis in such a context. On a more optimistic approach, Antonio Teodoro, who was the General Secretary and President of the Portuguese Federation of Teachers for more than two decades, and is now a Professor of the Universidade Lusófona de Humanidades e Tecnologias in Lisbon as well as a member of the Paulo Freire Institute in Portugal, offers a most illuminating European perspective on the possibilities of democratic education challenging globalization. In this vein, Peter Roberts, a noted Freirean scholar from New Zealand, explores in great detail the role of emotion and reason in the politics of social justice education grounded in Freire's theory. Paulo Blikstein, discussed the connections between technology, emancipation, and alienation in the work of Freire. Finally, and as a corollary to undertake a most serious revision of the implications of Freire's knowledge for indigenous theories of knowledge, Canadian Social Theorist Raymond Morrow, carefully outlines a critique of Eurocentric perspectives of development, showing the implications for teaching and learning, and their importance for a social justice education model.

Paulo Freire and Transformative Social Justice Learning.

Freire addresses a serious dilemma of democracy, the constitution of a democratic citizenship. Second, he has advanced in the sixties, quite early compared with the postmodernist preoccupations of the eighties, the question of diversity and border crossing in education, central tenets of transformative social justice learning. Freire taught us that domination, aggression and violence are intrinsic part of human and social life. Freire argued that few human encounters are except of one type of oppression or another; by virtue of race, ethnicity, class, and gender, people tend to be victims or perpetrators of oppression. Thus, for Freire, sexism, racism, and class exploitation are the most salient forms of domination. Yet exploitation and domination exist on other grounds including religious beliefs, political affiliation, national origin, age, size, and physical and intellectual abilities to name just a few.[xxii]

Starting from a psychology of oppression influenced by psychotherapists like Freud, Jung, Adler, Fanon and Fromm, Freire developed a pedagogy of the oppressed. In the spirit of the Enlightenment, he believed in education as a means to improve the human condition, confronting the effects of a psychology and a sociology of oppression, contributing ultimately to what Freire considered the ontological vocation of the human race: humanization. In the introduction to his highly acclaimed *Pedagogy of the Oppressed*, Freire states, "From these pages I hope it is clear my trust in the people, my faith in men and women, and my faith in the creation of a world in which it will be easier to love."[xxiii]

Freire was known as a philosopher and a theoretician of education in the critical perspective; an intellectual who never separated theory from practice. In *Politics and Education* he forcefully states that "Authoritarism is like necrophilia, while a coherent democratic project is biophilia."[xxiv] It is from this epistemological standpoint that Freire's contribution resonates as basic foundation for transformative social justice learning. The notion of democracy entails the notion of a democratic citizenship in which agents are active participants in the democratic process, able to choose their representatives as well as to monitor their performance. These are not only political but also pedagogical practices because the construction of the democratic citizen implies the construction of a pedagogic subject. Individuals are not, by nature themselves, ready to participate in politics. They have to be educated in democratic politics in a number of ways, including normative grounding, ethical behavior, knowledge of the democratic process, and technical performance. The construction of the pedagogic subject is a central conceptual problem, a dilemma of democracy.[xxv] To put it simply: democracy implies a process of participation where all are considered equal. However, education involves a process whereby the 'immature' are brought to identify with the principles and life forms of the 'mature' members of society.

Thus, the process of construction of the democratic pedagogic subject is a process of cultural nurturing, involving cultivating principles of pedagogic and democratic socialization in subjects who are neither tabula rasa in cognitive or ethical terms, nor fully equipped for the exercise of their democratic rights and obligations.[xxvi] Yet in the construction of modern polities, the constitution of a pedagogical democratic subject is predicated on grounds that are, paradoxically, a precondition but also the result of previous experiences and policies of national solidarity (including citizenship, competence-building and collaboration).[xxvii]

A second major contribution of Freire is his thesis advanced in Pedagogy *of the Oppressed,* and reiterated in countless writings, that the pedagogical subjects of the educational process are not homogeneous citizens but culturally diverse individuals. From his notion of cultural diversity, he identified the notion of crossing borders in education suggesting that there is an ethical imperative to cross borders if we attempt to educate for empowerment and not for oppression. Crossing the lines of difference is, indeed, a central dilemma of transformative social justice learning.

How can we define transformative social justice learning from a Freirean perspective? As a social, political and pedagogical practice, transformative social justice learning will take place when people reach a deeper, richer, more textured and nuanced understanding of themselves and their world. Not in vain Freire always advocated the simultaneous reading of the world and of the word. Based on a key assumption of critical theory that all social relationships involve a relationship of domination, and that language constitutes identities, transformative social justice learning, from a meaning making or symbolic perspective, is an attempt to recreate the various theoretical contexts for the examination of rituals, myths, icons, totems, symbols, and taboos in education and society, an examination of the uneasy dialectic between agency and structure, setting forward a process of transformation.

Language constitute identities. However language works through narratives and narrations, themselves the product of social constructions of individuals and institutions. Social constructions which need to be carefully inspected, both at their normative as well as at their conceptual and analytical levels. From a sociological perspective, transformative social justice learning entails an examination of systems, organizational processes, institutional dynamics, rules, mores, and regulations, including prevailing traditions and customs, that is to say, key structures which by definition reflect human interest. Though they represent the core of human interests, expressing the dynamics of wealth, power, prestige and privilege in society, these structures constrain but also enable human agency. Therefore, a model of transformative social justice learning should be based on unveiling the conditions of alienation and exploitation in society. That is, creating the basis for the understanding and comprehension of the roots of social behavior and its implications in culture and nature. This understanding could be enhanced if one considers both the theoretical contributions of Pierre Bourdieu on habitat and habitus, and how social capital impacts and is impacted by the construction of ideology in education.[xxviii] Likewise, one may resort to Basil Berstein's analysis of class, codes and controls, which offer, particularly linked to class analysis, an horizontal and a vertical modelling of social interactions in education.[xxix]

Transformative social justice learning is a teaching and learning model that calls on people to develop a process of social and individual conscientization.

A process encapsulated in the famous term of 'concientização,' popularized in the sixties in Brazil by the Bishop of Olinda and Recife Helder Camara. Paulo Freire himself adopted the notion of conscientização at some point in his work calling for a comprehensive challenge to authoritarian and banking education, but he gave up its use when he saw that it was being employed as a ruse to mask the implementation of instrumental rationality under the guise of radical education.[xxx]

Reclaiming conscientização as a method and substantive proposal for transformative social justice learning entails a model of social analysis and social change that challenges most of the basic articulating principles of capitalism, including frivolous hierarchies, inequalities and inequities. This poses an interesting contradiction in teachers' training. One may argue that a principle of social organization of schooling in capitalist society is to reproduce the conditions of production of such society, hence how could one advocate and in fact produce social change?.[xxxi]

Conscientização is not only a process of social transformation. Concientização is also an invitation to self-learning and self-transformation in its most spiritual and psychoanalytical meaning. A process in which our past may not wholly condition our present. A dynamic process which assumes that by rethinking our past, we can fundamentally gain an understanding of the formation of our own self, the roots of our present condition, and the limits as well as the possibilities of our being a self-in-the-world, reaching the 'inedito viable', that powerful concept elaborated by Freire in the sixties and developed in this book as 'untested feasibility in Bohorques' article.[xxxii]

Thus conscientização as a process of social introspection and self-reflectivity of researchers, practitioners and activists invites us to develop a permanent ethical attitude of epistemological and ethical self-vigilance. Concientização invites us to be agencies of social transformation facing potentially transformable structures. To this extent the notion of dialogue, so well developed in the Freirean opus, becomes an agonic tool of social agency, critically emblematic of its limits and possibilities.

Dialogue appears not only as a pedagogical tool, but also as a method of deconstruction of the way pedagogical and political discourses are constructed.[xxxiii] More than thirty years after Freire's main books were published,[xxxiv] the concept of dialogical education appears as a democratic tool for dealing with complex cultural conflicts in the context of unequal and combined development of Latin American education though its applicability in industrial advanced societies could be documented by many experiences.

Freire's contribution provided us with a pedagogy that expanded our perception of the world, nurtured our commitment to social transformation, illuminated our understanding of the causes and consequences of human suffering, and inspired as well an enlivened ethical and utopic pedagogy for social change. With Freire's death we were left with the memory of his gestures, his passionate voice, his prophetic face accentuated by his long white beard, and with his marvelous books of Socratic dialogue.

As an appreciation and celebration of his work, and his contributions to transformative social justice learning, I would like to quote Paulo Freire himself when he spoke at the University of San Luis, Argentina, in 1996. He remarked: "...as an educator, a politician, and a man who constantly re-thinks his educational praxis, I remain profoundly hopeful. I reject immobilization, apathy, and silence. I said in my last book, which is now being translated in Mexico, that I am not merely hopeful out of capriciousness, but because hope is an imperative of human nature. It is not possible to live in plenitude without hope. Conserve the hope.[xxxv] A mystique of hope is another fundamental principle of transformative social justice learning.

NOTES

[i] Marcuse, Herbert, Reason and revolution: Hegel and the rise of social theory New York: Humanity Books, 1999.

[ii] Fernando Henrique Cardoso and Enzo Faletto, Dependency and development in Latin America; translated by Marjory Mattingly Urquidi. Berkeley: University of California Press, 1979. For a neo-conservative critique, see Packenham, Robert A. The dependency movement: scholarship and politics in development studies. Cambridge, Mass. : Harvard University Press, 1992.

[iii] André Gunder Frank On capitalist underdevelopment. Bombay; New York: Oxford University Press, 1975; Sing C. Chew, Robert A. Denemark, editors, The underdevelopment of development: essays in honor of Andre Gunder Frank. Thousand Oaks: Sage Publications, c1996.

[iv] Theotonio dos Santos. Dependencia y cambio social. 2. ed.. Caracas: Universidad Central de Venezuela, Facultad de Ciencias Económicas y Sociales, División de Publicaciones, 1977.

[v] Comisión Económica para América Latina y el Caribe. La CEPAL en sus 50 años: notas de un seminario conmemorativo. Santiago de Chile: Naciones Unidas, CEPAL, 2000.

[vi] Pablo González Casanova. Sociología de la explotación. 2a ed. México: Siglo Veintiuno Editores, 1970, c1969.

[vii] Rodolfo Stavenhagen. Sociología y subdesarrollo. 2. ed. México: Editorial Nuestro Tiempo, 1974

[viii] Primera y Segunda Declaración de La Habana – prologue by Atilio Alberto Borón (Buenos Aires: Nuestra América, 2003, p. 5).

[ix] Born in Mendoza, Argentina in 1934, Enrique Dussel studied philosophy, history and theology in Europe. He published more than 60 books and 300 research articles. Without a doubt, he is one of the precursors of Latin American liberation theology with a vast output that crosses diverse thematic fields and specialties. His research includes a series of books on the history of the Latin American Church, philosophy, ethics and Marxism. Since emigrating from Argentina in 1975, he has resided in Mexico City where he is Professor of Philosophy at the Autonomous Metropolitan University - Iztapalapa (UAM-I) and at the National University of Mexico (UNAM). Among his recent texts are Ética de la Liberación en la edad de la globalización y la exclusión (Madrid: Trotta, 1998). His studies about the history of the church include the books: De Medellín a Puebla: una década de sangre y esperanza, 1968-1979; The Church in Latin Ameerica, 1492-1992; History and the theology of liberation: A Latin American perspective; A History of the Church in Latin America: Colonialism to Liberation (1492-1979); Ethics and the Theology of Liberation; Philosophy of Liberation; Para una ética de la liberación latinoamericana, 2 volumes (Buenos Aires: Siglo XXI, 1973) and two renown books that inspired an entire generation of radical intellectuals on the continent: América Latina: Dependencia o Liberación (Buenos Aires: Fernando García Cambeiro Editor, 1973) and El dualismo en la antropología de la Cristiandad (Buenos Aires: Editorial Guadalupe, 1974).

[x] Frantz Fanon The wretched of the earth; preface by Jean-Paul Sartre; translated by Constance Farrington. 1st Evergreen ed. New York: Grove Weidenfeld, 1991, c1963.

[xi] Albert Memmi. The colonizer and the colonized; introduction by Jean-Paul Sartre; afterword by Susan Gilson Miller; [translated by Howard Greenfeld]. Expanded ed. Boston: Beacon Press, c1991.

[xii] See Carlos Alberto Torres, The Church, Society and Hegemony. A Critical Sociology of Religion in Latin America. Westport, CT and London, England: Praeger, 1992. Foreword by Enrique Dussel, translated by R.A. Young; Carlos A. Torres Novoa, Religión, Sociología y Hegemonía. (MexicoCity: Ediciones Gernika, 1990).

[xiii] See Carlos Alberto Torres, La política de la educación no formal en América Latina (Mexico City: Siglo XXI, 1995); Carlos Alberto Torres, editor. Education and Social Change in Latin America. (Melbourne, Australia: James Nicholas Editor, 1995; Moacir Gadotti and C. A. Torres. Estado e educação popular na América Latina. (Campinas, São Paulo, Brazil: Papirus, 1992).

[xiv] Cartas a Guinea-Bissau: apuntes de una experiencia pedagógica en proceso, 7th edition (Mexico City: Siglo XXI, 1986). Cited in Peter Lownds "A Pedagogia do Mangue: Olinda, Pernambuco, 2002," paper presented at the Mid Term Conference of the Research Committee in Sociology of Education, International Sociological Association, Universidade Lusófona de Humanidades e Tecnologías, Lisbon, September 18-20, 2003.

[xv] Paulo Reglus Neves Freire. Educação & Atualidade Brasileira. (São Paulo: Cortez-Instittuo Paulo Freire, 2001—Preface by the Founders of the Paulo Freire Institute, Organization and contextualization, José Eustaquio Romão, interviews with Paulo Rosas and Cristina Heiniger Freire. Version in Spanish, Mexico City: Siglo XXI, 2001.

[xvi] El Instituto de Capacitación para la Investigación de la Reforma Agraria (The Training Institute for the Investigation of the Agrarian Reform) – translator's note.

[xvii] Moacir Gadotti, Paulo Freire. Su vida y su obra. (Bogotá: CODECAL, 1992).

[xviii] Carlos Alberto Torres et al. Freire e Illich. Xativa, Valença, Spain, CREC editions, 2004.

[xix] Carlos Alberto Torres, María Pilar O'Cadiz, and Pia Lindquist Wong. Educação e Democracia. Paulo Freire, Movimentos Sociais e Reforma Educativa (Lisbon: Edições Universitárias Lusófonas, 2002).

[xx] Published in English as Pedagogy of Freedom. Ethics, Democracy, and Civic Courage (Lahnman, Maryland: Rowman and Littlefield, 1998). In Spanish, Pedagogía de la autonomía. (Mexico City: Siglo XXI, 2000).

[xxi] The Paulo Freire Institute of São Paulo was conceived in a conversation between Paulo Freire, Moacir Gadotti and Carlos Alberto Torres in 1991, on ocassion of Freire's lectures at UCLA. The institute was organized with Freire as 'patrono' and five founding Directors, including Moacir Gadotti, José Eustaquio Romão, Walter García, Francisco Gutierrez and Carlos Alberto Torres.

[xxii] In this introduction I focus on transformative social justice learning but I am aware that this construct needs to be enriched reflecting the diversity of oppressive situations.

[xxiii] Paulo Freire, Pedagogy of the Oppressed. Montevideo, Editorial Tierra Nueva, 1972, page 19.

[xxiv] Paulo Freire, Pedagogy and Politics. Los Angeles, Latin American Center, 1998, p. 56.

[xxv] An analysis of this theme can be found in my book Democracy, Education and Multiculturalism. Dilemmas of Citizenship in a Global World. Lanhman, Maryland, Rowman and Littlefield, 1998.

[xxvi] We are thankful to Walter Feinberg for this suggestion in personal communication to the author.

[xxvii] O'Cadiz, M. P., and C. A. Torres. "Literacy, Social Movements, and Class Consciousness: Paths from Freire and the São Paulo Experience." Anthropology and Education Quarterly 25, no. 3, 1994; Torres, C. A. Pedagogia da luta. De la pedagogia do oprimido a la educação publica popular. São Paulo, Brazil: Cortes Editores and Institute Paulo Freire, 1998; Pilar O'Cadiz, Pía Linquist Wong, and Carlos Alberto Torres. Democracy and Education. Paulo Freire, ocial Movements, and Educational Reform in São Paulo. Boulder, Colorado: Westview Press, 1998.

[xxviii] See Pierre Bourdieu, La Distinction, critique sociale du jugement, Minuit, 1979. See also the 25th anniversary edition of Michael Apple, Ideology and Curriculum. New York, Routledge, 2003.

[xxix] Basil Bernstein, Class, Codes and Control (4 volumes). London, Routledge, several years.

[xxx] See Carlos Alberto Torres Torres, C. A. Education, Power and Personal Biography: Dialogues with Critical Educators. New York: Routledge, 1998.

[xxxi] Carlos Alberto Torres, "Schooling in Capitalist America: Theater of the Oppressor or the Oppressed?" In Dennis Carlson and Greg Dimitriadis (editors), Promises to Keep: Cultural Studies, Democratic Education, and Public Life. New York, Routledge, 2002, pages 263-275.

[xxxii] Jose Eustaquio Romão aptly distinguished three sociological categories associated to Freire's notion of the '*inédito viable*", *incompletude* (incompletness), *inclonclusão* (inconclusiveness), and *inacabamento* (unfinishness). "Pedagogia Sociológica ou Sociología Pedagógica." Paper presented to the Mid-Term Conference of the Research Committee of Sociology of Education, International Sociological Association, Lisbon, Universidade Lusófona de Humanidades e Tecnologias, September 18-20, 2003. See also Isabel Bohorquez in this book.

[xxxiii] See Carlos Alberto Torres and Adriana Puiggrós editors, Education in Latin America: Comparative Perspectives. Boulder, Colorado, Westview University Press, 1996.

[xxxiv] Paulo Freire, La educación como práctica de la libertad, Buenos Aires, Siglo XXI, 1978; Pedagogía del Oprimido. Buenos Aires, Siglo XXI, 1978; Carlos Alberto Torres, Estudios freireanos. Buenos Aires, Ediciones del Quirquincho, 1994.

[xxxv] Varios. El grito manso, Paulo Freire en la Universidad de San Luis. Unpublished manuscript, 1996.

RICHARD KAHN AND DOUGLAS KELLNER

PAULO FREIRE AND IVAN ILLICH: TECHNOLOGY, POLITICS AND THE RECONSTRUCTION OF EDUCATION

In her essay "The Social Importance of the Modern School," Emma Goldman (1912) considers the importance of history as a subject of education, noting that schools must "help to develop an appreciation in the child of the struggle of past generations for progress and liberty, and thereby develop a respect for every truth that aims to emancipate the human race." With this in mind, we interrogate the legacy of radical pedagogues like Paulo Freire and Ivan Illich and inquire whether their struggles still live for the students of standardized curricula, whose schools are littered with corporate advertising and products, and who are themselves either tracked into broken-down buildings lacking adequate textbooks and materials or into a cutthroat competition for admissions' placement that begins with pre-school and continues on through college.

Sadly, schools today are not regularly engaged by the emancipatory pedagogies and social movements sparked by the work of these two great mentors, perhaps the late 20th century's most important figures in the field of education due to their wide-ranging and perceptive theories linking politics and culture, capitalist economics, and human ethics to a rigorous critique of schooling. Today, as schools cuddle up to business and replace programs for literacy with a profit-friendly "computer literacy" (Aronowitz, 1985: 13), steadily moving computers from the production line to "the center of the classroom" (Apple, 1992), those who currently theorize and practice education will find Freire and Illich's philosophies of education extremely relevant to the wide range of questions that the current proliferation of technology produces for pedagogy.

Routinely, culture everywhere is becoming saturated with media, in which many aspects of myriad people's lives are mediated by technology (Stone, 2001). Technologized media themselves now constitute Western culture through and through and they have become "the primary vehicle for the distribution and dissemination of culture" (Kellner, 1995: 35). Thus, as the sociologist Manuel Castells has noted, "Politics that does not exist in the media…simply does not exist in today's democratic politics" (1999: 61). While the North American followers of Paulo Freire continue to oppose rightist mainstream educational technology policies and practices through the discourse of "critical pedagogy," it is surprising, then, that few works therein deal at length with Freire's own pedagogical relationship to new technologies. As for Illich, it has been surmised that his gadfly politics and anarchistic sentiments have so terrified educational institutions that academics have responded more or less collusively to "write him out" of ongoing discourse (Gabbard, 1993), thereby excluding him and rendering his work

C.A. Torres & P. Noguera (Eds.), Social Justice Education for Teachers, 13–34.

professionally illegitimate.[i] Consequently, this has resulted in little North American work on Illich altogether, and even less that examines the relevance of his views on technology and education for today's computer and Internet-readied classrooms.

Another reason for a gap in the literature on Freire and Illich may lie in the theoretical and political disputes in which they themselves engaged during the 1970s. Though initially close friends, political allies and colleagues – Illich in fact attempted to free Freire from jail in 1964 and he hosted Freire for two summers at the Center for Intercultural Documentation (CIDOC) in Cuernavaca, Mexico – their collaboration cooled over the ensuing decades. After Freire's Pedagogy of the Oppressed and Illich's Deschooling Society became bestsellers in the early 1970s, both became intellectual superstars and leading spokespersons for a generation of young scholars and activists who sought to combat academic privilege and revolutionize campus life post-May 1968. By the late 1970s, however, when Freire and Illich began to openly clash on ideological issues like the necessity of schooling, the role of "conscientization" in pedagogy, and Freire's connection to the World Council of Churches, respective camp lines between the two became drawn.

As Freire was championed by North American theorists like Henry Giroux, Stanley Aronowitz, and Michael Apple in the 1980s, Illich took on the role of outsider critic and maverick, much akin to his friends Paul Goodman and the "home schooling" movement theorists John Holt and Everett Reimer. More recently, neo-Illichians like John Ohlinger (1995), C.A. Bowers (2000)[ii], Dana Stuchul, Gustavo Esteva and Madhu Suri Prakash (2002) have attempted to challenge critical pedagogy's iconic status in leftist educational circles by producing strong (sometimes ad hominem) critiques of Paulo Freire and those he has influenced. However, these interventions have so far been met with little debate or rebuttal from both mainstream and critical educators. With the death of Freire in 1997, and Illich in 2002, the opportunity was sadly lost for each to break bread once again, jointly comment upon their important points of agreement and disagreement, and potentially reconstruct what are arguably two of the strongest radical traditions vis-à-vis education and technology.

For this reason, we feel that one component of a contemporary critical theory of education and technology requires a less polemical and more dialectical critique in which both the positives and negatives of Freire and Illich's theories are contextualized by present-day needs, even as the two theorists are themselves compared and contrasted for affinities and differences.[iii] Thus, in this essay we will undertake a "diagnostic critique," a dialectics of the present that "uses history to read texts and texts to read history," with the end goal of grasping alternative pedagogical practices and utopian yearnings for a reconstruction of education in the future, such that progressives will be challenged to develop pedagogies and political movements which address these challenges (Kellner, 1995: 116-117), while developing radical critiques of education proposed by Freire, Illich, and John Dewey.[iv]

Against one-sided critiques of present educational technology that are overly technophilic or technophobic, we seek to understand the present moment in education and society as marked by "objective ambiguity" (Marcuse, 1964:225). Reality should be seen as complex and contested by a variety of forces, rich with alternatives that are immediately present and yet ideologically, normatively, or otherwise blocked from achieving their full realization in their service to society (Marcuse, 1972:13). It is therefore the utopian challenge to radicalize social practices and institutions through the application of new diagnostic critical theories and alternative pedagogies such that oppressive cultural and political features are negated, even as progressive tendencies within everyday life are articulated and re-affirmed. Notably, this process has been conceptualized as "reconstruction" by progressive educators like John Dewey (1897) and revolutionaries like Antonio Gramsci, who importantly noted that "every crisis is also a moment of reconstruction" in which "the normal functioning of the old economic, social, cultural order, provides the opportunity to reorganize it in new ways" (Hall, 1987).[v] To speak of technology, politics and the reconstruction of education, then, is to historicize and critically challenge current trends in education towards using the tools at hand to create further openings for transformative and liberatory praxis.

THE POLITICS OF INFORMATION, INFOTAINMENT AND TECHNOCAPITAL

Humanity begins the 21st century by undergoing one of the most, if not the most, dramatic technological revolutions in history. As it is centered on computer, information, communication, and multimedia technologies, the resulting product of this revolution is often hailed as the beginning of a "network" or "information society" (Castells, 1996; 1999, Kellner, 2002). In the hands of its many boosters, the information society has often been represented as a sort of cyber-ecumene capable of bridging differences, weaving communion, and welcoming underdeveloped regions into a form of "global village" political economy. But through the information society's impetus towards modernization and development practices, traditional forms of social organization, culture and politics are routinely being outmoded, imploded into and hybridized with novel cultural and political modes to create a highly mediated realm of "technocapitalism" (Kellner, 1989; 2000: 300; Best & Kellner, 2001). In this respect, then, it is now clear that the digitized "one world" (Cosgrove, 2001: 263) of harmonious planetary communication brought about by the exchange of information is in many ways a myth that cloaks the seductive inequalities of what is better characterized as an "infotainment society" (Kellner, 2003a: 11-15), a globally networked economy driven by corporate forces of science, technology and a new Internet technocultural complex.

Over the last few decades, the culture industries beholden to technocapital have multiplied media spectacles[vi] throughout all manner of colonized public spheres, and spectacle itself is becoming one of the organizing principles of the economy, polity, society, and everyday life. The Internet-based economy deploys spectacle as a means of promotion, reproduction, and the circulation and selling of commodities. Media culture itself proliferates ever more technologically sophisticated spectacles to seize audiences and increase their power and profit. The forms of entertainment permeate news and information, and a tabloidized infotainment culture is increasingly popular. New multimedia that synthesize forms of radio, film, TV news and entertainment, and the mushrooming domain of cyberspace, become spectacles of technoculture, generating expanding sites of information and entertainment, while intensifying the spectacle-form of media culture.

In the United States, the nation of megaspectacle, schools have been forced to transform under the pressures wrought by ubiquitous media, technoculture and a computer industry that seeks to place a computer in every child's hands (Trend, 2001). A recent government study, A Nation Online: How Americans are Expanding Their Use of the Internet (2002), reveals that 90% of children between the ages of 5 and 17 (48 million) now use computers and that Internet use is increasing for people regardless of income, education, age, race, ethnicity, or gender. Additionally, the Public Broadcasting System's website, Digital Divide, cites figures that "98% of all US schools have computers...85% of all US public schools have computers with Internet access," and that there is a 10:1 ratio of students to computers with a 486 Pentium-class processor or higher (www.pbs.org/digitaldivide/race-interact.html). However, despite trends charting an increase of use by every demographic, Internet access in the United States remains largely stratified along lines of race, class, and level of educational attainment (Lenhart, et. al., 2003: 6-8). Schools now serve, then, as the primary places in which all manner of youth have the ability to interact with the global Internet, develop creative and technical skills like webpage design, and so acquire the necessary cultural capital to survive in a post-Fordist economy.

The Freirean educator Antonia Darder is undoubtedly correct when she calls attention to the fact that wealthy schools and districts often have greater access to computer technology and Internet access, and that the minority cultures that tend to comprise poorer schools and districts are placed in a role of having always to compete on an unequal playing field (Darder, 2002: 78). However, this critique can be overly totalizing when it downplays the opportunities for student and community agency that can also arise from newly infused-technology in schools and community centers. Further, it can miss a more complex level analysis if such critique fails to account for the way in which poor school districts sometimes capitalize upon their underserved and minority status to apply for and win state, federal and corporate technology grants. For example, the Lennox School District (in Los Angeles County), a district in which median household incomes are below the national average, unemployment is above the national average, and Spanish is the primary language spoken amongst a 97% Latino/Chicano population, has been awarded hundreds of thousands of dollars in development grants through applications to the state and federal government. Further, Lennox has "teamed" with Apple Corporation as a partner in the company's PowerSchool Information System initiative that wired the district and now provides a system in which teachers, students, administrators, and parents can all have real-time access to information about student, class, and school progress (www.apple.com/education/powerschool/profiles/lennox/).

16

We cite this example to point out the need for critical educators to integrate their theories and practices with the often contradictory and multi-faceted realities at work today in the lives of oppressed peoples. Lennox's technology initiative has unquestionably transformed its schools, providing a level of technological infusion unmatched by even the wealthy Beverly Hills School District to its north, and it has used its status as a poor, minority district toward achieving this end. Yet, the question remains as to how this technology is affecting the lives of students and families in the area for both good and ill. That Lennox's PowerSchool seeks to more closely monitor students' work and lives might trigger cause for alarm, as a post-Columbine paradigm in education points towards the use of information technologies and the psychological profiling of students to create sophisticated tools of administrative surveillance and discipline that function freely under the general claim of "security" (Lewis, 2003). As schools in Lennox have historically suffered gang-related violence, resulting in policy emphases upon disciplinary focus and increased safety measures, suspicion and a closer examination of the school district's corporate-fed information system are warranted.

In a non-formal educational context, our own work (Kahn & Kellner, 2003; 2005a; forthcoming) has demonstrated the manner in which changes in global society and technoculture are combining to mobilize transformative alternatives to mainstream media, politics, economics, and formal education itself. While also used for hegemonic ends, as well as "technological terror," surveillance, and cyber-war (Kellner 2003b), people have deployed new media technology - encompassing the Internet, computers, cell phones, digital cameras and recorders, and GPS (global positioning system) devices – to orchestrate the anti-globalization and anti-war movements, new political organizations and protests, along with novel forms of Situationist-inspired culture like "flash mobs" (Delio, 2004). Thus, we wish to underscore the important role technology has had in developing contemporary praxis. Emergent forms of Internet culture utilizing "blogs" and "wikis"[vii] are potentially involved in a radically democratic social and educational project that amounts to the mass circulation and politicization of information and culture. So-called "bloggers" have re-invigorated journalism and politics through the manifestation of an efficient grassroots media force and, in their hands, computing technology appears to be a vehicle for citizens to (at least on occasion) directly demonstrate both meaningful voice and agency in society. Thus, it is our belief that many online political and cultural projects today have an educational component as well, and are beginning to reaffirm and reconfigure what participatory and democratic global citizenship will look like in the global/local future (see Kahn & Kellner, 2005a and forthcoming).

PAULO FREIRE: PROMETHEAN PEDAGOGY

While a plethora of work in English exists that looks to Paulo Freire's work for guidance on issues of literacy, radical democracy, and critical consciousness, there has arguably been less interest in the fourth major platform of the Freirean program

– economic development through technological modernization processes. Though significant divides clearly exist between rich and poor within the advanced developed nations of the North as well, this gap in the literature of critical pedagogy undoubtedly results from the differing political and economic needs of the Southern countries in Latin America and Africa, developmental needs which Freire sought first and foremost to address. But the present age of globalized technocapitalism and media spectacle increasingly requires a dialectical understanding of how new technologies are affecting the political economy in both over and underdeveloped regions as part of a conjoined process. As Manuel Castells emphasizes, we need a critical theory that can "account for the structure of dependent societies and for the interactive effects between social structures asymmetrically located along the networks of the global economy" (1999: 55). Therefore, as Peter McLaren has noted:

> The globalization of capital, the move toward post-Fordist economic arrangements of flexible specialization, and the consolidation of neoliberal educational policies demand not only a vigorous and ongoing engagement with Freire's work, but also a reinvention of Freire in the context of current debates over information technologies and learning, global economic restructuring, and the effort to develop new modes of revolutionary struggle (2000: 15).

Notably, Freire himself echoed this sentiment in Pedagogy of the Heart, declaring that "Today's permanent and increasingly accelerated revolution of technology, the main bastion of capitalism against socialism, alters socioeconomic reality and requires a new comprehension of the facts upon which new political action must be founded" (1997: 56).

A self-professed "man of television" and "man of radio" (Gadotti, 1994: 79), Freire also believed in the "powerful role that electronically mediated culture plays in shaping identities, and the importance of the changing nature of the production of knowledge in the age of computer-based technologies" (Giroux, 2000: 153). Stating "It is not the media themselves which I criticize, but the way they are used" (Freire, 1972: 136), he should be considered a forerunner of the continually growing transdisciplinary field of critical media literacy. As early as Pedagogy of the Oppressed, Freire argued for the importance of teaching media literacy to empower individuals against manipulation and oppression, and using the most appropriate media to help teach the subject matter in question (Freire, 1972: 114-116; 1998: 123; Gadotti, 1994: 79). Hence, a re-examination of Freire's theory of education and technology is required in the context of the contemporary politics of mass and alternative media.

While Freire never developed a lengthy treatment of his views on computers and education, his work does contain a surprising degree of commentary related to the topic. Freire often employed cutting-edge media technologies as part of his system, even during his formative days as an educator in the early 1960s, and articulated his views on the politics of technology in a number of texts. Working in the tradition of Karl Marx, Freire propounded a dialectical view of technology

(Freire 1972: 157; 1997: 35; 1998: 38,92; Gadotti: 78), in which he was always cautious of technology's potential to work as an apparatus of domination and oppression (Freire in Darder, 2002: xi; Gadotti, 1994: 79), yet hopeful that it could also liberate people from the drudgery of existence, powerlessness, and inequality (Freire, 1993: 93; 1998: 82). Thus, he notes in Education for Critical Consciousness, "The answer does not lie in the rejection of the machine but in the humanization of man" (Freire, 1973: 35). In this way, Freire hoped to politicize the forces of science and technology (1996: 113), and thereby connects their popularization and democratization to a larger project of radical humanism.[viii]

Prior to the release of Pedagogy of the Oppressed in the United States, Paulo Freire was already famous in Latin America for being a radical educator whose innovative adult literacy programs made him first a Brazilian hero in 1962 and, soon thereafter, an enemy of the state who was jailed for a period and then exiled by military leaders after they took power via a coup d'etat in 1964. His infamy resulted from his coordination of "cultural circles," two-month long literacy programs that were pronouncedly successful by combining training in reading and writing with lessons in self-reflection, cultural identity and political agency. As Director of the National Literacy Programme, Freire sought to deliver rapid literacy to millions of indigent people as part of a populist turn in Brazil's governing structure, which in turn threatened elite classes (and helped cement the coup) because Brazil's constitution then barred illiterate people from participating in the political process as voters. Freire's campaign, then, was an educational venture designed to transform peasants into citizens, significantly broadening the electoral base of the jobless, landless, and working poor, while empowering them to begin to speak and demand attention for their issues.

Importantly, the Freirean cultural circle made use of slide projectors, imported from Poland at $13/unit (Freire, 1973: 53),[ix] which were used to display film slides that were the centerpiece of Freire's literacy training because of their ability to foster a collective learning environment and amplify reflective distancing (Sayers & Brown: 32-33). For the slides, Freire enlisted the well-known artist Francisco Brenand to create "codified pictures" (Freire, 1973: 47) that were designed to help peasants semantically visualize the "culture making capacities of people and their communicative capacities" (Bee, 1981: 41). Composed of ten situations that intended to reveal how peasant life is cultural (and not natural) and thus human (and not animal),[x] Freire's film slides were displayed on the walls of peasants' homes, whereupon dialogues were conducted that analyzed the slides' various pictorial elements. The pictures themselves depicted a range of pre-modern and modern technologies, as well as other cultural artifacts, and the final slide ends on a meta-cognitive note by depicting a cultural circle session in progress.
Central to Freire's method was that once individual objects had been visually identified within the pictures, the words referring to them would themselves be projected in turn, then broken down syllabically, and finally, the phonemic families of the syllables would be revealed as "pieces" (Freire, 1973: 53) by which participants could construct new terms. In this way, after members of a cultural circle realized their ability to manipulate and create modern technologies through

Brenand's pictures, they could transfer this knowledge to language itself and thereby recognize it as yet another technology available for their empowerment. Freire's intention, therefore, was to adopt technology pedagogically to demonstrate people's inherent productive and communicative abilities, as well as the possibility of their utilizing modern technologies critically and as part of a means to re-humanized ends.

Despite his early adoption of technology, Freire did not possess a naïve or technophilic attitude. To the contrary, in Education as the Practice of Freedom he is actually quite explicit about the tendency of high technology and the electronic media to domesticate and maneuver people into behaving like mass-produced idolaters of technospectacle (1973: 34). Under such conditions, Freire felt that:

> the rationality basic to science and technology disappears under the extraordinary effects of technology itself, and its place is taken by myth-making irrationalism…Technology thus ceases to be perceived by men as one of the greatest expressions of their creative power and becomes instead a species of new divinity to which they create a cult of worship (Freire, 2000: 62-63).

Reflecting upon this passage, Morrow and Torres correctly surmise that "Freire thus rejected from the outset any slavish imitation of given forms of 'modernization' driven by the unregulated capitalist exploitation of technologies" (2002: 70).

In a less well-known text, but one deserving of being more widely read, Freire treats the theme of modernized development in a particularly rigorous manner as part of a sustained critique of neo-colonialism. Chronicling his activities in Chile during the late 1960s, the book Extension or Communication sets out to address the question of whether the extension of modernized science and technology, exported to Chile (and other countries) as part of Northern agricultural development initiatives, has served more to educate or alienate the traditionally-based farming cultures of the Third World.[xi] Though he was hardly unfriendly to Western modes of science and technology, Freire here inveighs against the politics of "cultural invasion" (Freire, 1973: 117), which in his mind amount to the "imposition of one world view upon another" (Freire, 2001: 160). Cultural invasion, he notes,

> signifies that the ultimate seat of decision regarding the action of those who are invaded lies not with them but with the invaders. And when the power of decision is located outside rather than within the one who should decide, the latter has only the illusion of deciding. This is why there can be no socio-economic development in a dual, "reflex," invaded society (Freire, 2000: 161).

Rejecting "the imposition of ostensibly value-neutral technocratic solutions on peasants that do not take into account either local knowledge or the impact on the community" (Morrow & Torres, 2002: 56), Freire defended the cultural integrity of "ethnoscience" and "ethnotechnology" (Freire, 1992: 85, 227); but never in a "basist"

(84) manner.[xii] Instead, he articulated a dialectical view in which the complex situation of autonomous Third World cultural practices, imperialist and capitalist First World desires, and the promise of modernity offered by the beneficial aspects of science and technology could be understood together as part of a wholistic cultural development of radical "conscientizacao." Often misrepresented as a "consciousness raising" project, in this context, the conscientization process (Roberts, 2000: 144-45) is more properly revealed as a people's movement towards self-determination through engagement in emancipatory and critical praxis.[xiii]

Whereas agricultural and other technologies may have represented the leading-edge of a potential cultural invasion of the Third World in the 1960s, today similar debates rage around the attempt to develop a base of information and communication technologies (ICTs) throughout Latin America, Africa, and other regions of the planet. For example, the World Summit on the Information Society's 2003 Plan of Action targets that by 2015, with the help of the United Nations and the International Telecommunication Union, "all of the world's population will have access to television and radio services;" and that "half the world's inhabitants (will) have access to ICTs within their reach" (2). In Freire's own work, the myriad possibilities and problems inherent in this vision were already beginning to be delineated and a critical politics was tentatively developed.

During the early 1990s, as Secretary of Education for the city of Sao Paulo, Freire recognized that computers represented society and education's inevitable future and thus he acted decisively to commit to the infusion of computers in all of the schools under his direction. As he told Moacir Gadotti,

> we need to overcome the underdevelopment Brazil faces in relation to the First World. We haven't come to the Department of Education to watch the death of schools and education, but to push them into the future. We are preparing the third millennium, which will demand a shorter distance between the knowledge of the rich and that of the poor (Freire, 1993: 93).

Accordingly, Freire established the Central Laboratory for Educational Informatics while also investing in "televisions, video cassettes, sound machines, slide projectors, tape recorders, and 825 microcomputers" (152).

This is not to say that Paulo Freire sought to adopt computers uncritically, rather his policy was formed as a result of a political and pedagogical strategy that sought to intervene in the status quo of a multi-mediated age. Though the rhetoric surrounding computers in education is often ebullient, Freire countered that he had worries about infused-technology, fearing "that the introduction of these more sophisticated means into the educational field will, once more, work in favor of those who have and against those who have not" (Gadotti, 1994: 79). To this end, he was concerned that the science and technology of technocapitalism was increasingly producing knowledge representative only of "little groups of people, scientists" (Darder, 2002: ix). That most people, in either the First World or the Third, have neither the ability to produce a computer, nor even to manufacture or manipulate the software upon which computers run, was in his opinion anti-democratic and dangerously un-participatory.

Hence, during a debate in the late 1980s with the computer-aficionado and educational futurist Seymour Papert, Freire rejected outright Papert's claim that computer technology surely meant the death of schools. Pointedly, Freire responded by observing that for all their pedagogical value and apparent historical necessity, computers were not technologically determined to compel students to use them in a critically conscious manner (Papert, 2000). Therefore, Freire felt that all cultures which now confront an ever-evolving and expanding global media culture have a responsibility to utilize new technologies with a critical (but hopeful) curiosity, thereby remaining committed to a pedagogy that both rigorously interrogates technology's more oppressive aspects and attempts through the conscientization of technology to foster reconstruction of the social, political, economic, and cultural problems that people face.

IVAN ILLICH: EPIMETHEAN PEDAGOGY

In contemplating Paulo Freire and Ivan Illich, Carlos Alberto Torres (2004) has written of the dialectical and complementary relationship between the two theorists, noting that the analogy that comes readily to mind is of Dr. Martin Luther King and Malcolm X. Equal in merit, but often opposite in approach, the work of Freire and Illich combines to provide a form of forward and backward looking Janus-figure. Both sought radically to defend the dignity inherent in humanity's potential and to provide the possibility of a better world and social justice, but the paths by which each pedagogue traveled largely diverged. Whereas Freire sought to intervene on behalf of the poor, critically pose problems into the "facticity" of their oppression, and divert technologies and other forms of cultural capital away from those in power towards those in need, the renegade pastor/academic/ intellectual, Ivan Illich developed a less messianic method. As an alternative to Freire's Promethean politics, Illich instead promoted an Epimethean sentiment and style (Illich, 1970: 105-16) that looked to the historical past, and to the earth itself, for guidance in revealing the limits which, upon being transgressed, become counterproductive to life.[xiv]

Though famous for his notorious "deschooling" thesis, which called for the dis-establishment of the norm mandating institutionalized education, in later years Illich reconstructed his position by making it hostile to the idea of "education" in toto. Having previously realized that society's "hidden curriculum" (Illich, 1970: 74) manufactures schools in order to introject forces of domination into student bodies, Illich went on to insist that, in a highly professionalized and commoditized media culture, all aspects of life either promote themselves as educative or increasingly demand some element of training as a cost of unchecked consumption. Under such conditions, the being possessing wisdom, homo sapiens, becomes reduced to "homo educandus," the being in need of education (Illich, 1992a); and in an age when the computer becomes the "root metaphor" of existence (1992b), this reduction then becomes further processed and networked into the lost reality of "homo programmandus" (Illich, 1995; Falbel in Hoinacki & Mitcham, 2002: 133). Against this vision, Illich chose to defend "the fact that people have always known many things" (Cayley, 1992: 71) and managed to live decently even amidst conditions of hardship, when left to their own autonomous devices. Thus, Illich came to propose a negative definition of "education," as the industrialized formula: "learning under the assumption of scarcity" (71; Illich, 1992a: 165).

One need not commit to Illich's indictment of education, however, to realize that one of his enduring contributions is the manner in which he perceived the deep ideological relationships between modern institutions like schooling, the Church, factory production, medicine, the media, and transportation systems as aspects of unchecked industrial society. It is in this respect that Illich generally chose to speak of "tools," and not technology, both because it was a "simple word" (Cayley, 1992: 108) and because it was broad enough to:

> subsume into one category all rationally designed devices, be they artifacts or rules, codes or operators, and...distinguish all these planned and engineered instrumentalities from other things such as food or implements, which in a given culture are not deemed to be subject to rationalization (Illich, 1973: 22).

Therefore, for Illich, "tool" includes not only machines but any "means to an end which people plan and engineer" (Cayley, 1992: 109), such as industries and institutions.

In Illich's account, it is wrong to demonize tool-making – he was practical, dialectical, and not a technophobe - but tools do become problematical for Illich when they additionally produce "new possibilities and new expectations" that "impede the possibility of achieving the wanted end" (Tijmes in Hoinacki & Mitcham, 2002: 207-208) for which they were made. Doing so, tools turn from being "means to ends" into the ends themselves, and they thus alter the social, natural and psychological environments in which they arise (Illich, 1973: 84). By amplifying human behavior and needs beyond the limits of the natural scales that existed prior to the tools' creation, tools move from being reasonably productive and rational to paradoxically counterproductive and irrational (Illich, 1982: 15).

As Morrow and Torres (1995: 227) rightly observe, Illich's "tools" are thus related to Max Weber's concept of "instrumental rationalization," as well as variant formulations proposed by Frankfurt School members like Max Horkheimer, Theodor Adorno and Herbert Marcuse.[xv] For Weber, the process of instrumental rationalization resulted in the bureaucratization and disenchantment of existence, a sort of mechanized nullity brought about by "specialists without spirit" (Weber, 1958: 182). Likewise, Horkheimer and Adorno found it to be the irrationalism produced by culture industries bent on reifying the rational in the form of fetishized commodities; and Marcuse, in his notion of "one-dimensionality," offered that modern technology and capitalist instruments organize a society of domination in which any possible opposition becomes rationally foreclosed.

Somewhat partial to these more pessimistic views, Illich occasionally felt limited to testifying, with simplicity and silence, to contemporary horrors like nuclear terror (Illich, 1992a: 32-3) and the dehumanized cybernetic reality of "Techno-Moloch" (Illich, 1995: 237). Yet, Illich ultimately remained married to hope for "postindustrial" conditions[xvi] and so he spent much of his life in imagining and creating "convivial tools" (Illich, 1973) that can reconstruct and transform rampant technocracy and the globalization of industrialized culture which occurs under the moniker of modern development (Illich, 1971). Remarking that "Highly capitalized tools require highly capitalized men" (Illich, 1973: 66), Illich implied that it is necessary that people struggle to master their tools, lest they be mastered by them (22). For when people uncritically operate tools and invest them with unquestionable power, Illich believed that oppressive monopolies and managerialized societies can arise that constrain freedom through defining specific tools as necessary for life.

Conversely, Illich's "tools for conviviality" are appropriate and congenial alternatives to tools of domination, as convivial tools promote learning, sociality, community, "autonomous and creative intercourse among persons, and the intercourse of persons with their environment" (1973: 27). These tools work to produce a more democratic society that is "simple in means and rich in ends" (Cayley, 1992: 17) and in which individuals can freely communicate, debate, and participate throughout all manner of a cultural and political life that respects the unique "balance among stability, change and tradition" (Illich, 1973: 82). Through the idea of conviviality, Illich proposed positive norms to critique existing systems and construct sustainable options using values such as "survival, justice, and self-defined work" (1973: 13). These criteria, he felt, could guide a reconstruction of education to serve the needs of varied communities, to promote democracy and social justice, and to redefine learning and work to promote creativity, community, and an ecological balance between people and the Earth. Indeed, Illich was one of the few critics working within radical pedagogy in his period who took seriously the warnings of the environmental movement and he critically appraised industrialized society within an ecological framework that envisaged postindustrial institutions of learning, democratization, and social justice.

Illich was aware of how new tools like computers and other media technologies could themselves either enhance or distort life's balance depending upon how they are fit into a larger ecology of learning. He had a sense of computers' great promise, but was also suspicious of the new cybernetic regime of truth that seemed to him to be becoming instituted around ideas of data, networks, information, virtualization, feedback and transmission (Illich, 1992a: 177). Thus, he remarked that he was fascinated by cybernetic texts like Hofstadter's Gödel, Escher, Bach, but found them unreadable as they corresponded more to the "cut & paste" technics of word processing software than to a sequence of sentences representative of a continuous vision and inner-voice (Cayley, 1992: 249). This underscored, perhaps, his chief fear of the information society: that computer literacy was outmoding the (as he saw it) eight centuries of print literacy that had given rise to moral subjectivity and the possibility of an individual's inner life (Illich, 1992a; 1992b). Illich saw as politically dangerous, and spiritually painful, that such interior texts were being exteriorized and broadcast upon digital screens.

On the other hand, Illich was "neither a romantic, nor a luddite" and he believed "the past was a foreign country" not worth endorsing (Cayley, 1992: 188).

Nor did he believe that there was an either/or choice to be made between print and computer literacies; and so he suggested that for "anti-computer fundamentalists a trip through computerland, and some fun with controls, is a necessary ingredient for sanity in this age," as well as "a means of exorcism against the paralyzing spell the computer can cast" (Illich, 1992a: 207). Thus, Illich himself – ever the polymath – remained committed to learning and better understanding the latest developments in computing and while he personally chose to forego word processing (as well as a regular relationship to newspapers, television, and automobiles), it is important to note that he was in advance of many intellectuals by making a great many of his books, essays and lectures freely available for reading and sharing online.[xvii]

Further, while the last decade has produced a plethora of writing which cites Gilles Deleuze and Felix Guattari's concept of the "rhizome" as demonstrative of how the Internet can unlock radical possibilities in education, Illich's "learning webs" (1971: 72-104) and "tools for conviviality" (1973) even better anticipate the Internet's various social networks, blogs, wikis, chat rooms, list-servs, and compendious archives in many respects. Thus, whereas big systems of computers promote modern bureaucracy and industry for Illich, personalized computers made accessible to the public for their own ends could demonstrate how online tools might provide resources, interactivity, and communities that could help revolutionize education by enhancing autonomous modes of learning. Consequently, Illich was aware of how technologies like computers could either advance or distort pedagogy depending on how they were fit into a well-balanced ecology of learning.

RECONSTRUCTING EDUCATION WITH RADICAL PEDAGOGIES

Theorizing a democratic and multicultural reconstruction of education in the light of Freirean and Illichian critique demands that we develop theories of the multiple literacies needed to empower people in an era of expanding media, technology, and globalization (Luke, 2000; Kellner, 2002 and 2004; Kahn & Kellner, 2005b). It appears certain that technology will drive the current reconstruction of education, but we should make sure that it works to enhance democracy and empower people and not just corporations and a privileged techno-elite. Producing democratic citizens and empowering the next generation for democracy should be a major goal of the reconstruction of education in the present age. Moreover, as Freire reminds us (1972 and 1998b), critical pedagogy comprises the skills of both reading the word and reading the world. Hence, multiple literacies include not only media and computer literacies, but a diverse range of social and cultural literacies, ranging from ecoliteracy (e.g. understanding the body and environment), to economic and financial literacy, to a variety of other competencies that enable us to live well in our social worlds. Education, at its best, provides the symbolic and cultural capital that empowers people to survive and prosper in an increasingly complex and changing world and the resources to produce a more cooperative, democratic, egalitarian, and just society.

More than ever, we need philosophical reflection on the ends and purposes of educational technology, and on what we are doing and trying to achieve with it in our educational practices and institutions. In this situation, it may be instructive to return to John Dewey and see the connections between education, technology, and democracy, the need for the reconstruction of education and society, and the value of experimental pedagogy to seek solutions to the problems of education in the present day. A progressive reconstruction of education will urge that it be done in the interests of democratization, ensuring access to information and communication technologies for all, thereby helping to overcome the so-called digital divide and divisions of the haves and have-nots so that education is placed in the service of democracy and social justice (Dewey, 1997 [1916]; Freire (1972; 1998b) in light of Illich's critiques of the limitations and challenges of education in postindustrial societies. Yet, we should be more aware than Dewey, Freire, and Illich of the obduracy of the divisions of class, gender, and race, and so work self-consciously for multicultural democracy and education. This task suggests that we valorize difference and cultural specificity, as well as equality and shared universal Deweyean values such as freedom, equality, individualism, and participation.

Therefore, the project of reconstructing education will take different forms in different contexts. In the overdeveloped countries, people should be empowered to work and act in a highly technologized information economy, and should learn skills of media and computer literacy to be able to negotiate autonomously in the new social environment. Traditional skills of knowledge and critique should also be enhanced, so that people can name the system, describe and define the changing features of the new global order, and learn to engage in critical and oppositional democratic practices. This process challenges us to gain vision of how life can be, of alternatives to the present order, and of the necessity of struggle and organization to realize progressive goals. Languages of knowledge and critique must be supplemented by the discourse of hope and praxis. On the other hand, in much of the world the sheer struggle for daily existence is paramount and meeting unmet human and social needs is a high priority. As the United Nations has noted, however, education can everywhere provide the competencies and skills to improve peoples' lives, to create better societies, and a more peaceable and just planet. Moreover, as the world becomes ever more integrated globally networked technocapitalist system, gaining the multiple literacies necessary to critically use a range of technologies becomes crucially important for all.

Whether in the First or the Third World, adequately meeting the global challenges of ever-multiplying technologies raises questions about the design and reconstruction of technology itself. As Andrew Feenberg has long argued (1991, 1995, 1999), democratizing technology often requires its reconstruction and re-visioning by the different peoples whose needs it is meant to serve. Thus, within the world of computer high technology, "hackers" have redesigned technological systems and much of the Internet itself is the result of individuals contributing collective knowledge and making improvements that aid various educational, political, and cultural projects. Of course, there are often corporate and technical limitations upon computer technology's democratic design, such as the manner in which dominant programs impose their rules and aesthetics, as well as the manner in which they can alienate people based upon their cost. Still, recent movements in the direction of "open source" software and "free nets" which share programs and high-speed Internet connections freely amongst communities of users (Kahn & Kellner, 2005) imply that the struggle over technology between corporate and popular ownership is presently underway.

With this in mind, critical educators should help teach students (and should themselves learn) to become producers as well as consumers, thus helping to redesign and reconstruct the very hardware and programs of the technoculture. While the restrictions on what those without highly developed technical knowledge can do cannot simply be wished away, more creative and reconstructive uses of ICTs can be devised and implemented within limits, and the simple recognition of the restrictions facing critical educators can be important sources of debate and classwork. Still, many situations will allow for a surprising amount of participation once it is encouraged. One example, for instance, is the Information Arts and Technologies program at the University of Baltimore that involves students in every level of design operations, getting their input into what works, what does not and how learning can be improved. At the high-school level, notably, Los Angeles Latino/Chicano students recently spent two years producing a free online history game (www.tropicalamerica. com) that allows players a participatory look into the 500-year postcolonial history of El Salvador. Additionally, as discussed in a recent issue of T.H.E. Journal (Ferdig & Trammell, 2004), it is possible to have students develop their own weblogs. Such weblogs can range from personal diaries discussing what students are reading, learning, and doing in relation to coursework, to posting hyperlinks to useful Internet sites, to debate over issues being discussed in class or of current topical interests. To assist with this, there are several weblog sites (such as www.schoolblogs.com or www.blogger.com) that provide free software and webspace and there have been recent articles on how students are taking to the activity and making it a highly involved and interesting cultural forum (Nussbaum, 2004). From a Deweyean perspective, progressive education involves exactly these kinds of trial and error, concerns about participation and design and ongoing critique of methods and objectives.

In discussing new technologies and multiple literacies, then, we must constantly raise the questions: Whose interests are emergent technologies and pedagogies serving? Are they helping all social groups and individuals? Who is being excluded and why? We also need to seriously question the extent to which multiplying technologies and literacies serve simply to reproduce existing inequalities in the present, as we strategize the ways in which they might also produce conditions for a more vibrant democratic society in the future. Creating multiple literacies, therefore, must be contextual and engaged with the life-worlds of students and teachers participating in the new adventures of education. Learning involves developing abilities to interact intelligently with the environment and other people, and calls for convivial social and conversational environments. One can obviously become over-involved with technologies and thereby fail to develop even basic social skills and competencies. As Rousseau, Wollstonecraft, and

Dewey have argued, education involves developing proficiencies that enable individuals to successfully develop within their concrete environments, to learn from practice, and to be able to better interact, work, and create with other people in their own societies and cultures. In a dynamically evolving and turbulent global technoculture, multiple literacies will thusly require multicultural literacies. Communicating and interacting with different groups and individuals demands being able to understand and work with a heterogeneity of people and spaces, as well as the acquisition of confidences in a multiplicity of media that can effect more democratic forms of cultural participation (Courts, 1998; Weil, 1998).

From a policy perspective, it is the duty of the federal, state, and local governments, as well as other interested parties, to provide the necessary equipment and tools for teachers, students, and schools to cultivate these skills (Kellner & Share, 2005). Further, it is important that teachers have the opportunity themselves to develop the requisite literacies to make progressive uses of technology in their classrooms and there should be labs with support personnel who can mentor novice abilities to this effect. For recent studies have indicated that, without proper teacher training, technology itself will not adequately teach itself and may in fact be a source of frustration, thus blocking the educational goals 1desired (Rawls, 2000; Zimmerman, 2000).

Teachers and students, then, need to develop new pedagogies and modes of learning for new information and multimedia environments (Hammer & Kellner, 2000). This should involve a democratization and reconstruction of education such as was envisaged by Dewey, Freire, and Illich, in which education is seen as a dialogical, democraticizing, and experimental practice. New information technologies acting along the lines of Illich's conceptions of "webs of learning" and "tools for conviviality" (1971; 1973) encourage the sort of experimental and collaborative projects proposed by Dewey (1997 [1916]), and can also involve the more dialogical and non-authoritarian relations between students and teachers that Freire envisaged (1972; 1998b). In this respect, the re-visioning of education involves the recognition that teachers can learn from students and that often students are ahead of their teachers in a variety of technological literacies and technical abilities. Many of us have learned much of what we know of computers and new media and technologies from our students. We should also recognize the extent to which young people helped to invent the Internet and have grown up in a culture in which they may have readily cultivated technological skills from an early age.[xviii] Peer-to-peer communication among young people is thus often a highly sophisticated development and democratic pedagogies should build upon and enhance these resources and practices.

One of the challenges of contemporary education is to overcome the separation between students experiences, subjectivities, and interests rooted in the new multimedia technoculture, and the classroom situations grounded in print culture, traditional learning methods and disciplines (Luke and Luke, 2002). Already in the 1960s, Marshall McLuhan (1964) pointed to the disconnect frequently experienced by students raised on radio, television, and popular media culture when confronted with print culture materials. Today, the disengagement on the part of students is even more strikingly evidenced in the contrast between an interactive and multimedia technoculture and the traditional forms of authoritarian lecturing and problematical print materials (such as outdated textbooks). Thus, a "generational divide" is suggested that may be as meaningful as its digital counterpart.

The disconnect and divides can be overcome, however, by more actively and collaboratively bringing students into interactive classrooms, or learning situations, in which they are able to transmit their skills and knowledges to fellow students and teachers alike. Such a democratic and interactive reconstruction of education thus provides the resources for a democratic social reconstruction, as well as cultivates the new skills and literacies needed for the global media economy. So far, arguments for restructuring education mostly come from the hi-tech and corporate sectors who are primarily interested in new media and literacies for the workforce and capitalist profit. But reconstruction can serve the interests of democratization as well as the elite corporate few. Following Dewey, we should accordingly militate for education that aims at producing democratic citizens, even as it provides skills for the work place, social and cultural life.

Both Paulo Freire and Ivan Illich saw that a glaring problem with contemporary educational institutions was that they have become fixed in monomodal instruction, with homogenized lesson plans, curricula, and pedagogy, and that they neglect to address challenging political, cultural, and ecological problems. The development of convivial tools and radically democratic pedagogies can enable teachers and students to break with these models and engage in a form of Deweyean experimental education. The reconstruction of education can help to create subjects better able to negotiate the complexities of emergent modes of everyday life, labor, and culture, as contemporary life becomes ever more multi-faceted and dangerous. Supportive, dialogical and interactive social relations in critical learning situations can promote cooperation, democracy, and positive social values, as well as fulfill needs for communication, esteem, and politicized learning. Whereas modern mass education has tended to see life in a linear fashion based on print models and has developed pedagogies which have divided experience into discrete moments and behavioral bits, critical pedagogies produce skills that enable individuals to better navigate and synthesize the multiple realms and challenges of contemporary life. Deweyean education focused on problem solving, goal-seeking projects, and the courage to be experimental, while Freire developed critical problem-posing pedagogies of the oppressed aiming at social justice and progressive social transformation, while Illich offered oppositional conceptions of education and alternatives to oppressive institutions. It is exactly this sort of critical spirit and vision, which calls for the reconstruction of education along with society, that can help produce more radicalized pedagogies, tools for social and ecological justice, and utopian possibilities for a better world.

NOTES

[i] In this respect, Raymond Allan Morrow and Carlos Alberto Torres have also found Illich's disappearance from critical theories of education to be curious (Morrow & Torres, 1995: 232).

ii   Also see Bowers and Apffel-Marglin (2005).

iii   Morrow and Torres's encyclopedic *Social Theory and Education* (1995) is exceptionally notable for attempting a critical assessment of both Freire and Illich, though the context of the book's focus upon theories of cultural reproduction leaves a dialectical comparison of the two, and a close analysis of their thoughts on technology in relation to the recent growth of computing, beyond its scope.

iv   As we note further in this paper, Herbert Marcuse's theory of technology and politics undoubtedly exerted influence upon Illich, as it did for Freire, who in fact cites Marcuse in *Pedagogy of the Oppressed*. Students of Freire and Illich, then, should concern themselves with Marcuse's theories in order to better understand their generative aspects. For our take on the contributions of Marcuse to education in particular, see our studies in the special collection of articles on Marcuse and education at: http://www.wwwords.co.uk/pfie/content/pdfs/4/issue4_1.asp.

v   The concept of "rational reconstruction" offered by the critical theorist Jurgen Habermas (1984) also deserves mention, but should not be conflated with the more experiential and dialectical project of reconstruction outlined here. More so, projects of Freirean (Freire, 1997: 56; Morrow and Torres, 2002: 31; McLaren & da Silva, 1993: 69) and Illichian reconstruction (Illich, 1973) are obviously crucial, though our task here is to reconstruct them in terms of one another and contemporary needs in the context of present diverse situations in different locales.

vi   On the concept of "media spectacle" see Kellner, *Media Spectacle* (2003a); it builds upon Guy Debord's notion of the "society of the spectacle," which "describes a media and consumer society organized around the production and consumption of images, commodities, and staged events," and defines "those phenomena of media culture that embody contemporary society's basic values, serve to initiate individuals into its way of life, and dramatize its controversies and struggles, as well as its modes of conflict resolution" (2).

vii   "Blogs" are hypertextual web logs that people use for new forms of journaling, self-publishing, and media/news critique, as we discuss in detail below. It was estimated that there were some 500,000 blogs in January 2003, while six months later the estimated number claimed to between 2.4 and 2.9 million with a projection of ten million by 2005; see NITLE Blog Census (www.blogcensus.net) for current figures. For examples, see our two blogs: BlogLeft: Critical Interventions (www.gseis.ucla.edu/courses/ed253a/blogger.php) and Vegan Blog: The (Eco) Logical Weblog (www.getvegan.com/blog/ blogger.php). "Wikis" are popular new forms of collective databases and hypertextual archives. For an example, see Wikipedia (http://en.wikipedia.org/wiki/Main_Page).

viii   Note the comparison to the discussion of a radicalized Enlightenment project of education, conceived as *humanitas*, by Herbert Marcuse in his essay "The Individual in the Great Society" (2001: 77-8).

ix   Some years later, in Freire & Davis (1981), Freire placed the figure of each projector at $2.50. Considering the value of the dollar at that time, and that Freire purchased 35,000 units, this is obviously a large discrepancy in cost. Either way, one might surmise that Freire was comfortable with spending large sums of money on technology as long as it was being purchased for a progressive cause.

x   As Kahn (2003) has written, Freire's emphasis upon the dichotomy between human culture and animal nature must be understood as both an ideological tenet of Freire's radical humanism and as a reconstruction of the oppressive biases held by those in power that have historically labeled people of differing race, class, and/or gender as akin to "animals" in a "state of nature." Freire correctly perceived that in political regimes, dehumanizing people and reducing them to uncultured savages is equivalent to denying them power as part of a process of objectification. However, from a theoretical perspective Freire can be critiqued for maintaining a non-dialectical view of the relationship between humans and animals, and culture and nature.

xi   Freire's book is especially sophisticated because, though based in his practical attempts to deal with the real cultural and political problems besetting Chile at that time, Freire also speaks allegorically to the theoretical struggle between conservatives' attempt to delimit education as "*educare*" - the Latin root meaning "to cultivate" or "train" (like a plant, an animal, or a child) - and progressives' alternative vision of education as "*educere*" - meaning "to develop" that which is latent within. Thus, Freire undertakes an analysis of the modernization of agricultural practices, wondering if the extension of modern science and technology into Chile should be better understood as a literal attempt to train the Third World in First World cultivation techniques (e.g.; the way in which one trains a vine or disciplines a child), or as an attempt to help develop within the Third World its own latent abilities towards cultivating greater productivity and freedom via modern science and technology.

[xii] Freire thus presciently theorized the critical, post-colonial research methodology of "cultural interaction" (Fay: 231), which serves as the ideological basis of some notable recent ethnoscience collections (Nader; Figueroa and Harding) and the paper by Kahn (2005).

[xiii] Freirean conscientization should thus be interpreted as a form of political engagement parallel to the de-colonial, but developmental and modernization-oriented, "consciencism" formulated by the revolutionary African leader Kwame Nkrumah (1964: 70). As noted by Peter Roberts (138), Freire inherited the term "conscientizacao" from the radical Archbishop of Recife and Olinda, Dom Helder Camara – whom Illich also studied under, resulting in his introduction to Paulo Freire (Cayley: 205).

[xiv] Prometheus, the Greek titan whose name means "fore-thought," stole the element of fire from the gods to give to humankind because his brother Epimetheus (or "after-thought") was required to give traits to all the beings of the earth but, lacking fore-thought, gave them all away before he reached humanity. As a result of his theft of the divine fire, Prometheus was condemned to eternal bondage on a mountain-top where an eagle fed perpetually upon his liver. The favorite classical mythological figure of Karl Marx, through his influence Prometheus has also come to symbolize daring deeds, ingenuity and rebellion against the powers that be to improve human life. Alternatively, in the final chapter of *Deschooling Society* (1970), Illich revisits the myth and casts Prometheus as the original *homo faber* – the progenitor of the kinds of technologies and institutions that Illich believes have drowned hope in a global cult of expectation and social control. By contrast, he calls for the rebirth of "epimethean men." In Illich's depiction, Pandora was an ancient fertility goddess whose name meant "All Giver" and in marrying her Epimetheus was wedded to the Earth and its gifts. Whereas patriarchal Greek society cast Pandora as a curious female who loosed evil on the world by opening her box, Illich notes that Pandora was also the keeper of hope and he finds that her box was really a sort of Ark of sanctuary. Hence, Epimetheus was not the dull brother of Prometheus for Illich but rather the archetype of those who give and recognize gifts, care for and treasure life, and attend to preserving hope in the world.

[xv] However, their assertion that "Illich's whole theory is grounded in Marcuse's *One Dimensional Man*" (Morrow & Torres, 1995: 227) possibly obscures Illich's ability to synthesize a wide-range of philosophies of technology, as well as his own novel contributions that made him a leader in the radical, alternative, and appropriate technology movements of the 1970s. Especially important influences upon Illich's theory of technology include Murray Bookchin, Jacques Ellul, Marshall McLuhan, Walter Ong, Leopold Kohr, E.F. Schumacher, Lewis Mumford, John McKnight, and the twelfth-century monk Hugh of St. Victor.

[xvi] Such would be entirely different than found in the hyper-industrial society theorized as postindustrial by someone like Daniel Bell.

[xvii] For instance, a large collection of Illich's writing is freely available at: http://www.preservenet.com/theory/Illich.html. This is just one of the long-standing Illich archives to be found online that shares both his early and later material.

[xviii] For instance, Mosaic, Netscape and the first browsers were invented by young computer users, as were many of the first Websites, list-serves, chat rooms, and so on. A hacker culture emerged that was initially conceptualized as a reconfiguring and improving of computer systems, related to design, system and use, before the term became synonymous with theft and mischief, such as setting loose worms and viruses (see Levy, 1991). On youth and Internet subcultures, see Kahn & Kellner (2003).

BIBLIOGRAPHY

Apple, M. (1992). Is new technology part of the solution or part of the problem in education. In J. Beynon & H. Mackay (Eds.) *Technological literacy and the curriculum*. London: The Falmer Press, 105-124.

Aronowitz, S. (1985). Why should Johnny read? *The Village Voice Literary Supplement*, (May).

Bee, B. (1981). The politics of literacy. In R. Mackie (Ed.) *Literacy & revolution: The pedagogy of Paulo Freire*. New York: Continuum.

Best, S. and Kellner., D. (2001). *The postmodern adventure: Science, technology, and cultural studies at the third millennium*. New York and London: Guilford Press and Routledge.

Bowers, C. A. (2000). *Let them eat data: How computers affect education, cultural diversity, and the prospects of ecological sustainability*. Athens, Georgia: University of Georgia Press.

Bowers, C. A. and F. Apffel-Marglin (Eds.) (2005). *Rethinking Freire: Globalization and the environmental crisis*. Hillsdale, New Jersey: Lawrence Erlbaum.

Castells, M. (1996). *The information age: Economy, society and culture vol.I: The rise of the network society*. Cambridge: Massachussetts. Blackwell Publishers.

Castells, M. (1999). Flows, networks, identities: A critical theory of the information society" in M. Castells, R. Flecha, P. Freire, H.A. Giroux, D. Macedo, & P. Willis (Eds.) *Critical education in the new information age*, Lanham, Maryland: Rowman & Littlefield.

Cayley, D. (1992). *Ivan Illich in conversation*. Concord, Ontario: House of Anansi Press.

Cosgrove, D. (2001). *Apollo's eye: A cartographic genealogy of the Earth in the western imagination*. Baltimore, Maryland: Johns Hopkins University Press.

Courts, P. L. (1998). *Multicultural literacies: dialect, discourses, and diversity*. New York: Peter Lang.

Darder, A. (2002). *Reinventing Paulo Freire: A pedagogy of love*. Boulder, Colorado: Westview Press.

Delio, M. (2004). Global chaos, just for fun. *Wired News*, (June 17). Online at: http://www.wired.com/news/culture/0,1284,63872,00.html.

Dewey, J. (1897). My pedagogic creed. *The school journal, 54*, 3.

Dewey, J. (1997 [1916]). *Democracy and education*. New York: Free Press.

Feenberg, A. (1991). *Critical theory of technology*. New York: Oxford University Press.

Feenberg, A. (1995). *Alternative modernity*. Los Angeles, California: University of California Press, 144–66.

Feenberg, A. (1999). *Questioning technology*. New York: Routledge.

Ferdig, R. F. & Trammell, D. K. (2004). Content delivery in the 'blogsphere' *T.H.E. Journal*, (February), 12-20.

Figueroa, R. & Harding, S. (2003). *Science and other cultures: Issues in philosophies of science and technology*. New York: Routledge.

Freire, P. (1972). *Pedagogy of the oppressed*. New York: Herder and Herder.

Freire, P. (1973). *Education for critical consciousness*. New York: Continuum.

Freire, P. (1992). *Pedagogy of hope: Reliving the pedagogy of the oppressed*. New York: Continuum.

Freire, P. (1993). *Pedagogy of the city*. New York: Continuum.

Freire, P. (1996). *Letters to cristina: Reflections on my life and work*. New York: Routledge.

Freire, P. (1997). *Pedagogy of the heart*. New York: Continuum.

Freire, P. (1998). *Pedagogy of freedom: Ethics, democracy and civic courage*. Lanham, Maryland: Rowman & Littlefield.

Freire, P. (1998b). *A Paulo Freire reader*. New York: Herder and Herder.

Freire, P. (2000). *Cultural action for freedom*. Cambridge, Massachussetts: Harvard Educational Review.

Freire, P. (2001). *Pedagogy of the oppressed*. New York: Continuum.

Freire, P. & Davis, R. (1981). Education for awareness: A talk with Paulo Freire. In R. Mackie (Ed.) *Literacy & revolution: The pedagogy of Paulo Freire*. New York: Continuum.

Gabbard, D. A. (1993). *Silencing Ivan Illich: A foucauldian analysis of intellectual exclusion*. Lanham, Maryland: Rowman & Littlefield.

Gadotti, M. (1994). *Reading Paulo Freire*. Albany, New York: State University of New York Press.

Giroux, H. (2000). *Stealing innocence: Corporate culture's war on youth*. New York: Palgrave.

Goldman, E. (1912). The social importance of the modern school. Emma Goldman Papers. Rare Books and Manuscripts Division, New York Public Library.

Habermas, J. (1984). *The theory of communicative action, vol 1: Reason and the rationalization of society*. Boston, Massachussetts: Beacon Press.

Hall, S. (1987). Gramsci and us. *Marxism Today*, (June), 19.

Hammer, R. & Kellner, D. (2001). Multimedia pedagogy and multicultural education for the new millennium. *Current Issues in Education, 4* (2). Online at: http://cie.ed.asu.edu/volume4/number2/.

Hoinacki, L. & Mitcham, C. (Eds.) (2002). *The challenges of Ivan Illich: A collective reflection*. Albany, New York: State University of New York Press.

Illich, I. (1970). *Deschooling society*. New York: Marion Boyers Press.

Illich, I. (1971). *Celebration of awareness*. London: Marion Boyars.

Illich, I. (1973). *Tools for conviviality*. New York: Harper and Row.

Illich, I. (1981). *Shadow work*. London: Marion Boyars.

Illich, I. (1982). *Gender*. New York: Pantheon.

Illich, I. (1992a). *In the mirror of the past: Lectures and addresses 1978-1990*. London: Marion Boyars.

Illich, I. (1992b). *In the vineyard of the text: A commentary to Hugh's didasacalicon*. Chicago: University of Chicago Press.

Illich, I. (1995). Statements by Jacques Ellul and Ivan Illich. *Technology in Society*, 17(2), 231-38.

Kahn, R. (2003). Paulo Freire and eco-justice: Updating pedagogy of the oppressed for the age of ecological calamity. *Freire Online Journal*, 1(1). Online at: http://www.paulofreireinstitute.org/ freireonline/volume1/1kahn1.html.

Kahn, R. (2005). Know sweat: Defending an indigenous practice as scientific research. In B. Kozuh, A. Kozlowska, & R. Kahn (Eds) *The role of theories, facts and interpretation in educational research*. Los Angeles, California and Warsaw, Poland: Rodn "WOM" Publishers

Kahn, R. & Kellner, D. (2003). Internet subcultures and oppositional politics. In D. Muggleton (Ed.) *The post-subcultures reader*. London: Berg Publishers.

Kahn, R. (2005a). Oppositional politics and the Internet: A critical/reconstructive approach. *Cultural Politics*, 1(1). Londong: Berg Publishers.

Kahn, R. (2005b). Reconstructing technoliteracy: A multiple literacies approach. *E-Learning*, 2(3). Online at: http://www.wwwords.co.uk/pdf/validate.asp?j=elea&vol=2&issue=3&year=2005&article=4_Kahn_ELEA_2_3_web.

Kahn, R. (forthcoming). Technopolitics, blogs, and emergent media ecologies: A critical/reconstructive approach. *Emerging small tech: Technologies at the intersections of cyberculture and new media*. In B. Hawk (Ed.) Minneapolis, Minnesota: University of Minnesota Press.

Kellner, D. (1989). *Critical theory, marxism and modernity*. Baltimore, Maryland: Johns Hopkins University Press.

Kellner, D. (1995). *Media culture: Identity and politics between the modern and the postmodern*. New York: Routledge.

Kellner, D. (2000). Globalization and new social movements: Lessons for critical theory and pedagogy. In N. Burbules & C.A. Torres (Eds.) *Globalization and education: Critical perspectives*. New York: Routledge.

Kellner, D. (2002). Theorizing globalization. *Sociological Theory*, 20(3), 285-305.

Kellner, D. (2003a). *Media spectacle*. London and New York: Routledge.

Kellner, D. (2003b). *From 9/11 to terror war: The dangers of the Bush legacy*. Lanham, Maryland: Rowman & Littlefield.

Kellner, D. (2003c). Toward a critical theory of education. *Democracy & Nature*, 9(1), 51-64.

Kellner, D. (2004) Technological transformation, multiple literacies, and the re-visioning of education. *E-Learning*, 1(1), 9-37.

Kellner, D. & Share, J. (2005) Toward critical media literacy: Core concepts, debates, organization, and policy. *Discourse: studies in the cultural politics of education*, 26(3), 369-386.

Lenhart, A., Horrigan, J., Rainie, L., Allen, K., Boyce, A., Madden, M, & O'Grady, E. (2003). *The ever-shifting Internet population: A new look at Internet access and the digital divide*. The Pew Internet & American Life Project at: http://www.pewinternet.org/pdfs/ PIP_Shifting_Net_Pop_Report.pdf.

Lewis, T. (2003). The surveillance economy of post-columbine schools. *The Review of Education, Pedagogy & Cultural Studies*, 25(4), 335-356.

Luke, C. (2000). Cyber-schooling and technological change: Multiliteracies for new times. In B. Cope & M. Kalantzis (Eds.) *Multiliteracies: Literacy, Learning, and the Design of Social Futures*. Australia: Macmillan, 69–105.

Luke, A. & Luke, C. (2002). Adolescence lost/childhood regained: On early intervention and the emergence of the techno-subject. *Journal of Early Childhood Literacy*, 1(1), 91-120.

Marcuse, H. (1964). *One-dimensional man*. Boston, Massachussetts: Beacon Press.

Marcuse, H. (1972). *An essay on liberation*. Harmondsworth, Pennsylvania: Penguin.

Marcuse, H. (2001). The individual in the great society. In D. Kellner (Ed.) *Towards a critical theory of society*. New York and London: Routledge.

McLaren, P. (2000). Paulo Freire's pedagogy of possibility. In S. F. Steiner, H. M. Krank, P. McLaren, R. E. Bahruth (Eds.) *Freirean Pedagogy, Praxis, and Possibilities: Projects for the New Millennium*. New York: Taylor & Francis.

McLaren, P. & da Silva, T.T. (1993). Decentering pedagogy: Critical literacy, resistance and the politics of memory. In P. McLaren & P. Leonard (Eds.) *Paulo Freire: A critical encounter*. New York: Taylor & Francis.

McLuhan, M. (1964). *Understanding media: The extensions of man*. New York: Signet Books.

Morrow, R. A. & Torres, C. A. (1995). *Social theory and education: A critique of theories of social and cultural reproduction*. Albany, New York: State University of New York Press.

Morrow, R. A. & Torres, C. A. (2002). *Reading Freire and Habermas: Critical pedagogy and transformative social change*. New York: Teachers College Press.
Nader, L. (1996). *Naked science: Anthropological inquiries into boundaries, power, and knowledge*. New York: Routledge.
National Telecommunications & Information Administration. (2002). *A nation online: How americans are expanding their use of the Internet*. Online at: http://www.ntia.doc.gov/ntiahome/dn/nationonline_020502.htm.
Nkrumah, K. (1964). *Consciencism: Philosophy and ideology for decolonization*. New York: Monthly Review Press.
Nussbaum, E. (2004). My so-called blog. *New York Times*, (January 11), D1.
Ohlinger, J. (1995). Critical views of Paulo Freire's work. Online at: http://www3.nl.edu/academics/cas/ace/ resources/JohnOhliger_Insight1.cfm.
Papert, S. (2000). The future of school. Online at: http://www.papert.org/articles/freire/ freirePart1.html.
Rawls, J. J. (2000). *The role of micropolitics in school-site technology efforts: A case study of the relationship between teachers and the technology movement at their school*. Ph.D. Dissertation, UCLA.
Roberts, P. (2000). *Education, literacy, and humanization: Exploring the work of Paulo Freire*. Westport, Connecticut: Bergin & Garvey.
Sayers, D. & Brown, K. (1993). Freire, Freinet and "distancing": Forerunners of technology-mediated critical pedagogy. *NABE News*, 17(3).
Stone, A. R. (2001). Will the real body please stand up?: Boundary stories about virtual cultures. In D. Trend (Ed.), Reading digital culture. *Cambridge: Massachussetts. Blackwell Publishers.*
Stuchul, D. L., Esteva, G & Prakash, M. S. (2002). From a pedagogy of liberation to liberation from pedagogy. Online at: http://www.swaraj.org/shikshantar/ gustavo2ls3.htm.
Torres, C. A. (2004). Els mons distorsionats de Paulo Freire i Ivan Illich. *diàleg: Paulo Freire i Ivan Illich*. Xàtiva: Centre de Recursos i Educació Continua.
Trend, D. (2001). Welcome to cyberschool: Education at the crossroads in the information age. *Lanham, Maryland: Rowman & Littlefield.*
Weber, M. (1958). *The protestant ethic and the spirit of capitalism*. New York: Charles Scribner's Sons.
Weil, D. K. (1998). *Toward a critical multicultural literacy*. New York: Peter Lang.
World Summit on the Information Society. (2003). *Plan of action*. Document WSIS-03/GENEVA/DOC/5-E (December 12). Online at: http://www.itu.int/wsis/.
Zimmerman, R. (2000). *The intersection of technology and teachers: Challenges and problems*. Ph.D Dissertation, UCLA.

Richard Kahn
Graduate School of Education & Information Studies
University of California, Los Angeles

Douglas Kellner
Graduate School of Education & Information Studies
University of California, Los Angeles

PEDRO A. NOGUERA

BRINGIN' FREIRE TO THE HOOD: THE RELEVANCE AND POTENTIAL OF FREIRE'S WORK AND IDEAS TO INNER-CITY YOUTH

Paulo Freire's work has had an enormous influence upon educators, social scientists and activists throughout the world. The appeal of Freire's major books – The Pedagogy of the Oppressed (1970), Education for Critical Consciousness (1973), Education as the Practice of Freedom (1969), to name just a few, is based to a large degree upon its unique approach to addressing the plight of the marginalized and oppressed, and the uneven distribution of power, wealth and status in the world.

Through his writing and his work Freire advanced a distinct approach to the process through which oppression and exploitation could be challenged and subverted and changes in social relations and material conditions could be achieved. It is vision rooted in a belief that genuine transformations in the structure of society are only possible when those who have historically been marginalized and rendered powerless are able to participate as independent, self-conscious agents capable of critically analysing the conditions that constrain their lives and acting upon those constraints with creativity and resolve. More importantly, because Freire, recognized that the condition of oppression is not only material and structural in nature, but also contains important psychological and cultural dimensions, he reasoned that the systematic oppression of human beings could only be countered through deliberate actions taken by the oppressed to eliminate the condition of oppression. On this point Freire writes: "The liberation of the oppressed is a liberation of men (and women), not things. Accordingly, while no one liberates him/her self by his own efforts alone, neither is s/he liberated by others. (Freire 1970: 55)

Freire's commitment to grassroots social change, and bottom-up empowerment of the poor and powerless, and his insights into how this could be achieved has made Freire's scholarship a source of inspiration to many. In countries such as Nicaragua, Guinea-Bissau, Grenada and Mozambique, his ideas served as a guide for national literacy campaigns and a source of insight into how disenfranchised people who had long been excluded from sharing in the wealth generated by their labour and their nation's resources could be achieved. Despite the fact that much of his early work was rooted in the experience of a specific context – conditions of the poor in northeast Brazil – Freire's work has had an appeal that has transcended national boundaries and cultural orientations. Of course, this is because oppression and suffering are common and pervasive features of human experience, and such social realties that are not limited by national boundaries. Illiteracy, hunger, disease, political repression and violence are ubiquitous among poor people throughout the world, even in wealthy nations. For

C.A. Torres & P. Noguera (Eds.), Social Justice Education for Teachers, 35–50.

this reason, Freire's call for the empowerment of the poor has transcended boundaries based on language and culture and been embraced throughout the world by people seeking insights and ways to alleviate and respond to oppression.

This chapter discusses the relevance and potential of several core ideas in Paulo Freire's work to the plight of inner-city youth in North America. Throughout the United States, inner-city youth, especially African American and Latino males, are often regarded as a "problem" (West 1993); a threat to civil society and the social order and a source of unrest and disorder (Glazer and Moynihan 1963; Dilulio 2000; Patterson 2006). Though such individuals constitute a relatively small percentage of the population, they occupy a larger space in the public imagination and psyche. In popular media, inner-city youth are often portrayed in menacing and fear-provoking ways, and are generally depicted as a social grouping that is responsible for a variety of social problems, including - violence and gang warfare, drug use and drug trafficking, sexually transmitted disease and unwanted teen pregnancy, and a host of other social maladies (Garbarino 1999; Taylor-Gibbs 1988). Not surprisingly, such individuals are also regarded with fear and trepidation, and often perceived as a menace to the social order.

The most telling indication of how great the antipathy is toward inner-city youth is that more often than not, the primary response of policy makers to the problems frequently associated with inner-city youth is punitive. This is true even in cases when young people are clearly not responsible for the problems policy makers seek to solve. For example, in all fifty states, "high stakes" standardized assessments are being used to hold students "accountable" for their educational performance. However, very little has been done to insure that students have access to competent teachers, adequate learning materials or to insure that their opportunity to learn is guaranteed (Darling-Hammond 2005). Similarly, in response to fears about crime and violence, coercive policies such as curfews, police sweeps and targeted harassment are used to target inner-city youth ostensibly for the purpose of promoting safety (Davis 1994; Currie and Skolnick 1995). Even though the vast majority of the victims of crime and violence are young Black and Latino males (as are the majority of the perpetrators) (Noguera 1995; Madhabuti 1990), it is rare to find anything other than a punitive response initiated by local authorities. Several states have adopted increased criminal penalties for perpetrators of various crimes and increasingly harsh and highly restrictive incarceration practices (e.g .social isolation, denial of opportunities for education and physical recreation, etc.). Such policies have been pursued even though they have been shown to contribute to increases in recidivism and the perpetuation of criminality (Schiraldi and Zeidenberg 2001). Punitive policies continue to be directed at inner-city youth even though there is no evidence that such approaches are effective in reducing youth violence or drug dealing, raising test scores or lowering drop out rates. Undoubtedly, such practices continue to be relied upon largely because there is relatively little compassion for inner-city youth and their plight in American society.

Though it might seem obvious that inner-city youth would benefit from the kind of pedagogical approach advanced by Freire, relatively few of the North

American authors who have written about Freire and his ideas have made this connection. This is not to say that youth counsellors and educators who work with inner-city youth have not drawn inspiration from Freire and used his ideas to guide and influence their work with youth. There are several individuals and organizations that have done just that but the relative lack of writing on the relevance of Freire's ideas to the plight of inner-city youth is significant omission, one that I hope to address in the pages that follow.

BRINGING FREIRE TO THE INCARCERATED

My own thinking on how to apply Freire's ideas to the conditions affecting inner-city youth is based upon years of trying to understand and find solutions to some of the most pressing problems afflicting this constituency. My own view is that many of the problematic behaviours – interpersonal violence, drug dealing, and other forms of crime – are by-products of social and economic conditions which have rendered most inner-city communities in the United States "ghettos of hopelessness and despair" (Wacquant 2001) Eschewing the "culture of poverty" argument espoused by anthropologist Oscar Lewis (1968) and others, scholars such as Tabb (1970), Wilson (1989), and more recently Greenberg and Schnieder (1994) have effectively shown how changes related to de-industrialization, globalization and suburbanization, have contributed to the emergence of a population of permanently unemployed inner-city youth who have been drawn to crime as a result of changes in the larger political economy.

This is the constituency that I have dedicated much of my adult life to serving and understanding in a variety of contexts and settings. Most recently, during a series of visits to schools serving incarcerated youth at Rikers Island - the largest penal institution in the world - I attempted to use Freire's problem posing methods to get the young men I addressed to recognize their own capacity to free themselves from a life of institutionalization and to reject the criminality that so many of them had allowed to define and shape their identities. Based on past experience I knew that such a change in self perception would involve, at least in part, getting these young men to move beyond seeing themselves as victims of circumstance with limited options for survival, so that they might recognize their own condition as what Freire describes as a "limit situation" that can be transformed through "action upon the concrete, historical reality" (p. 90). I knew from experience that it is possible for those who have been marginalized and who have been submerged within a condition of oppression to become agents who could respond differently to their environment, to make different choices about their lives, and thereby begin to transform their circumstances. But I also knew that such changes involve a gradual process of critical awakening that typically cannot be achieved in one educational encounter. As an invited guest and educator, I knew this was my own "limit situation", and despite my realization of how little might be accomplished on my visit, I embraced the challenge anyway.

I was asked to lecture several hundred students, but in keeping with the pedagogical orientation of Freire's work, I decided to use my visit to engage in a

37

large-scale dialogue. I began my conversation with the following provocation, "There is a plan, some might call it a conspiracy, and to keep this facility filled with people like you – young Black and Latino men. A lot of jobs including those of the guards who supervise you are dependent on keeping these cells filled. There are towns in upstate New York that only able to survive because of the jobs prisons provide. My question to you is this: Are you part of the conspiracy?"

I posed the question this way even though I understood that for many of the young men I spoke to the odds that their lives might have turned out differently had been extremely low from the very beginning. The vast majority of these young men had been born into poverty in neighbourhoods like the South Bronx, Bedford Stuyvesant and Washington Heights, where poverty is concentrated and reproduced across generations, violence is rampant and normalized, good paying jobs and good schools largely non-existent, and fathers and positive adult male role models are few. In such communities, many young men make the transition from school to prison as a rite of passage into adulthood (Anderson 1990); as commonplace as a bah mitzvah or circumcision in another society or culture. Despite doomed nature of their plight, I knew that one of the keys to keeping them from following the predictable pattern of returning to prison within a couple of years[i] was getting them to recognize that they had the power to exercise some degree of control over their lives. For this to happen they would have to decide to take responsibility for their actions and change the choices they made about how to live and survive in their communities. Many would have to reject the idea that using violence to get what you want was legitimate or that taking advantage of the weak and vulnerable was justifiable. Others would have to eschew the logic of predatory capitalism, a mode of thinking in which making a dollar by any means necessary- selling drugs, stealing, extortion, etc. - is seen as an acceptable means of survival.

I knew from experience that such a transformation in consciousness is not easily made and certainly unlikely after listening to a lecture. Nonetheless, I saw my visit to Ricers as an opportunity, and I used my time to engage in a large group discussion on the "generative themes" that I knew resonate among urban youth. Speaking openly about "grinding" (a street term for drug dealing), gang banging, and hustling, I spoke directly about the world they knew to try to get them to consider that they could make different choices regarding how to act and respond to the numerous challenges and obstacles they faced. After two hours of a raucous, back and forth discussion, I knew that despite my effort, very few of the young men I met that day would embark on a different course. Reflecting on the anger, frustration and resignation I saw on their faces, I left Ricers that day deeply depressed, knowing that at most I provided some encouragement to those who were already on the path of rejecting criminality. A few of the young men approached me after our session, sharing with me their plans for improving their lives after they're pending release. I knew these were the exceptions, that for most of the young men I'd spoken to, prison would remain both their residence and their destiny. This is true both because the society in which we lived appears content with keeping large numbers of people incarcerated, despite the costs, and because many of the young men I spoke to had embraced life in prison as their fate,

One of the teachers who had sponsored my visit pulled a young man aside and asked me to speak with him. Placing her arm around his shoulder she explained: "This young man is extremely intelligent. He's good with math and a great writer. Don't you think that he could go to college one day?" Before I could respond the young man turned to me and declared, "I am a Crip for life", and with that he turned away and headed off to the holding area with the others. I knew this was both a statement about his identity and affiliation, and even more importantly, a declaration of his fate. By embracing the Crisp he was in effect accepting a way of life that would insure he would spend many years behind bars. I knew too that he, like so many others I encountered that day, had already come to believe that their future held little more than a life of crime "hustling" to get by, or a life in and out of prison.

Young men in inner-city communities across the United States understand at fairly early ages that prison may one day be where they end up, and many are not afraid (Singer 1996). In cities like Baltimore, Detroit, Oakland, Newark, St. Louis and New Orleans where 1 out of every 3 young Black men between the ages of 18 – 34 are incarcerated (only one in ten young Black men in these cities attend college), moving from school to prison is regarded as little more than a rite of passage (Gilligan 1996). For many of these young men prison no longer conjures feelings of fear and trepidation. Rather, it is regarded as a place where one goes to become respected as a man, an institution where one learns how to fight, where acquaintances with older family and friends are renewed, where health care and meals are guaranteed. Though I know from experience that for the vast majority of inmates the romanticized visions of prison they held onto during their youth fade quickly after arrival, and most would prefer to be on the outside, it is troubling to see how a "culture of incarceration" that is present in so many inner-city neighbourhoods has so profoundly shaped the mindset and outlook of so many youth. French sociologist Loic Wacquant has described the prison as the most efficient and penetrating institution ever created for the purpose of "exploiting and excluding poor Black people" (2001). In many cities, prisons and the criminal justice system have also become primary institutions in the socialization of young Black and Latino men. For these reasons, any effort to utilize education as a force for transformation in urban areas must confront the role that prisons and incarceration play in perpetuating the oppression of inner-city youth.

Despite the apparent futility of my visit to Rikers, I left there with the understanding that the problem was not my application of Freire's message. I knew from experience that more was needed for such a message to have meaning and influence. Education that leads to empowerment and transformation cannot be provided in two-hour lectures or occasional visits. I know too that it also takes more than listening to and asking a few questions of a college professor.

CRITICAL PEDAGOGY AND INNER-CITY YOUTH

Despite the frustration of my experience at Rikers, I know from other experiences that Freire's call for an educational practice that leads to critical consciousness and social transformation is indeed a powerful method for engaging inner-city youth. I have had other experiences working with young people who are confronted by dire circumstances and brutal hardships and seen the potential of such pedagogical approaches. Such experiences have convinced me that this approach can be highly effective when utilized as part of an ongoing project of work with inner-city youth. As a teacher in inner-city public schools I have seen young people who were written off as hopeless, and a menace to their communities and society, develop the capacity to exert control over their lives and become productive and positive members of their communities. Over years of teaching and working with inner-city youth in a variety of settings – schools, non-profit organizations, correctional institutions - I have come to see that Freire's problem posing approach to education can gradually transform the outlook of marginalized youth from one of desperate resignation, to one of critical awareness and pragmatic optimism. In most cases, such a transformation is based both on a rejection of fatalism and victim-hood and the acquisition of a critical consciousness about the nature of the circumstances that constrain their lives. Critical awareness must also be combined with a sense of personal resourcefulness and faith, on the part of the teacher and student, in the ability of urban youth to overcome obstacles through the cultivation of a resilient character. Resilience is essential because young people faced with a broad array of obstacles must also learn to persevere when setbacks and hardships inevitably emerge and thwart their efforts to overcome.

In fairness to those who have engaged in similar work and met nothing more than frustration and failure, I must point out that my recognition of the value of Freire's ideas to inner-city youth is not based upon a romanticized view of human redemption. I know only too well the real dangers that are ever-present in many inner-city communities and I know that many young people adopt behaviours that make them complicit in their own demise and oppression. I know too that in the process of trying to help young people change their outlook on their circumstances one often encounters setbacks and disappointments. Those who commit their lives to working with inner-city youth are compelled to recognize that the dangers in the inner-city are real, that sometimes those you are trying to help turn on you, and that trust must be earned and should never be assumed.

I learned this lesson early after volunteering to teach at a continuation high school[ii] in California and being asked to work with a group of "at-risk" young men. Each of these young men had criminal records and was regarded by their teachers as a disruptive influence in the classroom. As I got to know the students I also learned that they were all involved to varying degrees in crime and drug dealing. Despite their backgrounds and present situations the young men reacted positively to the opportunity to take a class with me. Part of the attraction seemed to be that I was a young Black man who the students felt they could identify with and relate to. Of course, the students were also being released from their regular classes to attend what I described as a "seminar", and undoubtedly this added to the appeal of the group since they assumed this would allow them to escape from their regular class work.

At one of our early meetings one of the young men suggested that our group should have a name. I thought this was a good idea, thinking that if we adopted a name it might help in generating a sense of belonging to the group. After hearing and rejecting several proposed names, one student suggested that we call ourselves ABT - All Brothers Together. I liked the sound of the name and so did the students, it seemed to invoke a strong sense of group solidarity, so we agreed to take it as our own. The following day I was asked by one of the guidance counsellors at the school how the group was going and I told her about our new name. She responded with immediate concern. "You better check that name out first. I think I recall hearing from a Probation Officer of one of your students that All Brothers Together, ABT, is the name of a prison gang." As it turned out the counsellor was right and when I shared this information with my students they all had a big laugh. Obviously, they knew that ABT was more than just a way to affirm group solidarity. I was the one who was naïve and in the dark.

As minor as this incident was, it served as an important lesson for me. It made me realize that I would need to be guided by more than good intentions to work effectively with these young men and that I could not uncritically embrace their sensibilities and worldview. I knew that if I were to have any chance of being effective as their teacher I would have to understand how they perceived their social reality and how they interacted with the world, but I would also need to devise strategies to challenge their ways of reasoning. Many of my students possessed what Freire has described as a "submerged consciousness", one that sees emulation and identification with the "oppressor" as the best route away from their own oppression. My students identified with ruthless gangsters from movies like "Scarface" and "The God Father", and they used language such as "nigger", "bitch" and "ho", to describe their peers and even themselves.

I learned that challenging this mode of thinking requires more than banning the use of distasteful words. Students must be encouraged to think critical about why such words are used in the first place, and why the contribute to the dehumanization and debasement of others. Likewise, I knew that condemning the movies they watched or the music they listened to would have little influence on their thinking unless together we explored why individuals who prey upon the weak are glorified, and why so often pimps, drug dealers and criminals are set up as role models in Black and Brown communities. My experience has taught me that to engage in this type of pedagogical practice effectively, educators must first have an ability to understand the social-psychological milieu in which such discourse emerges and is normalized. Without such an understanding their efforts to impose their mindset and moral reasoning on their students almost always fails. This is a basic and fundamental source of knowledge and understanding that all teachers need but most lack, particularly when the students come from race and class backgrounds that are different than their own. It is perhaps even more disturbing that many teachers do not even realize that they need to understand the social and cultural backgrounds of the students they teach because they assume that the technical training they received has provided them with the skills they need (Howard, 2002). The fact that so many teachers struggle with "managing" their classrooms and experience many of their students as defiant, disruptive and disrespectful (Gotfredson 2001; Noguera 1996) is the clearest indication that many cannot answer the most basic question of teaching: what does it take to educate the students we serve? Without an understanding of the social and cultural backgrounds of their students, and unable to comprehend how their students perceive the obstacles and challenges around them, many teachers find themselves unable to teach much less provide the guidance and direction their students so desperately need.

In my own case, I learned quickly I could not assume that even though I shared a great deal in common with my students (I too had been raised in a poor/working class community and been exposed to the harsh realities of the inner-city at a young age), that I necessarily understood what was happening in their lives. However, drawing on guidance from Freire's work I realized that if I were to learn how to teach them I would have to find ways to learn more about their lives. Like an anthropologist studying a foreign culture I knew that I needed to acquire an "insiders" understanding of their culture if I was to figure out how to make education – in this case the knowledge and skills needed not just to complete high school but to improve one's life – relevant to my students. Moreover, if I wanted education to serve as a tool of empowerment and social transformation I would have to comprehend what Freire refers to as the "generative themes" that shaped their social consciousness and inform their sense of the possible.

My background did make it possible for me to reject the notion that what these young men needed was to embrace "middle class values" and the "pull yourself up by the bootstraps views" that remain common and popular in American society. Such perspectives, which most recently have been expressed by commentators such as the comedian Bill Cosby, liberal journalists Bob Hebert (NY Times), Juan Williams (National Public Radio), or the conservative scholar John McWhorter (Manhattan Institute)[iii], may appeal to some but show little evidence of being an effective way to address the problems that beset inner-city youth. According to these pundits the problems that confront inner-city youth, particularly males, are due to the pathological culture they embrace – anti-intellectualism for McWhorter, a street mentality for Cosby, too much desire for "bling" (fancy jewellery) and guns for Williams. For these social critics the problems confronting inner-city youth could be solved if they were to simply adopt a different attitude, a stronger work ethic and a "middle class" cultural orientation. Such perspectives continue to be espoused and given considerable media attention even though they have no visible impact on the problems they claim to address. Those who espouse such views typically ignore or minimize the structural obstacles that limit the options and opportunities (i.e. unemployment, discrimination, failing schools, etc.) of the young men they castigate and malign. That they continue to be promoted and even acclaimed in certain circles[iv] is yet another reflection of the pervasive antipathy toward inner-city youth in American society. Even if one recognizes as I and others do, that the culture embraced by inner-city youth may be nihilistic (West 1993) or self destructive (Dyson 2003; Majors and Bilson 1992), those who espouse what Charles Payne (1984) has described as "blame the victim" arguments fail to see that while cultures can be transformed, and may in fact need to be, cultural change will require more than condemnation in a book, or the editorial pages of the New York Times or the Wall Street Journal.

My experience teaching and doing research in urban public schools and my work with community-based organizations in inner-city communities have provided me with insights into the mindset of inner-city youth and an understanding of how they perceive the formidable obstacles that limit and constrain their lives. Though my own privilege (I am now a well-paid university professor) and age (47) separate me from the young people I have worked with in practical and existential ways, I have taken time to try to understand the mindset of young people in the inner-city. By taking a phenomenological approach[v] to my work with inner-city youth, I was following one of the key principles modelled by Freire in his work with adult illiterates.

TOWARD A PHENOMENOLOGY OF INNER-CITY YOUTH

By taking time to listen without judgment to inner-city youth one can begin to understand that there are legitimate reasons for the anger they so often exhibit, an anger that frequently contributes to bad choices and behaviour that is self destructive and injurious to the communities where they live. For me, understanding the source of their anger is not the same as justifying or condoning how that anger may be manifest or expressed. However, without an understanding of its source it may be impossible to figure out how to help young people to channel feelings of anger and alienation in more positive and constructive ways, or how to intervene so that some of the more destructive tendencies among inner-city youth can be prevented. I have also come to understand that there is logic behind the choices they make, one that grows out of a sensibility and sometimes even a critical awareness of the forces stacked against them in American society and in their local environment. Like Freire's search for the "generative themes" in the lives of adult learners (the words, ideas and phrases that capture the passions and sensibilities of a particular community or group Freire 1972: 36) I have come to see that understanding the logic that guides the behaviour of inner-city youth is the first step to engaging young people in an educational process aimed at changing the way they respond to the forms of hardship and the forces of oppression that shape and constrain their lives.

I gained this understanding working in inner-city communities in the Bay Area. From 1986 – 1988 I was employed as the Executive Assistant to the Mayor of Berkeley, California. In this role, I had primary responsibility for helping the Mayor figure out how best to respond to problems such as homelessness, drug trafficking and urban blight. Initially, I embraced my work with enthusiasm and zeal because I believed that I was in a position where I could play a role in developing social policy and truly make a difference. However, after a few months on the job I began to realize that rather than being in a position where I could solve problems, I was merely in a position where I would have to explain to the community why their City government was so ineffective. Much of our failure could be explained by the fact that we lacked the resources to address the roots of problems like homelessness and drug trafficking. I soon realized that when I was asked to address an irate group of residents who wanted to know why the police were unable to prevent drive-by shootings or drug dealing that was occurring openly on street corners, explaining the inadequacy of City government was unlikely to appease them.

Frustrated with my job I began seeking out opportunities to work with young people in schools, hoping that education could serve as a means of preventing some of the problems I was grappling with in city government. I sought out other adults who shared my concern about what was happening to young people in our community and helped to establish new organizations that could attempt to respond.[vi] On one occasion I was asked by a middle school principal to speak to a group of boys who were considered "at risk" due to their poor grades and disruptive behaviour. She asked if I would meet with the boys on a regular basis and serve as a mentor. I agreed hoping that in this new role I would be far more effective at addressing some of the social problems I was being asked to respond to in the Mayor's office. However, I soon realized that working with this group of boys would be more challenging than I had expected. At my first meeting with the group I discovered that all twelve were involved, either directly or indirectly, with selling drugs. The boys were the ones who brought the topic up when I asked what they were interested in. They laughed and shouted "balling", "hustlin'" and "slanging rock"; all street terms used for drug dealing.

Initially, I tried unsuccessfully to engage them in a debate about the ethics of drug dealing, hoping that I might convince them that selling drugs was wrong. I spoke about the great harm that was being inflicted on abusers and their families. I brought up the violence drug dealing generated due to the competition among dealers for control of territory. However, all of the arguments I made failed completely. As I listened to these young men laugh and joke about their experiences selling drugs I realized that they too had an addiction, an addiction to drug dealing and the money it generated for them. I knew too that their unwillingness to "just say no", was rooted in their embrace of the logic of rugged individualism and amoral, predatory capitalism. Drug dealing was a business they argued, and given that all of them were poor and needed money to support themselves and in some cases their families, from their point of view, selling drugs made sense. As one young man put it bluntly "What's a nigga to do?"

To counter their logic or at least find a way to undermine it, I decided to change the topic. I began asking them questions about their lives outside of school in the hope that by learning more about them I might find a way to engage them in a critical discussion about what they were doing. I soon began to learn about their families, and as I asked the boys to talk about their role within their families I learned that none of them lived with their fathers (a few admitted not knowing who their fathers were), and that several were responsible for the care of younger siblings. This insight about the roles they played in their families gave me an opening that I thought I used to return to our conversation about drugs. After one student described how to he had to drop off his younger sister at school each morning and pick her up in the afternoon, I asked the young man "Would you sell drugs to your sister?" He looked at me with shock and disbelief. "No way. Drugs are poison". I then turned to one of the other boys in the group and asked him "What about you? Would you sell drugs to his sister?" The boy paused to think for a moment and then responded, "Yes. I'd do it because it's a business, and if I didn't sell to her someone else would." I then asked the first boy how he felt about the fact that someone he called a friend said he would sell drugs to your little sister. The boy responded, "That's wrong. He's supposed to be my boy." The other boy then said "I'm not saying I will sell drugs to your sister. I'm saying that if she asked me I would. At least I could make sure she got some good drugs."

With that admission the ethical discussion that I had hoped to initiate about drug dealing and social responsibility ensued. For the first time issues related to social responsibility and the impact of drug dealing and drug use in Black communities could be raised and debated. Several of the boys admitted how disturbed they were at seeing adults they knew – relatives, neighbours and friends – become addicted to drugs. Although there was laughter and ridicule expressed about "tweakers" and "base heads" (slang terms used to describe crack abusers), chicken heads and crack hoes (terms used to describe women who exchange sex for drugs), for the first time the young men acknowledged that crack cocaine was having a devastating impact on their community. Interestingly, once we got beyond the bravado of drug dealing and they acknowledged the impact that crack use was having upon their community and their lives, they were less willing to brag about their involvement in the drug trade and more willing to admit that what they were doing was wrong.

Over the years I have found that engaging inner-city youth in a critical analysis of their lives and the forces that shape and constrain them and their communities, must begin from an awareness of what their lives are like and how they have come to perceive and interpret their social reality. In order to gain this understanding educators must be willing to open themselves to learning about the lives of the students they teach. It is important to recognize that such pedagogical practice must include: 1) an openness to hearing young people share their perceptions of the social reality they inhabit, and 2) a willingness to engage in acts of solidarity in the fight against the oppression they face.

For me, this is more than an academic exercise. The conditions facing many inner-city youth are extreme – homicide rates remain high (in cities like Oakland, Detroit, Baltimore and Washington D.C. they are rising) and incarceration rates for juveniles show no signs of being reduced in the near future (Krisberg). Given the dire circumstances confronting inner-city youth the need to draw upon Freire for a "theory of change" cannot be overstated. There is a crisis facing inner-city youth in the United States, and it is essential that those who would like to do something to address this crisis recognize that no solutions are possible unless young people are active participants in designing and implementing them.

RENEWING AND REINVENTING FREIRE

While I continue to draw insight and inspiration from the ideas of Paulo Freire in my work with inner-city youth, work focused on intervening to reduce some of the risks they face –under achievement in school, dropping out of school, becoming unemployed, being arrested and incarcerated, being murdered or a victim of violence - I readily recognize and acknowledge that his ideas cannot be applied mechanically. In fact, mechanical application would never be possible because Freire called for a pedagogy co-constructed with those we work with, one in which students were subjects rather than objects of education. Though still extremely valuable for its philosophical and methodological approach to engaging those who are marginalized and silenced, bringing Freire's pedagogy to the inner-city compels the organizer/educator to revise, critique and even re-invented Freire's core ideas in order to insure that they will be useful in this setting.

For the last several years I have been working with others to find ways to counter gang violence in L.A. and the south Bronx, to lower the homicide rate in New Bedford, Washington D.C. and Oakland, or to increase student participation and engagement at schools in Baltimore, Atlanta and Detroit. In each case, I have found Freire's to be a powerful source of inspiration and a practical guide to the development of pedagogical strategies. Yet, I have also recognized that Freire's ideas must be modified and adjusted so that they can be truly relevant both to the sensibilities of inner-city youth and to the context in which they live. Freire wrote most of his major works at a particular moment in history – the late 1960s and 1970s. This was a period in which anti-colonial liberation movements were being waged in Africa and revolutionary movements were challenging oligarchies in Latin America and the Caribbean. It was a time when radical change seemed imminent, when there was great hope in many circles that revolution would lead to sweeping reforms that would establish a more just and humane social order. For those committed to involving the "masses" and the "wretched of the earth" in the process of change, not merely as beneficiaries but as participants, Freire's ideas were a source of guidance and a framework for how this could be done. Yet, while his ideas have resonated across the globe it is clear that they are not without their flaws or limitations.

For example, in much of Freire's work he used the dichotomous language of "oppressed" and "oppressor" to describe classes of people that existed in dialectical opposition to each other, one suffering under structural conditions that negate the worth of human beings and render lives hopeless, the other benefiting from the same structural arrangements deriving benefit and privilege from exploitation and suffering. He argued passionately that only the oppressed could bring about an end to oppression, and most importantly that this could be done not by trading places in the master-slave relationship, but by ending oppression altogether.

> Because it is a distortion of being fully human, sooner or later being less human leads the oppressed to struggle against those who made them so. In order for this struggle to have meaning, the oppressed must not, in seeking to

regain their humanity (which is a way to create it), become in turn oppressors of the oppressors, but rather restorers of the humanity of both.

This then, is the great humanistic and historical task of the oppressed: to liberate themselves and their oppressors as well. (Pedagogy of the Oppressed, p. 28)

For some readers, such categories and terms are still powerful because of the images and sentiments they invoke. We still live in a world where suffering, malnutrition, disease, desperation and poverty afflict millions across the globe. It is also a world characterized by extreme inequity, a world where pets in Western Europe and the United States eat better than people in many parts of Africa, Asia and Latin America. It is a world in which the rich consume the vast majority of the world's resources as they continue to grow richer, and the poor become ever more impoverished and dispossessed even as their numbers continue to swell.

Yet, despite the reality of this grotesque imbalance, the terms Freire used – oppressed and oppressor, liberation and emancipation - are increasingly outdated and anachronistic in contemporary usage. Is a low-level drug dealer or pimp a member of the oppressed or oppressor class? Both exploit and prey upon the weak and powerless to sustain themselves, yet neither can be regarded as a member of the "ruling class" or power elite. What about Bill Gates or Warren Buffet, two of the wealthiest men in the world, who's combined net worth exceeds the gross national product of several developing nations? Yet, both men are also among the largest philanthropists in the world, donating millions of dollars each year to support health care and education for the poor. I raise these questions not for the purpose of indicting or exonerating either drug dealers or billionaires, but merely to point out that neither falls easily into the types of categories that Freire relied upon as a he made the case for a pedagogy of the oppressed.

The same can be said of what is now referred to as "critical pedagogy"; a body of work developed by scholars and educators who have drawn heavily upon the ideas of Freire to articulate an educational practice they laud as "liberating" and emancipatory". Scholars such as Henry Giroux, Peter McLaren, Marilyn Ellsworth, and numerous others have developed a substantial body of work that they hope will further the efforts of educators, organizers and activists who seek to promote social change through popular education. Yet, unless one regards the hardships of the poor and powerless as purely psychological in nature and ignores the material aspects of their suffering, it is hard to indulge such grandiose claims. Unlike Freire who was personally committed to applying his radical theories in the "real world", too many of those who think of themselves as critical educators and radical theorists of critical pedagogy, keep themselves comfortably confined to the ivory towers of the university and never attempt to put the ideas they espouse into action. For these individuals who claim to be intellectual descendants of Freire, praxis no longer requires them to engage in genuine acts of solidarity in the communities they express concern about and solidarity with. Rather, it is the production of their scholarly publications and lectures that constitute their commitment to struggle and symbolize their revolutionary praxis,

Those who do the hard work of educating inner-city youth and who see themselves as allies and collaborators in the struggle against their marginalization and maligning, are unlikely to be fooled into thinking that there is some magic in the ideas of Freire or any other scholar that could shed light on how to "liberate" urban youth. Even when the ideas prove insightful and prove to be useful as a means of conceptualizing some aspect of the ongoing struggle, the ultimate test of their value is in their utility to guide practice and their applicability in efforts to transform lives and circumstances of young people. Unlike many of those who claim to be his intellectual descendants, Freire, understood the difference between writing and acting, talking and doing. He knew that truly revolutionary practice must be more than a scholarly enterprise; it must be rooted in the real world of the poor and powerless and it must be firmly engaged in efforts aimed at struggling against oppression and dehumanization. On this point Freire writes:

Education as the practice of freedom – as opposed to education as the practice of domination – denies that man is abstract, isolated, independent, and unattached to the world: it also denies that the world exists as a reality apart from men…Problem-posing education bases itself on creativity and stimulates true reflection and action upon reality, thereby responding to the vocation of men as beings who are authentic only when engaged in inquiry and creative transformation. (p. 69 – 71)

This is why Paulo Freire continues to be a source of inspiration for me as a grapple with the enormous challenges confronting inner-city youth in the United States and why I believe that others who are engaged in similar work can find in Freire a source of inspiration and insight that can make their efforts more effective and productive.

NOTES

[i] The clearest evidence that prisons in the United States largely fail at rehabilitating juvenile offenders can be seen in the 2/3 of incarcerated youth who return to prison within two years of their release. See National Council on Crime and Juvenile Delinquency 1996),

[ii] In California the term continuation school is applied to schools that specialize in serving students who have been dismissed from regular schools because of poor attendance, failing grades, discipline problems or a combination of these.

[iii] For a detailed description of the views of these conservative commentators and their recommendations on what should be done to "help" inn-city youth, see *Losing the Race* by John McWhorter (2001) and by Juan Williams. And by Orlando Patterson.

[iv] See for example recent reactions to the book by Puerto Rican politician Herman Badillo who criticized Hispanics for not valuing the importance of education. In an editorial, the Wall Street Journal described his book as "insightful and courageous".

[v] For a discussion of phenomenology as a philosophical, theoretical and methodological resource see

[vi] One of the organizations that I helped to create in 1987 was Black Men United for Change. My thinking was that by bringing concerned Black men together to address the plight of "at-risk" Black

youth, we might have greater ability to respond to the problems. Today, similar organizations exist throughout the United States most operating under the name 100 Black Men.

REFERENCES

Anderson, E. (1990) *Street wise. Race, Class and change in an urban community.* Chicago: University of Chicago Press.

Currie, E. and Skolnick, J (1994) *Crisis in American institutions.* New York: Harper Collins.

Darling-Hammond (1997) *The right to learn.* San Francisco: Josey Bass.

Dyson, M. E, (2005) *Is Bill Cosby right?* New York: Civitas Books.

Earls, F. (1991) Not fear, nor quarantine, but science: preparation for a decade of research to advance knowledge about causes and control of violence in youths. *Journal of Adolescent Health, 12,* 619-629.

Earls, F. (1994) Violence and today's youth. *Critical Health Issues for Children and Youth, 4*(3)..

Freire, P. (1970) *The pedagogy of the oppressed.* New York, NY: Continuum Publishing.

Freire, P. (1973) *Education for critical consciousness.* New York: Continuum Press.

Freire, P. (1976 *Education as the practice of freedom.* London: Writers and Readers Cooperative.

Garbarino, J. (1999) *Lost boys: Why our sons turn to violence and how to save them.* New York, NY: free Press.

Gilligan, James (1996) *Violence.* New York: Grosset,

Giroux, H. (1983). *Theory and resistance in education.* New York: Bergin and Harvey.

Glazer, N. and D. Moynihan (1963) *Beyond the melting pot.* Cambridge, MA: MIT Press.

Gottfredson, D. (2001). *Schools and delinquency.* Cambridge: Cambridge University Press.

Greenberg, M., & Schneider, D. (1994). Young black males is the answer, but what was the question? Social Science Medicine, *39*(2).

Hebert, Robert (2002) A rising tied of death, New York Times, May 11th.

Hischi, Travis *Causes of delinquency.* Berkeley, CA: University of California Press.

Howard, G. (2002) *You can't teach what you don't know.* New York: Teachers College Press.

Kozol, J. (1991) *Savage inequalities.* New York: Crown Books. The importance of cultural capital. *Sociology of Education, 60,* 73-85.

Krisberg, B., Marchianna S., Baird C. (2007) Continuing the struggle for justice.

Lewis, O. (1966). *La vida: A Puerto Rican family in the culture of poverty – San Juan and New York.* New York, NY: Random House.

Majors, R. and M. Billson (1992) *Cool pose. The dilemmas of black manhood in America.* NY: Simon and Schuster.

Madhubuti, Haki (1990) *Black men, obsolete, single dangerous?* Chicago: Third World Press.

Mc Whorter, J. (2000) *Losing the race.* New York: New Press.

Moynihan, D. P. (1999) *Miles to go: Personal history of social policy.* Cambridge: Harvard University Press.

Noguera, P. (1995) Reducing and preventing youth violence: An analysis of causes and an assessment of successful programs, in 1995 Wellness Lectures. Oakland, CA: University of California Office of the President.

Noguera, P. (1995). Preventing and producing violence in schools: A critical analysis of responses to school violence. *Harvard Educational Review, 65*(2), 189-212.

Noguera, P. (2000) Finding safety where we least expected it: The role of social capital in making schools safe, in *Zero tolerance*, edited by R. Ayers, et.al. New York: Teachers College Press.

Patterson, O. (2006)

Payne, C. M. (1984). *Getting what we ask for: The ambiguity of success and failure of urban education.* Westport, CT: Greenwood Press.

Russell, K. (1998) *The colour of crime*. New York: New York University press.

Schiraldi, V. & Ziedenberg, J. (2001). How distorted coverage of juvenile crime affects public policy. In W. Ayers, R. Ayers, & B. Dorhn (Eds.), *Zero tolerance*. New York: New Press.

Singer, S. (1996) *Re-criminalizing delinquency*. Cambridge, UK: Cambridge University Press.

Tabb, W. (1970) *The political economy of the black ghetto*. New York: W.W. Norton Co.

Taylor-Gibbs, J. (1988). *The black male as an endangered species*. New York: Auburn House.

Wacquant, L. (2000) Deadly symbiosis: When ghetto and prison meet and mesh, in *Punishment and Society, 2-3* (Fall).

West, C. (1993) *Race matters*. Boston: Beacon Press.

Williams, J. (2006) *Enough: The phoney leaders dead-end movements and culture of failure that are holding back black America*. New York: Crown

Wilson, W. (1987) *The truly disadvantaged*. Chicago: University of Chicago Press

PETER MAYO

ANTONIO GRAMSCI AND PAULO FREIRE: SOME CONNECTIONS AND CONTRASTS [i]

Antonio Gramsci (1891-1937) and Paulo Freire (1921-1997) are certainly two of the most cited figures in the debate concerning critical approaches to education. Their respective cultural and political work occurred in different contexts and at different times (Gramsci in Europe in the first part of the 20th century and Paulo Freire in Latin America, N. America, Europe and Africa in the second half of the century). Nevertheless, a whole generation of writers, positing a critical approach to education, especially those subscribing to what is commonly referred to as critical pedagogy, constantly draw on Gramsci's and Freire's powerful insights into the relationship between education/ cultural work and power.[ii] The two figures are often accorded iconic status in this literature.

In this paper, I shall attempt to draw theoretical and, when appropriate, biographical connections between the work of the two, also highlighting some obvious contrasts. In so doing, I shall reproduce key points made in my earlier published work on these two figures, notably my book length study[iii] in which I sought to derive insights from their respective writings for a process of transformative adult education relevant to contemporary times. In this piece, I also hope to provide fresh comparative insights not found in the earlier work.

SYSTEMATIC COMPARISONS OF GRAMSCI AND FREIRE

The literature on either Gramsci or Freire is indeed a burgeoning one. I shall confine myself here to that literature which seeks to bring the ideas of the two authors together.[iv] Paulo Freire posits this connection between his ideas and those of Gramsci:

> ...I only read Gramsci when I was in exile. I read Gramsci and I discovered that I had been greatly influenced by Gramsci long before I had read him. It is fantastic when we discover that we had been influenced by someone's thought without even being introduced to their intellectual production.[v]

There is some very important work focusing on Latin America that inevitably establishes connections between Gramsci and Freire. A significant literature emphasizes the influence of Antonio Gramsci on Latin American left wing politics [vi] and popular education[vii], the latter being the one area with which Paulo Freire's work and ideas are strongly associated.[viii] La Belle goes as far as to state that Gramsci is the most invoked Marxist theorist in popular education in Latin America; he underscores the relevance of Gramsci's ideas concerning the Factory Councils to the task of organizing the masses through popular education.[ix]

C.A. Torres & P. Noguera (Eds.), Social Justice Education for Teachers, 51–68.

Prominent among the English language works establishing connections between Gramsci and Freire, within the context of popular education, are the writings of Raymond A. Morrow and Carlos Alberto Torres[x] who argue that there has been a certain degree of polarization with respect to the reception of Gramsci in Latin America. One side links him with a "technocratic" perspective which places the emphasis on a critical appropriation of dominant knowledge, a position that is not at odds with the Leninist revolutionary vanguard theory but which has been perceived as contrasting with the position adopted by Freire. The other side, which argues for a confluence between his ideas and those of Freire, stresses the link between Gramsci's specific view of civil society and that of popular education, conceived of as an important element in the process of democratization of Brazilian society.[xi] This polarization is the result of the apparently paradoxical features of Gramsci's work, features which led Morrow and Torres[xii] to provocatively pose the question: are there "two Gramscis"?

Across the Atlantic, there have been a number of works combining insights from Gramsci and Freire. In Marjorie Mayo's Imagining Tomorrow[xiii], market-led perspectives are contrasted with those centering on adult education for social transformation with the focus, in the relevant chapter, being on the work of Gramsci, Freire and Ettore Gelpi. Less supportive of attempts to bring Gramsci and Freire together is Diana Coben who, in a book length study of these two figures' writings, considers their work incompatible and therefore rejects their linkage in the adult education literature.[xiv]

With respect to writings outside the field of education, one must mention the work of Ransome, Leonard and Ledwith.[xv] The first of these deals with Gramsci's work in general and brings Freire into the reckoning in the section on intellectuals. The second draws on insights from Gramsci and Freire for a critical approach to social work. Margaret Ledwith advocates transformative action in the area of community development rooted in critical pedagogy and the writings of Gramsci and Freire, to which an entire chapter is devoted.

As far as education is concerned, specifically a critical approach to education, one must mention the work of Paula Allman.[xvi] In her earlier chapter on education for socialism, Allman draws on the ideas of Gramsci and Freire, alongside those of Illich, in the context of a sustained discussion on ideology.[xvii] This is an issue with which Allman and participants in a diploma course she coordinated at the University of Nottingham had to contend as they sought signposts for a socialist approach to adult education. Allman sees adult education as part of the "prefigurative work" which, Gramsci insisted, had to precede every revolution: "Every revolution has been preceded by an intense labor of criticism, by the diffusion of culture and spread of ideas among masses of men…..".[xviii] Allman's later book length work[xix] projects a vision for transformed democratic social relations predicated on a pedagogical approach characterized by a revolutionary as opposed to a reproductive praxis, an approach that echoes Marx's dialectical conceptualization and that is reflected in the writings of both Gramsci and Freire.[xx]

MARXIAN UNDERPINNINGS

The reference to Allman immediately leads me to stress one fundamental and obvious point of contact between Gramsci's and Freire's respective works – their being rooted in Marxism and more specifically Marxian thinking.[xxi] That Gramsci is indebted to such thought goes without saying. In volume IV of his edited critical edition of the Quaderni del Carcere (Prison Notebooks), Valentino Gerratana provides the list of texts by Marx and Engels that Gramsci cites in the Notebooks. These include Capital, the Theses on Feuerbach, the Contribution to the Critique of Hegel's Philosophy of Right (Introduction), The Holy Family, The Eighteenth Brumaire of Louis Napoleon, Critique of the Gotha Programme, numerous letters and articles such as the one on the Spanish revolution in the New York Tribune, among others.[xxii] After all, Gramsci is credited with having "reinvented" some of Marx's concepts when discussing important aspects of his native Italy's post-Risorgimento state. One of his more enduring contributions is arguably that of having stressed the cultural dimension of revolutionary practice. He has thus made a significant contribution to various aspects of Marxist theory, including the debate around the 'Base-superstructure' metaphor. At the same time, one must not lose sight of his over-arching political analysis, lest one lapses into cultural reductionism.

Despite the criticism that Freire is too eclectic in his approach, drawing on a broad range of sources, including Christian-Personalism and Liberation Theology (which generally accommodates Marxist class analysis), one cannot deny the Marxian and Marxist underpinnings of his writing and specific mode of conceptualization. Unlike Gramsci, Freire could draw on a wide range of early writings by Marx, notably The German Ideology, The Economic and Philosophic Manuscripts of 1844, the Theses on Feuerbach and The Holy Family. These early writings by Marx provide important sources of reference for some of the arguments raised in Freire's best-known work, Pedagogy of the Oppressed.[xxiii] Later writings by Marx, however, feature prominently in such works as Pedagogy in Process [xxiv] where Freire attempts to come to grips with the social relations of production in an impoverished African country (Guinea Bissau) that had just gained independence from Portugal. In this work, and precisely in letter 11, Freire adopts Marx's notion of a 'polytechnic education'[xxv], arguing for a strong relationship to be forged between education and production.[xxvi] Marx had specifically developed this notion in the Geneva Resolution of 1866.[xxvii]

Most importantly, though, Pedagogy of the Oppressed is written in a dialectical style which, as Allman points out, is not easily accessible to readers schooled in conventional ways of thinking, often characterized by a linear approach.[xxviii] She demonstrates clearly that one cannot fully appreciate Freire's work without anchoring it within Karl Marx's dialectical conceptualization of oppression. The more one is familiar with Marx's "tracking down" of "inner connections" and "relations", that are conceived of as "unities of opposites" [xxix], the more one begins to appreciate Pedagogy of the Oppressed's Marxian underpinning.[xxx] This is not the only book Freire has written, but it is the most compact and consistent as far as the dialectical conceptualization of power is concerned.[xxxi]

IDEOLOGY

Gramsci's and Freire's respective works are embedded in a Marxian conception of ideology based on the assumption that "The ruling ideas are nothing more than the ideal expression of the dominant material relationships, the dominant material relationships grasped as ideas; hence of the relationships which make one class the ruling one, therefore the ideas of its dominance."[xxxii] Not only does the ruling class produce the ruling ideas, in view of its control over the means of intellectual production,[xxxiii] but the dominated classes produce ideas that do not necessarily serve their interests; these classes, that "lack the means of mental production and are immersed in production relations which they do not control," tend to "reproduce ideas" that express the dominant material relationships [xxxiv] After all, as Marx and Engels had underlined, "…each new class which puts itself in place of one ruling before it, is compelled, merely in order to carry through its aim, to represent its interest as the common interest of all the members of society, that is expressed in ideal form: it has to give its ideas the form of universality, and represent them as the only rational, universally valid ones."[xxxv]

Gramsci saw ideas that reflect the dominant material relationships as residing in those areas he identifies with 'common sense' which contains elements of 'good sense' but which is, in effect, a distorted and fragmentary conception of the world. It is, according to Gramsci, a "philosophy of non philosophers", namely " a conception of the world absorbed uncritically by the various social and cultural environments in which the moral individuality of the average man (sic.) develops."[xxxvi] This contrasts with 'philosophy' that is "intellectual order, which neither religion nor common sense can be."[xxxvii] For Gramsci, common sense is "…the folklore of philosophy."[xxxviii] Gramsci draws connections between popular religion, folklore (a specific body of beliefs, values and norms[xxxix] that is uncritical, contradictory and ambiguous in content) and common sense.[xl] Religion is, for Gramsci, "an element of fragmented common sense."[xli] The challenge, for Gramsci, is to supersede this common sense through a 'philosophy of praxis,' the "conscious expression" of the contradictions that lacerate society,[xlii] that would undergo a process of elaboration similar to that experienced by Lutheranism and Calvinism before developing into a "superior culture"[xliii] or 'civilta.'[xliv]

Freire's view of consciousness is also reminiscent of Gramsci's distinction between common sense and good sense. He too sees popular consciousness as being permeated by ideology. In his earlier work, Freire posited the existence of different levels of consciousness ranging from naïve to critical consciousness, indicating a hierarchy that exposed him to the accusation of being elitist and of being patronizing towards ordinary people.[xlv] Similar accusations can easily be directed at Gramsci with respect to the distinction he draws between common and good sense. In his early work, Freire reveals the power of ideology being reflected in the fatalism apparent in the statements of peasants living in shanty towns who provide 'magical explanations,' attributing their poor plight to the 'will of God". [xlvi] While Gramsci regards religion as an element of 'common sense,' Freire, a self-declared 'man of faith,' is less categorical. He extols the virtues of the 'Prophetic Church', with its basis in liberation theology, and attributes 'false consciousness' to the "traditionalist", "colonialist" and "missionary" church that he describes as a "necrophiliac winner of souls" with its "emphasis on sin, hell-fire and eternal damnation."[xlvii] This is the sort of Church to which Gramsci is likely to have been exposed in his native Sardegna and that could easily have been a propagator of the kind of 'folklore' that he despised.

Like Gramsci and a host of other writers, including important exponents of Critical Theory, Freire provides a very insightful analysis of the way human beings participate in their own oppression by internalizing the image of their oppressor. As with the complexity of hegemonic arrangements, underlined by Gramsci and elaborated on by a host of others writing from a neo-Gramscian perspective, people suffer a contradictory consciousness, being oppressors, within one social hegemonic arrangement, and oppressed within another.[xlviii] This consideration runs throughout Freire's oeuvre ranging from his early discussion on the notion of the 'oppressor consciousness' to his later writings on multiple and layered identities[xlix] where he insists that one's quest for life and for living critically is tantamount to being an ongoing quest for the attainment of greater coherence. Gaining coherence, for Freire, necessitates one's gaining greater awareness of one's 'unfinishedness'.[l]

RESOURCES OF HOPE

Both Gramsci and Freire accord an important role to agency in the context of revolutionary activity for social transformation. The two explicitly repudiate evolutionary economic determinist theories of social change. Gramsci regards them as theories of "grace and predestination." while Freire sees them as being conducive to a "liberating fatalism",[li] a position to which he adhered until the very end, stating, at an honoris causa speech delivered at Claremont Graduate University in 1989, that "When I think of history I think about possibility – that history is the time and space of possibility. Because of that, I reject a fatalistic or pessimistic understanding of history with a belief that what happens is what should happen."[lii] He sees persons as conditioned but not determined beings.[liii]

The emphasis on voluntarism and on the cultural and spiritual basis of revolutionary activity is very strong in the writings of the young Gramsci.[liv] This emphasis is also to be found in Freire's early writings, especially the work based on his doctoral thesis, 'Education as the Practice of Freedom.'[lv] This particular aspect of the two writers' work is generally regarded to have been the product of strong Hegelian influences. In Gramsci's case, however, it would be more appropriate to speak in terms of 'neo-Hegelianism', the kind of idealist philosophy derived from Croce.[lvi] In Freire's case, the Hegelianism may have partly been derived via the writings of such Christian authors as Chardin, Mounier and Neibuhr.[lvii] In later writings, however, this idealist position becomes somewhat modified as both Gramsci and Freire begin to place greater emphasis on the role of economic conditions in processes of social change.

Both rejected the view that the conditions of their time determined the limits of what is possible. Both recognized developments within capitalism, witnessed during their lifetime (Taylorisation / Fordism in Gramsci's time and Neo-Liberalism in Freire's), for what they were - manifestations of Capitalist reorganization to counter the tendency of the rate of profit to fall, owing to the 'crises of overproduction'.[lviii] In his notes dealing with 'Americanism and Fordism', Gramsci points to the need for Capitalism to reorganize itself periodically to counter such a tendency. Taylorisation constituted the earlier means in this regard.[lix] The intensification of globalization is the latest form of Capitalist reorganization.[lx] Understanding the contemporary stages of capitalist development according to what they represented was a crucial step for both writers to avoid a sense of fatalism and keep alive the quest for working to attain a better world driven by what Henry A Giroux calls an anticipatory utopia prefigured not only by critique of the present but by an alternative pedagogical/cultural politics.[lxi] The fatalism of neo-liberalism, buttressed by the propagation of an'ideology of ideological death'[lxii] was a key theme in Freire's later writings and was meant to be the subject of the work he was contemplating at the time of his death.[lxiii] Like Gramsci, who explored, through a multi-varied analysis of Italy's historical and contemporary conditions, directions to pursue in the quest for an 'intellectual and moral reform,' Freire could well have been on the verge of embarking on an exploration of the conditions that the present historical conjuncture, characterized by Neo-liberalism, would allow for the pursuit of his dream of a different and better world. Alas, this was not to be.

EDUCATION IN ITS BROADEST CONTEXT

Gramsci's engagement in a broad process of analysis of the historical and contemporary conditions of Italy, with a view to exploring the conditions likely to engender an 'intellectual and moral reform' of a scale that would render it the most radical reform since primitive Christianity,[lxiv] renders his conception of education quite expansive. Gramsci, very much involved in adult education, as part of his work in the Italian Socialist and subsequently Communist parties, wrote of the existence of "altre vie" (other routes) when it comes to education and learning. Gramsci saw progressive and emancipatory elements within these "altre vie" that can complement the kind of Unitarian school he proposed to advance the interests of the Italian working class.[lxv] Gramsci held a view similar to what Suchodolski would call an "education-centred society"[lxvi] or what is fashionable to call, nowadays, the 'learning society.' Gramsci scholar, Joseph A. Buttigieg, writes: "…the role of education in Gramsci's thought cannot be properly appreciated unless one recognizes that it resides at the very core of his concept of hegemony. 'Every relationship of 'hegemony' is necessarily an educational relationship,' he wrote."[lxvii] For Gramsci, therefore, a meaningful process of education must extend beyond schooling and adult education centres to be wide ranging. It is primarily located within the terrain of civil society[lxviii] wherein these educational / hegemonic relationships are consolidated, as is the case with much of contemporary society, and challenged. In the latter case, the challenge can possibly be part of what Raymond Williams would call a 'long revolution.'[lxix] Gramsci constantly writes about the need to secure alliances of progressive forces in a historical bloc and even encourages (something he himself did) collaboration with progressive individuals such as Piero Gobetti.[lxx] He insisted that the name of the Communist Party organ should be 'L'Unita`, which signifies a unification of all the popular forces, including the Catholic masses, in a historical bloc.[lxxi] Nevertheless, he attributed a central role, at the heart of this educational and political action for a moral reform, to the party that he conceived of as the Modern Prince. The Modern Prince had the task of unifying these forces in a national-popular bloc, just like Macchiavelli's Principe had the task of unifying the country. In the words of John Holst, "the party was to maintain hegemony.." and "…not allow the other alliance forces to steer the movement into reformism or economism…"[lxxii]

The idea of a larger terrain for educational action is also at the heart of Freire's work. Throughout his writings, Freire constantly stressed that educators engage with the system and not shy away from it for fear of co-optation.[lxxiii] Freire exhorted educators and other cultural workers to 'be tactically inside and strategically outside' the system. As with Gramsci, Freire believed that the system is not monolithic. Hegemonic arrangements are never complete and allow spaces for "swimming against the tide" or, to use Gramsci's phrase, engaging in 'a war of position.'[lxxiv] In most of his work from the mid eighties onward, Freire touches on the role of social movements as important vehicles for social change.

He himself belonged to a movement striving for a significant process of change, of radicalization, within an important institution in Latin America and beyond, namely the church. This stands in contrast to Gramsci who however saw enough progressive elements in the Catholic masses to stress the need for an alliance with them. When Education Secretary in São Paulo, a position that allowed Freire to tackle education and cultural work in their broader contexts, Paulo Freire and his associates worked hard to bring social movements and state agencies together.[lxxv] These efforts on behalf of the Partido dos Trabalhadores (PT) continue to be exerted by the party itself in other municipalities, most notably the city of Porto Alegre, in Rio Grande do Sul, where the PT has been in government since the late eighties, and presumably the other municipalities and states where the party won the elections in the Fall of 2001. One should also mention that, at present, there exists the possibility of engaging in such efforts throughout the entire country now that the PT leader, Luiz Inacio "Lula" da Silva, has won the federal presidential elections. The last years of Freire's life were exciting times for Brazilian society with the emergence of the Movimento dos Trabalhadores Rurais Sem Terra.[lxxvi] The Movement allies political activism and mobilization with important education and cultural work.[lxxvii] The movement is itself conceived of as an "enormous school."[lxxviii] As in the period that preceded the infamous 1964 coup, Paulo Freire's work and thinking must also have been influenced and reinvigorated by the growing movement for democratization of Brazilian society. In an interview with Carmel Borg and me, Ana Maria (Nita) Araujo Freire states:

"Travelling all over this immense Brazil we saw and cooperated with a very large number of social movements of different sizes and natures, but who had (and continue to have) a point in common: the hope in their people's power of transformation. They are teachers - many of them are "lay": embroiderers, sisters, workers, fishermen, peasants, etc., scattered all over the country, in favelas, camps or houses, men and women with an incredible leadership strength, bound together in small and local organizations, but with such a latent potential that it filled us, Paulo and me, with hope for better days for our people. Many others participated in a more organized way in the MST (Movimento dos Sem Terra: Movement of Landless Peasants), the trade unions, CUT (Central Única dos Trabalhadores), and CEBs (Christian Base Communities). As the man of hope he always was, Paulo knew he would not remain alone. Millions of persons, excluded from the system, are struggling in this country, as they free themselves from oppression, to also liberate their oppressors. Paulo died a few days after the arrival of the MST March in Brasília. On that April day, standing in our living-room, seeing on the TV the crowds of men, women and children entering the capital in such an orderly and dignified way, full of emotion, he cried out: "That's it, Brazilian people, the country belongs to all of us! Let us build together a democratic country, just and happy!"[lxxix]

Freire insisted that education should not be romanticized and that teachers ought to engage in a much larger public sphere.[lxxx] This has been quite a popular idea among radical activists in recent years, partly also as a result of a dissatisfaction with party politics. The arguments developed in these circles are often based on a very non-Gramscian use of the concept of 'civil society.' In his later work, however, Freire sought to explore the links between movements and the state[lxxxi] and, most significantly, movements and party, a position no doubt influenced by his role as one of the founding members of the PT. Authors such as John Holst[lxxxii] have argued that social movements theorists writing on the relevance of Antonio Gramsci's ideas for adult education tend to ignore the central role which Gramsci attributed to the Party in the process of social transformation. In view of this criticism, Freire's ideas concerning the relationship between party and movements are quite interesting and suggest a link with Gramsci's conception of the historical bloc involving an alliance between the party and mass organizations.

Freire argues that the party for change, committed to the subaltern, should allow itself to learn from and be transformed through contact with progressive social movements. One important proviso Freire makes, in this respect, is that the party should do this "without trying to take them over." Movements, Freire seems to be saying, cannot be subsumed by parties; otherwise they lose their identity and forfeit their specific way of exerting pressure for change. Paulo Freire discusses possible links between party and movements. This brings to mind the possible links between such movements as the MST and the PT, the party that, according to Carlos Nelson Coutinho, constitutes one of the major contemporary repositories for Gramsci's ideas in Brazil.[lxxxiii]

Today, if the Workers' Party approaches the popular movements from which it was born, without trying to take them over, the party will grow; if it turns away from the popular movements, in my opinion, the party will wear down. Besides, those movements need to make their struggle politically viable.[lxxxiv]

Both Gramsci and Freire, therefore, explore links between the party and movements within the context of a strategy for social change. While Gramsci is adamant on a directive role for the party in this process, Freire is less categorical in this regard, although events in Brazil tend to suggest a leadership role for the PT in the process of the democratization of Brazilian society. The PT enjoys strong links with the trade union movement, the Pastoral Land Commission, the MST and other movements. It has exercised its leadership role when forging alliances between party, state and movements in the municipalities in which it has been in power. The Participatory Budget project in Porto Alegre, an exercise in deliberative and participatory democracy, provides some indication of the direction such alliances can take.[lxxxv]

PRAXIS

The discussion has veered towards a macro-level analysis. It would be opportune now to bring the discussion back to the micro level with an emphasis on concepts that lie at the heart of the pedagogical relation as propounded by both Gramsci and Freire. The two figures regard praxis as one of the key concepts in question. The kind of philosophy which Gramsci contrasts with 'common sense' and which warrants elaboration to provide the underpinning of an intellectual and moral reform is referred to as the 'philosophy of praxis' which, in contrast to the bifurcation advocated by Benedetto Croce (philosophy for intellectuals and religion for the people), is intended to be a philosophy that welds intellectuals and masses together in a historical bloc.[lxxxvi] It is intended to be an instrument for the forging of a strong relationship between theory and practice, consciousness and action.[lxxxvii]

Praxis is also at the center of Freire's philosophical approach and becomes a constant feature of his thinking and writing. It constitutes the means whereby one can move in the direction of confronting the contradiction of opposites in the dialectical relation. For Freire and others, it constitutes the means of gaining critical distance from one's world of action to engage in reflection geared towards transformative action. The relationship between action-reflection-transformative action is not sequential but dialectical.[lxxxviii] Freire and other intellectuals, with whom he has conversed, in 'talking books', conceive of different moments in their life as forms of praxis, of gaining critical distance from the context they know to perceive it in a more critical light. Exile is regarded by Freire and the Chilean Antonio Faundez[lxxxix] as a form of praxis, a situation that recalls Gramsci's predicament in prison where the brain, which was meant to be stopped from working for twenty years, found the space, albeit for a ten year period, for profound critical reflection on the world of the Sardinian's action.[xc] The idea of critical distancing is however best captured by Freire in his pedagogical approach involving the use of codifications, even though one should not make a fetish out of

59

this 'method'[xci] since it is basically indicative of something larger, a philosophy of learning in which praxis is a central concept that has to be 'reinvented' time and time again, depending on situation and context.

Authority and Freedom

There are connections between Gramsci and Freire also with respect to the teacher-student dynamics. It might appear that Gramsci's view of schooling, as expressed in his two notes on the Unitarian School, contained in Notebook 4, provides a stark contrast to Freire's pedagogical approach.[xcii] Harold Entwistle, for instance, argues that the emphasis which Gramsci places, in these notes, on the acquisition of a baggage of facts suggests that Gramsci "held a view of learning which is not inconsistent with the notion, now used pejoratively, of education as banking".[xciii] This would seem to contrast with what Freire advocated. And yet, Gramsci had, for instance, denounced the popular universities (adult education institutions for the working class) precisely because their directors and educators filled the stomach with bagfuls of victuals ('sporte di viveri') capable of causing indigestion but that left no trace and did not touch the learners' lives to the extent that a difference could have been made.[xciv] He also states that the popular universities are reminiscent of the old Jesuitical schools where learning is static rather than dynamic; it was not the culmination of a long process of inquiry.[xcv]

To what extent did Gramsci favor the kind of pedagogical approach Freire argued against, namely 'banking education'? A close reading of Gramsci's text, one that devotes great attention to his choice of words, would indicate that he was averse to the encouragement of uninformed dialogue. For Gramsci, a process of uninformed dialogue is mere rhetoric. It is mere laissez faire pedagogy that, in this day and age, would be promoted under the rubric of 'learning facilitation' (sic). This is the sort of pedagogical treachery that provoked a critical response from Paulo Freire. In an exchange with Donaldo P. Macedo, Freire states categorically that he refutes the term 'facilitator', which connotes such pedagogy, underlining the fact that he has always insisted on the directive nature of education.[xcvi] He insists on the term 'teacher,' one who derives one's authority from one's competence in the matter being taught, without allowing this authority to degenerate into authoritarianism.[xcvii] "Authority is necessary to the freedom of the students and my own. The teacher is absolutely necessary. What is bad, what is not necessary, is authoritarianism, but not authority."[xcviii]

Gramsci seems to be advocating a process of education that equips children with the necessary acumen to be able to participate in an informed dialogue. This is why Gramsci writes in terms of a "nexus between instruction and education".[xcix] Recall Freire's crude statement, in the conversation with Myles Horton, that there are moments when one must be "50% a traditional teacher and 50% a democratic teacher".[c]

Emphasis is being placed, in this context, on 'authority and freedom', the distinction posed by Freire[ci] but which echoes Gramsci's constant reference to the interplay between "spontaneita' e direzione consapevole" (spontaneity and conscious direction).[cii] In his piece on the Unitarian School, Gramsci calls for a balance to be struck between the kind of authority promoted by the old classical school (without degenerating into authoritarian education) and the 'freedom' advocated by the then contemporary proponents of ideas associated with Rousseau's philosophy as developed in Emile. The latter type of education, for Gramsci, had to develop from its 'romantic phase' (predicated on unbridled freedom for the learner, based on her or his spontaneity) and move into the 'classical' phase, classical in the sense of striking a balance.[ciii] This is the balance between freedom and authority that has been the subject of much debate in Freire's work.[civ] In Pedagogy of Hope, Freire argues that the educator's "directivity" should not interfere with the "creative, formulative, investigative capacity of the educand." Otherwise, the directivity degenerates into "manipulation, into authoritarianism".[cv] Referring to this aspect of Freire's work, Stanley Aronowitz is on target when stating, "…the educator's task is to encourage human agency,[cvi] not mold it in the manner of Pygmalion."[cvii]

There is an interesting contrast between Gramsci and Freire also with respect to another curricular issue. Gramsci's piece on the Unitarian school places importance on what he sees as the finer qualities of the 'old' classical school, the school which enabled him personally to transcend his formative environment, replete with the 'folklore' he despised, to gain that sense of cosmopolitanism which he regards as key to preventing people from remaining on the periphery of political life. It has been argued, by the leading Italian Gramsci scholar, Mario Alighiero Manacorda, that what Gramsci has provided in his notes on the Unitarian school is an epitaph for the old classical school, an epitaph celebrating what that school was and what it cannot be any longer given that the social reality has changed.[cviii] It was a school that had to be replaced by one more in tune with the reality of Gramsci's times. For Gramsci, however, the reforms the Gentile educational administration sought to introduce (la riforma Gentile), based on the stark division between classical and vocational schools, represented a retrograde step and not a progressive one: "It will be necessary to replace Latin and Greek as the fulcrum of the formative school, and they will be replaced. But it will not be easy to deploy the new subject or subjects in a didactic form which gives equivalent results in terms of education and general formation…"[cix] Highlighting the most salvageable aspects of the 'old school' ties in with what has been a constant feature of Gramsci's cultural writings, namely his advocacy of the need for subaltern groups[cx] to gain the means to critically appropriate established 'high status' cultural forms and knowledge with a view to moving from the margins to the center.

This represents an important point of contrast with Freire in whose work emphasis is placed, almost exclusively, on the popular, with 'high status' culture hardly featuring except for discussions concerning standard language as opposed to dialect. This is true not only of his writings on popular education but also of writings by sympathetic researchers, combining theoretical insights with empirical data,[cxi] concerning the school reform he helped carry out in São Paulo when he was Education Secretary there. The schools involved were, after all, designated 'popular public schools'. This is as it should be given the need to strengthen the school's link with the pupils' immediate culture through which these pupils can experience a sense of school ownership and identify with the culture it fosters. And yet Freire has always insisted that the popular constitutes only the starting point of the educational process. We find, in the literature on these reforms, ample material regarding the handling of social themes, derived from the pupils' immediate surroundings, which constitute the basis of these schools' curricula. There is however little material concerning the learning process occurring with respect to those subjects and their content areas which somehow relate to the dominant culture. The short-lived nature of the reforms, which were, to a certain extent, echoed in Porto Alegre,[cxii] could have played its part in denying one sufficient time to temper the initial enthusiasm for a highly innovative and refreshing approach to communal learning with some consideration concerning the effectiveness of this approach in enabling the poor children of the megalopolis to appropriate the skills and high order knowledge necessary to transcend their state of material impoverishment and powerlessness. Given Freire's insistence that the popular constitutes only the entry point to knowledge and is not the be all and end all of the learning process, then one would have relished some insightful considerations concerning the 'popular public' curriculum on the lines we have come to associate with Gramsci and more recently, with respect to high status literary texts,[cxiii] including 'texts of empire', intellectuals such as C.L.R. James and Edward Said. On the other hand, as O'Cadiz et al.[cxiv] demonstrate forcefully, there is much in the reforms carried out in São Paulo that can be of value to a process of curriculum development that draws on Gramscian insights.[cxv] The organization of knowledge into generative themes gleaned from research by teachers and collaborators carried out in the school's surrounding community can help "render popular culture an integral feature of the learning process where the focus does not lie solely on the written word, a limitation in Gramsci's cultural (including popular culture) writings."[cxvi] All this would be in the interest of developing a radically democratic 'popular public' education with a national and international character.

CONCLUSION

The last point might help to underscore the often complementary nature of the ideas expressed by Gramsci and Freire that are relevant to education; I had stressed the complementary nature of their works throughout my previous book length study[cxvii] and related papers on the subject. In this paper, I have limited myself to a consideration of some important connections in the thinking of Gramsci and Freire. This is just a limited selection that incorporates only a few of the several points of similarity and contrast I outlined in the book. I would like to think, however, that my writing of this paper for the 3rd Paulo Freire International Research Conference Proceedings has allowed me to explore some fresh connections between the work of these two major social theorists. I consider the exploration of further connections between Gramsci and Freire to be useful given that their work continues to remain a source of inspiration to many, especially those seeking new directions for a transformative and socialist pedagogical politics.

NOTES

[i]   I am indebted to Dr Paula Allman and Professor Peter Roberts for their valuable comments on the first draft of this paper. Any remaining shortcomings are my responsibility.

[ii]   See the recent anthology, in which references to the work of Paulo Freire are constantly made, and which includes the work of leading critical educationists in the USA, Europe and Latin America. Carmel Borg, Joseph A. Buttigieg and Peter Mayo (eds.), Gramsci and Education (Lanham: Rowman & Littlefield, 2002).

[iii]   Peter Mayo, Gramsci, Freire and Adult Education. Possibilities for Transformative Action (London: Zed Books, 1999).

[iv]   There is a significant literature consisting of studies on the work of Paulo Freire in relation to the ideas of other major social theorists and/or revolutionary activists. At the 3rd Paulo Freire research conference, this paper was presented in a panel which also included presentations on Freire and Dewey (Douglas Kellner) and Freire and Rousseau (Danilo Streck). Dewey seems to be an obvious figure with whom to compare Freire's work. Other works on this subject are provided by Carlos Torres and Walter Feinberg, and by Ali Abdi.. See Walter Feinberg and Carlos Alberto Torres, 'Democracy and Education: John Dewey and Paulo Freire' in *Education & Society*, ed. Joseph Zajda (Melbourne: James Nicholas Publishers, 2001) pp. 59-70; Ali. A Abdi 'Identity in the philosophies of Dewey and Freire: Select analyses' in Journal of Educational Thought 35,2 (2001): 181-200.   This section will also make reference to work discussing Freire's ideas alongside those of the recently deceased Ivan Illich and Ettore Gelpi. Further important studies comparing Freire's ideas with those of others are Peter McLaren, Che Guevara, Paulo Freire and the Pedagogy of Revolution (Lanham: Rowman and Littlefield, 2000) and Raymond A. Morrow and Carlos Alberto Torres, Reading Freire and Habermas. Critical Pedagogy and Transformative Social Change (New York: Teachers College Press, 2002).

[v]   See Paulo Freire, 'Reply to discussants' in Freire at the Institute, eds. Maria Figueiredo Cowen and Denise Gastaldo (London: Institute of Education, University of London, 1995) pp. 63-64. I am indebted for this point to Marjorie Mayo, Imagining Tomorrow. Adult Education and Social Transformation (Leicester: NIACE, 1997), Ch. 8, p. 171.

[vi]   Jose' Arico', La Cola del Diablo. Itinerario de Gramsci en America Latina (Caracas: Editorial Nueva Sociedad, 1988); Carlos Nelson Coutinho, 'In Brasile' in Gramsci in Europa e in America, ed. Antonio A. Santucci (Rome and Bari: Sagittari Laterza, 1995), pp.133-140 ; Osvaldo Fernández Díaz, 'In America Latina' in ed. Santucci, op.cit., pp.141-157 ; Antonio Melis, 'Gramsci e l'America Latina', in Antonio Gramsci e il 'Progresso Intelletuale di Massa', eds. Giorgio Baratta and Andrea Catone (Milan: Edizioni Unicopli, 1995) pp. 227-234;

[vii]   Timothy Ireland , Antonio Gramsci and Adult Education. Reflections on the Brazilian Experience (Manchester: Manchester University Press, 1987); Thomas, J. La Belle, Non Formal education in Latin America and the Caribbean. Stability, Reform or Revolution? (New York: Praeger, 1986).

[viii]   Carlos Alberto Torres, The Politics of Nonformal Education in Latin America (New York: Praeger, 1990); Liam Kane, Popular Education and Social Change in Latin America (London: Latin American Bureau, 2001).

[ix]   La Belle, op.cit., p.185. See also Carmel Borg, Joseph A. Buttigieg and Peter Mayo, 'Introduction. Gramsci and Education. A Holistic Approach' in Borg, Buttigieg and Mayo, op.cit., p. 14.

[x]   Raymond A. Morrow and Carlos Alberto Torres, Social Theory and Education. A Critique of Theories of Social and Cultural Reproduction, (Albany: SUNY Press, 1995); Raymond. A. Morrow and Carlos Alberto Torres., 'Gramsci and Popular Education in Latin America. From Revolution to Democratic Transition' in Borg, Buttigieg and Mayo, op.cit., pp. 179-200.

[xi]   On this point, apart from Morrow and Torres' chapter in Borg, Buttigieg and Mayo, op.cit., see also Morrow and Torres, op.cit. 2002, p. 79.

[xii]   Ibid.

[xiii]   Marjorie Mayo, op.cit., Ch. 1., pp. 23-27.

[xiv] Diana Coben, Radical Heroes. Gramsci, Freire and the Politics of Adult Education (New York: Garland Publishing, 1998).

[xv] Paul Ransome, Antonio Gramsci. A New Introduction (London: Harvester / Wheatsheaf, 1992); Peter Leonard, 'Critical Pedagogy and State Welfare - Intellectual encounters with Freire and Gramsci, 1974-86' in Paulo Freire: A Critical Encounter,eds. Peter Leonard and Peter McLaren (New York and London: Routledge, 1993), pp. 155-168; Margaret Ledwith, Participating in Transformation: Towards a Working Model of Community Empowerment (Birmingham, Venture Press, 1997).

[xvi] Paula Allman, 'Gramsci, Freire and Illich: Their contributions to education for socialism' in Radical Approaches to Adult Education. A Reader, ed. Tom Lovett (London: Routledge, 1988) pp. 85-113; Paula Allman, Revolutionary Social Transformation: Democratic Hopes, Political Possibilities and Critical Education, (Westport, Connecticut and London: Bergin & Garvey, 1999).

[xvii] Allman, 1988, op.cit.

[xviii] Antonio Gramsci, Selections from Political Writings (1910 - 20), eds. Quintin Hoare and John Matthews (New York: International Publishers, 1977).

[xix] Allman, 1999, op.cit.

[xx] This theme constitutes the leitmotif of her most recent work. See Paula Allman, Critical Education Against Global Capitalism. Karl Marx and Revolutionary Critical Education (Westport, Connecticut and London: Bergin & Garvey, 2001).

[xxi] Throughout this section, I reproduce, verbatim, sentences from my review of Paula Allman's 1999 book. See Peter Mayo, review of Paula Allman, Revolutionary Social Transformation in Adult Education Quarterly, 51, no. 3 (2001): 256-258.

[xxii] Valentino Gerratana in Antonio Gramsci, Quaderni del Carcere (Edizione Critica), (Turin: Einaudi, 1975) 3062-3063

[xxiii] Paulo Freire, Pedagogy of the Oppressed, (New York: The Seabury Press, 1970).

[xxiv] Paulo Freire, Pedagogy in Process. The Letters to Guinea Bissau, (New York: Continuum, 1978).

[xxv] See David Livingstone's reference to Castles and Wustenberg. Stephen Castles and Wiebke Wustenberg, The Education of the Future: An Introduction to the Theory and Practice of Socialist Education (London: Pluto, 1979); David W. Livingstone, Class, Ideologies and Educational Futures (Sussex: The Falmer Press, 1983), pp. 186, 187.

[xxvi] Freire, 1978, op.cit.

[xxvii] Livingstone, op.cit., p. 187.

[xxviii] Allman, 1988, op.cit.

[xxix] Allman, 1999, op.cit, pp. 62, 63. In a situation characterized by the ongoing struggle for a critical and humanizing pedagogy, the actions of educators and learners are guided by the goal of 'negating the negation' of a dehumanizing relation, occurring under conditions of 'banking education.' Under Banking Education, the educator supports, deliberately or unwittingly, a dehumanizing structure of oppression that can only be solved through the termination of this oppressive and dehumanizing relation that denies both teacher and learner their humanity. This, I would argue, remains an ongoing struggle with no point of arrival. In my view, 'banking education' and 'dialogical education' ought to be conceived of as ends of a continuum. There are several tensions which prevent the 'negation of the negation' in the educational relationship from being realized fully, such as the tension between 'authority and freedom' to which I shall return later.

[xxx] For a thorough exposition of dialectical thinking, see Allman , 2001, op.cit. pp. 39-48.

[xxxi] Paula Allman with Peter Mayo, chris cavanagh, Chan Lean Heng and Sergio Haddad, "the creation of a world in which it will be easier to love..." in Convergence, XXXI, 1 & 2 (1998): 9 - 16

[xxxii] Karl Marx and Frederick Engels, The German Ideology, ed. C.J. Arthur (London: Lawrence and Wishart, 1970), p.64 .

[xxxiii] Ibid.

[xxxiv] Jorge Larrain, Marxism and Ideology (New Jersey: Humanities Press, 1983), p.24.

[xxxv] Marx and Engels, op.cit. 1970, pp. 65, 66.

[xxxvi] Antonio Gramsci, *Quaderni del Carcere, Edizione Critica*, ed. Valentino Gerratana (Turin: Einaudi, 1975) p.1396. See Carmel Borg and Peter Mayo, 'Gramsci and the Unitarian School: Paradoxes and Possibilities' in Borg, Buttigieg and Mayo, op.cit., pp. 87-108. Translation from Italian original by Carmel Borg.

[xxxvii] Antonio Gramsci, Selections from the Prison Notebooks, ed. and trans. Quintin Hoare and Geoffrey Nowell Smith (New York: International Publishers, 1971), p. 25. See Larrain, op.cit. for an excellent discussion of this distinction within the context of Marxism and ideology. See also Jorge Larrain, The Concept of Ideology (London: Hutchinson, 1979).

[xxxviii] Ibid.

[xxxix] Leonardo Salamini, The Sociology of Political Praxis - An Introduction to Gramsci's Theory (London: Routledge & Kegan Paul, 1981).

[xl] Borg and Mayo, 2002, op.cit., p. 91.

[xli] Gramsci, op.cit., 1971, p. 325.

[xlii] Larrain, op.cit., 1979, p .81.

[xliii] Sergio Caruso, 'La riforma intelletuale e morale' in Gramsci: I Quaderni del Carcere.í Una riflessione politica incompiuta, ed. Salvo Mastellone (Turin: UTET Libreria, 1997). pp.85, 86.

[xliv] It can be assumed that Gramsci intended much of what Allman calls 'prefigurative work', referred to earlier, to be geared towards this goal. However, Jorge Larrain provides the important caveat that such prefigurative work can never result in "total ideological domination" prior to the conquest of the state since, as Gramsci maintains, "class consciousness cannot be completely modified until the mode of life of the class itself is modified, which entails that the proletariat has become the ruling class" through " possession of the apparatus of production and exchange and state power." First part of the quote in English translation is found on the page where Larrain makes this important point. See Larrain, op.cit. 1983, p.82 The second part of the quote is my translation from the original tract by Gramsci, entitled, 'Necessita` di Una Preparazione Ideologica di Massa', found in Antonio Gramsci, Le Opere. La Prima Antologia di Tutti Gli Scritti, ed. Antonio Santucci (Rome: Editori Riuniti, 1997) p. 161.

[xlv] Kane, op.cit., p. 50.

[xlvi] Freire, 1970, op.cit., p.163.

[xlvii] Paulo Freire, The Politics of Education (Massachusetts: Bergin & Garvey, 1985), p. 131.

[xlviii] For book length expositions of Paulo Freire's philosophy, see Paul V. Taylor, The Texts of Paulo Freire (Buckingham: Open University Press, 1993); John Elias, Paulo Freire: Pedagogue of Liberation (Florida: Kreiger, 1994); Moacir Gadotti, Reading Paulo Freire. His Life and Work (Albany: Suny Press, 1994); Peter Roberts, Literacy and Humanization. Exploring the Work of Paulo Freire (Wesport, Connecticut: Bergin & Garvey, 2000); Antonia Darder, Reinventing Paulo Freire. A Pedagogy of Love (Boulder: Westview Press, 2002); Peter Mayo, Liberating Praxis. Paulo Freire's Legacy for Radical Education and Politics (Westport, Connecticut: Bergin & Garvey, 2004). See also various papers in McLaren and Leonard (eds.),op.cit.; Peter McLaren and Colin Lankshear (eds.), Politics of Liberation. Paths from Freire (New York and London: Routledge, 1994); Part 2, 'The Man with the Gray Beard' in McLaren, op.cit., 2001.

[xlix] Paulo Freire, 'A Response' in Mentoring the Mentor, A Critical Dialogue with Paulo Freire, eds. Freire, P (ed.) with James W. Fraser, Donaldo Macedo, Tanya McKinnon and William T.Stokes (new York: Peter Lang, 1997), pp. 303-329.

[l] Paulo Freire, Pedagogy of Freedom. Ethics, Democracy and Civic Courage (Lanham: Rowman and Littlefield, 1998, 51, 66). As I have argued elsewhere, this makes nonsense of the criticism, directed at Freire in North America, that he fails to recognize that one can be oppressed in one situation and an oppressor in another and that he posits a binary opposition between oppressor and oppressed. If anything, the relations between oppressor and oppressed have always been presented by Freire as dialectical rather than as binary opposites. Peter Mayo, ' "Remaining on the same side of the river": A Critical Commentary on Paulo Freire's Later Work' in Review of Education/Pedagogy/Cultural Studies, 22, no. 4 (2001):369-397. Also see Allman, 1999, op.cit., pp. 88-89, for an insightful exposition in this regard.

[li] Antonio Gramsci, The Modern Prince and Other Writings, ed. Louis Marks (New York: International Publishers, 1957), p. 75; Freire, op.cit., 1985, p.179.

[lii] Paulo Freire in Darder, op.cit., p.x. On the issue of history as possibility, see also Paulo Freire, Pedagogy of the City (New York: Continuum, 1993), p.65; Paulo Freire, Politics and Education (Los Angeles: UCLA Latin American Center Publications, 1998), p. 88

[liii] Freire, Pedagogy of Freedom, op.cit. p. 54

[liv] Raymond. A. Morrow, 'Introducing Gramsci on Hegemony. Towards a Post-marxist Interpretation'. Paper delivered at the Colloquium on the Fiftieth Anniversary of Gramsci's death, Edmonton, Dept. of Educational Foundations, The University of Alberta, 27th April, 1987.

[lv] Included in Paulo Freire, Education for Critical Consciousness (New York: Continuum, 1973).

[lvi] Angelo Broccoli, Antonio Gramsci e l'Educazione come egemonia (Firenze: La Nuova Italia, 1972); Morrow, op.cit., p.2.

[lvii] Frank Youngman, Adult Education and Socialist Pedagogy (Kent: Croom Helm, 1986), p. 159.

[lviii] Paula Allman and John Wallis, 'Challenging the Postmodern Condition: Radical Adult Education for Critical Intelligence' in *Adult Learning Critical Intelligence and Social Change*, eds. Marjorie Mayo and Jane Thompson (Leicester: NIACE, 1995), pp.; Griff Foley, Learning in Social Action. A Contribution to Understanding Informal Education (London and New York: Zed Books, 1999).

[lix] Quintin Hoare and Geoffrey Nowell Smith in Antonio Gramsci, op.cit, 1971, p.280. Argument reproduced from Paula Allman and Peter Mayo, 'Freire, Gramsci and globalisation: some implications for social and political commitment in adult education' in Crossing Borders breaking boundaries - research in the education of adults. Proceedings of the 27th Annual SCUTREA Conference, eds. Paul Armstrong, Nod Miller and Miriam Zukas (London: Birkbeck College University of London, 1997), p. 8.

[lx] See Griff Foley with respect to the implications of such reorganization for Capitalism. Griff Foley, ' Adult Education and Capitalist Reorganisation', Studies in the Education of Adults, 26 no. 2 (1994): 121 –143; Foley,op.cit.1999.

[lxi] Henry Giroux,,Public Spaces/Private Lives. Beyond the Culture of Cynicism (Maryland: Rowman and Littlefield, 2001).

[lxii] Paulo Freire, Teachers as Cultural Workers. Letters to those who dare teach (Colorado: Westview Press, 1998), p. 14.

[lxiii] Ana Maria (Nita) Araujo Freire, 'A bit of my Life with Paulo Freire' in Taboo. The Journal of Culture and Education, ll, Fall (1997): 3-11, p.10.

[lxiv] Saverio Festa, Gramsci (Assisi: Cittadella Editrice, 1976).

[lxv] See Stanley Aronowitz, ' Gramsci's Theory of Education: Schooling and Beyond' in Borg, Buttigieg,, Mayo, op.cit., pp.109-120 ; John Baldacchino, 'On a Dog Chasing its Tail. Gramsci's Challenge to the Sociology of Knowledge' in Borg, Buttigieg, Mayo, op.cit., pp. 133-146; Borg and Mayo, 2002, op.cit.; Joseph A. Buttigieg, 'Education, The Role of Intellectuals and Democracy. A Gramscian Reflection', 2002a in Borg, Buttigieg, Mayo, 2002, op.cit., pp.121-132; Henry A. Giroux, 'Rethinking Cultural Politics and Radical Pedagogy in the Work of Antonio Gramsci' in Borg, Buttigieg, Mayo, op.cit., pp.41- 65.

[lxvi] Bogdan Suchodolski, ''Lifelong Education – Some Philosophical Aspects' in Foundations of Lifelong Education, ed. Ravindah H. Dave, (Oxford: Pergamon Press; Hamburg: UNESCO Institute for Education, 1976).

[lxvii] Joseph A. Buttigieg, 'On Gramsci' in Daedalus, Summer (2002a): 67-70, pp. 69-70.

[lxviii] Gramsci uses 'Civil Society' in a manner that is different from the way it is used nowadays. The term, as used by Gramsci, refers to the complex of ideological institutions (print and broadcasting media, religious institutions, mass organizations, adult education institutions, parties, unions, factory councils etc.) that primarily serve to sustain and cement the present hegemonic relations but which also contain spaces within them wherein these relations can be challenged and gradually, probably through a 'long revolution,' be transformed.

[lxix] Raymond Williams, The Long Revolution (Middlesex: Penguin, 1960).

[lxx] Antonio Gramsci, The Southern Question, ed and trans. Pasquale Verdicchio (West Lafayette, IN: Bordighera Incorporated, 1995), pp. 44, 45.

[lxxi] Giorgio Amendola, Antonio Gramsci nella vita culturale e politica Italiana (Naples: Guida Editori, 1978), p. 39.

[lxxii] John D. Holst, Social Movements, Civil Society and Radical Adult Education (Westport, Connecticut, London: Bergin & Garvey, 2002), p. 112.

[lxxiii] Myles Horton and Paulo Freire, We make the road by walking. Conversations on education and social change (Philadelphia: Temple University Press, 1990);Miguel Escobar, Alfredo L. Fernandez and Gilberto Guevara-Niebla, with Paulo Freire, Paulo Freire on Higher Education. A Dialogue at the National University of Mexico, (Albany: SUNY Press, 1994).

lxxiv   Freire, in Escobar et al, op.cit., pp. 31, 32.

lxxv   See María del Pilar O'Cadiz, Pia L. Wong, and Carlos Alberto Torres (1997), Education and Democracy Paulo Freire, Social Movements and Educational Reform in São Paulo (Boulder: Westview Press, 1997); María del Pilar O'Cadiz, 'Social Movements and Literacy Training in Brazil: A Narrative' in Education and Social Change in Latin America, ed. Carlos Alberto Torres (Melbourne: James Nicholas Publishers, 1995), p. 163-173.

lxxvi   Literal translation: Movement of Rural Workers without Land. The abbreviated title is Movimento dos Sem Terra (MST - Movement of Landless Peasants). This is arguably one of the two most vibrant movements in Latin America, the Frente Zapatista in Chiapas being the other.

lxxvii   Kane, op.cit., Ch.4.

lxxviii   ibid., p.97.

lxxix   Nita Freire in Carmel Borg and Peter Mayo, 'Reflections from a "third age" marriage: Paulo Freire's pedagogy of reason, hope and passion. An Interview with Ana Maria (Nita) Araujo Freire,' in McGill Journal of Education, 35, no.2 (2000): 105-120, p.109.

lxxx   Paulo Freire in Ira Shor and Paulo Freire, A Pedagogy of Liberation. Dialogues on Transforming Education (Massachusetts: Bergin & Garvey, 1997), p. 37.

lxxxi   Paulo Freire, Pedagogy of the City (New York: Continuum, 1993); O'Cadiz et al., op.cit.

lxxxii   Holst, op.cit.

lxxxiii   Coutinho, op.cit.

lxxxiv   Freire, in Escobar et al, op.cit., p. 40

lxxxv   Daniel Schugurensky, 'Transformative Learning and Transformative Politics. The Pedagogical Dimension of Participatory Democracy and Social Action', eds. Edmund O'Sullivan, Amish Morrell, and Mary O'Connor, Expanding the Boundaries of Transformative Learning (New York: Palgrave, 2002), pp. 59 – 76. See also Angie Gallop's interview of the same author : Schugurensky, D (2002), 'From South to North: Can the Participatory Budget be Exported?', www.rabble.ca, November,1-9; Luiz Armando Gandin and Michael W. Apple, 'Thin versus Thick Democracy in Education: Porto Alegre and the creation of alternatives to Neo-liberalism' in International Studies in Sociology of Education 12, no.2, 99-115.

lxxxvi   Carmel Borg and Peter Mayo, 2002, op.cit., p.89.

lxxxvii   Quintin Hoare and Geoffrey Nowell Smith in Gramsci, op.cit, 1971, p. X111.

lxxxviii   Allman, op.cit., 1999.

lxxxix   Paulo Freire and Antonio Faundez, Learning to Question. A Pedagogy of Liberation (Geneva: World Council of Churches, 1989). On this see also Frei Betto and Paulo Freire, Una Scuola Chiamata Vita (Bologna: EMI, 1986), p. 58.

xc   Mayo, op.cit.1999, p. 91.

xci   Stanley Aronowitz, 'Freire's Radical Democratic Humanism'in McLaren and Leonard, op.cit., pp. 8-24.

xcii   Borg and Mayo, op.cit., 2002; Mayo, op.cit., 1999.

xciii   Harold Entwistle, Antonio Gramsci. Conservative Schooling for Radical Politics (London: Routledge and Kegan Paul, 1979), p. 47.

xciv   Antonio Gramsci, L'Alternativa Pedagogica, ed. Mario Alighiero Manacorda (Florence: La Nuova Italia, 1972), p. 83.

xcv   Ibid. pp.84, 85.

xcvi   See for instance Paulo Freire in Ira Shor and Paulo Freire, op.cit. p.103; Paulo Freire and Donaldo P. Macedo, 'A Dialogue: Culture, Language and Race', in Harvard Educational Review, 65, no. 3 (1995): 377 - 402. p. 394; Freire op.cit, 1993, p. 116; See also Freire in Moacir Gadotti, Paulo Freire and and Sergio Guimarães, Pedagogia: Dialogo e Conflitto, eds. B.Bellanova and F.Telleri (Torino: Societa' Editrice Internazionale), p.50.

xcvii   Freire and Macedo, op.cit., p. 378.

xcviii   Freire, in Horton and Freire, op.cit., p.181. See also Freire in Shor and Freire, op.cit. p.91.

xcix   Gramsci, op.cit., 1971, p. 36.

c   Freire, in Horton and Freire, op.cit., p.160.

ci   Freire, Pedagogy of Freedom.

cii   See, for instance, the anthology, Antonio Gramsci, Passato e Presente (Rome: Editori Riuniti, 1998), pp. 70-74.

ciii   Gramsci, op.cit., 1971, pp.32, 33.

[civ]   For a useful discussion on this, see Moacir Gadotti, Pedagogy of Praxis. A Dialectical Philosophy of Education (Albany: SUNY Press, 1996).

[cv]   Paulo Freire, Pedagogy of Hope (New York: Continuum, 1994), p. 79.

[cvi]   On the issue of 'agency', see Carmel Borg, Joseph A. Buttigieg and Peter Mayo, 'Introduction. Gramsci and Education. A Holistic Approach' in Borg, Buttigieg and Mayo, op.cit.

[cvii]   Stanley Aronowitz, 'Introduction' in Freire, Pedagogy of Freedom, p. 10.

[cviii]   Borg and Mayo, op.cit., pp.102-103. Mario Alighiero Manacorda in Antonio Gramsci, op.cit.1972, p.xxix.

[cix]   Gramsci, 1979, op.cit. pp.39-40.

[cx]   For an insightful discussion on the issue of subaltern groups and subaltern culture with reference to the relevance of the term 'subaltern' to such areas as colonialism, see Chapter 5 in Kate Crehan, Gramsci, Culture and Anthropology (Berkeley: University of Califronia Press, 2002).

[cxi]   O'Cadiz, Wong and Torres, 1998, op.cit. See also Peter Mayo's very favorable review of this work in Journal of Transformative Education, 2004, op.cit. Forthcoming.

[cxii]   Gandin and Apple, op.cit., 2001.

[cxiii]   For insightful discussions on Gramsci and literature see Ch.4 on the use and misuse of Gramsci in certain sections of the US literature on literary theory and cultural studies and Ch. 7, 'Yesterday, Today and Tomorrow. Notes on Antonio Gramsci's Theory of Literature and Culture,' both in Gregory L. Lucente, Crosspaths in Literary Theory and Criticism. Italy and the United States (California, Stanford University Press, 1997).

[cxiv]   O'Cadiz, Wong and Torres, 1998, op.cit.

[cxv]   Buttigieg, 2002b, op.cit, p. 130.

[cxvi]   Borg and Mayo, 2002, op.cit., p. 103

[cxvii]   Mayo, op.cit., 1999.

DANILO R. STRECK

THE UTOPIAN LEGACY: ROUSSEAU AND FREIRE

It is the dream that liberates. From everything: from the world, from others, from us. It is necessary to believe in the dream. And to save it always. In order to save ourselves. In order to leave the radiant face of our joy in the last wilderness, and in the last shadow, where other lives will come later and ask the things that we today are asking ourselves. (Cecília Meireles)

UTOPIA AND EDUCATION

Education and utopia have been bound together to the point of becoming almost inseparable. The possibility of situating oneself somewhere else, moreover in a not yet existing place, is the very foundation for educability. Both the etymology of education and pedagogy indicate respectively the movement from within to the outside, to a place, which may be known, or unknown; or the conduction of another one to a situation of learning. Education has thus come to express the very possibility of humans making a project of themselves and of the world they live in. Once there is education the images the educator makes of the educability of the educatee are a foundational element of the process.[i]

The question about the very possibility of education has much to do with the Western way of thinking and of relating to the world, which today is being widely criticized. Ideas such as historical linearity, continual progress and the faith in an unlimited human capacity to interfere in the world have been denounced for their claim of universality when, in fact, they are enmeshed in a complex set of power relations. Today we discover that there is cultures that do not even have a corresponding word for what we call education and that nevertheless live happy lives.

The purpose of engaging Rousseau and Freire in the dialogue about the problematic above enunciated is due to the fact that both stand at what might be considered two poles in tension. Rousseau represents better than anyone else the making of the pedagogical project within the modern social contract. His Emile is an obligatory reference for understanding the development of pedagogy as a specific field of knowledge. On the other hand, Paulo Freire stands for what could be understood as the search for pedagogy at the encounter of times[ii]. In the expression of the Portuguese sociologist Boaventura de Sousa Santos (2000:56), ours is a time of paradigmatic transition, when the lenses through which we see reality and the instruments to apprehend it reveal themselves inadequate. The frequent questioning of whether Paulo Freire is modern, postmodern or traditional

C.A. Torres & P. Noguera (Eds.), Social Justice Education for Teachers, 69–80.

– or a combination of them - is an expression of what he represents as an emblematic educational thinker for our times. Both Rousseau and Freire have in common an exceptional sensitivity to capture the political-pedagogical movements in historical periods of transition.[iii] This leads to radical and comprehensive theoretical formulations, which on their turn, are the ground for countless interpretations.

In this article I will point out some arguments where the dialogue between Rousseau and Freire can bring inputs for the present discussions in the field of education, inasmuch as this praxis relates to the cultural, political and social transformations of our time. First, I will focus on what allows us to see them as utopian educators, attempting to interpret some of the assumptions on which they build their utopian praxis. Secondly, there will be an effort to characterize issues where Paulo Freire incorporates a set of ideas that make it possible to have a fresh look at education and eventually to move towards what might become a pedagogy for a new social contract, an expression which represents the search for another way of being and living in the world. Its is an attempt to face the shortcomings of the modern social contract for the excluding character it assumed throughout the last two or three centuries. The discussion about pedagogy for a new social contract comprehends among other issues the understanding of human nature, the vision of education as a political-pedagogical project and the basic pedagogical teacher-learner relationship.

It must be remarked that in this essay it will not be possible to account for the over two centuries that stand between these two authors. For example, as much as Marx is a reference for Freire, he himself will build on many of Rousseau's assumptions. To stay with education, between our authors there is nothing less than a list of "universal" names such as Pestalozzi, Herbart, Montessori, Vygotski and John Dewey. In Latin America we could mention from José Martí to Anísio Teixeira. Considering the density and complexity of the pedagogical experiences that create the matrix for the dialogue of these two authors, and which can not be referred to directly in this text, their names in the title are connected through the less ambitious "and" (Rousseau and Freire) instead of "from…to" (from Rousseau to Freire), which would require a more explicit historical approach.

UTOPIA AS PERFECTIBILITY (ROUSSEAU)

In a provocative heading Adriana Puiggrós (1995) states "Emile educates Rousseau." Her intention is to show that with Rousseau there is a radical shift from what has been the traditional understanding of the role of the persons involved in the pedagogical process. It is not, at least in theory[iv], the educator who determines the direction and sets the pace for the process, but rather the pupil himself. "What must be done to train this exceptional man! We can do much, but the chief thing is to prevent anything being done." (Rousseau, 1974:9) Puiggrós will see in this formulation the possibility for the Marxist claim of the proletariat taking education and social transformation in their hands. For Freire, it will later turn out to be pedagogy of the oppressed and not for them, as we shall see later.

Rousseau's type of utopianism can be best seen in his permanent effort not to conform to the status quo. The foundation for this nonconformity lies in a past state of nature where one would still find the signs of a different world and of a different humanity. This idyllic reality, situated somewhere in the past, works as an image seen in a mirror which helps to find the right path and provides de vision for the future. Humans can be different from what they are. Society can be different. Therefore, it is quite irrelevant where Emile comes from, who his parents are, whether he has brothers and sisters. He can be "taken out" of the world in which he was born and if properly educated he will generate a different society.

The possibility of utopia is based on the human's potential for perfectibility, which, on its turn, derives from the capacity of self-improvement. It is the faculty of self-improvement "which, by the help of circumstances, gradually develops all the rest of our faculties, and is inherent in the species as in the individual".[v] Through this capacity humans differentiate themselves from the brutes and, as a consequence, it is the faculty to which can be finally traced humanity's achievements and misfortunes.

Man (sic!) is characterized by the "disproportion between his strengths and his desires"[vi] which at the same time is the cause of humans' weakness and the very foundation of their perfectibility. Learning happens when there is an appropriation of this sense of incompleteness, when the desires extrapolate the existing capacities and when this sense is properly instrumented and supported. Thus we can understand Rousseau's criticism of the seemingly futile discussions about the best methods for teaching a child how to read.

> People make a great fuss about discovering the best way to teach children to read. They invent "bureaux" and cards, they turn the nursery into a printer's shop. Locke would have them read by means of dice. What a fine idea! And the pity of it! There is a better way than any of those, and one, which is generally overlooked – it consists in the desire to learn. Arouse this desire in your scholar and have done with you "bureaux" and your dice – any method will serve.[vii]

Due to his trust in human nature – and corresponding distrust in society - Rousseau poses a radical critique for the society of his time. Emile must learn how to stand on his own feet, how to think for himself and not to take anything for granted. Books take away one's freedom, and Emile will be introduced to them very carefully through the reading of Robinson Crusoe. If humans are born enslaved, it is not because of a predetermined destiny or of some sort of natural law, but simply because of the way they have been organizing themselves in society. Therefore, they are also capable of promoting a social contract characterized by institutional arrangements based on equality among individuals under a collectively defined sovereign.[viii]

It is important to state that utopia was part of the eighteenth century thinking, as summarized in these sentences of James F. Jones (1977:27): "The safe, orderly word of a deo rex, a rege lex was crumbling, and something had to fill the vacuum. It is in this context that numerous eighteenth-century utopias appeared.

Cumulatively, they represent an essential characteristic of one of the most crucial intellectual crises in Western civilization." Rousseau, however, had very little in common with those who saw perfectibility and progress as being accomplished through the advance of science and technology, which he criticizes for contributing for human suffering. Emil's education is at the same time a critique of the traditional scholasticism as of the emerging technicism. This ability to criticize the lights from within the lights makes of Rousseau also such an important companion at the present.

UTOPIA AS THE INÉDITO VIÁVEL (FREIRE)

The expression that in my view best defines Freire's utopian praxis is inédito viável for combining in a very creative way the idea of newness and originality (the not yet edited) with the idea of historicity and possibility. Ana Maria Araújo Freire, in an elucidative note about the concept, writes "this category holds in itself the belief in the possible dream and in the coming utopia." (In Freire, 1992:205). To be utopian is not related to a sort of dreaming disconnected from the real world of necessity and conflicts. At the same time, it requires a rupture with this real world, which tends to "conform" thinking and social practice to it as a kind of inevitability. Utopia should neither be confounded with that which is purely imagined neither with that which is realistically possible. It happens in the tension between these two poles. The space between the "inedited" and the "viable" provides the climate for the creation of the new, the different or the other.

Freire's utopianism is founded on his understanding of both humans and the world as unfinished, as incomplete. The notion of "being more" in some way summarizes this understanding: "being more" implies above all openness to new possibilities of being him/herself and of being in the world. At the same time, this openness is never regarded as a purely individual challenge or achievement. Men and women are necessarily together in this adventure of dreaming and making themselves and the world.

Dreaming the possible as a way of being in the world has a political dimension. Freire (1992:91) speaks of a "strategic dreaming" (sonho estratégico) to indicate that there should not be dichotomization of ends and means, of theory and practice, of thinking and doing: "Dreaming is not only a necessary political act, but also a connotation of a socio-historical way of being women and men. It is part of human nature which, within history, is in permanent process of becoming."

This reveals itself pedagogically in tensions to be daily dealt with in the educational process: the tension between discourse and praxis; between saying the word and being silent; between subjectivity and objectivity; between the here of the educator and the here of the educatee and respectively their different there; between theory and practice; between pure spontaneity and manipulation; between patience and impatience. Let us have a closer look at the latter to exemplify the centrality of these tensions in Freire's thinking. To be patiently impatient or impatiently patient means not to give in to the temptation of leaving things as they are and should continue to be, neither to elevate oneself above the concrete and real problems as if any actions were possible. The educator who lives this tension is one that waits for the educatee, who walks with him/her, always challenging the educatee and in this process being him/herself challenged by a reality that has become an object of their epistemological curiosity.[ix] Using images coined by Freire himself, the educator cannot stand quietly on the beach, with his/her arms crossed, waiting for the fleet to come to him, but he is part of the fleet that looks for a safe haven where to land; or he/she is not one that simply calls for the educatee to cross the road in order to meet him/her on the side where he/she already stands. Education implies crossing frontiers (cultural, political, geographical, economical, etc.) for the encounter; it means the willingness to get soaked within the culture of the Other.

Although Freire has not lived long enough to feel the vibrations of the World Social Forum, this seems to be a space and a movement, which comes near to what his dreams refer to.[x] In one of his last interviews he was asked about what he thought about the march of the landless peasants to Brasilia and he answered that he would like to see the world full of such marches, from those who fail in schools to those who do not have love. The World Social Forum is the place where many marches meet under the slogan "Another World is Possible." It is movement, it is possibility and it is reality. Also the climate of the Forum, which combines the most serious discussions and the friendliness of a party, is a sign that the desired other world does not need to repeat the harshness of this one. For Freire, there will be no other education or other world without amorosity.[xi]

ROUSSEAU AND FREIRE ON UTOPIA: SOME ENCOUNTERS

So far, the intention has been to highlight basic principles on which Rousseau and Freire build their understanding of utopia without attempting a direct encounter. In what follows, there will be an exploratory comparative analysis of some themes, which emerge from the thought of these two authors. The underlying assumption is that the capacity of utopian praxis continues absolutely necessary at a time when some scholars proclaim the end of utopia, just confirming the apparent lack of political alternatives and the concomitant public apathy. After all, as Cecilia Meireles so beautifully wrote in the text used as epigraph: "It is the dream that liberates. From everything: from the world, from others, from us. It is necessary to believe in the dream. And to save it always. In order to save ourselves."

Human nature and educability

For Freire as for Rousseau the problematic of human nature underlies the theorizing about education and politics. In spite of their utopianism there are, however, some important distinctions, which lead to different proposals for education and political activity. Rousseau's departure point is that there is something like a human nature, ultimately derived from God. "God makes all things good; man meddles with them and they become evil." (Rousseau, 1974:5). His anthropology follows the classical theological model of creation, paradise and fall. The "paradise" (the natural world and man) is both something to go back to when one looks for his/her origins and something which lies ahead as a goal. At the same time, the fall, which corresponds to the emergence of consciousness, has provoked an abyss, which is now impossible to bridge. If in theology there is the recourse to Christ as the one who remakes the covenant broken by Adam and Eve, for the enlightened Rousseau this possibility is exclusively up to humans. And for humans it remains always a challenge and an aim to be persecuted, something between the possible and the impossible. "Men say the golden age is a fable; it always will be for those whose feelings and tastes are depraved. People do not really regret the golden age, for they do nothing to restore it. What is needed for its restoration? One thing only, and that is an impossibility; we must love the golden age." (Rousseau, 1974:439) The impossibility seems to lie in not loving that which one does not know, since from early childhood humans have been taught and trained in ways that lead away from this golden age. Education helps to promote a kind of forgetfulness regarding what once was and in this process blurs the sight for what could or should be.

In Freire we have a quite different approach to human nature. Humans or institutions are neither good nor bad by nature. Actually there is no human nature apart from the world in which men and women live since what it means to be human is itself a product of a given culture. Human nature is always in the process of becoming, a historical happening. There is, therefore, no specific content for his notion of "being more", different as Rousseau's idea of "perfectibility" which is referred to a supposed peaceful state of nature.

Does this mean that Freire shares some post-modern claims of cultural relativism based on difference as the basic criteria for ethical decisions? Where this the case, how to explain a pedagogy of the oppressed which he expands as a pedagogy of dialogue, of hope, of autonomy, of indignation...? The answer to this question must be sought in connection with his understanding of humanization as a process and as a possibility. Mutatis mutandi, for Freire there is always the risk for its distortion, i.e., for dehumanization. As stated in the opening paragraph of the Pedagogy of the Oppressed:

> While the problem of humanization has always, from an axiological point of view, been man's central problem, it now takes on the character of inescapable concern. Concern for humanization leads at once to the recognition of dehumanization, not only as an ontological possibility but as an historical reality. And as man perceives the extent of dehumanization, he asks himself if humanization is a viable possibility. Within history, in concrete, objective contexts, both humanization and dehumanization are possibilities for man as an uncompleted being conscious of his incompletion. (Freire, 1972:27)

Freire goes on saying that although humanization and dehumanization are concrete possibilities and realities they are axiologically not interchangeable, then only the first one corresponds to the human vocation. This vocation is broadly defined as the search for "being more", which while not having a definitive content should also not be seen as a void. "Being more" is historically defined and acquires its content against the concrete forms of oppression, which always represent a distortion of the basic possibility of humanization. For Freire "only the power that springs from the weakness of the oppressed will be sufficiently strong to free both." (Freire, 1972:28) They are those who, dialectically, are the primary carriers of the possibilities for advancing humanization. From the outside, they challenge the system where there is no place for them.

Different from Rousseau, there is no reference to a "golden age", neither in the past or in the future. Humanization is an open-ended process to which there is also not a foreseeable linearity. Men and women are on the way of becoming throughout history as they struggle to overcome the limit-situations, which are an obstacle for their "being more". There is also no room for the bon savage, and idealized universal human being whose purpose is to mirror what humanity is not, but who is hem/herself left out of the social contract.

Education as a political-pedagogical project:

There is no possibility of separating Rousseau's Emile from his Social Contract. The long and detailed educational process of Emile is a kind of preparation for introducing the social contract which is "the foundation of all civil society, and it is in the nature of this contract that we must seek the nature of the society formed by it" (Rousseau, 1974:424). At the same time, this double-faced process shows that no political project can be created and sustained without the recourse to pedagogy. Its constitution is itself a pedagogical process.

Rousseau is one of the great mentors of the modern social contract, regarded by Boaventura de Sousa Santos (1999) as the core metaphor of modern politics. In Emile (p. 424) Rousseau summarizes the social contract in this formula: "As an individual every one of us contributes his goods, his person, his life, to the common stock, under the supreme direction of the general will; while as a body we receive each member as an indivisible part of the whole." This contract has become a necessity since life in society under a given authority cannot anymore be taken for granted, either based on some sort of natural order or of divine dispensation. It is now up to individuals to find ways of living together, of building communities and nations.

In Freire we find the same pervasiveness of the political realm. Education is political, through and through, in the same way as politics is pedagogical. This can be exemplified with Freire's view of the consequences of colonization in Brazil. For him, it was the colonization model that largely conditioned the lack of democratic experience in the country. "Our colonization", he writes, "strongly predatory, was based on economic exploitation of the large landholding and on slave labor – at first native, then African. A colonization of this type could not create conditions necessary for the development of the permeable, flexible mentality characteristic of a democratic cultural climate." (Freire, 1973:21) This does not mean that Brazilians are destined to live in a non-democratic society. His argument is exactly that as beings of praxis, and not of adaptation, men and women are capable of producing a different future for themselves. To read and to pronounce the word means at the same time to create and to transform the world.

What is this world to be created? I would argue that Freire finds himself, as said earlier in this essay, at the other extreme of the modern social contract. As the master story of political organization, the modern social contract has shown its shortcomings and has revealed itself misleading and narrow. Women have criticized it as being a male contract.[xii] Blacks have denounced it as a white race contract.[xiii] The social contract has reduced nature to a mere physical support.[xiv] Besides, the real social apartheids we find within most countries and among countries is a sign that something went wrong with this story. Freire can be identified with those who try to develop an education for a new social contract, which incorporates elements such as the need to look at the material basis on which a society produces and reproduces itself; the recognition of inter-subjectivity as a way of being in the world; a greater attention to the constitution of power relations; a new understanding of the place of men and women in the cosmos.[xv]

There could be mentioned many examples of how schools or school systems and other educational settings try to plan and carry out their educational praxis as quite complex political-pedagogical projects. In Brazil there is the movement of the so called "escolas cidadãs" (citizen schools), very much inspired on Freire, where the "content" to be known is the life of the community itself. Throughout all of Latin America the pedagogical movement known as "Educação Popular" (Popular Education) has as one of its principles the commitment to the transformation of society. What these pedagogical practices have in common is the tensioned unity of reading the world and reading the word, of not dichotomizing teaching and learning from the critical insertion in reality.

From tutor and pupil to the teacher-learner community:

Rousseau's and Freire's utopian visions are embodied in very concrete pedagogical practices. Both draw their pedagogical insights and proposals from a keen observation of the education and the world in which it takes place. Rousseau watches closely how children play, how mothers relate to their children or what schools do to children. Freire's pedagogical writings, as he himself refers to them, are always reflexive reports of given practices, even when there is no explicit reference to them. This ranges from his first writings on the literacy program in Northeast Brazil to the pedagogical letter he was writing just before his death on the assassination of an Indian by middle class youth in Brasilia. The pedagogical utopianism of both authors is based on the denouncement of existing practices from where they announce alternatives.

Up from this point, however, there are significant differences in terms of the pedagogical practice. A basic feature of Rousseau's pedagogy lies in the fact that he chooses to educate one (1) white Christian boy from the upper class. The poor can manage for themselves to survive; women with their lower capacity of reasoning could not be entrusted with such a complex enterprise, and since institutions are necessarily an expression of human corruption education can be proceeded successfully only on an individual basis. Although being identified as a communitarian type of social contract, Rousseau's utopia turns out to be the utopia of the self-fulfilled individual, basically a young male who can afford it.

Paulo Freire starts from the presupposition that education is part of human intersubjectivity. Men and women educate themselves mutually in the process of relating to and transforming the world they live in. Educatees and educators are bound together in a learning community, a "gnoseological situation". According to Freire (1977:78), "'education as practice of freedom' is first and above all, a truly gnoseological situation. That one in which the act of knowing (ato cognoscente) does not end in the knowable object (objeto cognoscível), once it is communicated to other subjects, equally cognoscents." The search for objective facts, so important for Rousseau, gives rise to the mediation through a reality, which cannot be reduced to simple facts since it is necessarily permeated by human subjectivity.

However, it is not any type of learning community that interests Freire. To be "education as practice of freedom", "pedagogy of liberation" or "pedagogy of the oppressed" there is an ethical predefinition of the perspective in which this community views itself and the world. If significant learning always takes place within a learning community, the learning that liberates has as its reference the oppressed, since it only from their weakness that can originate the strength for liberation. The carriers of change are not technological innovations, but social movements, which push the limits of the established and instituted.

POST-SCRIPTUM: AOUT UTOPIA AND INDIGNATION

While revising this text, television stations were showing scenes of US troops invading the streets of Baghdad. Huge tanks with the most sophisticated weapons are pointing defiantly to all sides. Some soldiers armed and dressed up with the best equipments the military industry can produce walk in the deserted streets like Martians coming to earth in search for strange (and possibly dangerous) life. There are other scenes in which we can see the human and material destruction of the war of "liberation": a child with an amputated leg, destructed palaces, divided families...Other times the same screen shows the manifestations of tens or hundreds of thousands of persons whose voices appear to fall into a huge void. Nobody listens...while the tanks keep rolling towards their indisputable victory.

Even though violence is a part of daily life in most parts of the world, this war has helped to push the limits of cynicism, renaming reality under the sight of missiles and not seldom blaming the victims for their death. At a moment I felt that writing about utopia having this scene, as background was nothing but another expression of a naïve educator. Should this text not be kept for a more appropriate moment? After all, were the prophets of the end of utopia finally right? Where does any utopian thinking fit into this conflict - and so many others - in which people are supposed to choose between sides whose visions appear as equally dead end roads?

Looking back at our authors, it is indeed very difficult to believe in a Rousseau-type of human perfectibility, an evolution that begins with a wild and beast-like state of nature and unfolds to higher levels of civilization. The men (sic!) who promote this war are certainly not better, humanly, as those who promoted other wars in past times. We also do not have any prove that they are worse, and that there would be a degeneration leading humanity towards the final judgment, a definite encounter with truth.

Then I turned to Paulo Freire for whom dehumanization is always a possibility, as real and concrete as humanization. I was reminded of the already mentioned letter "About the assassination of Galdino Jesus dos Santos –the Pataxó Indian" [xvi], which Paulo Freire began and interrupted on April 21, 1997, a few days before his death on May 2. In this letter Freire wrote a paragraph which could as well have been written for the young North American and English soldiers hunting Iraqis, most of them obviously regarded as dangerous terrorists and therefore out of the range of any law. Freire wrote: "What a strange thing, to play at killing Indians, at killing people. As I think about it, I am immersed in a profound perplexity, frightened in face of the intolerable perversity of those young men dehumanizing themselves, in a context where they diminished instead of growing up." (Freire, 2000:66) Does it really matter so much whether the killing is done under the effect of drugs, in the name of a sacred cause, for the fun of it, or by carrying out orders of power-thirsty individuals and groups?

In the same letter Freire mentions the all powerfulness (todopoderosismo) of the liberties of these young men, "making fun of everything and of everybody." Not too different, it seems, from some of the most powerful leaders in the world speaking as if the world began and finished in their backyard. "The acceptance of the other, the respect of the weak ones, the reverence of life, not just human but vegetal and animal, the care with things, the enjoyment of beauty, the valorization of feelings, all this reduced to no significance or to very little." (Freire, 2000:66). Or to a kind of importance hidden behind arguments, which sound extremely unreasonable.

On the other side, there is an evident indignation stamped in the faces of the protesters for peace who take to the streets because they believe in another world and in constructing this other world through other means. To say to these people that there is no utopia is to close the ears to their cries, as do the powerful. Utopia, in this case, begins with indignation. But like hope, which may degenerate and loose its direction, also indignation has to be cared for, has to be educated. Utopia, in the Freirean sense, becomes itself an act of knowing.

NOTES

[i] Klaus Mollenhauer, when analysing the emergence of the idea of educability (*Bildsamkeit*), answers the question about what it is in a very suggestive way: "I don't know, and I take it to be impossible, that one can *know* - in the sense science tries to know - what it is, to erect trustful empirical knowledge about it. The scientific discourse about educability is nothing more than the exercise to make explicit this impossibility." (Mollenhauer, 1985: 80)

[ii] The issue is further developed in D. Streck, *Pedagogia no encontro de tempos* (Vozes, 2001)

[iii] Transition is here understood in Freire's sense of "transit", implying changes that have potentially a qualitative character.

[iv] The pedagogical praxis takes place within the context of an "ordered freedom" where the tutor's role is to select the experiences he wants his pupil to have. There are positive (von Hentig) and

negative (Starobinski) appraisals of this concept of freedom, respectively, as a necessary filter for the child's experience of the world and as a form of control.
[v] A discourse on the origin of inequality. In Rousseau, *The social contract an discourses*, p. 209.
[vi] Rousseau, *Emile*, p. 128.
[vii] Id., ibid., p. 81.
[viii] See Joel Pimentel de Ulhoa, *Rousseau e a utopia da soberania popular*.
[ix] Freire differentiates between a natural curiosity, that all humans have, and a curiosity, which becomes self-reflexive and methodologically instrumented.
[x] The first three forums took place in Porto Alegre, Brazil, from 2001 to 2003. The fourth was held in Mombai, India, in January 2004.
[xi] *Amorosity* is an adaptation of the Portuguese word *amorosidade* (Spanish *amorosidad*), which means the capacity and the predisposition for love. It preserves some of the sonority of the original.
[xii] See Carole Pateman, *The sexual contract*.
[xiii] See Charles Mills, *The racial contract*.
[xiv] See Michel Serres. *O contrato natural*.
[xv] For further development of this topic see Danilo R. Streck, *Educação para um novo contrato social* (Vozes, 2003).
[xvi] The letter refers to an Indian assassinated (burned) while sleeping on the street in Brasilia by five young middle class youth. Freire's letter was initiated on the same day of the crime.

REFERENCES

Freire, Paulo (1973). *Education for critical consciousness*. New York: The Seabury Press,.

Freire, Paulo (1972). *Pedagogy of the oppressed*. New York: Herder and Herder,

Freire, Paulo (1992). *Pedagogia da esperança: Um reencontro com a pedagogia do oprimido*. Rio de Janeiro: Paz e Terra,.

Freire, Paulo (1977). *Extensão ou comunicação?* 3. ed. Rio de Janeiro: Paz e Trra,.

Freire, Paulo. *Virtudes do educador*. São Paulo: Vereda, s.d.

Freire, Paulo (2000). *Pedagogia da indignação: cartas pedagógicas e outros escritos*. São Paulo: Editora UNESP.

Hentig, Hartmut von (2003). *Rousseau oder die wohlgeordnete Freiheit*. Muenchen: Verlag C.H. Beck,.

Jones, Jr., James (1977). *La Nouvelle Heloise: Rousseau and Utopia*. Geneve: Librairie Droz,.

Meireles, Cecíla (2001). *Crônicas de educaçãol*.Rio de Janeiro: Nova Fronteira; Fundação Biblioteca Nacional.

Mills, Charles W. (1997) *The racial contract*. New York: Cornell University Press.

Mollenhauer, Klaus (1985). *Vergessene Zusammenhaenge. Ueber Kultur und Erziehung*. Muenchen: Juventa Verlag,.

Pateman, Carole (2001). *The sexual contract*. 11. Ed. Stanford: Stanford University Press.

Puiggrós, Adriana (1995). *Volver a educar: El desafío de la enseñanza argentina a finales del siglo XX*. Buenos Aires, Ariel.

Rousseau, Jean-Jacques (1974). *Émile*. London: Dent; New York: Dutton.

Rousseau, Jean-Jacques (1950). *The social contract and discourses*. London: Dent; New York: Dutton,.

Santos, Boaventura de Sousa (1999). Reinventar a democracia: entre o pré-contratualismo e o pós-contratualismo. In: Heller, Agnes et alii. *A crise dos paradigmas em ciências sociais e os desafios para o século XXI*. Rio de Janeiro: Contraponto.

Santos, Boaventura de Sousa (2000). *A crítica da razão indolente: contra o desperdício da experiência*. São Paulo: Cortez.

Starobinski, Jean (1991). *Jean Jacques Rousseau: A transparência e o obstáculo*. São Paulo: Cia. Das Letras.

Serres, Michel (1991). *O contrato natural*. Rio de Janeiro: Nova fronteira.

Streck, Danilo R. (2001). *Pedagogia no encontro de tempos*. Petrópolis: Vozes.
Streck, Danilo R. (2003). *Educação para un novo contrato social*. Petrópolis: Vozes.
Ulhôa, Joel (1996). *Pimentel de Rousseau e a utopia da soberania popular*. Goiânia: Editora UFG.

RAYMOND A. MORROW

PAUL FREIRE, INDIGENOUS KNOWLEDGE AND EUROCENTRIC CRITIQUES OF DEVELOPMENT: THREE PERSPECTIVES[i]

INTRODUCTION

The goal of this essay is to situate the approach of Paulo Freire in relation to current debates about the nature and implications of so-called "indigenous knowledge(s)" for education and development studies. In these recent discussions, indigenous knowledge does not refer specifically or uniquely to either Native Indian or aboriginal cultures, though these are included. For this reason, some prefer the term local knowledge, though this term loses the important reference to ethnic and religious particularity, as well association with pre-modern and non-Western traditions. Though the term indigenous knowledge originated in agricultural research around 1980, it did not figure in Freire's own writing. Nevertheless, he did use some closely related and analogous concepts, most notably that of "popular culture" and reference to the communication of outside expertise to campesinos in agricultural extension work. Not surprisingly, therefore, aspects of Freire's thinking have been appropriated for some versions of the indigenous knowledge literature, as we will see.

The organizing theme is that three broadly identifiable approaches to the problematic of indigenous knowledge have emerged in the context of education and development. The first grouping, which originates as a critique of development theory, has proclaimed itself as "postdevelopment theory" (Rahnema 1997). This rather diffuse approach has origins in radical ecology and ecofeminism, postcolonial critiques of Western science, Ivan Illich's critique of "schooling", and the experiences of some disillusioned development experts. This orientation argues that the incommensurability between Western and indigenous knowledge creates a situation where colonial domination and economic unsustainability are inevitable and destructive. The conclusion is that the very effort of outsiders to promote "development" is misguided.

A second approach, with roots in education, will be characterized here as - for lack of a better term - "multicultural theories of subjugated knowledge"(Dei, Hall, and Rosenberg 2000a; Semali and Kincheloe 1999b). Its intellectual origins are similar to those of postdevelopment theory, though the focus shifts from development to education. Consequently there is often a certain overlap between the two positions. But instead of rejecting development altogether, this approach advocates a pedagogical strategy and alternative model of development that are oriented toward a dialogue within which Western and indigenous knowledge are accepted as equals, as variant forms of local knowledge with differential access to power. From this perspective the appreciation of indigenous knowledge is viewed

C.A. Torres & P. Noguera (Eds.), Social Justice Education for Teachers, 81–100.

as the basis a new conception of transformative education with implications for redirecting development away from Western models.

A third approach, which has multiple sources, will be labeled "emancipatory postfoundationalism"(Morrow and Torres 2002). Though there is no specific approach to indigenous and local knowledge that currently labels itself in these terms, it will be argued that Freire is the pioneer of such a strategy. Contemporary sources are used to sketch aspects of an approach to indigenous knowledge that might flesh out and qualify Freire's early contributions, as well as ground a critique of the preceding two perspectives. The outcome draws upon postempiricist theories of science and more nuanced critiques of Eurocentrism to develop a more pragmatic framework for understanding education and development that proposes a much more modest role for indigenous knowledge than proposed by the first two approaches. From this perspective, modern science and technology – understood in constructivist, post-Kuhnian terms – remains the necessary authoritative reference point for debates about knowledge and development. In short, rather than still being tied to a monolithic Cartesian-Newtonian epistemological perspective, academic disciplines have increasingly developed a more plural, inclusive, and contextual understanding of knowledge, one that creates the basis for the kind of authentic dialogue with indigenous knowledge envisioned by Freire. In this context the notion of cultural hybridity provides a framework for rethinking the implications of conscientization for marginalized populations.

FREIRE ON LOCAL KNOWLEDGE, POPULAR CULTURE AND DEVELOPMENT

One of the founding principles of Freirean pedagogy is to treat the learner – no matter how illiterate or marginal – with respect. This respect implies a kind of personal or human equality, thought it does not require formal equality of knowledge. The application of these principles in the context of indigenous knowledge was first elaborated in a publication appearing in Chile in 1969, and later translated into English as "Extension or Communication" (Freire 1973: 93-164). As is sometimes noted in the indigenous knowledge literature, his "seminal" work in the 1970s sensitized agricultural researchers to the need for a dialogical relation with local knowledge (Titilola and Marsden 1995: 503).

Beginning with a semantic analysis of the concept of "extension" as used in agricultural assistance, Freire concludes that it is grounded on treating the "subjects" of transmission as "objects":

> ...the act of extension, in whatever sector it takes place, means that those carrying it out need to go to 'another part of the world' to 'normalize it', ...the term extension has a significant relation to transmission, handing over, giving, messianism, mechanical transfer, cultural invasion, manipulation, etc. all these terms imply actions which transform people into 'things' ... They negate the true action and reflection which are the objects of these actions (Freire 1973: 95)

This formulation presents several themes that have been subsequently popularized in the indigenous knowledge literature: the colonizing aspects of going elsewhere (even if within a region of the same country); the dangers of the process of "normalization" (subsequently a focal point of Foucault's influence); the relation of manipulation and cultural invasion that transforms people into passive objects. To anticipate the latter discussion of the more recent indigenous knowledge literature, however, it is necessary to emphasize some of the distinctive implications of these observations.

First, Freire does not deny that outside or "Western" agricultural experts have some forms of knowledge of potential value: "I do not, however, wish to deny the agronomist working in this field the right to be an eductator-educatee, with the educatee-educator peasants" (Ibid.: 96). What he rejects is that this pedagogical relationship be conceived on the model of "propaganda" to be imposed on "blank pages": "In their role as educators, they must refuse to 'domesticate' people. Their task is communication, not extension" (Ibid.: 97).

Second, Freire addresses this relation in terms of its implications as an epistemological ("gnosiological") problematic. A key assumption is that the knowledge of experts and their peasants clients is historically conditioned and uncertain, a circumstance that creates the imperative of more learning and discovery. In other words, he rejects any uncritical defenses of "indigenous knowledge," just as he criticizes extensionists who make unreflexive claims about the absolute authority of their knowledge. Freire uses the example of magical practices to illustrate this possibility. More specifically, he views a "oneness" with nature, characteristic of traditional cultures and now prized by radical ecologists, as an obstacle to full humanization:

> Only people are capable of this act of 'separation' in order to find their place in the world and enter in a critical way into their own reality... However, the more we observe the behavior patterns and the though-habits of peasants, the more we can conclude that in certain areas (to a greater or lesser degree) they come so close to the natural world that they feel more part of this world than transformers of the world... A mistaken apprehension of what links one fact to another, induces likewise an erroneous understanding of the facts. This, in its turn, is associated with magical action (105-6).

Whereas postdevelopment and multicultural critics focus on the conditioning of Western knowledge, Freire equally stresses that "the knowledge of the peasants...is equally conditioned" as part of a cultural totality (Freire 1973: 108). In other words, a critique of indigenous knowledge is as important as a critique of Eurocentrism.

A third significant aspect of Freire's formulation is that there is an inevitable asymmetry between Western and indigenous knowledges. Though this should not take the form of a hierarchy that condones the kind of symbolic violence characteristic of colonialism, it remains a hierarchical ordering in the sense that modern academic knowledge systems should ultimately arbitrate the rules and procedures for knowledge claims, whether they are codified in relatively translocal (universal) or relative local (contextual) terms. Whereas an authentic dialogue was indeed impossible on the terms set by the older Cartesian-Newtonian worldview, it is now possible – at least in principle - from the perspective of postempiricist (postfoundationalist) theories of science and technology.

In this respect there is a parallel between Freire's conception of the pedagogical authority relation between educator-educatee in the classroom and that between Western and peripheral knowledge systems. His model presupposes a form of equality based on mutual respect, but this does not extend to one of formal equality with regard the empirical status of all knowledges. In the case of agricultural change or health, for example, there remains the assumption that the cumulative research traditions of "Western" science and technology provide a degree of provisional authority in many areas (e.g. AIDS). Moreover, the ultimate foundation of that authority is not the potentially fallible content of that knowledge, but its claim to be based on strategies of experimentation and validation that attempt – a least in principle – to avoid subordinating knowledge claims to politics, power or religious authority. But that authority needs to be self-critical in accepting the possibility of learning from indigenous knowledge, of creating a relationship of mutual learning.

Freire's later experience in Africa sheds some new perspectives on this basic position. In particular, he was confronted with the realization that his literacy training method could not be transplanted as a means of providing literacy through a foreign language - as a second language, as was attempted in Portuguese colonies in Africa (Freire 1983). Nevertheless, he does not abandon his basic position regarding the importance of negotiating a relation between modern science and local knowledge. As he reiterates, the classic model of modern science as enlightenment is flawed. This desire to help is

> strongly imbued with the authoritarian ideology which overestimates scientific knowledge and advanced technology, and under-rates popular wisdom. According to this authoritarian ideology, this ideology of 'whiteness, it is the center that knows, while the 'periphery' never knows. It is the center that decides, while the decisions made by others (Freire and Faundez 1989: 88)

It is importance to stress, however, that this reference to a white, authoritarian ideology is directed primarily toward the cultural context, the mind-set of the particular agents applying knowledge. In other words, he is not reductively dismissing the findings and methodologies of Western science as "white". Nor is he making any strong claims about the self-sufficiency or adequacy about "popular wisdom". Indeed, he specifically does go on to note that "Amilcar Cabral used to speak of the need to overcome what he called 'the negative elements in culture" (Ibid.: 89). Moreover, given the effects of colonization it becomes extremely difficult to separate out the traditional and colonial origins of local knowledge, with its positive and negative aspects. Consequently, he agrees with Faundez's suggestions regarding creating textbooks for popular biology. The first step is to evaluate such local knowledge to establish its value as "empirical knowledge" and "complement it with scientific knowledge" (Ibid.: 133). In short, local and Western empirical knowledge are not held to be incommensurate; nor is there any allusion to "alternative ways of knowing" in this domain to be accepted on faith.

POSTDEVELOPMENT THEORY: INCOMMENSURABILITY AND AMBIVALENCE TOWARD MODERNITY

Postdevelopment theory is based not only on a critique of past and present discourse on development, especially modernization theory and Marxism, but on a rejection of the very project of development. Accordingly, there is no attempt to propose a coherent alternative (Nederveen Pieterse 1998). In this context is it not necessary to delve into the diverse threads of the origins of this perspective: versions of ecofeminism and radical ecology, postcolonial critiques of Eurocentric knowledge, the Heideggerian critique of technology, and Illich's pioneering critiques of the development project(Illich and Rahnema 1997). Primary sources of the approach include <u>The Post-Development Reader</u> edited by Majid Rahnema (Rahnema 1997), some of writings of the anthropologist Arturo Escobar (Escobar 1995a; Escobar 1995b), some forms of ecofeminism and radical ecology (Mies and Shiva 1993; Sachs 1992), and some critiques of development education (Bowers 1983; McGovern 1999).

A trenchant summary by Meera Nanda captures, however, the spirit of this diffuse approach as a rejection of development as a Western conspiracy:

> The theorists of post-development have supplemented, and in some cases superseded, the problem of economic inequality between and within countries with the problem of cultural inauthenticity... Cure for this problem cannot be found within the conventional paradigms of development (capitalist or collectivist), all of which assume the intent to develop. A satisfactory solution requires, the critics of inauthenticity claim, that we 'liberate the imaginary' from the universal design of a homogenized 'Western' modernity. Then, and only then, can other, nonwestern and anti-capitalist ways of achieving a good society emerge (Escobar 1995) (Nanda 1999: 5)

In a brief presentation appropriate for the present context, three key features of postdevelopment approaches are notable:

- A reductionist account of European scientific imperialism that is often accompanied by problematic claims about the revival of alternative, traditional scientific systems, including a "people's science" (Prakash 1999; Sardar 1999). From this perspective the revival and recovery of indigenous knowledge is viewed as part of revolutionary, anti-colonial intellectual reassertion of the periphery on traditional grounds.
- A contention that the incommensurability of modern (inauthentic) and indigenous knowledge precludes meaningful dialogue: "the spread of Western episteme — Western ideas of science, technology, and a modern consciousness of needs and rights — is held responsible for the decline of

> local knowledges and destruction of local cultures (Sachs 1992)…
> extreme post-developmentalists… recommend 'delinking' from the
> "imperialism of conceptual categories" of the core (read Western
> sciences) in favor of self-reliant local knowledges" (Nanda 1999: 5-6).

- A selective focus on the negative aspects of development and a romantic defense of traditional ways of life. Paradoxically, this position may often play into the hands of traditional elites, e.g., in agrarian populism in India (Nanda 1999). Moreover, this approach has a tendency to nostalgically refer back to educational models based on traditional authority and defensive responses to modernity, all in the name of indigenous traditions (McGovern 1999).

Needless to say, this alternative overall perspective – if not aspects of the critique of classical development discourse – is quite at odds with Freire's approach to development and indigenous knowledge. Indeed, his strategy of intervention has been labeled as an example of "cultural invasion" from this perspective (Bowers 1983).[ii] Postdevelopment theory has been noted here in passing primarily to illustrate some of disturbing implications of this particular approach, one that is often described as postmodern and poststructuralist. Nevertheless, this is just one possible interpretation of the implications of postmodern critiques of knowledge. Moreover, in abdicating the very project of development altogether, such strategies do not have the effect of letting the "people" decide for themselves; rather they play into the hands of the market processes unleashed by neoliberal globalization. Obviously, Freire is not "postmodern" in the form proposed in postdevelopment theory.

MULTICULTURAL SUBJUGATED KNOWLEDGE THEORY: INDIGENOUS KNOWLEDGE AS EPISTEMOLOGICAL THERAPY

More interesting as a potential expression of the implications of Freire's pedagogy are approaches that can be termed multicultural theories of subjugated knowledge that draw upon rather different tendencies in postmodern and poststructuralist theorizing. Key representatives of this perspective include the collection <u>What is Indigenous Knowledge?</u> edited by Ladi Semali and Joe Kincheloe (Semali and Kincheloe 1999b) and <u>Indigenous Knowledge in Global Contexts</u> edited by George Dei and his associates (Dei, Hall, and Rosenberg 2000a). In contrast to postdevelopment theories, some room is granted for dialogue and development alternatives. The following critical discussion will focus on the more ambitious claims of the first collection, though most of the comments would apply to the second anthology, which is also based on a stereotypical conception of Western science and rationality and embraces indigenous knowledges as the solution to the sins of the white, patriarchal, West.[iii]

In his preface to Semali and Kincheloe's collection, Donaldo Macedo – a well-known exponent of Freire – is quite enthusiastic about their project:

> The brilliance of this edited book lies on the author's understanding that a
> global comprehension of indigenous knowledge cannot be achieved through

the reductionistic binarism of Western versus indigenous knowledge."
(Macedo 1999: xi-xii).

In softening the binarism previously described in the context of postdevelopment
theory, Semali and Kincheloe's approach certainly has a number of advantages that
bring it closer to Freire. Moreover, broadening the reference to forms of indigenous
knowledge found within regions and urban areas in advanced societies provides
important insights into the diverse forms of local knowledge. Nevertheless, both of
these gains are accompanied by various new problems evident in the following
central themes:[iv]

- Though the binarism between "Western" and "indigenous" knowledge is
  softened and the basis for significant commensurability and dialogue is
  acknowledged, the argument still remains within the framework of a
  reductionist critique of Eurocentrism's "white science" based on
  Foucault's conception of subjugated knowledge.
- Since the valorization of indigenous knowledge is based in on a critique
  of essentialism, this strategy rejects any fixing of a stable indigenous
  identity, but remains wary of notions of hybrid identity.
- The pedagogical implications are taken to be the need for a transformation
  of "Western" knowledge, by incorporating indigenous knowledge into the
  Western curriculum as part of a "synergistic" dialogue.

A REDUCTIONIST CRITIQUE OF EUROCENTRISM: ABUSING FOUCAULT

Despite certain qualifications and denials, Semali and Kincheloe present a "strong"
version of the Eurocentric thesis that is sweeping and indiscriminating in its claims.
The basis of this argument is the assumption of the epistemological equality of
various approaches to science: "Thus, this Western modernist way of producing
knowledge and constructing reality is one of a multitude of local ways of knowing
– it is a local knowledge system that denies its locality, seeking to produce not
local but translocal knowledge. Such knowledge is true regardless of context and is
the product of the process known as Cartesian reductionism" (Ibid.: 28). This
European (white, patriarchal, heterosexual) science was then deployed as a source
of legitimation and instrument for scientific colonialism. The underlying purpose
of this use of multicultural science studies, however, is to argue that "Western
epistemological tyranny decrees that the reality constructed by Cartesian-
Newtonian ways of seeing is the only reality worth discussing in academic
settings" (ibid.: 31). To be sure, anthropologists do study "ethno-science," but this
is treated as "other" and remains within the imperial frame. In other words,
scientific imperialism continues today within the academy:

While operating at a far more subtle and sanitized manner in the late
twentieth century, this epistemological tyranny still operates in the academy
to undermine efforts to include other ways of knowing and knowledge
production in the curriculum... The use of the term, subjugated knowledge,
asserts the centrality of power in any study of indigenous knowledge and any

> effort to include it in the academy… one constant emerges: all indigenous knowledge is subjugated by Western science and its episteme (its rules for determining truth)" (Semali and Kincheloe 1999a: 31-3)

It is symptomatic that the authors do not even find it necessary to mention the name of Michel Foucault (or cite him) here, even as they use his terminology.[v] Within the context in which such authors are writing, the "authority" of Foucault – or rather, a particular interpretation of Foucault – is such that his concepts can be applied dogmatically without raising further questions. As careful Foucault scholarship has concluded, however, despite his efforts to "problematize" the construction of Western knowledge, he did not draw such rash conclusions, especially about academic disciplines (Gutting 1994; Hacking 1995).

It is also important to recall that Foucault's formulations about subjugated knowledge were initially formulated in relation to cultural conflicts within the West. Foucault's strategy involved touching on those rather exceptional instances of either local "other" knowledges (e.g., the insane, delinquents, alternative sexualities) or erudite scholarly traditions where the subjugation of marginal knowledges did involve suppression of "truths" that were invisible for the dominant, early modern forms of science (Foucault 1980: 81ff). The "subjugated knowledges" in question, in other words, were themselves suppressed sides of modernity, not pre-modern traditions. Foucault cannot, therefore, be intelligibly read as a defender of earlier traditions of alchemy, witchcraft, or feudal agriculture as great repositories of suppressed knowledge and wisdom. Yet this is precisely the implication of the approach of theorists such as Semali and Kincheloe, whose implicit reference to Foucault fails to address a number of fundamental questions, e.g., how the success of the West was a result no only of its power, but the effectiveness of its knowledge in its distinctive form described by Max Weber as "occidental" reason; that this tradition had a self-critical methodology that eventually made the critique of the Newtonian-Cartesian worldview possible; and how the mere fact of subjugation confers no automatic assumption of adequacy and validity.

Foucault can be used to justify such interpretations of his subjugated knowledge argument with great difficulty. Moreover, his general thesis that "power is productive" cautions against any automatic presumption that the exercise of powers of regulation within scientific communities is necessarily tyrannical or "bad" – whether in undermining the knowledge claims of the powerful, or when used to reject those with flawed applications for recognition. Unlike Foucault, multicultural theorists of subjugated knowledge speak of "epistemological tyranny" in order to make this equation of subjugation and the presumption of validity, though the cases are chosen or excluded selectively. For example, fundamentalist creationism could easily be view as subjugated knowledge, thus claiming to be a victim of epistemological tyranny.

ANTI-ESSENTIALISM AND THE MISSING CRITICAL INDIGENOUS SUBJECT

At the same, however, Semali and Kincheloe do warn against essentializing indigenous knowledge. Freire and Faundez are cited as a reminder of the dangers of romanticization: "When advocates for indigenous peoples buy into such romanticization, they often attempt to censor 'alien' presences and restore the indigene to a pure precolonial status. Such a return is impossible, as all cultures (especially colonized ones) are perpetually in a state of change" (Semali and Kincheloe 1999a: 22). In stressing this point – shared with "postmodern" anthropology - they distance themselves from a central tendency in postdevelopment theory, one that rejects dialogue. Further, they reject the notion that there is a "fixed and stable indigenous identity," while simultaneously expressing considerable ambivalence about the alternative of an approach based on "cultural hybridity" (Semali and Kincheloe 1999a: 23-4).

Yet several kinds of problems are evident in such efforts to avoid romantic essentialism, promote dialogue and define indigenous identity in fluid terms. First, with such elastic, anti-essentialist definitions, there is great difficulty in identifying "authentic" indigenous knowledge: "we use our counter-essentialist understandings to argue that there is no unitary indigenous curriculum to be factually delivered to students in various locations" (Semali and Kincheloe 1999a: 24). Who and how is decide how to construct such a curriculum under these circumstances?

Second, they avoid altogether the question of the difficulty of assessing indigenous validity claims, a problem exacerbated by the absence of any attempt at differentiating or classifying the various types of local knowledge. A religious belief, an attitude toward nature, and a technique for planting corn represent very different forms of knowing. In the domain of technical knowledge, ethnoscientists assume that valid indigenous knowledge can in principle be explained within the categories of Western science, even though sometimes this may be difficult in the short run (Heyd 1995).

Third, in rejecting the notion of a stable indigenous identity and avoiding the possibility of cultural hybridity, such theories provide no guidance for actually characterizing concrete indigenous subjects. Despite sweeping generalizations about transforming American education, it is not clear who these indigenous subjects might be aside from the more isolated native Indian groups. A promising line of inquiry can be found in studies of cultural hybridity, but this strategy is not pursued. Why this ambivalence? Taking cultural hybridity into account would necessarily require calling into question the inescapable latent essentialism of any effort to validate the "indigenous" in such global and uncritical terms. Moreover, it would require asking what pertinence does their account have for the hybridized ethnic and black minorities that do not constitute "indigenous" groups in the strict sense? In short, opening up the category of indigenous knowledge to embrace virtually any marginalized group perspective creates problems with respect to the identification of forms of "authentic" indigenous knowledge.

INDIGENOUS KNOWLEDGE AS EPISTEMOLOGICAL THERAPY

Significantly, Semali and Kincheloe have very little to say about the implications of their approach for alternative development strategies, other than express great optimism about the potentials for reviving indigenous knowledge. Their primary objective is rather recuperating indigenous knowledge to challenge the impositions of Western Eurocentric knowledge: "In this context Western students come to understand that their ways of seeing the world are but one of a plethora of cultural perspectives. The simply act of recognizing the existence of indigenous knowledge in an educational setting undermines Western' science's pretensions to universality... This in itself is a profoundly transformative act" (Semali and Kincheloe 1999a: 47).

Moreover, they and others (Dei, Hall, and Rosenberg 2000a) assert that indigenous knowledges from around the world need to become central to the curriculum because they will have a major impact: "Only now at the end of the twentieth century are European peoples beginning to appreciate the value of indigenous knowledge about health, medicine, agriculture, philosophy, ecology, and education" (Semali and Kincheloe 1999a: 38). Despite the occasional "finds" that have led to awareness of biopiracy, some medical contributions (e.g. acupuncture), or the borrowing of indigenous ecological themes in radical ecology, there is little evidence that indigenous knowledge is or will have a major impact on the knowledge systems of the "North". And even when it may appear to do so, as in the case of the ad-driven mainstreaming of homeopathic and herbal remedies, or various cultic religious and "new age" movements, this has little to do with either authentic indigenous knowledge or knowledges with verifiable effects or enduring benefits. Greater selective exposure to aspects of indigenous cultures would indeed likely be of value for creating greater tolerance, as long suggested by proponents of intercultural education in anthropology, religious studies, etc., but this more modest goal falls far short of the grandiose claims made by the multicultural theorists of subjugated knowledge.

EMANCIPATORY POSTFOUNDATIONALISM: A FREIREAN ALTERNATIVE?

Those who have been most responsible for the revival of interest in and attention to indigenous and local knowledge have been engaged in anthropological fieldwork and participatory agricultural research. This predominantly anthropological literature is primarily concerned with forms of knowledge associated with the biological and natural sciences: "human and animal health, agriculture and food production, natural resources management and fisheries" (Slikkerveer 1995: 513). The study of such knowledge systems has been pioneered by anthropologists and the emergent field of "ethnobiology" or "ethnoecology" (Stepp, Wyndham, and Zarger 2002; Toledo 2002) and has had an increasing impact in Latin America (Pichón, Uquillas, and Frechione 1999). Not surprisingly, some of the leading representatives of this pioneering research have been perplexed by the suspicions about their work in the context of postdevelopment and subjugated knowledge theory:

> First of all, the rejection of collaborative ethnobiological research sets in opposition indigenous and 'scientific' ways of knowing, with scholarship judged inherently exploitative and thus morally suspect. This view is informed by postmodernist notions of knowledge as power and of truth as hegemonic narrative. At the logical extreme, this view asserts that to seek to understand other people can be no more than to see to control and manipulate them. It is ultimately a paranoid and sociopathic vision of human society (Hunn 2002: 5)

This defensive position reflects the fact that those in the position of doing empirical research on indigenous knowledge have not have the time or theoretical skills to elaborate the full implications of their work. But as will be argued here, what can be called emancipatory postfoundationalism, taking its point of departure from the work of Freire, can provide the kind of alternative justification necessary for shifting the context of debate in directions more consistent with the actual practice and experience of those in the field.

The notion of emancipatory foundationalism stems from the insights generated from a comparative analysis of Freire and Habermas in the context of transformative educational theory (Morrow and Torres 2002: 168). This strategy seeks to side step the rather confusing and multi-leveled debates that surround the modernism-postmodernism distinction. Emancipatory postfoundationalism rejects the classic modernist scientific project as flawed, but does point to various counter-modernist tendencies that were always part of Western thought. Consequently, there no need to argue for a complete epistemological discontinuity as argued by some on the basis of the modern-postmodern divide. Or even where an argument for discontinuity is made, it acknowledges that such a paradigm shift, oriented toward a "new common sense," draws upon sensibilities originating in the West's own self-critique (Santos 1995).

From this perspective, moreover, there is no basis for assuming that there is a fundamental incommensurability between Western and indigenous knowledge in the narrower sense relating natural science and technology given (a) the more inclusive and open boundaries of contemporary postempiricist (post-Kuhnian) theories of knowledge and science; and (b) the imperative of indigenous knowledge to become self-reflexive and engage in dialogue with other scientific traditions. This approach is thus postfoundationalist in the epistemological sense of rejecting any understanding of the relative superiority of Western science on the basis of some unified, reconstructed model of universal science. Science is understood in more historical and sociological terms as a complex set of institutions and practices, of interlinked communities of academic knowledges constantly in flux as part of a long process of historical change that has become a "postmodern adventure" (Best and Kellner 2001; Burke 2000).

Further, this approach is emancipatory in the sense that it is grounded in a development model of the human subject that has, to use Freire's term, an "ontological vocation" to overcome obstacles to "humanization". Or, to use the terminology of Habermas, this perspective gives normative priority to the realization of the diverse possibilities, the developmental potentials, revealed by a critical social psychology (Morrow and Torres 2002: ch. 2,5). Such an approach is acutely aware of the failures of modernization theory (and its sibling, neoliberal globalization theory), Marxism and dependency theory (Leys 1996), even though dependency itself needs to be rethought as a dimension of globalization (Castells and Laserna 1994). Moreover, to use the terminology of Habermas's critical theory, such failures can be traced in part to the "selective" and "one-sided" applications of technology that did not incorporate adequately social rationalization at the level of the lifeworld (Ray 1993). Despite the limitations of "development" defined as GNP, this does not preclude developing multiple indicators of the material and social conditions of "human development", goals that can be achieved through diverse strategies (United Nations Development Programme (UNDP) 2000). What is also required, moreover, are new forms of social theory that can address the problem of collective creativity (Domingues 1995; Domingues 2000).

The priority given to individual freedom and autonomy from this emancipatory perspective is not understood in terms of a narrow conception of the possessive (male) individual found in much liberal thought. Rather, the focus is on the capacity of individuals to engage in forms of mutual recognition through which solidarity can be reconciled with the struggle for individual self-realization (Honneth 1996). The importance of this emancipatory focus in the present context is that it rejects the tendency of both postdevelopment theories and multicultural theories of subjugated knowledge to rather uncritically embrace indigenous models of subjectivity as equally acceptable or even superior alternatives, even though they may embody repressive and authoritarian processes of subject formation. Abandoning an emancipatory standpoint, on the supposed grounds that it represents a culturally biased and local "Western" perspective, has especially grave consequences for the status of women (Benhabib 1995).

Another way of situating such an emancipatory postfoundationalism would be an alternative reading of the implications of the kinds of questions posed by Sandra Harding in her Is Science Multicultural? (Harding 1998). In surveying post-Kuhnian accounts of science, as well as feminist theory and postcolonial science studies, she provides a carefully argued case for an account of knowledge and science in terms of a multiplicity of local standpoints. This perspective argues for the dysfunctionality of universal knowledge and truth claims. It is beyond the scope of this paper to directly engaged her complex and subtle arguments here, except to note that the educational theorists of subjugated knowledge claim to be inspired by her conception of "borderlands epistemology" (Semali and Kincheloe 1999a: 52-3). Serious doubts can be raised, however, whether their dogmatic and simplistic application of a multicultural theory of knowledge in educational theory does full justice to many of the questions posed by Harding.

In any case, the task at hand is not so much to justify and detail an alternative reading of constructivist theories of science, as opposed to illustrating some of the key differences of interpretation. Above all, an emancipatory postfoundationalism resists a reductionist and simplistic interpretation of Foucault's subjugated knowledge thesis that is often used to frame such discussions. Though it argues for the necessity of a critique of Western science and the dominant discourses of development (Crush 1995), as well as for a partial decolonization and selective indigenization of knowledge, these are understood in terms that are often quite distinct from the multicultural subjugated knowledge approach. The present preliminary formulation can only attempt to give a basic idea of this approach and its relation to Freire's overall strategy. Some of the key alternative arguments include the following:

- "Western" or scientific rationality – now understood more inclusively and pluralistically in post-Kuhnian, constructivist terms - continues to play a strategic role for marginalized groups in need of universalistic challenges to oppression based on traditional authority and magical practices.[vi]
- Decolonization and indigenization need to be understood as processes involving a critical hermeneutics – necessitating an intercultural public sphere - that attempts to mediate between the translocal and the particular problems of the local.
- The focus on the politics of knowledge should not be allowed to distract from urgent problems relating to abject poverty and excessive inequality and the increasingly urban and global forms of crisis.
- As part of a contingently universal normative framework, it is argued that knowledge should facilitate the development of critical, autonomous, hybrid subjects sensitive to difference, the imperatives of mutual recognition, and the need for human solidarity.

POSTFOUNDATIONALIST CRITIQUES OF WESTERN RATIONALITY

The point of departure of an emancipatory postfoundationalism is that the "hegemonic" position of the Western model of critique and the sciences is not merely the result of colonial imposition. In contrast, defenders of multicultural epistemologies argue, "when knowledge plurality mutated into knowledge hierarchy, the horizontal order of diverse but equally valid systems was concerted into a vertical ordering of unequal systems" (Shiva 2000: vii). Rejecting the notion of "equally valid systems" preserves a form of knowledge hierarchy, but not an authoritarian one of the type plausibly linked with classic scientism, e.g. Cartesian-Newtonian epistemologies. Within the emerging hierarchy of networks of scientific knowledges as understood in postempiricist theories of science, new contenders for validation (e.g. forms of indigenous knowledge) may potentially gain recognition. Within this more pluralistic conception of knowledge, diverse claims to knowledge can be negotiated and adjudicated in relation to weak universalistic claims and local contexts of application (Longino 2002). Those who keep insisting that these are merely "Western" criteria necessarily invoke vague claims to "alternative ways of knowing" to defend the local from criticism.

DECOLONIZATION AND INDIGENIZATION: CRITICAL HERMENEUTICS AND INTERCULTURAL PUBLIC SPHERES

Another way of describing the strategy of an emancipatory postfoundationalism is in terms of the insistence that indigenous knowledge subject themselves to the same kind of constructivist critiques that have transformed the self-understanding of Western knowledge systems. Otherwise decolonization and indigenization become transformed into xenophobic processes of purification that restore "local" traditions of dubious authenticity or validity, often at the cost of other local individuals or groups, while providing legitimation to the potentially authoritarian elites that can gain credit for such a transformation.

Constructive strategies of decolonization and indigenization presuppose the formation of something like an "intercultural public sphere" within which such more particularistic claims can be adjudicated persuasively in relation to universal procedural criteria of evidence and participation. Such issues have been apparent, for example, in legal contexts involving self-government among North American natives where "collective" or indigenous rights conflict with those of individuals. As has been argued in response to such dilemmas on the basis of the approach of Habermas and others, "a universalistic orientation to cultural pluralism is crucial to a just democratic theory, since it can demonstrate how tribal sovereignty can facilitate fair and critical communication among Native and non-Native communities" (James 1999).

Similar principles could be applied to problems relating to the negotiation of relations between traditional and modern knowledge. Such a model of self-governance would require a forum for dialogue within which the relative merits of different modes of knowing would not be determined a priori, in favor of either the "new" or the "old" ways. Instead, both would be required to confront the forces of the reasons and evidence as interpreted from diverse, representative points of view. Such a strategy would provide a more theoretically elaborated basis for the kinds of dialogical approach anticipated in Freire's early critique of agricultural extension education.

INEQUALITY, GLOBALIZATION AND KNOWLEDGE

Paradoxically, one of the arguments invoked against the appropriation of Western science and technology and development strategies generally is that they merely reinforce the power of existing elites. Though this is particularly true for neoliberal globalization, this effect can be partly avoided in projects involving participatory action and appropriate or intermediate technologies. Furthermore, there is little basis for assuming that simply reproducing the existing local systems of production, indigenizing educational curricula, or facilitating "people's science" will not also reinforce existing class relations in rural areas (Nanda 1999). Critiques of inequality depend crucially on processes of empowerment for which "modern" educational systems are a necessary, though not a sufficient aspect.

Furthermore, attempts to legitimate the transformative effects of indigenous knowledge derive from an excessively rural focus. Whatever limited merits the re-appropriation and partial validation of indigenous knowledge systems may have in rural areas based on high levels of agricultural self-sufficiency, such strategies become of marginal significance in the context of the urban crises of the Third and Fourth Worlds. Given this demographic context, any comprehensive reliance on traditional productive techniques and cultural adaptations is unsustainable. Economic growth in the appropriate, more sustainable forms and income redistribution remain indispensable ingredients of any development process that is to be coupled with "human" development. Abandoning these issues in the name of indigenous knowledge and resistance against Western scientific imperialism is extremely problematic.

THE HYBRID SUBJECT OF TRANSFORMATIVE CRITIQUE

The facts of massive urbanization and globalization also provide reminders of the increasingly hybrid character of individuals with "indigenous" origins in the various possible senses. The resistance of theorists of subjugated knowledge to the notion of hybrid subjects needs to be regarded with suspicion as a symptom for deeper problems. This resistance stems from the assumption that indigenous knowledge as local knowledge is embedded in a total way of life. Consequently, it is feared that any effort to engage in piecemeal reform or adoptions of externally induced "development" strategies will undermine that way of life and the efficacy of these "other ways of knowing". This is not a new argument, of course, because it originates from a traditionalist resistance to change that can now be dressed up in the theoretical legitimacy of "postmodern" critiques of development. This defensive response disregards, however, the possibility that hybrid subjects may be able in practice to develop complex bi-cultural strategies of adaptation that allow them to creatively respond to the pressures of globalization and the formation of new identities (García Canclini 1990). In this respect, Freire's account of the "peasant" as a social subject needs to be updated in relation to recent work on the transformation peasant identities in the context of globalization (Kearney 1996). The Zapatista movement in Mexico can also be viewed as exemplifying many Freirean principles (Johnston 2000). Nevertheless, such contemporary approaches are consistent with Freire's emphasis on how conscientization should have at its goal critical subjects capable of assessing the multiple realities that impinge on their practical and political engagements of the world. It is also broadly compatible the Foucault's later ethics of the self, which seeks to problematize but not reject the Kantian (and Freirean) question of "enlightenment," of "whether we will ever reach mature adulthood" (Foucault 1997: 318). But the formation of such competences is seriously inhibited by any exclusive focus on forms of education designed to reproduce some putatively subjugated "traditional way of life", or "alternative ways of knowing," strategies that must necessarily suppress some modes of thinking as dangerously "modern" or "Western". Hence Foucault, in defending an experimental attitude, regards with suspicion "all projects that claim to be global or radical" in avoiding putting themselves to "the test of reality": " In fact, we know from experience that the claim to escape from the system of contemporary reality so as to produce the overall programs of another society, of another way of thinking, another culture, another vision of the world, has led only to the return to the most dangerous traditions" (Foucault 1997: 316).

CONCLUSION

It has been argued that the first approach discussed – postdevelopment theory - is quite alien to Freire's approach to education and development, a point reinforced by the virtual lack of reference to his work. Not surprisingly, one symptomatic source of postdevelopment theory is the pioneering work of Ivan Illich's critique of technology (Morrow and Torres 1990). Illich and Freire briefly crossed paths in the late 1960s and initially expressed admiration for each other's projects. To the surprise of many, they parted ways very early on for reasons that were never fully clarified, but now can be retrospectively understood in relation to subsequent developments. Illich's call for "de-schooling" was imbedded in a radical critique of technology and rationalization and aversion to modernity that ultimately could not be reconciled with the Freirean vision of emancipatory education. Recently remarking on his disillusionment, Illich acknowledges having to "learn the lessons of our powerlessness in order truly to renounce development" (Illich and Rahnema 1997: 108). Similar differences from Freire are evident in the influence of the Gandhian tradition on the postdevelopment approach, especially its focus on local self-sufficiency, rejection of modern technology, and a conception of education that reinforces local traditionalism (Zachariah 1986)

The second approach, on the other hand, draws extensively on Freire's concept of dialogue and cites his contribution to giving respect for popular culture and knowledge. While there are certain a number of affinities, it was argued that on certain key epistemological, educational, and political issues, Freire's thinking is clearly incompatible with what are here referred to as multicultural accounts of subjugated knowledge. While the present critique acknowledges that the decolonization and indigenization of knowledge are strategically important tasks, it has also tried to provide some warnings and cautions. Paradoxically, if all definitions of knowledge can be reduced to power, indigenous knowledges have no hope in the power/knowledge regime of neoliberal globalization. The only glimmer of hope lies in having more powerful reasons that can both sway emotions and change minds.

Finally, in a more constructive vein, it has been suggested that the anticipations of Freire's approach can best be appreciated in the context of his greater affinities with emancipatory postfoundationalism, an epistemological and theoretical strategy that remains compatible with such disparate literatures as ethnoscientific research in anthropology, participatory agricultural research, the Gramscian critique of common sense, the critique of science, technology and communication found in the later Frankfurt tradition (e.g. Habermas), some readings of Foucault, and some versions of postfoundationalist science studies.

In constructing this debate, an effort has been made to construct a dialogue in the name of Freire's ghost, or at least, the spirit of one of his voices – the Gramscian historicist one that always insisted that popular knowledge could become powerful only through becoming self-critical and engaging itself with appropriating the previous cultural and scientific achievements of humanity. That may have begun as a local project, and it certainly continues to be plagued by these Eurocentric origins, but it may be the first knowledge system to potentially achieve a degree of contingent universality through the articulation of its constructionist self-critique (Bourdieu 2000).

NOTES

[i] My initial interest in indigenous knowledge was recently stimulated by discussions with three doctoral students: Linda Krieitzer (University of Calgary) who confronted me in a seminar with the question of Freire and Foucault's relation to the topic; and, at the University of Alberta, the recently completed dissertations of Josée Johnston and Joan Reynolds forced me, respectively, to think about the issues of alternative "development" and Foucault as an "enlightenment" theorist.

[ii] But see the response to Bowers (Roberts 2000: 119-136).

[iii] Despite ostensibly rejecting romanticism, the authors affirm the following: "The theoretical conceptions of 'indigenous knowledges' that the authors in this book bring to the current discussion problematize the idea that unlimited human and material progress is possible through science, technology, and competition... Interest in indigenous knowledges is growing quickly, as manifested in recent academic and cultural projects... Of more direct relevance to our current work is Shiva (1989)...who argues that throughout the world a new questioning is growing, rooted in the experiences of those form whom the spread of the Enlightenment has been the spread of darkness, of the extinction of life and life-enhancing processes. There is an expanding awareness that those things which are presently called 'progress' are merely, in fact, the special projects of modern Western patriarchy." (Dei, Hall, and Rosenberg 2000b: 8-10)

[iv] Not all of the papers in this volume are guilty of the more extreme claims of the editors; for example, several of the papers are simply good examples of applying Freirean principles, e.g. (George 1999; Knijnik 1999). Two others, on the other hand, actually take postdevelopment positions (Prakash 1999; Reynar 1999).

[v] Even more tellingly, Semali and Kincheloe associate the subjugated knowledge thesis with Gramsci: "This historical dynamic is extremely important in the context of subjugated knowledge. Antonio Gramsci (1988) noted that philosophy cannot be understood apart from the history of philosophy...Subjugated knowledge by its very existence proves to us that there are alternative to knowledge produced within the boundaries of Western science" (Semali and Kincheloe 1999a: 37). The problem with this interpretation is that Gramsci's historicism did not extend to a disqualification of Western science and technology (he idealiized Fordist production techniques) and he saw one of the tasks of education was to overcome the superstition of traditional thought. One may disagree with Gramsci here, but to collapse his view into the multiculturalist account of Foucault is simply false.

[vi] See, for example, the insightful account of the Deweyan influenced resistance movement of the pariah caste in India that used modern science as the basis of a critique of Hinduism (Nanda 2001).

REFERENCES

Benhabib, Seyla (1995). Feminism and postmodernism. In: *Feminist contentions: A philosophical exchange*, edited by S. Benhabib, et al. New York and London: Routledge.

Best, Steven and Douglas Kellner (2001). *The postmodern adventure: Science, technology, and cultural studies in the third millennium*. New York and London: Guildford Press.

Bourdieu, Pierre (2000). *Pascalian meditations*. Translated by R. Nice. Stanford, CA: Stanford University Press.

Bowers, C. A. (1983). Linguistic roots of cultural invasion in Paulo Freire's pedagogy. Teachers College Record, *84*:935-953.

Burke, Peter (2000). *A social history of knowledge: From Gutenberg to Diderot*. Cambridge: Polity Press.

Castells, Manuel and Roberto Laserna (1994). The new dependency: Technological change and socioeconomic restructuring in Latin America. In: *Comparative national development: Society and economy in the new global order*, edited by A. D. Kincaid and A. Portes. Chapel Hill and London: University of North Carolina Press.

Crush, Jonathan (Ed.) (1995). *Power of development*. London and New York: Routledge.

Dei, George Jerry Sefa, Budd L. Hall, and Dorothy Goldin Rosenberg (Eds.) (2000a). *Indigenous knowledges in global contexts : Multiple readings of our world*. Toronto: OISE and University of Toronto Press.

Dei, Goerge J. Sefa, Budd L. Hall, and Dorothy Rosenberg (2000b). Foreword: Cultural diversity and the politics of knowledge. In: *Indigenous knowledges in global contexts : Multiple readings of our world*, edited by G. J. S. Dei, B. L. Hall, and D. G. Rosenberg. Toronto: OISE and University of Toronto Press.

Domingues, José Maurício (1995). *Sociological theory and collective subjectivity*. Houndmills, Basingstoke, Hampshire and New York: Macmillan Press/St. Martin's Press.

— (2000). Social creativity, collective subjectivity and contemporary modernity. London and New York: Macmillan/S.t Martin's Press.

Escobar, Arturo (1995a). *Encountering development: The making and unmaking of the third world*. Princeton, NJ: Princeton University Press.

— (1995b). Imagining a post-development era. In: *Power of development*, edited by J. Crush. London and New York: Routledge.

Foucault, Michel (1980). *Power/knowledge: Selected interviews and other writings 1972-1977*. New York: Pantheon.

— (1997). *Essential works of Foucault 1954-1983, Volume 1: Ethics, subjectivity, and truth*, Edited by P. Rabinow. New York: New Press.

Freire, Paulo (1973). *Education for critical consciousness*. Translated by M. B. Ramos. New York: Seabury.

— (1983). *Pedagogy in process: The letters to Guinea-Bissau*. Translated by C. S. J. Hunter. New York: Continuum.

Freire, Paulo and Antonio Faundez (1989*). Learning to question: A pedagogy of liberation*. New York: Continuum.

García Canclini, Néstor (1990). Culturas híbridas: Estrategias para entrar y salir de la modernidad. México, D.F.: Grijalbo.

George, June M. (1999). Indigenous knowledge as a component of the school curriculum. In: *What is indigenous knowledge?*, edited by L. Semali and J. L. Kincheloe. New York: Falmer Press.

Gutting, Gary (1994). *The Cambridge companion to Foucault*. New York: Cambridge Uiversity Press.

Hacking, Ian (1995). *Rewriting the soul: Multiple personality and the sciences of memory*. Princeton, N.J.: Princeton University Press.

Harding, Sandra (1998). *Is science multicultual? Postcolonialism, feminisms, and epistemologies*. Bloomington and Indianapolis, IN: Indiana University Press.

Heyd, Thomas (1995). Indigenous knowledge, emancipation and alienation. *Knowledge and Policy, 8*, pp.63-73.

Honneth, Axel (1996). The struggle for recognition: The moral grammar of social conflicts. Translated by J. Anderson. Cambridge, MA: MIT Press.

Hunn, E. S. (2002). Traditional environmental knowledge: Alienable or inalienable intellectual property. In: *Ethnobiology and biocultural diversity: Proceedings of the Seventh International*

Congress of Ethnobiology, edited by J. R. Stepp, F. S. Wyndham, and R. K. Zarger. Athens, GA: International Society of Ethnobiology/University of Georgia Press.

Illich, Ivan and Majid Rahnema (1997). Twenty-six years later. In *The Post-development reader*, edited by M. Rahnema. London and New Jersey: Zed Books.

James, Michael Rabinder (1999). *Tribal sovereignty and the intercultural public sphere. Philosophy and Social Criticism, 25*, pp.57-86.

Johnston, Josée (2000). Pedagogical guerrillas, armed democrats, and revolutionary counterpublics: Examining paradox in the Zapatista uprising in Chiapas Mexico. *Theory and Society , 29*, pp. 463-505.

Kearney, Michael (1996). *Reconceptualizing the peasantry: Anthropology in global perspective.* Boulder, CO: Westview Press.

Knijnik, Gelsa. 1999. Indigenous knowledge and ethnomathematics: Approach in the Brazilian landless people education. In: *What is indigenous knowledge?*, edited by L. Semali and J. L. Kincheloe. New York: Falmer Press.

Leys, Colin (1996). *The rise and fall of development theory.* Bloomington: Indiana University Press.

Longino, Helen E. (2002). *The fate of knowledge.* Princeton, NJ: Princeton University Press.

Macedo, Donaldo (1999). Preface: Decolonizing indigenous knowledge. In: *What is indigenous knowledge?*, edited by L. Semali and J. L. Kincheloe. New York: Falmer Press.

McGovern, Seana (1999). *Education, modern development, and indigenous knowledge : An analysis of academic knowledge production.* New York: Garland Pub.

Mies, Maria and Vandana Shiva (1993). *Ecofeminism.* London: Zed Books.

Morrow, Raymond A. and Carlos Alberto Torres (1990). Ivan Illich and the de-schooling thesis twenty years after. New Education, *12*, pp.3-17.

— (2002). *Reading Freire and Habermas: Critical pedagogy and transformative change.* New York: Teacher's College Press, Columbia University.

Nanda, Meera (1999). Who needs post-development?: Discourses of difference, green revolution and agrarian populism in India. *Journal of Development Studies, 15*, pp.5-31.

— (2001). A 'broken people' defend science: Reconstructing the Deweyan Buddha of India's Dalits. *Social Epistemology, 15*, pp. 335-365.

Nederveen Pieterse, Jan. (1998). My paradigm or yours? Alternative development, post-development, reflexive development. *Development and Change, 29*, pp.343-373.

Pichón, Francisco J., Jorge E. Uquillas, and John Frechione (1999). *Traditional and modern natural resource management in Latin America.* Pittsburgh, Pa.: University of Pittsburgh Press.

Prakash, Madhu Suri (1999). Indigenous knowledge systems - Ecological literacy through initiation into people's science. In: *What is indigenous knowledge?*, edited by L. Semali and J. L. Kincheloe. New York: Falmer Press.

Rahnema, Majid (Ed.) (1997). *The post-development reader.* London: Zed Books.

Ray, Larry J. (1993). *Rethinking critical theory: Emancipation in the age of global social movements.* London and Newbury Park, CA: Sage.

Reynar, Rodney (1999). Indigenous people's knowledge and education: A tool for development? In: *What is indigenous knowledge?*, edited by L. Semali and J. L. Kincheloe. New York: Falmer Press.

Roberts, Peter (2000). *Education, literacy and humanization: Exploring the world of Paulo Freire.* Westport, CN: Bergin & Garvey.

Sachs, Wolfgang (Ed.) (1992). *The development dictionary: A guide to knowledge as power.* London and New Jersey: Zed Books.

Santos, Boaventura de Sousa (1995). *Toward a new common sense: Law, science and politics in the paradigmatic transition.* New York and London: Routledge.

Sardar, Ziauddin (1999). Development and the locations of Eurocentrism. In: *Critical development theory : Contributions to a new paradigm*, edited by R. Munck and D. O'Hearn. London and New York: Zed Books.

Semali, Ladislaus and Joe L. Kincheloe (1999a). Introduction: What is indigenous knowledge and why should we study it? In: *What is indigenous knowledge?*, edited by L. Semali and J. L. Kincheloe. New York: Falmer Press.

— (1999b). *What is indigenous knowledge? : Voices from the Academy*. New York: Falmer Press.

Shiva, Vandana (2000). Foreword: Cultural diversity and the politics of knowledge. In: *Indigenous knowledges in global contexts : Multiple readings of our world*, edited by G. J. S. Dei, B. L. Hall, and D. G. Rosenberg. Toronto: OISE and University of Toronto Press.

Slikkerveer, L. Jan. 1995. INDAKS: A Bibliography and Database on Indigenous Agricultural Knowledge Systems and Sustainable Development in the Tropics. Pp. 512-516 in The Cultural Dimension of Development : Indigenous Knowledge Systems, edited by D. M. Warren, L. J. Slikkerveer, D. Brokensha, and W. H. J. C. Dechering. London: Intermediate Technology Publications.

Stepp, John R., Felice S. Wyndham, and Rebecca K. Zarger (Eds.) (2002). Ethnobiology and biocultural diversity: *Proceedings of the Seventh International Congress of Ethnobiology*. Athens, GA: International Society of Ethnobiology/University of Georgia Press.

Titilola, S. Oguntunji and David Marsden (1995). Indigenous knowledge as reflected in agriculture and rural development. In: The cultural dimension of development : Indigenous knowledge systems, edited by D. M. Warren, L. J. Slikkerveer, D. Brokensha, and W. H. J. C. Dechering. London: Intermediate Technology Publications.

Toledo, V. M. (2002). Ethnoecology: A conceptual framework for the study of indigenous knowledge of nature. In: *Ethnobiology and biocultural diversity: Proceedings of the Seventh International Congress of Ethnobiology*, edited by J. R. Stepp, F. S. Wyndham, and R. K. Zarger. Athens, GA: International Society of Ethnobiology/University of Georgia Press.

United Nations Development Programme (UNDP) (2000). *Human development report 2000*. New York and Oxford: Oxford University Press.

Zachariah, Mathai. 1986. Revolution Through Reform: A Comparison of Sarvodaya and Conscientization. New York: Praeger.

PETER ROBERTS

REASON, EMOTION AND POLITICS
IN THE WORK OF PAULO FREIRE

Teachers must not be afraid of tenderness, must not close themselves to the affective neediness of beings who are indeed kept from being. Only the poorly loved ones can understand teaching as a trade for the insensitive, so filled with *rationalism* that they become empty of life or feeling (Freire, 1998a, p.50).

INTRODUCTION

Over the past three decades, a number of educational theorists have identified a strong rationalist thrust in the work of Paulo Freire. C.A. Bowers (1983), for example, sees Freire as a 'carrier' of what he terms 'the Western mindset', elements of which include critical reflection, problematisation and the gaining of rational distance from everyday experience. Elizabeth Ellsworth (1989) includes Freire among those educationists who advance a series of rationalist ideals (e.g., 'dialogue', 'student voice' and 'empowerment') as the basis for a critical pedagogy. Frank Margonis (2003) argues that Freire's philosophy bears the influence of a tradition of rationalist thinking dating back to Plato and, more recently, to the Enlightenment. In each of these cases, Freire's 'rationalism' is seen as problematic. Bowers sees the possibility of cultural invasion in Freire's pedagogy; Ellsworth sees the universalist, abstract language employed by Freire and other critical educationists as repressive; and Margonis wonders whether Freire could be 'complicit' in the colonial traits of Plato's work.

These criticisms have been addressed at length elsewhere (e.g., Roberts, 1996, 2000, 2003). This paper focuses on a slightly different line of questioning, namely, whether Freire emphasizes reason and rational processes over emotion and feelings. I shall argue that he does not, and that the importance of emotion for Freire can be seen not only in his ideas on teaching, learning, dialogue, and reading but in his style of writing and the way he lived his life. Over the past fifteen years, a number of theorists have examined the nature, role and significance of emotions in education (see, among many other sources, Morgan, 1994; Zigler, 1994; Beck and Kosnik, 1995; Nias, 1996; Boler, 1997, 1999a; Hargreaves, 1998; Zembylas, 2002). In considering Freire's position on emotions, an article published by Ann Sherman in 1980 provides a helpful starting point. Sherman draws our attention to some important tensions and weaknesses in Freire's early references to the role of emotions in education, dialogue and political transformation. This paper assesses the extent to which Freire addressed the concerns raised by Sherman in his later

C.A. Torres & P. Noguera (Eds.), Social Justice Education for Teachers, 101–117.

work. I suggest that Freire's project, which remained incomplete at the time of his death in 1997, was to develop a critical ideal in which reason, emotion and political commitment would be dynamically intertwined. The paper falls into three major parts. The first section summarizes Sherman's argument and considers the interconnectedness of reason and emotion in Freire's language (written and spoken), ontology, epistemology, and educational theory. The second part comments in more detail on the political significance of these ideas, focusing on the pivotal themes of solidarity and love. The final section assesses some of the strengths and weaknesses in Freire's critical ideal.

REASON AND EMOTION IN FREIRE'S WORK

In 1980 Ann Sherman published a concise critique of Freire's position on the relationship between emotion, education and social change. Sherman identified a tension between Freire's valuing of certain emotions (love, hope, faith, and trust) for critical educative dialogue and his rejection of 'emotionality'. In discussing the movement from 'closed' to more open forms of social organization in Brazil, Freire warned against the dangers of highly emotive, irrational responses to oppressive structures, practices and relationships. Freire also felt that the critical character of the communicative process could be compromised if strongly emotive individuals exerted undue influence on others within a group. Sherman pointed out that motivating students to learn was an important part of adult literacy education for Freire, and that emotions were pivotal in this process; yet, emotions were seen as inadequate for understanding causal relationships in the social world. Sherman argued that Freire provided only a vague and superficially developed account of the emotions necessary for educative dialogue. This, she maintained, was no accident, for if Freire had 'a lingering conception of emotions as totally uncritical forces it would not make much sense to discuss critical methods for developing them' (Sherman, 1980, p. 38). She continued: 'Since the methods of development are part of what the end product is, to advocate critical methods for developing emotions would entail that emotions were, at least in part, critical' (p. 38). Having identified the shortcomings and apparent contradictions in Freire's work, Sherman suggested that further research would be needed if we were to develop a more meaningful and substantial account of the role of emotion in educational dialogue.

When Sherman published her article, there were only four major texts by Freire available in English: *Pedagogy of the Oppressed* (Freire, 1972a), *Cultural Action for Freedom* (Freire, 1972b), *Education: The Practice of Freedom* (Freire, 1976), and *Pedagogy in Process: The Letters to Guinea-Bissau* (Freire, 1978). In subsequent years, Freire was to publish more than a dozen further books. He was particularly productive in the last decade of his life. Freire collaborated with a number of other scholars in co-authoring a series of 'talking' books, written in the form of structured dialogues around key educational themes (Freire and Shor, 1987; Freire and Macedo, 1987; Freire and Faundez, 1989; Horton and Freire, 1990). Several of his books had a semi-autobiographical flavor (Freire, 1994, 1996); one reflected on his experiences as Secretary of Education for the municipality of Sao Paulo (Freire, 1993); one addressed issues in higher education (Escobar et al., 1994); one focused on the process of teaching (Freire, 1998a); and several paid particular attention to questions of politics (Freire, 1997, 1998b, 1998c).

Freire never addressed the nature of emotion, or its relationship to reason, in a systematic and extended way. He did not, for example, devote an entire book, or even a substantial portion of a book, to this theme. This does not mean, however, that these issues were unimportant to him, or that he ignored them in his written and practical work. I want to suggest that while there are limits to what Freire has to offer in addressing the challenge posed by Sherman in 1980, he nonetheless saw emotions as of vital significance for his educational work. This, I believe, has been evident to some degree in all of his writing but has come into sharper focus in his later publications. Emotions and feelings (I shall use the two terms interchangeably in this paper) were significant for Freire at multiple levels: in relation to teaching, learning, studying, reading, writing, speaking, and knowing.

Those who knew Freire, or experienced his work as a teacher, or witnessed him speaking at conferences and seminars, almost always attest to his highly passionate nature (see, for example, Taboo, 1997; Convergence, 1998; Boshier, 1999; McLaren, 2000; A.M.A. Freire, 2001; Darder, 2002, 2003). Freire expressed himself with feeling and conviction, but also with reason. He would apply himself to reading and study with concentrated enthusiasm and he was an engaging, often animated, participant in educational conversations. While it is important not to 'heroise' Freire (Coben, 1998; Boler, 1999b), it seems clear that as a person, he generally lived what he talked about in his books. Donaldo Macedo, who worked closely with Freire for years and translated several of his books into English, observes that there was 'a great coherence between his [Freire's] words, deeds, and ideas' (Macedo, 2001, p. 3). Freire's philosophy became, in Pierre Hadot's (1995) terms, a way of life, rather than mere intellectualizing. In philosophy as the practice of theorizing, the aim is, in Alexander Nehamas's words, to 'deface the particular personality that offers answers to philosophical questions, since all that matters is the quality of the answers and not the nature of the character who offers them' (cited Neiman, 2000, p. 576). Philosophy as a way of life, by contrast, requires style, idiosyncrasy, and a sustained effort -- not just to understand the world more deeply, but to be in and with it in a new way. The character and lived experience of the person become central. As Neiman puts it, the 'entire rationale has to do with the life of a particular person' (p. 576). Freire's lived philosophy was one in which feelings played a central role. For Freire -- as a person, and a writer, and a teacher -- these feelings could not be disentangled from reason and from action. There was, to employ the categories developed by Steiner (1995), among others, a strong relationship between thinking, feeling and willing in Freire's work. Freire felt distress and pain and frustration and anger (and many other emotions) when he worked with severely impoverished illiterate adults in Brazil in the 1950s and early 1960s; he thought deeply about the nature of the social system that produced such oppression (and went on to convey those thoughts

103

in books such as *Pedagogy of the Oppressed*); and he willed himself to action through his efforts in major literacy campaigns and other educational initiatives.

The integration of emotion and reason in Freire's work is evident in the style he used to construct his later books. A book such as *Pedagogy of Hope* (Freire, 1994), for example, might be criticized for its somewhat rambling character. This book lacks the tight structure often demanded of academic writers. Freire does not provide extensive references for his ideas in this text or other later books. In fact, he only seldom makes direct reference to the work of other scholars. In some of his later published writings (including *Pedagogy of Hope*) Freire's second wife, Ana Maria Araújo Freire, has added detailed endnotes elaborating on points made in the text. Freire does not employ a 'stream of consciousness' style, but he does allow his feelings to exert greater influence on the direction and nature of his prose than many of his international academic peers. Many of Freire's later books address a very wide range of philosophical, pedagogical and political themes, and considerable work is left to the reader in creating a coherent overall picture of his views. Freire must be read holistically if we are to gain a full appreciation of what he has to offer educational theory and practice. There is more of 'Freire himself' in the later books. Freire shares his feelings with readers, reveals more of his biography, acknowledges his failures and shortcomings more openly, confesses his discomforts and frustrations more readily, and allows moments of anger and joy to find their way more directly into his writing. In these works, Freire does not attempt to 'remove himself' from the text: the ideas he expresses are, in an open and obvious way, *his* ideas. Yet, the faculty of reason is never absent in these writings. There is logic, coherence, and sound argumentation in Freire's later books, but the reader must assume a certain kind of relationship with these texts if the deeper reasoning behind many of Freire's ideas is to be found. The reader needs, among other things, to adopt a critical posture, to put the different books into conversation with each other, to consider them in the light of Freire's practical commitments in the last ten years of his life (particularly his role in the Brazilian Workers' Party and his responsibilities as Secretary of Education), and to make a definite effort to disentangle particulars (including examples from Freire's personal experience) from universals (e.g. the notion of humanization underlying Freire's work).

Freire has argued, from his earliest writings, that humans are 'unfinished' or incomplete beings. In *Pedagogy of the Oppressed* (Freire, 1972a) he advanced an ethical ideal of humanization, which he saw as a process of becoming more fully human (not fully human) through critical, dialogical praxis. Freire posited humanization as an ontological and historical vocation for all human beings. He saw dehumanization as a distortion of this vocation. Dehumanization is manifested, in concrete terms, by structures, practices, policies, and relations of oppression. It is through struggling against oppression -- in a reflective, dialogical, active manner -- that humans pursue their liberation. Freire depicts liberation as an ongoing process of struggle, not as an endpoint to be reached. There will always be a need for further reflection, action and social transformation. Freire's account of oppression and liberation was later to draw criticism from postmodernists who found fault with his appeal to universal propositions, his failure to theorize adequately his own position of privilege, and the somewhat abstract manner in which he articulated his ideas (compare, Ellsworth, 1989; Weiler, 1991; Freire and Macedo, 1993). In later works, Freire engaged postmodern ideas and made an attempt to address, in a more explicit and extended way, questions of diversity and difference. Arguably, however, the philosophical core of his ontology remained the same throughout his writing career. In some books, he uses different terms to describe the same ideal. In *Pedagogy of Freedom* (Freire, 1998c), for instance, he argues for a 'universal human ethic'. Despite the shift in terminology, the essential features of his ideal remain the same: all humans, he maintained, are 'called' to think, feel, act, and communicate with others in certain ways in pursuit of a shared vocation.

In *Pedagogy of the Heart* (Freire, 1997), Freire takes up the theme of human unfinishedness as the basis for educational life. Freire points out that not only are we unfinished; we are capable of *knowing* ourselves as such. This provides the ground for the permanent process of searching, which Freire regards as a distinguishing characteristic of all human beings. It is consciousness of our inconclusiveness that makes us educable. Engaging in this process of constant searching, which provides an important motivating force for the process of education, cannot be a purely rationalistic process:

> Consciousness of, an internationality of consciousness does not end with rationality. Consciousness about the world, which implies consciousness about myself in the world, with it and with others, which also implies our ability to realize the world, to understand it, is not limited to a rationalistic experience. This consciousness is a totality -- reason, feelings, emotions, desires; my body, conscious of the world and myself, seizes the world toward which it has an intention (p. 94).

In later writings, Freire makes it plain that knowing is a multifaceted process, incorporating physical, emotional and intellectual elements: 'I know', Freire says, 'with my entire body, with feelings, with passion, and also with reason' (Freire, 1997, p. 30). Ana Maria Araújo Freire, in conversation with Carmel Borg and Peter Mayo, extends these ideas. Paulo, she says, was 'never ashamed to say that everything he knew came from his curiosity, awakened by his feelings, by what his skin said, his intuition aroused, his emotion dictated' (Borg and Mayo, 2000, p. 112). Her husband's language, she argues, was 'loaded with feelings':

> Paulo was a radically coherent man: what he said contained what he felt and thought and this is not always easy to translate. There are emotions whose meanings can only be well perceived, understood and felt inside a certain culture. And we Brazilians are unique in this way.

Translators of Paulo's work would sometimes err to much on the side of form, ignoring other words that might be perceived as 'too full of feelings'. In doing so, they would unwittingly lose something of the imaginative quality of his work. Studying the Portuguese language, she suggests, is not the same as *living* it within Brazilian culture. For Paulo, language -- whether in written or spoken form -- was a way of expressing his love of knowledge and humanity. Ana Maria recalls an incident shortly after Paulo's death in which cultural differences on the relationship between reason, emotion and language came into sharp focus:

> First World intellectuals said to me: "Don't cry, don't become emotional! You are giving a scientific speech, an academic work in surroundings where there is no place for emotions!" Can you imagine? I was in Hamburg, at an Adult Education congress where everything, or almost everything, turned around Paulo. The conference paid great homage to him. His ideas and his name filled the atmosphere of the meeting. And I had lost Paulo less than three months before! The terrible sense of loss was strongly reflected in the form of working I had learnt exactly from him: to say what one felt when thinking. Why would it be wrong to think, crying? Can it be true that when we cry we lose our reason? I felt I could not even control myself to stop crying, but I knew I was thinking. And so, why control myself? That is the question! (p. 111).

Ana Maria makes it clear that Freire would not work *just* with feelings or intuition but rather subjected what arose from them to deep, critical, reflective thought. For Freire, intuition and emotion were an important part of the process of knowing, but without serious questioning and thinking they could lead to distortions and misunderstandings. Equally, and this is a point that is often forgotten, Freire believed that an exclusive or dominant focus on the intellect will yield an incomplete and inadequate understanding of human beings and the world. Freire 'never maintained the emotion should subjugate reason. But he also vehemently rejected the opposite "academicist" view' (p. 112). Freire's stance is captured effectively in this passage from *Teachers as Cultural Workers*:

> The problems of teaching imply educating and, furthermore, educating involves a passion to know that should engage us in a loving search for knowledge that is -- to say the least -- not an easy task. It is for this reason that I stress that those wanting to teach must be able to dare, that is, to have the predisposition to fight for justice and to be lucid in defense of the need to create conditions conducive to pedagogy in schools; though this may be a joyful task, it must also be intellectually rigorous. The two should never be viewed as mutually exclusive (Freire, 1998a, p. 4).

In his later books, Freire stresses repeatedly that educational dialogue should be structured, with a clear sense of purpose and direction (see especially, Freire and Shor, 1987). Freire argues against both authoritarian and 'anything goes' learning environments. Students and teachers have both rights and responsibilities in an educational dialogue. Freire acknowledges the right for all students to speak, provided their actions do not impede others from doing so. Equally, participants should have the right to refrain from speaking. *Engagement* with the object of the study and the content and movement of the dialogue is the key; this need not always involve speaking. Indeed, a tendency to want to 'thrust oneself forward' all the time, to insert oneself into the conversation, often betrays a certain egoism and inability to wait and to listen to what others have to say. (I return to this point later in the paper.) The notion of discouraging 'emotionality', detected by Sherman in Freire's earlier writings, continues here. But Freire's intentions must be considered carefully. Preventing or discouraging others from speaking by 'shouting them down' in an emotional outburst represents a failure to live up to one's responsibilities in a dialogue and to recognize the rights and feelings of others. Allowing some emotions to exert undue influence on a dialogue could, Freire believed, be damaging to the educational process and dehumanizing for participants. Allowing one's excitement, anger or frustration to boil over compromises the dialogical process not only for others but for oneself as well. What is needed is the moderating influence of reason and a certain kind of balance in the expression of one's feelings. This can involve striving to inculcate feelings of care, calmness, patience, and respect as well as enthusiasm, commitment and courage. Acknowledging one's own limitations, retaining a sense of curiosity and wonder, and developing the ability to listen are also qualities of fundamental importance.

SOLIDARITY, HOPE AND LOVE

In his last books, several of which were published posthumously, Freire continued to stress the importance of getting involved in the process of political struggle. He saw this as an integral part of his intellectual life (see Escobar *et al.*, 1994). This process, he recognized, was difficult, often slow and seldom straightforward. Freire never gave up the view that capitalism was an inherently unjust mode of production, and he saw the marketisation of social and economic life under neoliberalism as highly problematic. For Freire, the increasing dominance of a small class of corporate elites was further evidence of the need to resist the politics of capitalist expansion. Freire was appalled by the destruction of the natural environment and the growing gap between 'haves' and 'have nots' within and between countries across the planet. As a further impediment to liberation, groups on the Left had developed deep divisions and had expended considerable emotional, intellectual and political energy fighting among them selves. This fragmentation had hampered efforts to resist forms of oppression relevant to all groups, and had allowed those on the economic and cultural Right to prevail.

Dowbor (1997), in his Preface to Freire's *Pedagogy of the Heart*, stresses the importance of solidarity in a world increasingly driven by division, functionality and anonymity. Solidarity, for Freire, is forged not merely through words but through action. In contemporary capitalist societies built on a manufactured ethic of relentless consumption, people find themselves working harder than ever before. Yet, for all the technological advancements of recent years, we seem unable to build better lives. In many parts of the world, we have lost a strong sense of community. We have been encouraged to depersonalize suffering, to remove ourselves from it, and to build up our defenses against the shock of witnessing other human beings starving, desperately poor, or in pain. 'With the global society of long distances and large numbers', Dowbor says, solidarity has become 'no longer a matter of the heart, of feelings naturally generated before the known person; it has shifted over to the intellect, reason, which is satisfied with rationalization' (p. 27). For Dowbor, Freire offers an alternative approach:

> In Paulo Freire's reasoning, rationality is rationally clamoring for the right to its emotional roots. This is the return to the shade of the mango tree, to the complete human being. And with the smells and tastes of childhood, it is much broader a concept than that of the right or the left, a deeply radical one: human solidarity (p. 28).

In reflecting on the enormous challenges posed by neoliberal capitalism, Freire continued to stress the importance of hope. He believed, however, that developing and retaining the *feeling* of hope was not sufficient on its own. 'Hope of liberation', he said, 'does not mean liberation already. It is necessary to fight for it' (Freire, 1997, p. 44). It is not a case of separating the feeling from the action, but rather of acknowledging how one might be informed and nourished by the other. Holding firm to the feeling of hope when everything around us suggests we should be lapsing into despair allows us to go on, to continue to find meaning in our existence. This feeling is made all the richer and more complex, however, when we communicate with others about our dreams and fears, and when we find ways (appropriate to the problems of our time, place and social situation) to keep working for social change.

The concept of *love* is arguably even more significant than the notion of hope in Freire's later work. Indeed, it is possible, as Darder (2002, 2003) has shown, to view love as the foundation for Freire's entire pedagogy. The importance of love in Freire's work has also been addressed by a number of other theorists in recent years (compare, for example, Spring, 1994; Fraser, 1997; McLaren, 2000). Freire employed the concept of love in a number of different ways. At the broadest level, he speaks repeatedly of the need for a profound love of human beings and the world. He sees this as a defining characteristic of the vocation of humanization. The influence of both Marx and radical Catholicism can be detected here. In *Pedagogy of the Oppressed* Freire quotes, with approval, Che Guevara's famous statement about love as a revolutionary virtue (Freire, 1972a, p. 62), and he contrasts this with what he sees as the distortion of the word 'love' in the capitalist world. Genuine revolutionaries, Freire argues, are motivated by a deep concern to address conditions of oppression, which are characterized by a dehumanizing lack of love and often a deliberate, sadistic desire to dominate others. Freire accepts the Christian imperative to 'love your neighbour as yourself' (*The New English Bible: New Testament*, Matthew 22, 39) but he also takes from Marx the need to respond to conditions of exploitation and oppression. 'No matter where the oppressed are found', Freire says, 'the act of love is commitment to their cause -- the cause of liberation' (p. 62).

Freire, like others in the tradition of liberation theology (where his work was influential: see Oldenski, 2002), reads the Gospels as a call for social action. From a Freirean point of view, to engage in humanizing praxis -- critical, dialogical reflection and action for transformation -- is to put into practice the ideal of love fostered by Christ (cf. Freire, 1997, pp. 103-105). There is a deeper sense, however, in which the Christian imperative comes to life in Freire's work. For to love one's neighbor as oneself is to recognize that, in a very significant sense, one's neighbor *is* oneself. This point has, of course, been explored in great detail by theologians, philosophers and others over the centuries. Freire was not a theologian, and he did not address this question directly or at length in his writings. Nevertheless, his position, when his work as a whole is surveyed, seems clear. We are, Freire argues, always *social* beings. Our thoughts, emotions, experiences, and actions are always shaped by -- and to this extent *defined* by -- our relationships with others. Others *live through* us. We are not isolated, autonomous selves; rather, we are always *connected*, often in ways we cannot recognize, with others. This is why, in *Pedagogy of the Oppressed* and other works, Freire speaks of oppression dehumanizing both the oppressed and the oppressor(s). Similarly, to love others, treating them, as we would want to be treated, is also to love oneself. It is to live, as one should in fulfilling the ontological vocation of humanization.

Freire also speaks, more specifically, of the importance of love for educational dialogue, for teaching, for the students with whom one works, for processes of reading, writing and study, for knowledge, and for life itself. Love is both 'the foundation of dialogue and dialogue itself' (Freire, 1972a, p. 62). Without loving respect for other participants in a dialogue, one cannot truly *listen* to, and hence learn from, what they have to say. Freire argues that listening is an activity that goes beyond mere hearing. Listening involves 'being open to the word of the other, to the gesture of the other, to the differences of the other' (Freire, 1998c, p. 107). This does not mean one should be 'reduced' to the other; this would, from Freire's point of view, not be listening but *self-annihilation*. Freire explains:

> True listening does not diminish in me the exercise of my right to disagree, to oppose, to take a position. On the contrary, it is in knowing how to listen well that I better prepare myself to speak or to situate myself vis-à-vis the ideas being discussed as a subject capable of presence, of listening 'connectedly' and without prejudices to what the other is saying. In their turn, good listeners can speak engagedly and passionately about their own ideas and conditions precisely because they are able to listen (p.107).

With love, there must also be humility -- a willingness to acknowledge one's weaknesses as well as strengths and to 'step back', removing the focus from oneself and allowing others to show what they know. Humility is especially important in a critical dialogue, where ideas -- including those we cherish most -- are subject to rigorous questioning and debate. Humility 'calms and pacifies what our vanity may have difficulty tolerating, even when the criticisms we receive are just' (Freire, 1998b, p. 57). Freire sees teaching as an act of love (see his comments in Leistyna, 1999, p. 57). Love sustains the teaching process in the face of what Freire sees as an utterly contemptuous attitude on the part of those responsible for the funding of schooling. Without the profound love many teachers have for their vocation, they would not be able to put up with such 'shameful' wages, under-resourcing, and poor working conditions (cf. Freire, 1998a, pp. 40-41). In later works, Freire refers often to reading, writing and study as difficult, demanding processes. In reading a text we should, Freire suggests, be prepared to be challenged by it, but we should also be prepared to ask questions of it. Freire advocates a stance of loving the text while fighting with it (Freire and Shor, 1987, p.11). This kind of critical reading involves the active linking of 'word' and 'world' (Freire and Macedo, 1997), where the reader attempts to relate the content of a text to contemporary contexts, to the issues and problems of the day, and to the struggles with which he or she is associated. Freire also encourages readers to set texts appropriately in the author's context: to try and understand something of the circumstances under which the author was writing.

If we are to love the process of study, we must come to appreciate that joy and rigor are not mutually exclusive. In *Letters to Cristina* Freire recalls how he, as a young intellectual, would experience intense emotional pleasure as he watched boxes of books being opened in a bookstore in Recife, Brazil. He also notes that at that time he threw himself into the study of grammar and the Portuguese language. His interest was not in the merely technical study of grammar. 'My passion', he says, 'was always directed toward the mysteries of language in a never anguished but always restless search for its substantive beauty' (Freire, 1996, p. 79). The joy of study arises not just when we discover what we sought to know, but from the process of investigation itself; that is, from searching, asking questions, exploring beneath the surface -- in short, from the attempt to engage the object of investigation critically (see Freire, 1985, pp. 1-4, 1998a, p. 4, 1998c, p. 125). If this process of reading, studying and learning works well, we come to develop a deep love of knowledge and will continue to seek out opportunities to better understand the world over the course of our lives. Indeed, the process is crucial is shaping the degree to which we love life itself:

> What I want to say is that the sequence of learning in which we all participate inculcates the love of life or the love of death in us, shapes the way that we relate from a young age to animals, plants, flowers, toys, and people; the way that we think about the world; and the way that we act in the world. If we treat objects with meanness, destroying them or devaluing them, the testimony we give to our offspring is a lack of respect for the powerless and a disdain for life. We learn to either love life or to reject it (Freire, 1996, p. 75).

THE LIMITS OF FREIRE'S CRITICAL IDEAL

Freire's position on reason and emotion cannot be fully appreciated without considering the contexts within which he worked. His commitment to a critical educational ideal grew out of his experiences in Brazil and Chile, where the disparities between different social groups were readily apparent. Freire's concept of liberation is also linked to these experiences: he sees liberation as a form of struggle against oppression. In defining liberation in this way, Freire has been able to make a distinctive and lasting contribution to the theory and practice of teaching and learning. He was one of the most important figures in twentieth century educational thought in bringing the political dimension of education to our attention (Mayo, 1999). Much of what Freire has to say about reason and emotion is tied to his political project. Freire saw liberation as 'the most fundamental task' of the twentieth century (Freire, 1993, p.84), and when he spoke about the significance of love and hope for educationists he was not concerned with romantic ideals but with the messy, difficult, complex realities of political transformation. Seen in this light, it is perhaps not surprising that Freire placed such a heavy emphasis on the development of a critical mode of being. Freire's intellectual kinship with other theorists in the critical tradition is readily apparent in his published work. The influence of Marxism, existentialism and radical Catholicism has long been noted (see, for example, Mackie, 1980), but there are also important connections that can be drawn between Freirean ideas and the work of critical theorists such as Habermas (see Morrow and Torres, 2002). Freire's integration of insights from these scholarly traditions had an overt political purpose: he saw critical reflection, dialogue and action as essential in addressing the realities of oppression.

This should not, however, be seen as a commitment to a narrow form of rationalism: Freire saw emotions as a vital part of his critical ideal. It is not a case of supplanting emotion with the cold gaze of reason, but rather of understanding how thinking, feeling and acting depend on each other for their intelligibility. For Freire, when we attempt to think in a disciplined way -- to theorize, to argue, to reason -- we simultaneously commit ourselves to an emotional process. Through critical reading, writing and investigation we experience a range of emotions -- sometimes frustration, sometimes joy, often (in the longer run, if not immediately) a sense of fulfillment. The very process of struggling to make our reading critical, rather than passive or merely entertaining, is itself an indicator of its emotional character. Similarly, when we commit ourselves, with others, to social action, this commitment cannot be sustained without a deep, ongoing feeling that conditions of oppression can and ought to be resisted. In Freire's case, this feeling was first cultivated in childhood experiences (e.g., his observations of racism) and continued to grow and develop through his educational work in his adult life.

Yet, the very features that make Freire's approach distinctive also pose their own limits. Freire leaves us searching for more when we ask how we might develop ourselves as emotional and rational beings beyond the process of addressing -- through critical, dialogical praxis -- conditions of oppression. His repeated references in later books to the virtues of good teachers and learners go part of the way to addressing this concern, but if we are to understand the significance of his comments in this area it is helpful to look beyond Freire's work. A much fuller exploration of human virtues can be found in Aristotle's *Nichomachean Ethics* (Aristotle, 1976) and the contemporary philosophical literature on virtue ethics. Freire spoke about the importance of *caring* for students, but for an in-depth investigation of this theme we need to look elsewhere (e.g., Gilligan, 1982; Noddings, 1984). Freire pays scant attention to the wider literature on the philosophy of emotion within feminist theory (Boler, 1997, 1999b).

Similarly, while Freire was supportive of efforts to enhance ecological awareness, he did not consider, in any detail, how such work might be helpful in rethinking human experience, modes of understanding, and forms of social life. Freire also has little to say about the relationship between reason, emotion and spirituality, a theme that has been addressed thoughtfully by others (e.g. Zigler, 1994). Freire does not comment, directly, on the ways in which our lives as thinking, feeling and willing beings might be enhanced (or impeded) by contemplative or meditative activities. There is scope for extending Freire's ideas on liberation to include these dimensions (see, for example, Dallaire, 2001). Freire's view of the reading process also raises questions. Freire's emphasis on the importance of critical reading -- which is, it must be remembered, both a rational and an emotional process -- leaves us wondering what he might have said about other ways of approaching texts. It might be argued that something is *lost* in promoting a critical approach to reading, and that there is value, at times, in attempting to read a book in a distinctly *non-critical* way. I want to finish the paper with a few remarks on this last issue: the limits of Freire's view of reading.

Freire has a great deal to say about reading, but his purposes in addressing this subject are primarily educational. In exploring the role of reading in developing a rich life of feeling, questions of aesthetics inevitably arise. Freire does not position himself self-consciously within any particular school of aesthetics. This is not to say that he ignores aesthetic questions altogether. He comments in places on the relationship between curiosity, a sense of wonder, and the spirit of investigation. He talks about the role of 'aesthetic curiosity' in allowing one to become pleasurably immersed in a challenge, or lost in contemplation of a sunset or the clouds, or touched by a work of art (Freire, 1997, pp. 95-96). Freire also stresses the importance of the aesthetic dimension of language, not just for artists but for all engaged in intellectual work. 'It is the duty', Freire maintains, 'of all those who write to write beautifully. It does not matter what one writes or writes about' (Freire, 1996, p. 80). And in *Pedagogy of Freedom*, he argues that ethical formation ('decency') and aesthetic appreciation ('beauty') need to proceed hand in hand. Yet, Freire's account of aesthetic appreciation remains sketchy and incomplete. As readers, we have to develop a *feeling* for Freire's position on questions of aesthetics; he does not provide us with a well-developed, systematic theory. Moreover, as has been noted elsewhere (Roberts, 2000, p. 93), where Freire refers to the aesthetic moment in reading or the beauty of books he tends to do so in relation to a broader critical ideal (see, for example, Horton and Freire, 1990, pp. 23-27, 31-32). This begs the question of whether and how books might be encountered and experienced in ways other than those tied to notions of critical consciousness or critical literacy. A number of theorists have spoken about the ways in which reading -- particularly the reading of literary works -- can educate the emotions (among many other examples, compare Hepburn, 1972; Gribble, 1983; Solomon, 1986; Nussbaum, 1990; Cunningham, 2001). Freire has little to say about this. When we consider the theme of reading, then, the problem is not, as Sherman (1980, p. 38) suggests, that Freire sees emotions as 'totally uncritical forces' but rather that he pays adequate attention *only* to the ways in which emotions might become critical forces.

Freire talks about the need for humility (on the part of the reader) and a willingness to be challenged by the text. He warns us not to become 'too certain of our certainties' (see Freire, 1994), fooling ourselves that we have all the answers already and have nothing to learn from the ideas conveyed by others in books and dialogues. But Freire also stresses that this is a reciprocal relationship: readers can -- and *ought* to -- ask questions of texts, just as texts can raise questions for readers. Freire promotes rational and emotional engagement with texts; he does not support a more passive approach in which readers attempt to minimize their critical capacities in the reading process. A case could be made, however, for exactly this sort of attitude -- *in some contexts*, with some texts, for some purposes. There are some circumstances, it might be argued, when experiencing the process of reading a text, 'absorbing' it, living with it, and letting it talk to us without subjecting it to systematic examination or critique or analysis could be worthwhile. Applying too firm a critical hand too early can sometimes dampen, hinder, or even destroy some of the benefits we might otherwise gain from reading a text.

Much depends here, I think, on the sorts of texts with which we are dealing. Freire was concerned primarily with scholarly texts, and particularly with those addressing philosophical, sociological and educational themes. His notion of 'fighting with the text while loving it' emerged from his own struggles with texts of this kind. When he spoke, in *A Pedagogy for Liberation* (Freire and Shor, 1987) and elsewhere, about the importance of reading classic texts, he was referring not to literary works but to the writings of theorists such as Marx or Gramsci. Freire has little to say about literary texts and the forms of reading he believes are appropriate for them. His scattered remarks about aesthetic appreciation provide some clues in determining what he might have said had he written in these areas. It is certainly clear, I believe, that he would have stressed the need to respond to literary works -- and creative works more generally -- not just in a 'rational' way but also in an emotional way. Freire speaks fondly of his own immersion in books, of encountering new texts with great excitement and enthusiasm. We also know that the power of language and the beauty of the written word moved him. But he tells us virtually nothing about the way a literary text in particular might 'work on us', shaping and building our emotions. Reading, for Freire, can play an important role in encouraging educationists to 'side with the oppressed'. There are links here with the work of moral philosophers who talk about the development of altruistic emotions -- compassion, sympathy, and empathy -- through the reading of novels (see Boler, 1999a, pp. 158-160). Freire has in mind works of non-fiction: theories of oppression or factual accounts (historical or contemporary) of oppressive structures, policies and practices. He does not deal with the question of how literary works -- or other artistic forms such as film or drama -- might develop a 'feeling' for oppression in a different way.

Freire's notion of fighting with a text while loving it does give us some purchase on an attitude that may be helpful in reading at least some literary works. I am thinking, especially but not exclusively, of those authors who confront searching philosophical questions, problems and issues in and through their work. A good example here would be Dostoevsky, arguably one of the most deeply philosophical of all novelists. There is much to be gained, I believe, in both attempting to 'just read' a book such as *The Brothers Karamazov* (Dostoevsky, 1991) and in self-consciously reflecting upon it. This is where the interconnectedness of emotion and reason becomes apparent. If we are too eager to bring our own questions to the text, subjecting it to critical analysis prematurely, some of the emotional impact of the book could be lost. We need to allow Dostoevsky's narrative to unfold, working on us, forming an appreciation of the characters and the events in the novel. Yet, as this development of our 'feeling' for the characters emerges, so too does our thinking about them. This is one of the marks of Dostoevsky's genius: his novels are so richly textured, so complex and multilayered, that it is difficult to avoid becoming reflective in reading them. We become entwined in the lives of Dostoevsky's characters -- in their thoughts, emotions, dilemmas, challenges, tensions, contradictions, actions, and relationships -- and in doing so, we are prompted to ponder questions of importance in our own lives. We should not, from a Freirean point of view, set out to dissect the book or to impose a rigid critical framework or to question Dostoevsky's motives before hearing what he has to say. This is not to say that we start from a 'neutral' position. Freire has long argued that this is impossible. Our prior experiences and our current understanding and circumstances will always have some bearing on how we read and what we gain from a literary work (or any other text). But these things do not *determine* our experience of a book. Coming to *love* the book is not possible without this experience. We might 'fight' with the text, wrestling, as Dostoevsky's characters do, with competing ideas. We might also consider the possible influence of Dostoevsky's own experiences (e.g. his imprisonment in Siberia) on his writing. We might be critical of his Russian nationalism, his dislike of Poles, his anti-Semitic tendencies, his position on Catholicism or socialism. But none of this rational-critical activity need diminish our love of the book. Dostoevsky teaches us about the limits of reason and the power of feelings but he does not encourage us to abandon reason altogether.

CONCLUDING COMMENTS

Where, then, does the mature Freire rest in relation to Sherman's critique of more than two decades ago? Sherman criticized Freire for the rather vague and underdeveloped account of emotions in *Pedagogy of the Oppressed*. A holistic reading of Freire's later works yields a clearer, more robust account of the role of emotions in educational life. This is particularly true of emotions such as love and hope, both of which received extended attention in the last few years of Freire's life. Freire continued to be critical of 'emotionality', conceived as an excessive, uncontrolled, and often violent expression of human passion. He could not sanction revolutionary action based entirely on the highly emotional and unreflective chanting of slogans. Similarly, he spoke at length about the need for tolerance, openness and humility in educational dialogue. Any notion of Freire retaining a 'lingering conception of emotions as totally uncritical forces' (Sherman, 1980, p. 38) had, I think, well and truly disappeared by the mid-1990s. I have suggested, to the contrary, that Freire saw emotions as an integral part of his critical ideal and that what is missing in his work is an extensive investigation of dimensions of emotional life *other* than those tied to a critical mode of being. It seems certain that Freire would have said more about the nature and role of emotion had he lived for another ten years. When he died in 1997 he was still in his writing prime, and this theme, along with several others of importance to him (e.g., the impact of neoliberalism and globalization on education, reading and intellectual life, the relationship between faith, education and social transformation) would undoubtedly have received ongoing attention. Of course, it is unreasonable to expect any one theorist to explore all dimensions of educational experience. There is merit, however, in considering possibilities for further research, where the contributions Freire has made might be combined with insights from other bodies of work to extend and deepen our understanding of reason, emotion, politics, and educational life.

ACKNOWLEDGEMENT

I wish to thank Peter Mayo for his very helpful comments on an earlier version of this paper.

REFERENCES

Aristotle (1976) *Ethics* (The Nicomachean Ethics), revised edn., trans. J.A.K. Thomson (Harmondsworth, Penguin).

Beck, C. & Kosnik, C.M. (1995) Caring for the emotions: Towards more balanced schooling, *Philosophy of Education Society Yearbook: 1999* (Illinois, Philosophy of Education Society).

Boler, M. (1997) Disciplined emotions: Philosophies of educated feelings, *Educational Theory, 47* (2), 203-227.

Boler, M. (1999a) *Feeling power: Emotions and education* (New York, Routledge).

Boler, M. (1999b) Posing some feminist queries to Freire, in: P. Roberts (Ed) *Paulo Freire, politics and pedagogy: Reflections from Aotearoa-New Zealand* (Palmerston North, Dunmore Press).

Borg, C. & Mayo, P. (2000) Reflections from a 'third age' marriage: Paulo Freire's pedagogy of reason, hope and passion – An interview with Ana Maria (Nita) Freire, *McGill Journal of Education, 35* (2), 105-120.

Boshier, R. (1999) Freire at the beach: Remembering Paulo in the bright days of summer, *Studies in Continuing Education, 21* (1), 113-125.

Bowers, C.A. (1983) Linguistic roots of cultural invasion in Paulo Freire's pedagogy, *Teachers College Record, 84* (4), 935-953.

Coben, D. (1998) *Radical heroes: Gramsci, Freire and the Politics of adult education* (New York, Garland).

Cunningham, A. (2001) *The heart of what matters: The role for literature in moral philosophy* (Berkeley, University of California Press).

Convergence (1998) Special issue: 'A Tribute to Paulo Freire', 31.

Dallaire, M. (2001) *Contemplation in liberation -- A method for spiritual education in the schools* (Lewiston, NY, Edwin Mellen Press).

Darder, A. (2002) *Reinventing Paulo Freire: A pedagogy of love* (Boulder, CO, Westview Press).

Darder, A. (2003) Teaching as an act of love: Reflections on Paulo Freire and his contributions to our lives and our work, in: A. Darder, M. Baltodano & R.D. Torres (Eds) *The critical pedagogy reader* (New York and London, RoutledgeFalmer).

Dostoevsky, F. (1991) *The brothers Karamazov*, trans. R. Pevear & L. Volokhonsky (New York, Vintage).

Dowbor, L. (1997) Preface, in: P. Freire, *Pedagogy of the heart* (New York, Continuum).

Ellsworth, E. (1989) Why doesn't this feel empowering? Working through the repressive myths of critical pedagogy, *Harvard Educational Review, 59* (3), 297-324.

Escobar, M., Fernandez, A.L., Guevara-Niebla, G. & Freire, P. (1994) Paulo Freire on higher education: A Dialogue at the National University of Mexico (Albany, State University of New York Press).

Fraser, J.W. (1997) Love and history in the work of Paulo Freire, in: P. Freire, J.W. Fraser, D. Macedo, T. McKinnon, & W.T. Stokes (Eds) *Mentoring the mentor: A critical dialogue with Paulo Freire* (New York, Peter Lang).

Freire, A.M.A. (2001) *Chronicles of love: My life with Paulo Freire* (New York, NY, Peter Lang).

Freire, P. (1972a) *Pedagogy of the oppressed* (Harmondsworth, Penguin).

Freire, P. (1972b) *Cultural action for freedom* (Harmondsworth, Penguin).

Freire, P. (1976) *Education: The practice of freedom* (London, Writers and Readers).

Freire, P. (1978) *Pedagogy in process: The letters to Guinea-Bissau* (London, Writers and Readers).

Freire, P. (1983) The importance of the act of reading, *Journal of Education, 165* (1), 5-11.

Freire, P. (1985) *The politics of education* (London, MacMillan).

Freire, P. (1993) *Pedagogy of the city* (New York, Continuum).

Freire, P. (1994) *Pedagogy of hope* (New York, Continuum).

Freire, P. (1996) *Letters to Cristina: Reflections on my life and work* (London, Routledge).

Freire, P. (1997a) *Pedagogy of the heart* (New York, Continuum).

Freire, P. (1998a) *Teachers as cultural workers: Letters to those who dare teach* (Boulder, Westview Press).

Freire, P. (1998b) *Politics and education* (Los Angeles, UCLA Latin American Center Publications).

Freire, P. (1998c) *Pedagogy of freedom: Ethics, democracy, and civic courage* (Lanham, Rowman and Littlefield).

Freire, P. & Faundez, A. (1989) *Learning to question: A pedagogy of liberation* (Geneva, World Council of Churches).

Freire, P. & Macedo, D. (1987) *Literacy: Reading the word and the world* (London, Routledge and Kegan Paul).

Freire, P. & Macedo, D. (1993) A dialogue with Paulo Freire, in: P. McLaren & P. Leonard (Eds) *Paulo Freire: A critical encounter* (London, Routledge).

Freire, P. & Shor, I. (1987) *A pedagogy for liberation* (London, MacMillan).

Gilligan, C. (1982) *In a different voice: Psychological theories and women's development* (Cambridge, Harvard University Press).

Gribble, J. (1983) Literature and the education of the emotions, in: *Literary education: A revaluation* (Cambridge, Cambridge University Press).

Hadot, P. (1995) *Philosophy as a way of life* (Cambridge, MA, Blackwell).

Hargreaves, A. (1998) The emotional practice of teaching, *Teaching and Teacher Education, 14*, 835-854.

Hepburn, R.W. (1972) The arts and the education of feeling and emotion, in: R.F. Dearden, P.H. Hirst & R.S. Peters (Eds) *Education and reason* (Part 3 of *Education and the Development of Reason*), (London, Routledge and Kegan Paul).

Horton, M. & Freire, P. (1990) *We make the road by walking: Conversations on education and social change*, Eds B. Bell, J. Gaventa & J. Peters (Philadelphia, Temple University Press).

Leistyna, P. (1999) *Presence of mind: Education and the politics of deception* (Boulder, CO, Westview Press).

Macedo, D. (2001) Introduction, in: A.M.A. Freire, *Chronicles of love: My life with Paulo Freire* (New York, NY, Peter Lang).

Mackie, R. (1980) Contributions to the thought of Paulo Freire. In R. Mackie (Ed) Literacy and revolution: The pedagogy of Paulo Freire (London, Pluto Press).

Margonis, F. (2003) Paulo Freire and post-colonial dilemmas, *Studies in Philosophy and Education, 22,* 145-156.

Mayo, P. (1999) *Gramsci, Freire and adult education: Possibilities for transformative action* (London, Zed Books).

McLaren, P. (2000) *Che Guevara, Paulo Freire, and the pedagogy of revolution* (Lanham, MD, Rowman and Littlefield).

Morgan, J. (1994) Learning to live with emotion, *Educational Philosophy and Theory, 26* (2), 67-81.

Morrow, R.A. & Torres, C.A. (2002) *Reading Freire and Habermas: Critical pedagogy and transformative social change* (New York, Teachers College Press).

Neiman, A.M. (2000) Self examination, philosophical education and spirituality, *Journal of Philosophy of Education, 34* (4), 571-590.

Nias, J. (1996) Thinking about feeling: the emotions in teaching, *Cambridge Journal of Education, 26,* 293-306.

Noddings, N. (1984) *Caring* (Berkeley, University of California Press).

Nussbaum (1990) *Love's knowledge: Essays on philosophy and literature* (New York, Oxford University Press).

Roberts, P. (1996) Defending Freirean intervention, *Educational Theory, 46* (3), 335-352.

Roberts, P. (2000) *Education, literacy, and humanization: Exploring the work of Paulo Freire* (Westport, CT, Bergin and Garvey).

Roberts, P. (2003) Epistemology, ethics and education: Addressing dilemmas of difference in the work of Paulo Freire, *Studies in Philosophy and Education, 22,* 157-173.

Sherman, A. (1980) Two views of emotion in the writings of Paulo Freire, *Educational Theory, 30* (3), 35-38.

Solomon, R.C. (1986) Literacy and the education of the emotions, in: S. de Castell, A. Luke & K. Egan (Eds) *Literacy, society, and schooling: A reader,* (Cambridge, Cambridge University Press).

Spring, J. (1994) *Wheels in the head: Educational philosophies of authority, freedom, and culture from Socrates to Paulo Freire* (New York, McGraw-Hill).

Steiner, R. (1995) *Intuitive thinking as a spiritual path: A philosophy of freedom,* trans. M. Lipson (Hudson, NY, Anthroposophic Press).

Taboo: The Journal of Culture and Education (1997) Special issue on Paulo Freire, *2* (Fall), 1-188.

The New English Bible: New Testament (1961) (Oxford, Oxford University Press).

Weiler, K. (1991) Paulo Freire and a feminist pedagogy of difference, *Harvard Educational Review, 61* (4), 449-474.

Zembylas, M. (2002) Structures of feeling' in curriculum and teaching: theorizing the emotional rules, *Educational Theory, 52* (2), 187-208.

Zigler, R.L. (1994) Reason and emotion revisited: Achilles, Arjuna and moral conduct, *Educational Theory, 44* (1).

JOSÉ EUSTAQUIO ROMÃO

CIVILIZATION OF THE OPPRESSED

INTRODUCTION: CULTURE AS THE EXPRESSION OF SOCIAL CLASS

From our first days of school, we learn that science, technology, religion, art and other superior constructions of human invention, in all historical ages, were born of privileged or dominant social groups. Most of our teachers assured us that even though, sometimes, representatives from these groups have failed to distinguish themselves intellectually, they have always decided which of the creations and inventions of human intelligence should be preserved and disseminated, thanks to the control they have had over the financing of theoretical formulations and their condensation in the fabrication of artifacts.

Since the beginning of the history of stratified societies, the productions and expressions of the hegemonic classes or those they control have constituted what is called "erudite culture". And, as the expression of those in power, it almost always seems like the only one that should be transmitted to future generations, as if it guaranteed the elevation of special beings to superior levels of actualization [i] in terms of their specific possibilities.

In the same line of thinking, we hear endless claims about the lack of culture of the poor, about the "not-knowing" of the dominated. Even when, from time to time, we have heard tell of their specific ways of analyzing and interpreting reality, their representations are almost never taken seriously and, because of this, they are opposed by the processes of preservation, accumulation and transmission of the cultural patrimony and, consequently, banished from scholastic curricula. In other words, popular culture is almost never considered a constituent element of the preserves considered important for the evolution of the species. It appears as a counterpoint to "erudite culture" and its linguistic expression, when compared to the "cultured norm", carries a negative epistemological and political connotation.

To cite an example of this cultural bipolarity, in hegemonic historiography, "pas de documents, pas d'histoire" [ii]. So, if there is no history where there is no (written) document, there is no people's history because, usually, the people cannot write. The absolutism of written documents in historical science is an exclusionary ideological contrivance used by literate culture, in the guise of epistemological superiority. To reconstitute the history and historiography of the oppressed, we must use different and alternative sources than the primary, written ones. We need to find other evidence.

C.A. Torres & P. Noguera (Eds.), Social Justice Education for Teachers, 119–128.

It would not be too much to remember here that the marvelous expressive variety of the neo-Latin languages derives from Vulgar, not from Classical, Latin! Thus, it does not make sense that schools in countries with neo-Latinate languages quash the popular dialect in the name of a greater epistemological and expressive wealth in the "cultured norm". This entails true ethnocentrism, or would it be classicentrism, as evinced, in counter-proof, by the frequently excessive refinement of popular prose and poetry. So that, often, the beauty and precision of the terms and expressions seem to come from a real epistemological-ethical-esthetic "Occam's razor"[iii]

CIVILIZATION OF THE OPPRESSED: A HYPOTHESIS

In the end, every thesis remains a hypothesis because it can be negated by a posterior thesis. Many times, humanity has been misled by beliefs in "scientific theories" which later prove to be completely mistaken, not to say erroneous. Such was the case, for example, of centuries of belief in geocentrism[iv]. Human theories are merely representations of reality, closer or more distant from objective truth, according to the position of the observer. Fundamentally, greater "scientific intimacy" does not depend so much on the formulators' talent as on their position in the context.

It is exactly this kind of evidence that obliges us to review the "inescapable" truths which are fed to us, from elementary school on, regarding the significant cultural creations of hegemonic groups and societies in every historical era. So that, by observing the evolution of humanity and consulting the historiography which hung over the trajectory of the "civilizing process"[v], we may perceive that advances of the human species toward higher ground, in the sense of realizing their full potential, always came from oppressed social formations or segments, never from the socially oppressive classes. Certainly, it was in support of this evidence that Paulo Freire wrote:

> Whereas the violence of the oppressors prevents the oppressed from being fully human, the response of the latter to this violence is grounded in the desire to pursue the right to be human. As the oppressed, fighting to be human, take away the oppressor's power to dominate and suppress, they restore to the oppressors the humanity they had lost in the exercise of oppression. It is only the oppressed who, by freeing themselves, can free their oppressors. The latter, as an oppressive class, can free neither others nor themselves. (FREIRE, 2000: 56)

This same evidence, on the other hand, obliges us to relativize our theses, recharacterizing them as hypotheses, even when we are convinced that the perspective of the oppressed gives them some epistemological advantages and nourishes their impulse to accomplish their initiatives which can elevate them and, along with them, a great part, if not all, of humanity.

However, there is a series of questions, which are raised by the hypothesis of the authorship of civilization's advances by the oppressed. In the first place, the very term "civilization" is loaded with ethnocentrism, insofar as it is the result of a classification made by a "civilized" person of humanity's stages of cultural evolution. Thus, the discussion of the concept of culture, the stages of its occurrence in social formations and the cultural systems present in all of them is of consummate importance for the propositions of the aforementioned hypothesis. In the second place, it is not easy to identify a vocabulary word or, what is more, to construct a neologism -- as Paulo Freire frequently did -- which, semantically and without signs of ethnocentrism, accounts for the significance we wish to lend to the idea of a civilizing process. Finally, and perhaps this is the task which seems the most difficult, it is necessary to discover the factor(s) which impel the oppressed to advance Humanity in the direction of "civilization", rather than retreating to "savagery" or "barbarity".

CULTURE, CIVILIZATION OR PAIDÉIA

A lot of paper and ink has been used in the discussion about the differences, the approximations and the dissimilarities and divergences between the concepts of culture and those of civilization. I do not wish to restate them here. However, I will restate, in a rather summary way, what I have already developed in other works on the concept of culture and its corollaries and implications.

The term "culture" presents a semantic plurality but, given the limits of this essay, we will focus on its significance as "humanization of the world". In this sense, culture is everything that results from human thought and action about nature, especially when it comes to obtaining the goods and services necessary for the survival and reproduction of the species. In sum, culture is all human action that confers a new significance to that which, originally, things and processes had in their natural state. Beings and natural phenomena exist and are transformed objectively, as if obeying a determining, external teleos. In other words, they evolve as if impelled by an exogenous objective. When a human being makes use of one of these beings or interferes in one of these phenomena, she confers a second significance and another objective, creating culture. Let us imagine, as an example, the use of a tree branch by one of our ancestors to "augment" her arm and, with it, reach a fruit on a higher tree. What was, naturally and simply, a branch became a "food collector"; moreover, it gained new significance and a new objective in the hands of a representative of the species. In the same way, she could use the branch to beat the head of her runaway husband, now conferring on it the sense of a "weapon". In the two opportunities, we are faced with acts of cultural creation, as violent as one of them happens to be.

Still from an anthropological perspective, we must derive from this concept of culture, among others, at least three orders of consideration. In the first place, culture is more a process than a structured group of concepts, laws, axioms, postulates, artifacts, etc. In the second place, we have to admit that all peoples, even the most primitive, have culture. Finally, even though they are in different stages, all social formations, from the simplest to the most complex, constitute their culture with three systems of intervention in the Cosmos:

I -- Productive Cultural System

II -- Associative Cultural System

III -- Symbolic Cultural System.

The first is made up of the forms and instruments of "production and reproduction of immediate life", as Engels wrote in the Origin of the Family, Private Property and the State (1975: 19). In other words, what the Productive System -- which some anthropologists, like Darcy Ribeiro (1978), prefer to call the "Adaptive System"[vi] -- says with respect to the forms, means and instruments of production of material existence. It corresponds to the anthropological version of what the materialist-dialectical explanation calls the "infrastructure of societies". It is made up, therefore, of means of production and productive forces.

The Associative System is made up of the group of specific norms of human sociability in each one of its known social formulations, as well as the forms, specific also, of its application. Moreover, it has as constituent parts the "instruments" of supervision and application of these norms, which are also responsible for the application of sanctions on whomever disobeys them. It can be said, in more technical language, that the Associative System is made up of the law and bureaucracy of each society, for even though these words are applied only to modern, complex social formations, it is not difficult to imagine their adaptation to more primitive and simpler human communities. In terms of historical materialism, this system corresponds to the juridical-political superstructure.

The Symbolic System, contrary to the first two which are action systems, is a representational system: through it, women and men represent nature, themselves, their relations with nature, other human beings, their mutual relations, the cosmos, etc. The Symbolic System is made up of the sciences, the arts, religions and all forms of captivation, interpretation, representation and worldly expression.

There is another human reality that is not specifically contained in any of the cultural systems mentioned above, even though it passes through them. Perhaps it constitutes another system.[vii] That is affectivity, sometimes called "libidinal reality". It is just as fundamental to the survival of the species as the elements of the other systems, since its imbalance can lead, in extreme cases, to self-elimination; and, evidently, is even more fundamental for the reproduction of the species! Under Freudian rationality[viii], the libido appears as an element diametrically antagonistic to sociability, made manifest as the tragically individualistic search for personal happiness.

In sum, culture may be synthesized as in the diagram contained in Figure 1.

PROCESS	MANIFESTATION	ELEMENTS	TARGET
Productive	Action	Means of Production Productive Forces	Material Life (Production/ Reproduction)
Associative		Laws Bureaucracy	Collective Life
Symbolic	Representation	Science Arts Religion...	Explanation Expression Communication

Figure 1 – Cultural processes

The concept of culture, however, is laden with ambiguities. Not to belabor the theme, suffice it to say that it is most commonly used as a synonym of erudition. We say "so and so is a cultured person" when, usually, it would be more appropriate to say "that person is erudite." On the other hand, the word "culture" denotes a structure, to the extent that it introduces a more procedural connotation. Thus, the reading and administration of the world, by women and men, constitutes a process in permanent mutation. Trying to escape the traps of the ambiguities of the other term, "pedagogy", the Greeks wound up offering us a word which comes very close to the idea we want to capture and register. That is, "Paidéia", whose nearest translation is "civilizational process", or process in search of the full realization of humanity. And it is on this meaning that we construct our thesis or, rather, our hypothesis that any human advances in the sense of this fulfillment can only be developed by the oppressed.

Finally, it comes down to identifying the impulse that causes men and women to develop the process of civilization, of culture, the movement in search of the human utopia, the Paidéia.

However, to discover the impulse -- and even to know what to call it -- leads peripheral social formations and dominated social groups to surpass their "limit situations", transforming them into "viable originals", we would need to analyze the specific situation of every social formation that occurred in the history of humanity. As this examination also surpasses the limits of the present work, the summary considerations we make here about the theme are no more than provocations, hypotheses to be confirmed in the empirical proof of the analysis of concrete social formations. Nevertheless, we will simply foresee something here that may be developed more profoundly later with a simultaneous inquiry into both the concrete history and the history of human thought on the theme of impulse.

Until the XVII century, the human impulse toward the "Paideiatic advance" was seen as the result of a passive movement in the direction of a teleos external to the being and which attracted it. From that point on, various thinkers sought the internal impulse, propulsion of self toward human fulfillment.

> Around the year 1600 people began to place this propensity inside men (impelling them) rather than outside (attracting them) as had been the case before 1600. In 1670, Espinoza called this impulse "soul." In 1818, Schopenhauer called it "will." In 1890, Bergson called it "vital energy", while Freud, at about the same time, called it "sex."[ix] Throughout this last period, many naturalists called it "energy." (Quigley, 1961: 30-31)

Arnold Toynbee, the historian who is a reference for Quigley[x], developed the theory that civilizations are only constructed by social formations which respond to the (real, but not excessive) challenges they confront. Here, even though he criticizes the teleos (exogenous attraction), Quigley, inspired by Toynbee, ends up returning to the negation of the endogenous impulse: the challenges that present themselves in the trajectory of social formations are those which catapult them toward civilization. It follows that people and social segments only develop if they are challenged. In this sense, indigenous Brazilians, for instance, would be backward, in terms of civilization, because they are seldom if ever challenged, to the extent that they are protected by a benevolent nature, settling for the material comfort that it gives them. Would it not also be worthwhile to ask why Brazilian slum-dwellers are in such an "uncivilized" situation? Could it be because they were unable to respond to the real and excessive challenges of domination?

Paulo Freire made a notable contribution to the discussion about the concept of impulse, developing his theory about human beings' consciousness of their own incompleteness as a catalyzing element of dissatisfaction and, dialectically, as a propelling factor in the construction of hope and of utopia, in the tireless search to "be more". Among all the beings of the Universe – incomplete, unfinished and inconclusive like us—human beings are unique in their consciousness of their own incompleteness and, because of this, push themselves toward completion, toward plenitude.

The Freirian contribution goes further to discuss why this impulse is not present in the oppressors – or present in a distorted manner – but only in the oppressed. How do the oppressed, and not the oppressors, make humanity advance, if the dominant ideas, values, projections and aspirations in a class society are ideas of the dominant classes, as Marx claimed? How can the oppressed do anything different from the oppressors, if they inculcate the oppressors' ideological traffic, becoming their hosts, as Freire affirmed; most of the time, merely wanting to change places with the oppressor, transforming themselves into him?

What is important, therefore, is that the oppressed struggle to overcome this contradiction. Liberation is thus a childbirth, and a painful one. The man or woman who emerges is a new person, viable only as the oppressor-oppressed contradiction is superseded by the humanization of all people. Or to put it another way, the solution of this contradiction is born in the labor which brings into the world this new being: no longer oppressor nor longer oppressed, but human in the process of achieving freedom.

This solution cannot be achieved in idealistic terms. In order for the oppressed to be able to wage the struggle for their liberation, they must perceive the reality of oppression not as a closed world from which there is no exit, but as a limiting situation which they can transform. This perception is necessary but not a sufficient condition for liberation; it must become the motivating force for liberating action. Nor does the discovery by the oppressed that they exist in dialectical relationship to the oppressor, as his antithesis—that without them the oppressor could not exist—in itself constitute liberation. The oppressed can overcome the contradiction in which they are caught only when this perception enlists them in the struggle to free themselves. (FREIRE, 2000: 49)

In fact, the mediation of the situation of oppression is in the oppressor-oppressed relationship. The oppressed, in their impulse, in their transforming movement, can take two paths[XI]: either they seek to be elevated to the dominant position, which leads, eventually, to their attempting to defeat or substitute the oppressor, or they struggle to change the situation of oppression. And there is the key to Paulo Freire's thinking which denies the possibility of human freedom coming from the hands of the oppressors: if it comes, it will come from the hands of the oppressed, which is not to say that it will ever come. It will not come, even from the oppressed, as long as they are interested in changing places. In the first instance, the oppressed will not free themselves or their oppressors; only by following the second path can they free themselves and, in doing so, free their oppressors as well.

We remain ignorant of the impulse factor, what is its motor and why it is located in the oppressed. Could it be because the oppressed suffer domination? We can infer from Freire's thesis that only the oppressed can be interested in changing the situation of oppression, because of their suffering. But the answer to this question is an essential part of our thesis (hypothesis), which we want to present in our final considerations.

FINAL CONSIDERATIONS

Carroll Quigley (op. cit.) developed the theory that all societies have one or more "instruments of expansion", which make them advance in the direction of the construction of a civilization. As far as he is concerned, the impulse is sent through this instrument. Nevertheless, every instrument of expansion has an irrepressible tendency toward institutionalization. That is, a factor that exists and works for the sake of the whole society, as was the case with the infantry in the Roman Republic, and produces its development; however, with the passage of time, it is threatened to be overcome by new social needs, because its internal agents tend to resist the changes demanded by the new times. At this moment, the instrument is institutionalized, that is, it no longer attends to the needs and designs of society in general, favoring the exclusive interests of those agents.

Every hegemonic group in the mechanisms of the State[xii], which are the instruments of expansion, fearing the loss of positions in the implementation of modifications demanded by society, starts to use these unaltered instruments just to defend its corporate interests. In sum, every dominant group would have a structural tendency to institutionalization, as Quigley says. In other words, every social formation presents various sectors of activity and, in each one of them, more or less dynamic institutions can exist[xiii]. The more dynamic they are, the more "instituting"; the less dynamic, the more instituted or institutionalized. And their degree of dynamism must be measured by their efficiency and efficacy in responding to the institutional missions with which society as a whole entrusted them. The 'instituting' institutions begin to lose their capacity to respond to these missions when they migrate, more and more, within themselves, turning to the objectives of their own agents, sacrificing those of the society at large.

Let us see how this occurs in the broader historical process. In a general way, ascending groups of oppressed people, in their battle against the situations of oppression, obtain a high incidence of identification between their values and ideals and the projections and aspirations of the whole of society. However, once in power, they tend to collectivize their objectives and to crystallize history as the possibility of a series of transformations. In other words, once in the place of the oppressive class, they tend to negate history insofar as they begin to view the society resulting from their victory as terminal, at the same time "forgetting" their original objectives, entrenched as they are in the defense of their rights and 'exclusive' ideals. That is why the oppressed perspective of constructing the Paidéia is in movement, not in the structuring of its victory.

Paulo Freire made two important contributions in this sense. First, he studied and wrote "pedagogies", recommending to his closest friends that they do the same. Increasingly universal in his thought and action, was he not contradictorily recommending a segmented production, turned toward a specific field? Or was he saying that pedagogy, in the "paideiatic" sense (a process of humanization through culture), is the necessary rationality at the beginning of the millennium? Was it not for this reason that, instead of creating "pedagogical circles" or "educational circles", he proposed the creation of circles of culture?

In the second place – and this is the most important contribution he made to world thought – he tried to read the world through the eyes of the oppressed, from the perspective of the pedagogy. He did not produce a "pedagogy for the oppressed", but a pedagogy of the oppressed!

As scholars and re-inventors of Freirian thinking, we ought to pore over every sector of human activity, searching for this perspective of the oppressed, this regard which sees the world, epistemologically and politically, as a space of 'being more.' Because the "superiority" of science, of art, of religion and of the remaining forms representing the oppressed is exactly in its admission of change, in the understanding and hope brought about by/through the transformation. One could even argue that this is the rationale of the lowest common denominator – and we know that Paulo thought of "vanguardism" as well as "basism" as alienated/alienating ways to construct knowledge and political militancy. It can even be argued that the world vision of the oppressed is contaminated by traces of the consciousness and culture of the oppressor. So, why consider the oppressed consciousness as more scientific and of greater political density? Here there is no way to escape the distinction made by Lucien Goldmann[xiv] between "real consciousness" and "possible consciousness", developed throughout all his work. Paulo Freire himself, in Pedagogy of the Oppressed, recommends that we examine this distinction in Goldmann[xv]. In this sense, we must go back, to the science of the oppressed, to the music of the oppressed, to the literature of the oppressed, etc., not only for the generosity and political commitment of the "wretched of the earth", but also for the epistemological clairvoyance and ontological necessity of the realization of our humanity.

Paulo Freire gave us the example in this particular case, positioning himself in the perspective of the oppressed to detail the educational and pedagogical process. But this process does not appear on the surface of the consciousness of the oppressed, it has to be sought in their insertion in the historical process, in their historicity, which makes traces of liberationist consciousness possible, independent of psychologically and socially manifested consciousness. However, for these traces to become reality, a pedagogical process that unlocks a liberationist education is necessary and, what is more, one that creates Padéia, the process of Humanity's cultural development.

Nevertheless, we are even now convinced that the richest and most powerful people, politically speaking, and those who employ the most technology are not necessarily those who advance, making the whole of humankind advance with them. The history of societies is replete with examples contrary to these hegemonic beliefs. Let us look, by way of example, at the case of Iberia. Until the XIV century, it was a region on the periphery of Europe[xvi], without economic, technological or political power. Even so, from one moment to the next, it realized important syntheses, whether in science or in technology as known in various parts of the world at that time, so as to apply it to the "Great Navigations" and, through them, to allow the advance of the whole of Humanity in various aspects of its process of 'being more.' Along the same lines of thinking, when the Iberian social formations attempted to consolidate their colonial empires of domination over other people, they lost their identity with more planetary ideas, values, dreams and utopias and fell into decadence.

So which is, finally, the creative impulse of "civilization", of culture, of humanization? It seems to be that which speaks about solidarity or, for those who are not frightened by certain or words or expressions, it seems to be the ability to love. In fact, the contrary movement back to nature, the return to "barbarity," always seems impelled by the category of privatization. The privatization of the Productive System and, consequently of the goods (of production and of consumption) has taken the minority to the alienation of consumerism, accumulation and environmental destruction, imposing on the majority the atrocious suffering of hunger and violence, threatening the very bases of the Planetary survival of the species. But this has already been exhaustively demonstrated. The private appropriation of the Associative System, that is, the utilization of the rights and mechanisms of the State (in the Gramscian sense) has transported the minority to despotic alienation of all gradations and has taken the majority to the madness of submission to those parallel powers of contravention, the drug trade and fundamentalism. The privatization of affectivity leads to the delirium and the mania of narcissism and of solitude.

Does this mean that the oppressed will always mobilize collectively? No. Not always, because, in most cases, they will be reading the world with the eyes of the oppressor, with the oppressor's tongue and head. For them to read the world with their own eyes, from the perspective that history impressed upon them, it is necessary that the pedagogy of the oppressed continues to expand.

Only the oppressed have the potential to allow humanity to advance in the sense of the Padéia; but it is only the Pedagogy of the Oppressed, which will permit the construction of the Civilization of the Oppressed.

JOSÉ EUSTAQUIO ROMÃO

Translated into English by Peter Lownds, PFI-LA, October-November 2002

NOTES

[i] In the Aristotelian sense of the term.

[ii] No documents, no history.

[iii] William of Occam (1270-1347), scholarly thinker, known as the "Invincible Doctor", he was an important philosopher, the creator of the principle of simplicity in the construction of scientific hypotheses. Thence the expression "Occam's Razor" or "Occam's Principle". The supposition of the uniformity of Nature, for example, is based on this principle and has as corollary the presumption that the entire universe is composed of the same substances, which behave in the same manner when submitted to the same conditions. In the first place, the non-application of "Occam's Razor" would cause great difficulty: it would not be possible to lift up all the constituent parts of the universe to prove that they are made of the same elements and behave in the same way. It is simpler to start with the presupposition that they are. In the second place, we can prove that this is not so if we find one exceptional case. The presumption that everyone is innocent until proven guilty, in the judicial system, is also based on this principle. In this case, in oppressive regimes, the violation of "Occam's Razor" always appears as an instrument for the elimination of those in opposition. That is the case, for example, with political prisoners who have to prove their non-adhesion to ideologies considered subversive, when it ought to be their accusers who have the burden of proof.

[iv] A theory according to which Earth is the center of the solar system.

[v] Notably, Arnold J. Toynbee, with his A Study of History (1953); Carroll Quigley, with The Evolution of Civilizations (1963); and Fernand Braudel, with his Grammar of Civilizations (1989).

[vi] From our viewpoint, inadequately, since the human species does not adapt to nature but rather adapts nature to its necessities.

[vii] A more thorough discussion of this theme surpasses the limits of this essay, but I hereby promise to take it up again in others, with more room to breathe.

[viii] And here we include the post-Freudians, like Wilhelm Reich.

[ix] Really, Freud and his disciples, especially Reich, called the human impulse "compulsion".

[x] Even though he criticizes him.

[xi] There is also a third option, which is not that of impulse, of movement, but that of resignation to one's "luck", to one's "destiny", falling into the fatalism typical of the "naturalization" of human relations (removed from history).

[xii] And here the concept is that of Gramsci, in the sense of the "amplified State," that is, all the mechanisms of organization and exercise of power located not only in the political community, but also in the general social community.

[xiii] Quigley (op. cit., passim) speaks of "levels" rather than of sectors and of "instruments of expansion", instead of institutions. What we call "corporatization", he considers "institutionalization" of the "instrument of expansion", which threatens the social formation, perhaps leading it to decadence and to disappearance.

[xiv] Especially in Cultural Creation in Modern Society (1972).

[xv] See Pedagogy of the Oppressed, op.cit.: 126.

[xvi] It was even said that "Europe ended at the Pyrenees."

RICHARD VAN HEERTUM

FREIRE, APATHY AND THE DECLINE OF THE AMERICAN LEFT

The Future of Utopia in the Age of Cynicism

OVERVIEW

Paulo Freire's sanguine theories on education have emboldened generations of progressive educators across the globe, from South America to Africa and even a small coterie of critical pedagogues in the United States. And yet the educational system in the U.S. – now being exported from North to South in the name of "development" – may be the greatest impediment to the realization of his transformative vision. While the neoconservative movement in the West, solidified with the rise of Thatcher, Reagan and Trudeau, might be the driving force behind the push for increased standardization, testing, back-to-basics education, privatization and professionalism at home, the New Left has been complicit, if not actively supportive, in this turn from the foundations of progressive education.

But it is not the proponents of neoconservatism and neoliberalism alone that have driven us from the Freirian vision. The ubiquitous apathy of the left that rose in the wake of communism's collapse, together with the anesthetizing power of media, legal and illegal drug culture and the corporate colonization of a depoliticized public sphere, have been equally important in the victory of market populism and its ahistorical fatalism[i]. As Russell Jacoby has argued, this pervasive pessimism has driven the left away from its utopian roots and toward a defeatist acquiescence that ensures the success of their conservative opponents.[ii] It is reinforced through the dual but oppositional forces of "objective" positivism and its "value-free" research and postmodern nihilism, both serving the conservative agenda from opposite ends of the epistemological spectrum.

In seeking to overcome these debilitating paradigms, Paulo Freire's spirit can serve as a voice of reason calling for a return to the utopian foundations of radical Western thought, within the context of a multicultural world. In this paper, I take Freire outside the educational realm and place him squarely in the political. Using some of his key ontological and epistemological positions, I critique three dynamics currently plaguing the left including the "end of history" cynicism of neoliberal ideology, the postmodern problematics of political engagement and overemphasis on difference and the collapse of a collective utopian vision. By capitalizing on Freire's eclectic philosophical positions, the left could gain greater insight into its own theoretical deficiencies and work to overcome them toward a renewed faith in positive social transformation.

C.A. Torres & P. Noguera (Eds.), Social Justice Education for Teachers, 129–146.

FALSE PROPHETS AND THE END OF HISTORY

Have we truly reached the end of history, as Fukuyama so infamously proclaimed?[iii] Has hope been absconded by a lack of vision and an entrenched cynicism and apathy that preclude the resolve to change? Is ideology critique dead when there are no alternatives offered to unfettered capitalism and the dismantling of the welfare state?[iv] And, if not, who will then come forward to fight for humanity? It is here, most of all, that I believe the Freirian perspective can be instrumental in both deconstructing the failure of the left and building a new vision that is more hopeful and optimistic of the possibility of a better tomorrow.

For the cynicism and disenchantment with politics now so pervasive in America, has infected not only the right end of the political spectrum but the middle and left as well, making the later two unwitting but powerful catalysts in its canonization into universal law. Richard Rorty argued in 1989, as the last remnants of communism where wilting away, "I do not think that we liberals can now imagine a future of 'human dignity, freedom and peace.' We have no clear sense of how to get from the actual world to these theoretically possible worlds and thus no clear idea of what to work for."[v] And this is the popular perspective of a left that has fallen into disrepair, either reveling in the "end of politics" radical postmodernism has ushered in or falling into deep malaise at the collapse of oppositional voices. Emblematic of the new despondency was Marxist historian Eric Hobsbawm who in 1991 argued, "There is no part of the world that credibly represents an alternative system to capitalism . . . [which] has once again proved that it remains the most dynamic force in world development."[vi] Or South American theorists like Jorge Castaneda who in 1994 wrote, "The very notion of an overall alternative to the status quo has been severely questioned . . . The idea of revolution itself, central to Latin American radical thought for decades, has lost its meaning."[vii] More recently, in his 1999 book End of Politics, Carl Boggs closed with the following resigned analysis of Jerry Brown's evacuation of the radical project, "The sad truth is that even ostensibly 'radical' alternatives to the regime of corporate colonization seem to have been assimilated into the matrix of political business-as-usual . . . Betrayals of this sort will only reinforce what has become the hallmark of a depoliticized society: retreat from the public sphere, hatred of 'big government' and its politicians (however radical), a turn toward civil privatism, incapacity to pursue struggles for social change and the public good." And then there are the nihilistic postmodernists, as represented by figures like Baudrillard, who have extricated agency from humanity, and made us passive objects in a media universe that has severed the ties between reality and fiction, truth and lies and even the human and machine. "Somewhere in the course of the eighties of the twentieth century, history took a turn in another direction. Once it passed its apogee in time, once it reached the peak of the curve in its evolution, its solstice of history, a sliding back of events set in, an unfolding of inverted meaning."[viii]

And who can blame the left in the current milieu? America truly is experiencing the end of politics, replaced by a depoliticized public sphere where sensationalism and spectacle pass for discourse, where the Democrats and Republicans collapse into one corporate party with slightly varied views of

130

American geopolitical hegemony and where a disillusioned polis disengages and dissolves before the anesthetizing blue glow and the advertisers who underwrite it. The profound deterioration of public discourse and participation has ushered in a new age of cynicism, alienation and remystification where the central precepts of citizenship, social governance, community and the common good central to modern liberalism are supplanted by individualism, greed and detachment. An atomized left has lost its focus and splintered into sectarian fragments whose only point of solidarity is in the collective desire to fight for the parochial interests of their constituencies. And politics itself has degenerated in deference to the media bias to amuse us to death, neglecting the real issues of our time – including the colonization of corporations into all facets of the public and private spheres, degradation of the environment, attacks on civil liberties, dismantling of the welfare state and the diminution of economic prospects for the vast majority of global citizens – while instead focusing on the likeability of candidates, diversionary "values" issues and sexual morality.[ix]

But it is worth considering the roots of this cynical fatalism. The end of history Fukuyama so brazenly foretold is itself an ideology – perhaps the most effective in history. It calls for blind support of the status quo. It is not provisional, time or location specific, or in any way unsettled. It has a transcendental perpetuity and immutability that, through the iconic treatment of the market as panacea to all our social ills, seems to eschew any self-reflection or criticism. We are to believe that this is it – capital has won and no one will ever be able to conceptualize another economic system. All we need do now is continue the march toward total privatization, dissolution of the last vestiges of the social safety net, deunionization, opening of global markets and shrinking of "big government." The power of the new paradigm stems largely from its dependence on a lack of curiosity and conviction in the audience that receive it; two attributes at the heart of the Freirian project.[x] It is written by the winners, as Foucault noted, and is espoused by the same people that see the boundless opportunity for technological innovation but can't see past their own instrumental rationality to the potential innovation of the human condition. And as Slavoj Zizek among others has argued, this ideology exists above and below us embedded in language and our subconscious, where it is all but impossible to fully conceptualize its colonizing grasp.[xi]

Freire always rejected fatalism as shortsighted, failing to acknowledge our "unfinishedness" in the world. To him the future is never preordained, unless we accept it as such. He thus argued that the "global tendency to accept the crucial implications of the New World Order as natural and inevitable," simply revealed the power of hegemony to spread, through education, the media and civil society, the precepts of the dominant class, transforming them from modes of repression to commonsensical norms.[xii] But like Jean Paul Sartre, Freire believed that while we are conditioned, we are not determined, and are thus free to revolt against that conditioning:

Our being in the world is much more than just "being." [It is] a "presence" that can reflect upon itself, that knows itself as presence, that can intervene,

> can transform, can speak of what it does, but that can also take stock of, compare, evaluate, give value to, decide, break with, and dream.[xiii]

By taking this ontology position, he eviscerates the deterministic and monological philosophy of neoliberalism, which relies on a solipsistic vision of reality founded on extreme individualism, instrumental rationality and subjects as passive receptors of objective being. Freire's intersubjective ontology instead argues for a reality founded on dialogue where individuals work in fellowship and solidarity to first envision their surrounding reality and then work collectively to change it. And Freire's ontology builds the foundations for a communal vision of humanity, where reality is constructed and altered in collective action, not through an individual subject looking out at an objective world. The implications to the radical project cannot be underestimated, as this is a key building block in moving beyond individualism and greed as the two central features of social organization to again contemplate the individual within the larger social framework. It challenges the Marxist structuralist position of Althusser and his followers, which stripped humanity of its agency to alter their reality for the better. And it builds the foreground for the negation of the negation, and the realization of the ultimate utopian state Marx envisioned, where having is supplanted by being and a positive humanism flourishes.

Freire thus believed that history was problematic but not determined. As he argued in 1992, "For me, history is a time of possibilities, not predeterminations . . . History is a possibility that we create throughout time, in order to liberate and therefore save ourselves."[xiv] Our ability to hope is what separates us from the rest of the animal kingdom, and what makes possible the utopian vision of a better future: a future of unity in diversity where we confront and overcome our "limit situations." For hope really is the leitmotif of Freire's work and the key constituent to rebuilding a progressive movement that can break through its own cynicism and doubt to galvanize the populace anew to struggle for collective emancipation.

Within this space of possibility and indeterminacy, education comes to play a central role in imbuing children and adults with a vision of a future that can be altered. But there is no reason to limit this valuable lesson to students. Just as Freire claimed the sine qua non of good teaching as creating an environment that embraces the imagination of a better world, and that inspired students to hope and dream, the left must find venues to embrace and spread this message outside, as well as inside, classrooms. Instead of decrying the hegemonic messages from without, it seems a more apt strategy might be to move within the system and create counterhegemonic films, curricula, and television programming and news outlets. This has already started to occur, but more must be done to create an alternative vision that can reach a larger and larger audience – particularly those outside the liberal mode. As Freire argued, this is the critical first step in overcoming the greatest impediment to true ethical responsibility – neoliberalism and its "cynical fatalism and inflexible negation of the right to dream differently, to dream of utopia."

Unfortunately, the realization of this subject position in history is countervailed by the return to a mentality, as described by C. Wright Mills in 1960, where smug conservative, tired liberals and disappointed radicals portend the end of both ideology and politics itself. To transform the ubiquitous cynicism, more than hopeful revelry will be required. While rejection of historical determinism can offer seeds of doubt and hope, real change will require a profound reexamination of the two primary vehicles of hegemonic ideology – the media and education.

MEDIA, EDUCATION AND THE OPAQUE IDEOLOGY OF "OBJECTIVITY"

The spread of hegemonic ideology continues throughout civil society, but the media and education are its two greatest proponents. While many including Gramsci, Adorno, Habermas, and Marcuse – and more recently Giroux, Kellner and Zizek – have detailed the spread of ideology in media and education, Freire offers a valuable framework for categorizing its multivariate mechanisms. In education, Freire first located and then rejected the oxymoron of objective, apolitical teaching without reservation and in his analysis of antidialogical action he offered a framework to critique the power of media and education in colonizing the psyche and reinforcing existing power dynamics.

Freire believed teaching necessarily entailed taking a position: "It seems fundamental to me to clarify in the beginning that a neutral, uncommitted, and apolitical educational practice does not exist."[xv] And in media, a similar obedience to objectivity can itself cloak ideology. Yet while many in the Ivory Tower, including Stanley Fish, Jacques Derrida and Hayden White, have rejected objectivity as a retrograde notion supplanted by omnipresent subjectivity, public school educators and the media continue to believe that their call to arms is complete disassociation from political ideology. While the absurdity of the claims is almost laughable, even Fox News employs tag lines like "we report, you decide," "no spin zone" and the more well known "fair and balanced." And most of the media professes a similar allegiance to objectivity, even as they continue to actively support market populism and consumer culture from the vantage point of the massive profit-seeking corporations that control them.[xvi]

Even forgoing the obvious biases and ideologies that underwrite all language and media, if one refuses to take a position, it seems fair to claim they are actively supporting the maintenance of the current order and status quo. For isn't adherence to conventional wisdom synonymous with passive retreat? I believe Freire would answer in the affirmative, further stipulating that objectivity in teaching and media neglect the ethical responsibility of educators and journalists to mold not only the economic potential of audiences but their moral foundation as well. In schools, by moving from the indoctrination of "banking education" to the transformative potential of problem-posing education, Freire envisioned a system where revolutionary spirit could be created and fostered into a resolve for change.[xvii] And in media, moving from a false objectivity to a critically balanced position, or even overt political advocacy, would be preferable to the current "he said, she said" reporting and rhetorical conservative bias.

Freire was essentially arguing that objectivity itself was an ideology, powerfully inured to the goals of maintaining unequal power relations and unjust economic and social order. Adorno and Horkheimer had recognized this fact earlier and had offered trenchant critique of positivism and its over-reliance on science, reason and objectivity.[xviii] And then postmodernist theorists called the whole project of objectivity into doubt, starting with philosophy and working their way to history and all "objectivity" claims.[xix] But Freire goes further to demand the infusion of ethical consideration into all pedagogical realms, moving beyond the church and family to the schools, media and remnants of the public sphere. He believed that objectivity was but a cloak that protects us from the deeper theoretical and systemic issues at the heart of social injustice.

In critiquing the role of education and media in closing the American mind, Freire's theory of antidialogical action offers great insight. He argued from his magnum opus Pedagogy of the Oppressed forward, following Hegel and Erich Fromm, that key facets of oppression are driven by prescribed behavior and domesticating conditioning, that makes the oppressed unconsciously complicit in their own subjugation.[xx] By closing the channels of cooperation, efforts at organization and solidarity and pluralism, critical dialogue is hampered or vitiated completely. Freire thus described four major types of antidialogical action crucial to the maintenance of the dominant-subordinate social order.

The first is conquest, established through force and symbolic mystification. Recent attacks on the constitution through legislation like the Patriot Act and through the continued illegal detainments in Guantanamo Bay and across the U.S. are challenging our civil liberties at home, while forces abroad are spreading American hegemony through military might. And the explosion of the jail industry and the harsh drug crimes necessary to keep them full are leading to the incarceration of large proportions of minority youth. More important though are the myths that continue to proliferate and prosper in America today, introduced, spread and reinforced in classrooms, on television, the radio, and movie screens and in cyberspace. Foremost among these is the myth of the free market system and its power to serve as panacea to all social ills – spread through the mainstream media, universities, and international organizations like the IMF, Word Bank and WTO – though obviously challenged by its continued failure for most of the inhabitants on earth. But several other myths are also valuable at enforcing the status quo and protecting conservative interests. These include a vibrant American "democracy" in an environment of ignorance and apathy, pervasive violence among poor youth, ambiguous notions of freedom, meritocracy, personal responsibility and social mobility and the pervasive myth that patriotism and blind allegiance are synonymous. The discourse also comprises popular condemnation of big government, taxes and politicians, while neglecting discussion of its potential role in mitigating big business and its almost immeasurable harm to the common good. And it includes the aforementioned conviction that change is impossible, that politics is inherently corrupt and that that any attempt to improve the lot of the poor and disenfranchised destined for failure. Together these myths build the foundations of disillusionment, pessimism and alienation so critical to quashing any burgeoning visions of radical reform.

Divide and rule is a second form of antidialogical action, based on focalizing problems away from a totalizing view. It is instrumentalized through a number of channels from the right and left. Dramatic deunization is one key method used by the right to splintered the left, and this has been facilitated by media treatment of unions as inherently anti-competitive, inefficient and corrupt, neglecting their positive influence on everything from the five-day workweek, to employer sponsored healthcare to pensions and the minimum wage. More recently, we have learned that the FBI and local police are again infiltrating leftist groups, under the guise of the war on terror, reminding of earlier COINTELPRO operations. And the discourse of the right has also been extremely effective at derailing any debate on key issues of our time, muting the left with phrases like "race baiting," "class warfare," "partisan politics" and "political correctness," while continuing to vilify all things "liberal" and "elite" and even reverting to the retrograde "communist" label when anyone questions a new round of tax cuts or reductions in "big government." At the same time, they further smother any discussion of system inequality or structural barriers to equality through the use of the ubiquitous "personal responsibility" trope, placing the blame back on the victims of unfettered capitalism. On the left, the erection of theoretical systems like "social capital" have been used to place all of the blame for inequality on families, the community and individuals – while they turn their back on our poorest citizens in a grasp for power (as, for example, with Clinton's 1996 welfare reform). More importantly, identity politics, while having the positive effect of opening the debate to a much wider diversity of voices, has simultaneously fomented fragmentation into special interest groups that place barriers in the way of solidarity and collective action.

A third form of antidialogical action is manipulation, where communication is used to distort reality and inhibit democratic participation. Media myths and the spread of ideology, as innumerate above, are one key manner in which the masses are manipulated into irrational decision-making. A second is the anesthetizing, entertainment focused nature of media culture that distracts people from their own plight and diffuses the agency they possess to change their situation.[xxi] And this is reinforced through a celebration of anti-intellectualism, that is coupled with a vilification of all things intellectual, tending to privilege street smarts, intuition, irreverence and slang over intelligence, critical thinking, earnestness and eloquence. "Inoculating individuals with the bourgeois appetite for personal success" is another key distortion technique, accomplished with great success in America through the greed ethos and by using the opulent lifestyles of the rich and famous, on television, movies and magazines, as enticement for the many to acquiesce to the market economy in the hopes that they can themselves join the shrinking ranks of the rich and famous. The recent proliferation of reality television has only fortified this improbable dream of upward mobility, by offering fifteen minutes of fame to anyone willing to cede their time and self-respect. And the innate mistrust of government and politicians that has been ingrained in the public by the media, while ignoring the grosser malfeasance of corporations, creates a cynicism that disincentives political participation and even voting, while creating a false confidence in the innate superiority of markets over governments for solving social problems.

Finally is cultural invasion, which entails directly penetrating the cultural contexts of groups to impose a view of the world that negates alternative possibility. This paper has already discussed one form of this process, namely the breeding of ahistorical cynicism and apathy, but a few other sources are worth noting. One is an educational system that tends to reinforce "deficiency theory" mentalities through racially-biased standardized testing, unequal access to good schools, AP courses and resources, the debasing of alternative cultures, immigrants and foreign languages and a general neglect of alternative perspectives in textbooks and classroom curricula. This mentality is reinforced through movies, as Henry Giroux has argued, that portray minorities and all "exotic others" as subservient, violent or innately inferior.[xxii] It is buttressed by television shows like The Cosby Show or The George Lopez Show that treat assimilation as the only appropriate behavior for minority groups in America.[xxiii] And it is cemented through establishing white upper-middle class Americans as the normative ideal against which all other groups must compare themselves – leading many to internalize the outward manifestations of racism and embody the deficiency theories in thought and action.

Clearly, the fall of communism and the many failures of the left have left the radicals in a state of great distress. But waxing nostalgic for the past allows the vision to tunnel, while the hopelessness bleeds down and out creating a plague of apathy, hopelessness and dystopian nihilism that only reinforce the power of media and education to manipulate. If the left is to challenge this juggernaut of intellectual indoctrination, it needs to understand the spread of ideology and work to counteract it in a manner that resonates with the general public. And this attack must occur both within and outside public education and popular culture. Luckily many organizations like Move On.org and Air America are taking up this struggle, but more must sign on and we must simultaneously challenge the hidden agenda of objectivity.

In the struggle, we must acknowledge that media and education have the potential to deliver counterhegemonic and emancipatory messages. As Ernst Bloch has argued, any ideological vehicle that is persuasive must also include the underpinnings of utopian moments that could empower the audience to believe in change.[xxiv] And Walter Benjamin and Bertolt Brecht believed, as Douglas Kellner continues to argue, that media could be used as an emancipatory source itself, inviting audiences to envision a better future and to fight for its actualization.[xxv] So in concert with Freire, the potential to change a system that seems intent on self-preservation is still possible – and a goal the left should actively engage.

THE PSYCHOLOGY OF HOPELESSNESS IN A TECHNOLOGICAL AGE

Key in the movement away from a communicative environment so crucial to Freire's vision is the advent of modern technology including television, videogames, computers and the Internet. These new technologies, which ostensibly open the world up, can also be used to shut it off in lieu of an alternative reality where we live vicariously through others and suppress our true desires in deference to contentment and facile amusement. In the age of biotechnology, cloning, artificial intelligence and genetic engineering, is it possible that fear of obsolescence has become the new form of anxiety, supplanting or superceding our innate anomie? While this may exaggerate the impact of technology, it seems possible that it is instrumental in both amplifying traditional alienation, individualism, disillusionment and fear of death and creating new forms of anxiety based on the collapse of reality, the human-technology divide and truth itself. Marshall McLuhan argued that the information age had profound ramifications for not only how we communicate, but how we think, and that the discourse of technology has a speed and form that forced us to choose in a new global context. With this change, technology has created a new mode of thought, based on pattern recognition rather than classification, that is incommodious in its treatment of contemplative space and time, complicating the realization of critical consciousness. And it causes other potential problems as well. Technology like the Internet and email entail talking "at" rather than "to" one another, creating further strains in communication. Technology and the Internet can be effective vehicles for maintaining sectarian, parochial perspectives by allowing us to consume news and opinions within the confines of sources and cyberspace peers that share those views and perspectives.[xxvi] And, it can be argued that the manipulative potential of technology far surpass the written word, opening up the possibility of spreading false information with greater speed, stealth and success than ever before.

As with the general discussion of media, technology also offers new opportunities for dialogue and new channels for political participation and dissent. Much of the anti-war protest was organized through the Internet, and mobilization occurred on an unparalleled global scale solely because of its nearly boundless reach. Alternative media and oppositional voices are not muted on the Internet to the same extent as in mainstream media, allowing for the delivery of more accurate, balanced and potentially emancipatory messages to wide swaths of the population. The Internet is becoming a valuable tool for dialogue among leftist groups across the country and globe. And cheaper and faster media production is allowing almost instantaneous response to the attack ads and character assassination that have become so endemic to partisan political in America. This leaves technology from a leftist perspective as yet another contested terrain, that must be fought for if it is to serve its potential as a vehicle for mobilization and change.

THE LEFT IN AN ABYSS OF SUBJECTIVITY AND STATISTICAL FETISHISM

A second area where Freire can be of critical importance is in challenging the postmodern ontological and epistemological problematics, while seeking to overcome the limitations of difference and localized struggle as a focal point of political action. In the realm of epistemology, in particular, Freire can help toe the line between the excessive objectivity and neutrality of positivism and the boundless subjectivity of postmodernism.

For the positivism that Karl Popper ushered into American research was of great concern to Freire, particularly its reliance on a false "value free" methodology. Beyond the obvious manipulative potential of statistics −Benjamin Disraeli once quipped "there are three kinds of lies: lies, damn lies and statistics" − to Freire this potential was secondary to the more insidious nature of reliance on statistical analysis, which is its extrication of ethical considerations. Donaldo Macedo outlined in his introduction to Pedagogy of the Freedom, Freire's particular concern with the power of positivistic overemphasis to effectively cloak ideology "behind a facile call for 'scientific rigor' and 'absolute objectivity.'"[xxvii] As noted above, neutrality claims and ahistorical research are extremely powerful mechanisms to spread ideology in a package that absolves itself of ethical responsibility, making it more difficult for the naïve audience to discern or contradict.

Ironically it is research that incorporates ethical considerations, and underlying structural problems, that is now received with critical weariness and an almost reflexive rejection. As Henry Giroux argues, "theory and knowledge are subordinated to the imperatives of efficiency and technical mastery, and history is reduced to a minor footnote in the priorities of 'empirical' scientific inquiry."[xxviii] Key in attacking this almost slavish adherence to numbers and pseudo-scientific research is an understanding that the social sciences should not seek to mirror the "hard sciences," but should instead respect the unique nature of humanity and the social constructions that lay at the foundations of knowledge.

The postmodern questioning of objectivity thus seems an ideal vehicle for questioning overreliance on statistical analysis and "value-free" measurement. But it too holds dangers for the future viability of the left. Freire rejected intractable subjectivity as well, believing that the potential for reaching a dialogical, praxis-driven state of provisional humanizing reality countervails the immutable subjectivity of postmodern ontology. And from an epistemological position, Freire would reject the position of inherent knowledge subjectivity, instead relying on the possibility of reaching provisional truth through a subject-subject dialogue, based on eliciting conscientization and the collective reconstitution of empirical knowledge.

By relying on critical hermeneutics, and a reinterpretation of phenomenological epistemology, Freire rejected both the excessive reliance on an unattainable objectivity and the complete rejection of knowledge claims from the revisionist camp. He argued that we could reach a provisional, generalizable knowledge at a given moment that could be used constructively in the struggle to define the world. And he tied this knowledge to everyday life, rather than some universalizing principles, and founded it on conscientization and distantiation, where dialogue and experimentation led people to their own understanding. In the process, he created the space where individuals could become conscious of the social, cultural and political world around them and the power relations that underwrote those realities while reinjecting political economy into the discussion.

The entire research community could benefit greatly from this mediated position, moving away from their general reliance on positivist empirical research and methodological rigor that simply reproduces evidence of intuitive problems without any real prescriptions for change or from the other extreme dissolving all attempts at analyzing problems from the start. And all the disciplines, from history to sociology, could find renewed strength in this mediated position on knowledge. Science can still serve the cause of radicalism, if it takes a radically different course than that offered today – as an active advocate and effective apologist for conservative ideology.

MULTICULTURALISM OR CULTURAL MYOPIA?

It is clear that the left is losing ground each year in the battle of ideas. Their discourse is either ignored or popularly derided to the point democrats run away from the verboten term "liberal" with as much celerity as the postmodernists from the Marxist tradition. Neoliberal and neoconservative policies are solidifying the logic of a new unfettered technocapitalist world founded on social Darwinism and complete evacuation of a social safety net. The public sphere is in continued decline. And the daily lives of the women, the poor, minorities, and third world populations are moving in reverse, reestablishing and amplifying past inequalities and injustices. Yet the left seems crippled – unable to present a united front against this daily onslaught, instead festering in a realm of parochial interests and internecine battles.

Freire's idea of unity in diversity – with a contemporary modification to solidarity in diversity – could be a powerful vehicle for seeking to overcome the current balkanized left. Through the recognition that, though the forms of oppression, subjugation and exploitation can diverge widely, there are points of similarity and generalizable traits common across gender, race, class, ethnicity and sexual preference we can move forward. Further, that these commonalities form the basis from which the different groups can come together to fight a common enemy, working in solidarity while maintaining and respecting the diversity across groups. The key point is that the structural form of these various modes of oppression are actualized by the same economic and social mechanisms, largely the economic imperatives of capitalism.

As Antonia Darder and Rodolfo Torres argued in their 1999 essay "Shattering the 'Race' Lens: Toward a Critical Theory of Racism," race is a problematic concept that tends to decenter focus on the continued relevance of capitalism and class as the overarching systemic problems plaguing humankind. But they go further to problematize the very nature of discussion of race, by recognizing a paradox in the post-structuralist position – namely that scholars recognize race as a social construct but tend to essentialize racial difference none-the-less. By focusing on racism rather than its roots, much is lost in analyzing larger structural issues and the power dynamics that established and maintain racial unrest and inequality:

> Unlike scholars who argue resolutely for a critical theory of "race," we seek a critical language and conceptual apparatus that makes racism the central category of analysis in our understanding of racialized inequality, while simultaneously encompassing the multiple social expression of racism. Undoubtedly, this entails the development of a critical language from which activists and scholars can reconstruct theories and practices of contemporary society that more accurately reflect and address capitalist forms of social and material inequalities that shape the lives of racialized populations.[xxix]

And a similar point is made by Gimenez when she argues, "class is not simply another ideology legitimating oppression," but rather engenders "exploitative relations between people mediated by their relations to the means of production."[xxx] She claims the overemphasis on difference and experience is problematic because it ignores the dialectical relationship between individual experience and the larger historical and social circumstances that affect that experience. Kovel goes further to claim:

> Class relations entail the state as an instrument of enforcement and control, and it is the state that shapes and organizes the splits that appear in human ecosystems. Thus class is both logically and historically distinct from other forms of exclusion (hence we should not talk of 'classism' to go along with 'sexism' and 'racism,' and 'species-ism') . . . There will be no true resolution of racism so long as class society stands, inasmuch as a racially oppressed society implies the activities of a class-defending state.[xxxi]

But I am not arguing for a return to the reductivist, economistic past where class is placed above all other forms of oppression, nor to ignoring other forms of oppression in deference to class. While I believe there is some truth in the totalizing power of capitalism to colonize all aspects of the public and private spheres, the only way to build a more united front is to recognize and respect the struggles of all groups and to work in solidarity with them, while seeking to find common ground for broader agendas of profound social transformation. In this way, I believe Freire can offer a valuable alternative where the various groups that comprise the "identity politics" movement can begin to talk to each other, to find points of agreement and to work in solidarity and tolerance to overcome their differences and fight what is generally a common enemy. Martin Luther King, as an example, saw the power of bringing class and race together and thus became one of the most effective voices in American history advocating for a truly equitable and just society. By building bridges of understanding and solidarity, we can again create networks that galvanize the many to fight a wider range of injustice and work to forge a new more humane future.

DYSTOPIA AND UTOPIA: A DIALECTICAL RELATIONSHIP

A third critical realm for Freire's ideas is in the conceptualization of utopia. When Karl Mannheim wrote Ideology and Utopia in 1929, he presciently foresaw the future invasion on modernist and enlightenment principles by postmodern theorists. By claiming that all ideologies were equally subjective and thus equally open to debate, he ushered in the first hints of doubt that were to soon germinate and ultimately plague the followers of Enlightenment and Marxist philosophy. But even in the brashness of his discovery, he realized the implications of his action. In a stirring conclusion, missing from many English versions of the book, he left the reader with the following dire warning:

> The disappearance of utopia brings about a static state of affairs in which man himself becomes no more than a thing. We would then be faced with the

140

greatest paradox imaginable . . . After a long, tortuous, but heroic development, just at the highest stage of awareness, when history is ceasing to be blind fate, and is becoming more and more man's own creation, with the relinquishment of utopia, man would lose his will to shape history and therewith his ability to understand it.[xxxii]

While it took almost 60 years for his predictions to reach full fruition, in the wake of communisms collapse the left had lost its vision of utopia and in the process its hope of a better tomorrow. The long, arduous philosophical struggle for the "good society" has been supplanted by an inveterate sectarianism, abyss of subjectivity and a cynical detachment from the struggle. The postmodern challenge thus becomes one of the greatest philosophy has faced, but one that must be engaged and surpassed if we are to seriously reengineer an oppositional movement. With Freire, we find some of the clues necessary to break through the sometimes-valid charges levied by the deconstructionists. But while his inviolable faith in hope opens the door – as for example with his statement that "life without dreams is possible, but human existence and history without dreams are not" – to reach beyond we must go further to reconstitute a faith in utopia itself.

Russell Jacoby argued in End of Utopia that the left has not only lost faith in the socialist project but in the ability to transform the world for the better. And even earlier than this, they had become trapped in the economic/work paradigm as the foundation of utopia. But other thinkers like Walter Benjamin, Ernst Bloch and Herbert Marcuse had a more open visualization of utopia that included deeper libidinal desires and dreams. Could a utopia exist where humans break through the "Protestant Work Ethic" and find a future of leisure, love and carefree happiness?[xxxiii] Freire did not openly speak of this more radical alternative, but his vision of an open-ended, flexible utopia founded on hope, love and humanism sought above all else to create a more just and compassionate future for all.

And in creating the space for a provisional utopia that could be formulated in the act of revolution, he confronted, in advance, three of the strongest postmodern criticisms of utopia. His utopia was not preordained, would not sprout from a vanguard elitist party and would be bottom up rather than top down. Freire argued that we must now envision the future in the spirit of progressive postmodernism – unclouded by a return to reductivist, class-centered reform – where we reject depressed pessimism and naïve optimism and instead embrace a historical climate of critical optimism with a true dialectic understanding of confrontation and conflict:

Instead of decreeing a new History, without social classes, ideology, struggle, utopia, dreams – which day-to-day living throughout the world bruisingly negates – what we need to do is reinsert into the center of our preoccupations and efforts that very human being who acts, thinks, speaks, dreams, loves, hates, creates and recreates, knows and ignores, affirms and denies, constructs and destroys, and who has both inherited and acquired traits. In this way, we restore the profound significance of radicalism.[xxxiv]

Early in his career it was clear he was emboldened by the prospects of a Marxist revolution. But he later came to advocate for radical democracy and the individual freedom this engendered. Even in Pedagogy of the Oppressed, Freire had already deconstructed the failure of past revolution, critiquing Lenin and his followers for abandoning the human in the search for a more humane future. He saw what would become the key postmodern critique of socialism and communism, namely that there were elitist, reductivist and too production-centric. And he recognized that communism, as practiced to date, ceded too much individual freedom in the struggle for justice and equality. Instead Freire saw emancipation as a collective process that entailed drawing from localized experience and generalizing to broader social and systemic forms of oppression. Instead of sloganization and propaganda from a vanguard party, Freire wanted education to sprout from everyday experience, experimentation and open, critical dialogue among the oppressed. And this new vision of history would not be hampered by the old totalitarianism and authoritarian instincts of the left, instead relying on an open formulation that embraces collective liberation in a constant process of negation.

Freire thus recognized that radical change had to occur from the bottom up rather than the top down. Again confronting the legacy of Lenin, and Stalin, Freire saw that a real revolution could only come from the oppressed. Like Franz Fanon, and hearkening back to a claim of the young Hegel, he saw that only the exploited and subjugated could recognize what a truly human society looked like and could thus emancipate all humanity by struggling for eradication of injustice.[xxxv]

This provisional formulation is critical today, as theorists like Negri, Hardt and Halloway argue for the dissolution of the dialectical interaction between theory and practice, instead finding revolution sprouting in a quasi-automatic form from either localized struggle or constant negation.[xxxvi] Freire instead had an abiding faith in praxis as essential to revolution and social transformation. In creating a provisional concrete utopia, we can find the point of connection and the hope necessary to constructive struggle. Instead of fetishizing the subject or placing too much emphasis on Adorno's negative dialectics, praxis offers the necessary balance of theory and practice essential to a sensible oppositional front. Without theory, practice becomes undirected activism and without practice, theory becomes intellectual masturbation.[xxxvii]

But how can the left come to embrace a renewed faith in utopia? It seems the first step is to formulate it with light, erasable ink that can be easily altered as more voices are brought to the discussion. It must forego the old vision of utopia, never failing to heed the warning of Lord Acton that power is corrupting and absolute power corrupts absolutely. It must seek change from the bottom up, rather than the top down while recognizing that any movement needs leaders that can mobilize and embolden the masses to demand a better future. It must break through the invasive, internecine battles that identity politics have wrought, while embracing solidarity over unity and respect for difference as foundational principles. And it must fight through the ideology that has colonized us as deeply as the disengaged, the disenfranchised and the disillusioned. For recognition of our situation does not guarantee the ability to overcome it. We must also recognize our

142

free will as subjects in history. And we must have the fortitude to take the first step outside that safe encasement and actually fight for a different future. Only then can the many be galvanized to both the opportunity of change and its actualization.

CONCLUSION

Could it be that the resolve to defend is rarely as great as the resolve to overthrow? While the many will be swayed by the pacifying comfort of the status quo, the few will generally find more passion for their imagination and dreams of a divergent future. As Margaret Mead reminded us, it is the dedicated few that change the world, by inspiring the masses to revolt or demand change. So while Freire places his faith in the many, his educational strategy could also be used to foster the revolutionary spirit of the few that can then galvanize the many to revolt. It is here where I depart partially from Freire, in wondering if waiting for the many to revolt, particularly by adhering to their parochial interests informed by lived experience, in fact predispose us to the true realization of an end to history. Could it be that an enlightened leader exists that can open the mind without needing to fill it as well?

One could further argue that not only Fukuyama, but Jacoby as well, were wrong, and that utopian visions continue to flourish on the fringes even today. Maybe communism will never sprout wings anew, but alternatives exist to assuage the excesses of unfettered capitalism. Counterhegemonic media is now easier to create than ever before, and a growing number of theorists including Frederik Jameson and Henry Giroux are renewing the struggle to find a utopian vision for today. And who is to say that a new alternative will not come to the fore in the future, driven by a sage for the post-Fordist, technocapitalist present. Some can still envision a world where the disparity between rich and poor shrinks instead of increases, where the universal healthcare spread not only to the U.S. but across the globe, where per capita hours decrease toward the end of unemployment, where the local success of livable wage standards spreads across the country and world, where the violence of hunger is forever conquered and the plight of the "wretched of the earth" ceases to plague humankind.

Maybe more than anything, the critical legacy of Paulo Freire is one many artists have never forgotten. As exemplified by the bittersweet Herb Gardner play I'm Not Rappaport – among a thousand other plays, movies, novels and poems – the vocation of humanity that separates us from the rest of the animal kingdom is our ability to hope and to dream of a better future. Our enduring desire to leave a better world then the one we entered is really the only fate worthy of humanity. And it is here that Freire's words should embolden us anew to seek out the alternatives that will capture the imagination of the masses and draw them to their own critical vision of a tomorrow the many can abide.

NOTES

[i] Thomas Frank (2000) argued that the general public had come to believe the iconographic "market" now had the power to positively influence everything it touched from class to race to

education and the environment. The system promised equality of opportunity, democratic liberation and meritocratic advancement, as long as it is accepted without dissent. He labeled this *market populism*, though many use the more popular term *neoliberalism*.

[ii] See Jacoby, *The End of Utopia* (1999).

[iii] See Francis Fukuyama, *The End of History* (1992) for further articulation of his central premise that the end of communism has ushered in the complete victory of capitalism, liberal democracy and the end of social upheaval in deference to the power of the market, both at the national and global levels.

[iv] As Jacoby argued, this is not the first time claims of ideologies death have been made. Albert Camus was the first to use the term in 1946 and in the 50s it become a popular riposte of the liberal, anti-communist camp, including Daniel Bell, *End of Ideology*.

[v] Rorty, *Contingency, Irony and Solidarity*, pg. 181-182.

[vi] Eric Hobsbawm, "Goodbye to All That," pp. 117, 122-23.

[vii] Jorge Castenda, *Utopia Unarmed*, pp. 240-1.

[viii] Baudrillard, "Reversion of History."(Galilee, Paris, 1992).

[ix] See Carl Bogg's *The End of Politics* for a comprehensive critique of politics in the age of corporate colonization, degradation of the public sphere and media, consumer culture run amok. Also see Habermas (1991) for earlier discussion on the decline of the public sphere in advanced capitalism.

[x] See Freire, *Pedagogy of Freedom*, particularly Chapter 3, for further discussion of the importance of curiosity and conviction to teaching.

[xi] See Zizek *The Sublime Object of Ideology*.

[xii] See Antonio Gramsci (1971), Roland Barthes (1983) and Louis Althusser (2001) for discussion of the spread of hegemonic ideas through civil society, media and education, respectively.

[xiii] Freire, "Continuous Education and the Educative City" in *Pedagogy of Freedom* (1998), pg. 25-6.

[xiv] Freire, "Notes About Unity in Diversity" in *Politics and Education* (1998), pg. 38.

[xv] Freire, "Education and Quality" in *Politics and Education*, p. 39.

[xvi] See Chomsky, *Manufacturing Consent*, for discussion of the political economy of media and its encumbrance to state and corporate interests and Eric Alterman's *What Liberal Media?* for a response to the continued charges of liberal bias from conservatives like Bernie Goldberg (*Bias: A CBS Insider Exposes How the Media Distort the News*) and Ann Couter (*Slander: Liberal Lies about the American Right*).

[xvii] See Freire, *Pedagogy of the Oppressed*, Chapter 2 for in-depth discussion of the advantages of problem-posing, dialogical education over the current "banking" method that implants information in a hierarchical system that neglects lived experience, student diversity and true critical thinking skills and the cultivation of critical consciousness.

[xviii] Adorno & Horkheimer, *Dialectic of Enlightenment*.

[xix] For critique of philosophy in this vein see Richard Rorty, *Philosophy and the Mirror of Nature*, and in history Hayden White, *Metahistory: The Historical Imagination in late 19th Century Europe*.

[xx] See Erich Fromm, *Escape from Freedom*.

[xxi] See Neil Postman's *Amusing Ourselves to Death*, for discussion of the effects of the information age on education, discourse and political participation.

[xxii] Giroux, *Stealing Innocence* and *Channel Surfing*, among others, which provide great insight into the scapegoating of minority youth, used by conservative forces to argue for the dismantling of social programs that could otherwise help these groups including education, welfare and affirmative action programs while simultaneously calling for harsher mandatory jail sentences and drug crime laws.

[xxiii] See Herman Gray, "Watching Race" for discussion of assimilation themes in television programming.

[xxiv] Ernst Bloch, *The Principals of Hope*

[xxv] See Benjamin, "The Work of Art in the Age of Mechanical Reproduction," for more information on his artistic projects, which included radio plays with Bertolt Brecht. A good discussion of Kellner's position is available in *Media Culture*.

[xxvi] It should be noted that this can and does occur on both ends of the political spectrum. It could be argued that too many on the left have isolated themselves from mainstream media, losing touch with popular opinion and the effective tools of conservative discourse.

[xxvii] From the introduction of Freire, *Pedagogy of Freedom*.

[xxviii] Henry Giroux, *Theory and Resistance*, p. 87.

[xxix] See Darder & Torres, "Shattering the Race Lens," p. 35.

[xxx] See Gimenez, "Marxism and Class, Gender and Race."

[xxxi] See Joel Kovel, *The Enemy of Nature*, p. 123-4.

[xxxii] Mannheim, *Ideology and Utopia*, 1929.

[xxxiii] See Max Weber, *The Protestant Work Ethic*.

[xxxiv] Freire, "Opening Thoughts" in *Politics and Education*, p. 21.

[xxxv] See Franz Fanon, *Wretched of the Earth*, though Freire would never agree with Fanon's call for immediate violent revolution.

[xxxvi] See Negri & Hardt, *Empire* and Halloway, "Going in the Wrong Direction."

[xxxvii] See Raya Dunayevskaya *The Power of Negativity* and *Philosophy and Revolution* for an excellent contemporary vision of Marxist humanism, incorporating full recognition of the bi-directional relationship between theory and practice.

BIBLIOGRAPHY

Adorno, Theodor and Horkheimer, Max. *Dialectic of enlightenment: Philosophical fragments*. (New York: Herder and Herder, 1972).

Althusser, Louis, Ideology and ideological state apparatuses, in *'Lenin and Philosophy' and other essays*, trans. by Ben Brewster. (New York: Monthly Review Press, 2001).

Barthes, Roland. *Mythologies*, trans. Annette Lavers. (New York: Hill and Wang, 1983).

Bell, Daniel. *The end of ideology: On the political exhaustion of political ideas in the fifties*. (New York: Free Press, 1960).

Benjamin, Walter, The artist as producer, in *Walter Benjamin collected writings, Volume II*. (Cambridge, MA: Harvard University Press, 1999).

Bloch, Ernst. *The principles of hope*. (Cambridge, MA: MIT Press, 1986).

Boggs, Carl. *The end of politics: Corporate power and the decline of the public sphere*. (New York: The Guilford Press, 1999).

Castaneda, Jorge E. *Utopia unarmed: The Latin American left after the Cold War*. (New York: Vintage Books: 1994).

Darder, Antonia & Torres, Rodolfo, Shattering the 'race' les: Toward a critical theory of racism, in *Critical ethnicity*. (MD: Rowman & Littlefield, 1999).

Dunayevskaya, Raya. *Philosophy and revolution: From Hegel to Sartre, from Marx to Mao*. (New York: Columbia University Press, 1989).

Dunayevskaya, Raya. *The power of negativity: Selected writings on the dialectics in Hegel and Marx*. (Lanham, MD: Rowman & Littlefield, 2002).

Fanon, Franz. *The wretched of the earth*. (New York: Grove Press, 1963).

Frank, Thomas, *The rise of market populism: America's new secular religion*, The Nation, October 30, 2000.

Freire, Paulo. *Pedagogy of freedom*. (Lanham, MY: Rowman & LittleField Publishers, Inc., 1998).

Freire, Paulo. *Pedagogy of the oppressed*. (New York: The Continuum International Publishing Group, Inc., 1970).

Freire, Paulo. *Politics and education*. (Los Angeles: UCLA Latin American Center Publications, 1998).

Fromm, Erich. *Escape from freedom*. (New York: An Owl Book, 1941).

Fukuyama, Francis. *The end of history and the last man*. (New York: Penguin Books, 1992).

Gimenez, Martha. Marxism and class, gender and race: Rethinking the rilogy, *Race, Gender & Class, 8* (2), p.22-33.

Giroux, Henry. *Channel surfing: Racism, the media, and the destruction of today's youth*. (New York: Palgrave Macmillan, 1997).

Giroux, Henry. *Stealing innocence: Youth, corporate power and the politics of culture*. (New York: St. Martin's Press, 2000).

Giroux, Henry. *Theory and resistance: A pedagogy for the opposition.* (South Hadley, MA: J.F. Bergin, 1983).

Gramsci, Antonio. Edited and Translated by Quintin Hoare and Geoffrey Nowell Smith. *Selections from the prison notebook.* (New York: International Publishers, 1972).

Gray, Herman. *Watching race: Television and the struggle for "blackness.* (Minneapolis: University of Minnesota Press, 1995).

Habermas, Jurgen. *The structural transformation of the public sphere: An inquiry into a category of bourgois society.* (Cambridge, Mass: MIT Press, 1962).

Halloway, John, Going in the wrong direction: Or, Mephistopheles – Not Saint Francis of Assisi, *Historical Materialism, 10* (1).

Hardt, Michael and Negri, Antonio. *Empire.* (Cambridge, MA: Harvard University Press, 2000).

Hobsbawm, Eric, *Goodbye to all that, in After the fall: The failure of communism and the future of socialism,* ed. R. Blackburn (London, England: Verso, 1991).

Jacoby, Russell. *The end of utopia: Politics and culture in an age of apathy.* (New York: Basic Books, 1999).

Kovel, Joel. *The enemy of nature: The end of capitalism or the end of the world?* (London: Zed Books, 2002).

Mills, C. Wright. *The power elite.* (Boston: Beacon Press, 1956).

Postman, Neil. *Amusing ourselves to death: Public discourse in the age of show business.* (New York: Penguin Books, 1985).

Rorty, Richard. *Contingency, irony and solidarity.* (Cambridge, England: Cambridge University Press, 1989).

Rorty, Richard. *Philosophy and the mirror of nature.* (Princeton, NJ: Princeton University Press, 1981).

Torres, Carlos and Morrow, Raymond. *Reading Freire and Habermas: Critical pedagogy and transformative social change.* (New York: Teachers College Press, 2002).

Torres, Carlos. *Democracy, education and multiculturalism: Dilemmas of citizenship in a global world.* (New York: Rowman & Littlefield Publishers, Inc., 1998).

White, Hayden. *Metahistory: The historical imagination in late 19th century Europe.* (Baltimore, John Hopkins University Press, 1975).

Zizek, Slavoj. *The sublime object of ideology.* (New York: Verso Books, 1997).

MOACIR GADOTTI[i]

PAULO FREIRE AND THE CULTURE OF JUSTICE AND PEACE

The perspective of Washington vs. the perspective of Angicos

The word "perspective", in Portuguese, is rich with meanings. It originates in the late Latin "perspectivus", which derives from two verbs: perspecto, which means "to look to the end, to examine attentively", and "perspicio", meaning "to look through, to see well, to look attentively, to examine with care, to recognize clearly".[ii] According to the Dictionary of Philosophy by the Italian Philosopher Nicola Abbagnano, "perspective" is "any kind of anticipation of the future: project, hope, ideal, illusion, utopia. The term expresses the same concept of possibility, but from a more generic and less compromising point-of-view given that things may appear as perspectives which do not have sufficient consistency to be authentic possibilities".

According to the Aurelio Dictionary, very familiar to Brazilians, "perspective" is the "art of representing objects on a plane as they are seen by the eye; painting which depicts landscapes and buildings in the distance; the aspect of objects seen from a certain distance; panorama; appearance; aspect; aspect under which a thing is presented; expectation; hope". Perspective can also mean approach, when we speak, for example, of political perspective and possibility, belief in circumstances considered probable and good. To speak of perspectives is to speak of faith in the future.

These definitions seem to me to be complementary and very appropriate when speaking of Paulo Freire's work in this Third International Meeting of the Paulo Freire Forum, in the United States, in an era of uncertainty and, therefore, of paradigmatic transition.

Perspective means "point of view" which is the view from a point, from a place. From here we will choose as current perspectives those of Washington and Angicos. I am going to explain, later, why I chose these places, these points, to define two perspectives of education and of "the future of humanity" so as to limit myself to the general theme of this Forum.

Paulo Freire impelled us to read the world. We read the world from the space, from the place where we are located. It is by no means a fixed point since we are always on the go, in motion. Our viewpoint always determines our vision of the world. It is small wonder that our points of view are so diverse and even antagonistic. We are located in many places. This diversity is the wealth of humanity. Without it, there would be no change; the world would be static,

C.A. Torres & P. Noguera (Eds.), Social Justice Education for Teachers, 147–159.
© *2008 Sense Publishers. All rights reserved.*

eternally the same, senseless, without perspective. To respect diversity is not merely an ethical demand. It is a condition of humanity. It is the condition sine que non-for the advancement of humanity itself.

Paulo Freire made us dream because he spoke from the point-of-view of the oppressed, the excluded, a point from which we can invent a new humanitarian paradigm, one which is pro-civilization, the dream of another possible, necessary and better world. So why, then, do I speak of the Washingtonian perspective versus that of Angicos? Why not speak of the perspective of the oppressor and of the oppressed, as Paulo Freire did, of the colonizer and the colonized, the globalizer and the globalized?

I don't know the city of Washington. I hope one day to know it. It must be a beautiful city, where millions of people live, work and try to make sense of their lives. I have nothing against it. I have nothing against them. I speak of Washington as a metaphor, a symbol of power, of a certain politics, of a vision of the world, of a point-of-view. This is not about provocation. I do know the city of Angicos. I went there with Paulo Freire in 1993 along with my good friend, Carlos Alberto Torres. It is a small town, located in the poorest part of the suffering northeast of Brazil. For us Freireans, it is as famous as Washington because it was there that Paulo Freire made the most important experiment of his pedagogical method. Starting with the success of Angicos in 1963 that he became known in the world.

Angicos and Washington can be taken today as metaphors of a paradigm of civilization. Even analyzing dialectically-- unity and the opposition of contrary forces --these two points-of-view are fundamentally irreducible, like war and peace, military and utopian power, fundamentalism and dialogue.

Contradictions exist in everything. That is why changes exist. In proposing this reflection about these two opposite paths of humanity, we are not attempting to defend their non-reducibility. On the contrary, we are trying to overcome it dialectally so that in the "other possible world" there won't be so much hunger and so much poverty as exists today, sustained by wars and fundamentalist beliefs. The beauty of diversity must not be confused with the brutality of misery in the face of wealth.

We must make a choice between dialogue and war. And Paulo Freire can help us find a safer path. Opposed to the necrophiliac vision of the world which pits one fundamentalism against the another, which leads to environmental depravation, to violence, which arouses and nourishes political, economic, religious, military and State terrorism, there exists another vision, a biophiliac vision, which promotes dialogue and solidarity. As difficult as this path may be, it is the only one capable of avoiding war, barbarity and extermination.[iii] Terrorism cannot stand in the way of our thinking clearly.

1. THE FUNDAMENTALIST POINT OF VIEW

Paulo Freire distinguished himself as an educator and intellectual through the radical affirmation of dialogue. He taught us to distinguish radicalism (to go to the roots, all the way, to the truth) from sectarianism, attachment to a part, to an idea, to a creed). Fundamentalism is the very expression of sectarianism. It is linked to intolerance, to principalism, to conservatism. According to Leonardo Boff,[iv] the term derives from a collection of books entitled Fundamentals, written by Princeton University theologians at the beginning of the nineteenth century, which defended a literal interpretation of the Bible, which is why it was also called "literalism". Christian culture, however, already had a long history of fundamentalism before the word was invented. We frequently find in Christian literature the words "heretic", "infidel", and "traitor" which clearly manifest fundamentalist thought and practice. There is no more exacerbated fundamentalism than the affirmation: " I am the way, the truth and the life", which tolerates no other truth, which closes the doors on human history as possibility.[v]

The religious fundamentalism which is part of our Western culture is just one kind of fundamentalism. Another kind exists, which is politico-economic fundamentalism. As Leonardo Boff says, "the first and most visible of all is the fundamentalism of the political ideology of neoliberalism, by way of capitalist production and its finest expression, the integrated world market. It is presented as the sole solution for all countries and for all of the needs of humanity",[vi] even when all evidence is to the contrary. The logic of the market on which it is based ignores the needs of humanity in favor of profit. As Edgar Morin says, "development the way it is conceived, ignores that which is neither calculable nor measurable: life, suffering, happiness, love, and the only criterion by which satisfaction is measured is the growth of production, productivity and monetary receipts. Uniquely defined in quantitative terms, it ignores the qualities of existence, the qualities of solidarity, the qualities of the milieu, the quality of life."[vii]

The most flagrant characteristic of the current fundamentalism is the "globalization of the enemy" which became visible after the attacks on the World Trade Center in 2001. In the vision of the neoliberal ideology, "the terrorist attack was not against the United States but, rather, against humanity, in the supposition that they are humanity itself," declares Leonardo Boff.[viii] The barbarity perpetrated in New York on September 11, 2001, was utilized politically to manipulate people's consciousness. The political use is inevitable, but it is cowardly, given the unprecedented tragedy. This tragedy would be vehemently condemned if he were alive, according to what he wrote in the forward of his last book, Pedagogy of Autonomy, published in 1997, four years before the attacks on New York; "My viewpoint is that of the 'wretched of the earth', the excluded ones. I do not, however, accept, in the name of anything, terrorist actions, because from these come the death of innocent people and the insecurity of human beings. Terrorism negates what I have come to call the universal ethics of the human being."[ix]

It is necessary to restate the matter of violence and terrorism in its proper terms. Today, the promoters of war pass for teachers of peace. The theme of peace is being tactically appropriated today by those principally responsible for the planet's wars. Commenting on the crimes of September 11, 2001, the Brazilian sociologist Emir Sader claims that this situation "is the fruit of the polarization in which liberal globalization is trying to confine humanity: the violence of liberal globalization and the globalization of the violence. If we remain enclosed by the terms that the North American hegemony is attempting to impose on the world, it will be increasingly insecure for all of us and unjust for the great majority.

Overcoming the present situation will only be possible if we render these terms moot and replace the matter of violence, war and terrorism within their true parameters. It means fighting against the war, understanding it as the opposite of peace. Fighting against all kinds of violence, including religious and State terrorism. [x]"

The lucid analysis of the North American professor of linguistics, Noam Chomsky, moves in the same direction. He sees in the terrorism the "fury" and the "desperation" of peoples and nations historically massacred by the political economy of the United States, the only superpower with the capacity for strategic intervention in any part of the planet. The Americans were astonished by how much they were hated and asked themselves why. Their president responded that it was because it they were the guardians of democracy in the world and the hatred came from those who did not respect the democratic freedoms. But this is a false explanation. Recalling and paraphrasing Bertold Brecht, those who are shocked by the power of the river, which topples the banks and destroys the leafy trees (buildings), forget the fury of the banks which compress and oppress the gentle river's waters.

As Noam Chomsky maintains, effectively combating terrorism would imply a revision of North American external politics, which nourish world terrorism through all kinds of support for armed groups in democratic regimes, support for authoritarian regimes and despotic leaders. The American war against terrorism, in the manner in which it was conceived, merely feeds the hatred toward Americans and strengthens terrorism itself, because it is motivated only by the desire for vengeance. As Chomsky states, the United States "officially opposes the dominion of the law, every time that the law hurts its interests."[xi] An opinion poll conducted by the Pew Research Center, Princeton Survey Research Associates and the International Herald Tribune in December 2001 was very edifying. According to the December 21, 2001 edition of the newspaper Folha de Sao Paulo. The poll revealed that "for 58% of those surveyed in twenty-three countries, it was North American politics which 'caused' the attacks. In the Middle Eastern and Islamic countries this percentage reached 80% against 18% in the United States. The research question was this: "Does the majority of the population of our country believe that American politics caused the terrorist attack of September 11?"

People can like American as people but hate the external politics of the United States which enlarges the distance between rich and poor countries. The poll clearly showed the ignorance of the American people in relation to what the rest of the world thinks of them. On this people the American people are being very badly instructed, accustomed as they are to looking only at themselves and their pragmatic interests. Contrary to what they believe, they are not hated because they defined democracy, but because they do not respect it outside their territory. The United States is not going to be any less powerful, less competent, or less intelligent when it succeeds in becoming more solidary, more generous, and more humble.

Really there is neither hate for the American people nor for the United States. What is growing in the world is hatred for what the United States represents today: a nation whose economic and military leadership is oppressing other nations and peoples. It is the hatred of the oppressed for their oppressors, hatred toward a nation which, in the name of peace, and for so-called "humanitarian" reasons, intervenes militarily in other nations' affairs, killing thousands of innocent people and, what is more, demanding that everyone keep quiet. Paulo Freire would say: "I do not join my voice to those who, speaking of peace, demand the resignation of the oppressed and wretched of the earth. My voice has another semantics, another music. I speak of resistance, of indignation, of the "just wrath" of the betrayed and the deceived. Of their right and their duty to rebel against the ethical transgressions which increase their victimization and suffering."[xii]

All of us must vehemently condemn the terrorist attacks, just as we must condemn the Empire, which found an unhappy pretext to impose its worldly interests without limits and without borders. Bush took advantage of the crimes against the symbols of capitalism in order to "globalize the enemy", as Leonardo Boff writes. He "interpreted the barbarities of September 11 as a war against humanity, against good and evil, against democracy and the global market economy which (in his presupposition) had brought so many benefits to mankind. Whoever is against such a reading is an enemy and, an 'other' and a 'foreigner' who must be fought and eliminated. Such a strategy can lead to violence within the United States and the four corners of the earth. It is the total violence of the system against all its critics and Opposers." [xiii]

Paulo Friere's speech at UNESCO in Paris in 1968, when he received the "Educator for Peace" prize is extremely illustrative: "From anonymous people, suffering people, exploited people, I learned above all that peace is fundamental and indispensable but that peace implies a struggle. Peace is created, is constructed, in the incessant construction of social justice. It is because of this that I do not believe in any effort called education for peace which, instead of uncovering the world of injustices, makes it opaque and calls its victims short sighted."[xiv] Peace can only exist with justice; Peace is the fruit of justice. That is why we speak of justice-peace.

To put the blame on the United States would be very convenient, if only because there are as many oppressed people in the United States as anywhere else in the world. In the era of globalization, the "Nation-state" has a different meaning than it had two centuries ago. Today the rich and powerful of any nation have a say in the choice of the American president because they finance his campaign. In other words, when Shell Oil financed the electoral campaign of George W. Bush, it wasn't only North American capital, which was made available for his election. It was international capital. Today international business elects the president of the Empire's greatest power. Don't confuse the Empire with the United States. It is international.[xv]

What must be combated is the Empire, which oppresses, terrorizes and kills, and not a single people or a nation. What must be combated is the model of globalization, which divides the world into globalizers and globalized, rich and poor, a combat, which is also implied in the proposal for "another possible world", of alternatives to this world of capitalist terror. Our combat must be intentional.

2. THE EARTH AS A POINT OF VIEW

But the Empire is also a "contra-power". It is contradictory. Inside it we find a future of warring paradigms: capitalist globalization which divides, exploits and terrorizes, sustained by Nation-states, capital and by a dominant military-industrial-religious complex, and the belief in planetary possibilities, which conceives of humanity as singular and diverse, currently represented by non-governmental organisms, "organisms of the people", which form a nascent global civil society. What we call "planetary possibilities", Edgar Morin calls "world-society" whose constitution, according to him, still lacks principles: "What is missing for a world-society to be constituted not as the end of the planetary hegemonic empire but as the basis of a civilized confederacy, is not a program or a project, but the principles which would allow a path to be opened." To do this, according to Morin, it is necessary to "reform Western civilization and all civilizations" as well as "to radically reform all systems of education."[xvi]

The new paradigm also thinks in terms of inclusion, but not inclusion-submission as in the Empire. Inclusion as self-identity, as participation in global citizenship. "Global citizenship is the power of the people who re-appropriate the control over space and, thus, of designing the new cartography",[xvii] guaranteed by a "social salary" and an "income for all"[xviii] the inhabitants of the planet, the authors of Empire maintain. We need to develop this new human intelligence which is the bold intelligence of the Earth, without which human beings could not develop this new and necessary paradigm for sustaining life on the planet and that it should lead us to "educate for a simple life", for this "voluntary simplicity" about which our great Freirean comrade, the anthropologist Carlos Rodrigues Brandao, one of those "earthly pedagogues", speaks to us: "To learn to share ideas, to place goods at the service of others, to lend what is 'mine' so it can be seen as alive in the happiness of another. To create ever-expanding networks of people willing to live together and to lend, barter and give. To make sure that all that is good is always good in circulation." This he wrote in a "note" which he shared with me in Porto Alegre, in December 2000, in a meeting of the MOVA-RS (Movement for the Education of Youth and Adults of the State of Rio Grande do Sul). He told me that in that year he had learned to feel the "living universe" of which he felt himself an inseparable and eternal part.

A passage from Leonardo Boff's book, Know to Care, made me think to what extent our culture is dualistic "It was not the struggle for survival of the fittest which guaranteed the persistence of life and of individuals until now, but the cooperation and coexistence among them."[xix] Malthus, Darwin and some readings of Marx are in accordance with this new vision of "evolution." It points toward a symbiosis: the individual and the species gaining through the exchange, the association with one another, not needing to destroy others to in order to evolve and transform themselves. With the anxiety to dominate the Earth, human beings became distanced from it, from their home, their ship, breaking the ties of coexistence with other beings, the sacrificing interdependence and the solidarity.

Leonardo Boff confronts the dualistic model (person/nature; man/woman; body/spirit) of the classic paradigms with the new paradigm, the Earth Paradigm, which sees Earth as a single community. After all, everything and everyone is a product of a long and unique cosmic process of fifteen billion years of evolution. And he adds in another book: "We refuse to reduce the Earth to a group of natural resources or to a physical-chemical reserve of primal matter. It possesses its identity and autonomy as an extremely dynamic and complex organism. It presents itself, basically as the Great Mother who nourishes us and carries us. She is the great and generous Pacha Mama (Great Mother) of the Andean cultures or the living super-organism, Gaia, of Greek mythology and modern cosmology."[xx]

The Earth and the universe were made for human beings. We are still not sure about the existence of other intelligent, conscious and loving beings inhabiting other planets. Everything makes us believe that the universe was made for human beings, everything converges and points to the humanization of the universe. Guided by this, our responsibility unimaginably vast. To be able to assume such responsibility we need to construct a solidary planet, starting immediately.

With this book, Leonardo Boff is negating an entire religious tradition based on the limitless exploitation of the earth for, as Astrid Cabral writes in her introduction to the book of the North American thinker, Henry D. Thoreau (1817-1862), "the roots of the domination over nature and consequent environmental pollution must be sought in religions which, like the Hebraic, dissociate the idea of God from the idea of Nature, reserving for man an independent role as a superior being destined to govern the world."[xxi] Religions sustain themselves on an anthropocentric vision of the individual who turns to the world to dominate and possess it; the conception of calculating man who objectifies, accumulates and merchandises everything, including life itself.

"More than ever I feel that the human species is truly one. There are differences of color, language, culture and opportunities, but people's feelings and reactions seem very similar", wrote Sebastiao Salgado in the introduction to Exodus, his voluminous book of photographs, after circling the planet in search of its deepest identity. The human species is unique, but it is a species which knew how to "dominate the land" without yet succeeding in becoming "truly one" with it[xxii], divided and fragmented as it is into territories, powers and interests, etc.

The Earth Paradigm is still being constructed as a group of principles, knowledge and new explanations, not just about our planet, but about the very sense of our lives in the universe. Earth must no longer be understood as just an astronomical phenomenon, but as a historical phenomenon too. James Lovelock, one of the founders of this paradigm, defined Earth as Gaia: "We define the Earth as Gaia because it presents itself as a complex entity encompassing the biosphere, the atmosphere, the oceans and the soil; in their totality, these elements constitute a cybernetic system or one of re-nourishment which seeks the best physical and chemical means for life on this planet."[xxiii] The paradigm of the oppressed as a paradigm of civilization has a new name today: "Earth Paradigm", because the dominating way human beings today produce and reproduce their existence on the planet has made Earth the largest of all the oppressed.

3. EDUCATE TO CONSTRUCT THE DREAM

In its etymology, the word education means to conduct. We can conduct by dragging, manipulating or carrying, seducing for a cause, or constructing a new path, dialogically and collectively, a better way for everyone. Thus we serve ourselves from a particular curriculum which is not a curricular grade or a group of contents but, as the word indicates, a way of life. To educate is always to indicate paths, to point toward a possible future. Thus there is no education without utopia.

For the educator, the dream, the utopia is not something unrealizable. It is his/her real reality, that which must be done. Utopia is not something which is added to an educators training as a personal choice. Utopia forms an essential part of the training itself. An educator who does not dream is incompetent because, really, you can only educate around the dream of a type of society which you want to watch be born and grow. The educator sees the future first, a better future, and then turns to the present and the past. The educator's ethical-political engagement is part of his/her technical competence.

What matters, however, is to educate to construct the dream. As the writer Frei Betto said in one of his talks during the Second World Forum in Porto Alegre, in February 2002, capitalism privatized capital and socialism privatized the dream. The capitalist dream can be summed up as "the I without the we" and the socialist as the "we without the I." Frei Betto criticized current socialism not only for the privatization of the right to dream but also for its lack of sensitivity to men and women as the subjects of history. The dream continues to be the construction of a society of "the I with the we."

In an interview in O Estado de Sao Paulo newspaper on March 26, 1991, the historian Eric Hobsbawn, one of the greatest Marxist intellectuals of the twentieth century, declared that "Communism did not know how to reform itself." Thus its "fall" is explicable. The dream and the utopia spilled blood too, provoking huge tragedies in history's most violent century. Hobsbawn criticizes the utopia of the "new man", as the birth of an "entirely good" man, as if it were possible to transform human nature: "Everything is part of human nature. Human beings are not entirely good or entirely bad, they are exactly as we know they are. I do not believe that any regime is capable of changing them. It was a big mistake of the ideological regimes to claim that they were transforming human nature. This is one of the reasons that people no longer believe in them. The people of China, the Soviet Union and other places knew that human nature was not being changed. But this does not mean that the regimes should not try to better the human condition, that they should not be based on reason and morality. To say that we are returning to human nature is an excuse not to fight all the barbarities, which are now appearing. On the contrary, we have the obligation to combat them."[xxiv] It is from inside this critical vision that we understand the notion of utopia as very far from the dogmatic, bureaucratic or authoritarian vision, which certain political regimes believe it to be. Education for dream construction can contribute to the enlargement of spaces of non-statist public administration necessary for the construction of a new democracy in which citizens appropriate public space, govern it, overcome their isolation and begin to become part of the greater sphere, a sphere of universal citizenship, a planetary sphere. To educate for the construction of the dream of a "new civilization"[xxv] thus becomes a positive response that education can give to the crisis of values generated by neoliberal pedagogy and market society. This was also Paulo Freire's dream, as we can tell from reading his final book. Innovative experiments are emerging, like those linked to the citizen school movement and ecopedagogy. These movements are built on great faith in the renovation of future education.

4. EDUCATE FOR HUMANITY

Faced with the possible extermination of the planet, the culture of peace and the culture of sustainability offer alternatives. Sustainability is not only about biology, economy and ecology. Sustainability has to do with the relationship we maintain with ourselves, with others and with nature. The pedagogy ought to begin by teaching how to read the world, as Paulo Freire tells us, the world which is the universe itself, for it is our first educator. This primary education is an emotional education, which places us face to face with the mystery of the universe, in its intimacy, producing the emotion of our feeling part of this sacred living being and in permanent evolution.

Education is confused with the very process of humanization. Responding to the question of "how the teacher can become an intellectual in contemporary society", the great Brazilian geographer Milton Santos, who died in 2001, answered: "When we consider possible history and not just existing history, we come to believe that another world is viable. No intellectual works without an idea of the future. To be worthy of man, that is, of man seen as a project, intellectual and educational work must be founded on the future. That is the way that teachers can become intellectuals: by looking at the future."[xxvi]

Teachers need to constantly question themselves about the sense of what they are doing. If this is fundamental for all human beings, as beings always in search of meaning, it is also a professional duty for teachers. It is part of their professional competence to continually inquire about the meaning of what they are doing in the school, along with their colleagues and students. A teacher is always in the process of constructing meaning. As Celso Vasconcellos says,[xxvii] "meaning is not someplace ready and waiting to be discovered. Meaning does not arise from a transcendent sphere, nor from the immanence of the object, nor even from a simple logical-formal game. It is the construction of the subject!" Celso Vasconcellos, a student of Paulo Freire's, insists in his beautiful book that the teacher's role is to "educate through instruction."[xxviii] He/she may only teach multiplication tables, but they are only educating through instruction when the meaning of the tables is constructed along with its learning because, as Celso Vasconcellos says, to instruct comes from the Latin insignare, which means "to mark with a sign", to act in the construction of the meaning of what we do. Everything we do we need to do with meaning; everything we study has to have meaning.

The two greatest educators of the last century, John Dewey and Paulo Freire, each in his own way, attempted to respond to this matter and centered their analyses on the relationship between "education and life", reacting to the technological pedagogies of their times, as much from the left as from the right, which were only concerned with teaching methods and techniques. "I would like to be remembered as someone who loved life", said Paulo Freire two weeks before his death. Education only makes sense as life. It is life. School loses its sense of humanization when education becomes merchandise, when it stops being the place where people learn to be people and becomes the place where children and young people go to learn to compete in the marketplace.

It is symptomatic how Ladislau Dowbor ends his book, Technologies of Knowledge[xxix] with data from a United Nations Report from 1998 which show the negligence, the indifference and the cynicism of the neoliberal ideology to people's needs: "It was not possible to raise the $6 billion necessary to put in the schools everyone who belonged there, nor to raise the $13 billion necessary to insure basic health and nutrition for all. But $8 billion were spent on cosmetics in the United States, $11 billion were spent on ice cream in Europe, $17 billion on pet food, $50 billion on cigarettes in Europe, $400 billion on narcotics and $780 billion spent on the military throughout the world." What are the world's priorities? The United Nations Report does not even need to respond.

This is why it is necessary to make critical, social and economic analyses. But that is still not enough. It is necessary that the rigorous analysis of the situation not end there but, rather, point the way and indicate how we should proceed. Otherwise, no matter how rigorous and correct they are, these sociological and political analyses merely serve to maintain educational immobility and lack of perspective.

Paulo Freire insisted that the transformative school was a "school of companions." That is why his pedagogy is a pedagogy of dialogue, of exchanges, of meetings, of solidary networks. "Companion" comes from Latin and means "one who shares bread." Consequently, it is a radical posture and, at the same time, a critical and solidary one. Sometimes we are only critics and lose the sympathy of other people through lack of companionship. And the present state of teaching will not be overcome without a deep feeling of companionship. Struggling on our own, we will come to feel frustrated, discouraged and full of complaints. Whence the deeply ethical sense of this profession. Fundamentally, Marx's thesis still holds true when confronting neoliberal cruelty in education: "the educator must be educated." The alternative to neoliberal pedagogy, which fragments and divides, is education for humanity.

5. THE VIEWPOINT OF THE OPPRESSED: NEITHER THE CULTURE OF WAR, NOR TERRORISM. JUSTICE AND PEACE.

Let us return to the general theme of this book: the possible dream. Paulo Freire and the future of humanity.

It is fitting to end with the question: what are the new perspectives for the future, for the future of humanity?

The future, Freire said, cannot be foreseen, but can be invented. Thus, his thesis of the "possible dream" which confronts "neoliberal cruelty."[xxx]

156

We will attempt to design, for didactic ends, two antagonistic alternatives, two possible paths, even without wanting to dichotomize reality which is always in process:

- one is based on the ethics of the market while the other is based on the ethics of the human genus;

- one sanctifies competition and demonizes solidarity while the other preaches compassion and affection;

- one combats fundamentalism with fundamentalism while the other combats fundamentalism with dialogue;

- one sees the world as a battlefield of competing interests while the other sees it as a symbiosis of development with cooperation;

- one defends the capitalist model of globalization and divides the world into globalizers and globalized while the other defends a "world society" and considers the Earth as a single community;

- one considers education as merchandise, forming consumers while the other considers education a right whose objective it is to form citizens.

The first we call, metaphorically, the "Washington Perspective" and the second we call the "Angicos Perspective."

Which of the two points of view is the truest one?

The point of view of the oppressed is truer than the point of view of the oppressor because the oppressed have nothing to hide while the oppressor needs to hide his game, his cunning and his tricks, to continue oppressing. Nevertheless, Paulo Freire warned that the oppressed will not liberate themselves without liberating their oppressors. The alternative for a better future for humanity is not the elimination of the enemy, but overcoming the contradiction between the two.

Paulo Freire also insisted that dialogue between antagonists is impossible. Conflict is the only possibility. The most they can hope for is a pact. How, then, to speak of dialogue? Is it possible to dialogue with a terrorist? No, there is no dialogue with terrorism because terrorism is the very negation of dialogue. That is why dialogue must be established first, to be able to act on things early on and not a posteriori. Dialogue must be established before the acts of terrorism happen. It must be radical; going to the root. Terrorism must be prevented. We need to rest assured that it will not prevail over dialogue.

For this reason, the "Washington Perspective" is wrong again: because it does nothing to prevent, to act on the causes of terrorism. It waits for terrorist acts so it can make war on them afterwards. Because its culture is the culture of war -- as present in the great majority of national anthems -- and not the culture of dialogue, which Paulo Freire defended, the culture of justice and peace, as we call it today. The dialogical thinking of Freire points toward a new civilizational platform, a new spiritual period for humanity.

Faced with the state of the world today, dialogue is no longer just another political option. Dialogue is today an existential and historical imperative. Terrorism is the alternative, as are the globalization of cruelty and war. The two possibilities are both present in the current situation: on one side, democratic legitimacy and, on the other, the legitimacy of power.

Moreover, it is necessary to widen our point of view. We need to see the Earth from a distance, in its totality, in its planetary condition, as a single community. We are still thinking in terms of blocks of nations against other blocks of nations: European Community, Japanese block, United States block, China: characteristics of the fragmentary, neoliberal model. These blocks stimulate competition without solidarity and the machinery of war against life. On the contrary, we need to think of a culture of peace and sustainability, to think globally, in terms of the planet, in favor of the whole community of life.

Finally, we must abandon the anthropocentric vision so as to cultivate a holistic vision, founded on a slate of planetary ethics above orders, species and kingdoms. Paulo Freire spoke to us in his final book of an "ethics of the human gender", pointing to the possible dream of humanity united around a common objective of justice, of peace and of prosperity for all. This is the dream. It must be made historically viable.

Translation by Peter Lownds, Olinda, 17/vii/2002.

NOTES

[i] Moacir Gadotti received his doctorate in Education Sciences from the University of Geneva, Switzerland. He is a titled professor at the University of Sao Paulo (Brazil) and director of the Paulo Freire Institute in Sao Paulo. He has written many books, among them *reading Paulo Freire: His Life and Work* (Albany: State University of New York Press, 1994) which was translated into Japanese, Spanish, Italian and Portuguese; *Pedagogy of Praxis: A Dialectical Philosophy of Education,* with a preface by Paulo Freire (Albany: State University of New York Press, 1996) also translated into Spanish; *History of Pedagogical Ideas,* translated into Spanish and *Paulo Freire: A Bibliobiography* (Sao Paulo: Paulo Freire Institute and Cortez Publishers, 1996), translated into Spanish (Mexico City: Siglo XXI, 1999). With more than 780 pages, it is the most complete work about Paulo Freire.

[ii] Ernesto Faria, in the *Scholastic Dictionary of Latin and Portuguese.*

[iii] "To dialogue with them until exhaustion sets in, to negotiate to the ultimate limit of reasonableness, may perhaps lead the fundamentalist to recognize the "other", his/her right to exist and the resulting contribution of a minimal convergence in the diversity." Leonardo Boff, *Fundamentalismo: a globalizacao e o futuro da humanidade.* Rio de Janeiro, Sextante, 2002, p. 48.

[iv] Ibid, p.12

[v] I am going to limit myself here to Christian fundamentalism. Islamic fundamentalism is already too well-known. With the reservation that not every Christian, or every Muslim, is fundamentalist and that not every fundamentalist is a terrorist.

[vi] Op.cit., p.38

[vii] Edgar Morin, "por uma globalizacao plural". In the journal "Folha de S. Paulo", 31st of March, 2002, p.A-17.

[viii] Leonardo Boff, op.cit., p.41

[ix] Paulo Freire, *Pedagogia da autonomia: saberes necessarios a practica educativa.* Sao Paulo, Paz y Terra, 1997, p.16.

[x] Emir Sader, "Guerra e Paz", in *Folha de S. Paulo* October 8, 2001, p.3.

[xi] Noam Chomsky, In *Folha de S. Paulo* September 22, 2001, Caderno Especial, p.8.

[xii] Paulo Freire, op.cit. Pp. 113-114.

[xiii] Leonardo Boff, in *Folha de S. Paulo, November 26, 2001, p. 3.*

[xiv] Paulo Freire. In Moacir Gadotti (org.), *Paulo Freire: uma biobibliografia.* Sao Paulo, Cortez/IPF, 1996, p.52.

[xv] According to Michael Hardt and Antonio Negri (*Imperio*. Rio de Janeiro, Record, 2001), the Empire is "a network of powers and opposing powers structured on an unlimited and inclusive architecture" (p. 185), oriented by the "cold logic of capitalist profit" (p.11).

[xvi] Edgar Morin, "Por uma globalizacao plural". In *Folha de S. Paulo*, March 31, 2002, p.A-17.

[xvii] Michael Hardt and Antonio Negri, *Imperio*. Rio de Janeiro, Record, 2001, p. 424.

[xviii] *Idem ibidem*, p.427.

[xix] Leonardo Boff, *Saber cuidar: etica do humano, compaixao pela terra*. Petropolis,Vozes, 1999, p. 115.

[xx] Leonardo Boff, *Principio-Terra: a volta a Terra como patria comum*. Sao Paulo Atica, 1995, p.34.

[xxi] Henry D. Thoreau, *Walden ou a vida nos bosques e a desobediencia civil*, Sao Paulo, Aquariana, 2001 p. 13.

[xxii] Sebastiao Salgado, *Exodos*, Sao Paulo, Companhia das Letras, 2000, p.15

[xxiii] James E. Lovelock, *Gaia, um novo olhar sobre a vida na Terra*, Lisbon, Edicoes 70, 1989, p. 27

[xxiv] Eric Hobsbawn in *O Estado de S. Paulo*, May 26, 1991, p. 12.

[xxv] Guillermo Williamson C. *Paulo Freire, educador para una nueva civilizacion*. Temuco, Universidad de la Frontera, 2000.

[xxvi] Milton Santos, "O professor como intelectual na sociedade contemporanea". In *Anais do IX ENDIPE--Encontro Nacional de Didatica e Pratica de Ensino*, vol. III, Sao Paulo, 1999, p. 14.

[xxvii] Celso Vasconcellos, *Para onde vai o professor? Resgate do professor como sujeito de transformacao*. Sao Paulo, Libertad, 2001, pp. 51-52.

[xxviii] *Idem*, p.55.

[xxix] Ladislau Dowbor, *Tecnologias do conhecimento: os desafios da educacao*. Petropolis, Vozes, 2001, pp. 79-80.

[xxx] Paulo Freire, *Pedagogia da autonomia: saberes necessarios a pratica educativa*. Sao Paulo, Paz e Terra, 1997, p.15.

ADRIANA PUIGGRÓS

PAULO FREIRE AND THE NEW LATIN AMERICAN PEDAGOGICAL IMAGININGS

[In this work, I will defend the thesis that the Brazilian pedagogue Paulo Freire contributed a series of ideas that are dissonant relative to the modern educative model. The concept of dialogic education, the non-essentiality of the educator and of the educatee and the internal nature of politics in relation to education constitute some of the elements that make the construction of new pedagogical imaginings possible. The realization of such a possibility is a prerequisite for permitting the immediate theoretical developments demanded by the current educational crisis.]

1.TOLERANCE IS A MARK OF ORIGIN

Paulo Freire was a Catholic, but he was born into a family with ideological differences: his father, a spiritist, accepted the son's choice of his mother's Catholicism. At twenty, while studying Psychology of Language and Philosophy and teaching Portuguese, Paulo withdrew from the Church for a year "because of its distance from life, a distance that in my naiveté I couldn't understand -- the commitment it required and what the priests said in their Sunday sermons" (Education Notebooks, 1974). His reading Tristán de Atayde, Maritain, Bernanos and Mounier, among others, brought him back to his mother's religion, from a different but still not dissident perspective.

The aforementioned authors, and also Bergson, Gabriel Marcel and Vaz, a Brazilian Hegelian Jesuit, opened 'personalist' doors to the writings of Marx. Father Vaz allowed him to skip Ives Calvez' critique of Marx and begin his study inspired by the search for ideas tied to the people's struggles rather than trying to demonstrate the errors of Marxism.

According to Carlos Alberto Torres, existentialism (Man as a being under construction), phenomenology (Man constructing his consciousness), Marxism (Man living in the drama of the economic conditioning of the infrastructure and the ideological conditioning of the superstructure), and Hegelian philosophy (self-conscious Man departs from experience to elevate himself toward science by means of the dialectic) are confluent in Freire's thought. On a more political plane, the influence of progressive developmentalism in the 1960s and of Latin-American revolutionary theories in the 1970s should be added.

In the numerous interviews in which he was questioned about his origins and despite the diversity of his influences, Freire was never ideologically torn between religion and politics. His struggle was between politics-transformed-into-pedagogy and dogmatism.

C.A. Torres & P. Noguera (Eds.), Social Justice Education for Teachers, 161–175.

2. EDUCATION AND POLITICS

In his first book, Education as the Practice of Freedom, Paulo Freire speaks of politics. However, many years later, in dialogue with Frei Betto and Ricardo Kotscho, he would say that there was not a single word about the relationship of education and politics in this initial text. Education as the Practice of Freedom was a work written in the flavor of his recent literacy experiment during the João Goulart government and inspired by the ideas of Jaspers, Marcel, Barbu and Tristán de Atayde's Myths of ourTime.

Freire was a "radical" in the sense that Atayde attributed to the concept: he rejected activism and subordinated it to reflective action, the opposite of the "rightist or leftist fanatic" who "confronts history like its only maker" (Freire and Betto, 1988). The radical does not feel he is history's owner and recognizes himself as a subject, one of many, able to contribute to social change. Based on the orientation provided by the papal encyclical Mater et Magistra of John XXIII, more than on the second Vatical Council, Education as the Practice of Freedom supports a proposal of gradual change. It clarifies the concepts of development and evolution as present in the social doctrine of the Church as in the sociological thinking then dominant in Latin America. Liberation Theology and the "Social Doctrine" counter-discourse that succeeded it (cf. Ezcurra, 1986) had yet to occupy the Christian discursive scene. Freire's critique of assistencialism leaves the impression of a latent conflict. Nevertheless, for the moment, harmony reigns. Pedagogy is a tributary of politics and can lead to freedom.

However, the dictatorship installed in Brazil beginning in 1964 punished him twice. First: it threw him into prison and into exile, accusing him of subversion, of being "a traitor of Christ and of the Brazilian people" and of using methods "similar to those of Stalin, Hitler, Péron and Mussolini." The elites in charge, rather than moving from a consciousness of "ingenuous transitivity" to the more democratic consciousness of "critical transitivity" (Freire, 1975) evolved toward a politics befitting a dominant bloc. Second: it threw him into the arms of a Left that was dogmatic and in permanent conflict with real freedom.

3. HISTORY AND FREEDOM

With Freire, the theme of freedom is always present. As absence, as hope, as goal, as conflict. In its philosophical origins it arises from Gabriel Marcel's confession about his struggle to escape the world in which he was imprisoned, but the concern with the feeling of freedom immediately points to Emmanuel Mounier for whom one is not freed by the mere fact of being able to exercise spontaneity, but only if one is able to utilize this spontaneity in the sense of liberation. To do that, it is necessary to recognize the sense of history so one can insert oneself in it. Nor must one totally adhere to the "history that is", since one would then risk not being part of "the history that must be." Mounier adds: "it is necessary to seek the outward appearances of human nature; but in reproducing her known forms extremely well, we fail to invent their virgin possibilities. This is the route of all conformisms. So Man's freedom must be intrepid as well as modest (...) when men stop dreaming about cathedrals, they will no longer know how to make beautiful lofts." (Mounier, 1962, p. 38)

For Freire, freedom occurs when the mind of the oppressed is cleansed of the oppressor's presence. The current version of Man is dominated by the myths of modern society and renounces his capacity to decide, he is asphyxiated by anonymity, without hope and without faith, a prisoner of the dominators, domesticated, reified.

Freire adopts Marx's concept of alienation, which he probably read in the 1960s or early 1970s in the works of Erich Fromm, an author whom he cites repeatedly in his first books. Fromm (1962) pointed out that the end, for Marx, was not just the emancipation of the workers but the liberation of all people, through the restitution of their liberty. However, in every historical epoch, the end of alienation creates conditions for humanization. People are either affirmed as subjects or "minimized as objects" (cf. Freire, 1972) depending in large part on their understanding of the epoch's themes, that is, on their sense of history. For Freire, this means acquiring a critical consciousness.

When he left Brazil, Freire had a Latin American or Third World stance. As can be verified by his work, he thought that experience could not be transferred, that every concrete social-historical reality had a meaning all its own. From Geneva, Freire wrote Mario Cabral, then leader of Guinea-Bissau: "In our case, to the contrary, the experiences in which we participated yesterday, like those in which we find ourselves involved today, teach us that they cannot be simply transplanted. (...) Closing off experiences lived through in other contexts is as wrong as ingenuously opening up to them which leads to their pure and simple importation" (Freire, 1978, p. 108).

In this enunciated position resides one of the most important contributions of Freire's pedagogy. It deals a blow to positivism by denouncing the supposed universality of pedagogical theory. One aspect of this attack is evident in Freire's epistemological stance, always respecting the primacy of the real. A second aspect is rooted in the fact that he postulates the oppressor's pedagogy as one possibility rather than as the only legitimate and universal pedagogical form. In qualifying pedagogy as either banking or dialogical, he limits it, restricts its reach, makes it particular. In exile, Freire remained faithful to this position, doubtlessly helped by his ability to put himself in the other people's places, respecting their beliefs, as he had learned from his father in childhood.

Freire rebels against all withdrawals, when confronted by any obstacle to communication or any attack on liberty. In his theory, this concern stimulates associations, which contribute to generating his theory of the "transitivity" of consciousness, beginning by characterizing the position of "intransitivity" in which the illiterate and oppressed peasants find themselves. In the 1960s, he was still using a category typical of the developmental thinking of the times: "closed society." In Education as the Practice of Freedom Freire reconstructs the cultural actions of people inhabiting the least developed regions of Brazil.

These people are characterized by the lack of a sense of history and a narrowness of vision. Their gaze does not go beyond the local limits of communities which Brazilian pedagogue Fernando de Azevedo referred to as "delimited" and "turned in on themselves." Intransitivity forces people to founder in their incomprehension of problems situated outside their "vital biological sphere" (Freire, 1972, p. 65).

The path that Freire finds to break down the barriers of this cultural prison is the political path. This is profoundly similar to what Gramsci proposed, from prison, in his analysis of the 'southern [Italian] question.' Both authors consider that pure spontaneity needs limits. The peasants of the "mezzogiorno" constituted an amorphous and disunited mass, without any real cohesiveness; the Brazilian peasant possesses a kind of uncommitted consciousness as far as other human beings or the transformation of life conditions are concerned. It is necessary to transform this submerged, parochial peasant lacking critical consciousness into a person who takes an active role in changing his/her life and that of society. For that to happen, it is necessary for the old intellectual agrarian bloc to be disassembled and the chains that imprison and oppress the illiterate to be broken. (Portantiero, 1977).

The process of political, critical and transitive consciousness-raising is Freire's proposal for self-liberation from prison, exile and intransitivity. It is the path toward humanity that destroys the possibility of psychological and moral death.

4. FREIRE, THE LEFT AND POPULISM

Nevertheless, Freire continued to be accused by the traditional left of being "cultural", "idealistic", "spontaneous", "paternalistic" and other attributes which have in common the fact of signaling that he was far from doctrinaire Marxist positions and from the political proposals of the parties or organizations which held them.

Freire's detractors, like those of Gramsci, did not forgive the fact that he overlooked the ritual of punctually demonstrating how every cultural or pedagogical fact is linked to and mirrors material conditions. Such critics were unable to understand that multiple socioeconomic and political elements make up the pedagogical network and not a sole cause external to the educative process.
But if Freire's relationship to the Marxists was theoretically conflictive, even more complicated are the Christian-Marxist "liberationist pedagogues" defending the validity of their practice, not wanting to be thought of as "populists." In fact, the mixture of Latin Americanism, Third World Christianity, Marxism and democracy inscribed in the pedagogy of liberation discourse was strongly combated. As was Freire's conviction of the necessity of undertaking a politico-pedagogical task that would help develop the abandoned higher levels of consciousness so that social transformation might be possible. His preacher's attitude was referred to as paternalistic and manipulative. His program was accused of being reformist.

Although a reading of Freire's work leads us to situate the majority of his convictions and experiences within this large spectrum of what could be called "popular nationalism" or "populism", his own resistance to this situation warns us of the need to be careful in regard to this matter.

The first question that must be asked has to do with the continuity or discontinuity which could exist between Freire and the pedagogical expressions of popular nationalism. The latter are inscribed in a series of ideological-political formations that express complex themes. In Latin America there are diverse political-pedagogical manifestations in which nationalism, development, social class struggles, regional groups, sexes, cultural sectors, anti-imperialist and Third World agendas predominate, according to the combination of social, ideological, economic and political strengths peculiar to each.

While the critics of liberation pedagogy would frame its founder, from the start, in "developmental nationalism," the fact that they do not try to attribute historical and ideological links with "trabalhismo"[i] to him is noteworthy. Even though Freire was against the politics of Getúlio Vargas and of João Goulart, we must not forget that he had his first experiences (predecessors, according to his own testimony, of the method he successfully propagated in 1961), as director of the Department of Education and Culture at SESI (Social Service of Industry) in Pernambuco and later, as its Superintendent, between 1946 and 1954, that is, during Vargas' third government. Nor should we forget that it was during the João Goulart government that Freire had his most significant experience in the Popular Culture Movement of Recife which he later continued in the Cultural Extension Service of Recife University.

Moreover, it is worth analyzing the educational program of popular Brazilian nationalism in which Freire worked. It was during his first two governments that Vargas built the national educational system and developed formal education programs for factory workers. Educators' opinions are divided about the significance of these programs. The introduction of technical and industrial education is either interpreted as the government's response to a bourgeoisie that demanded qualified manual labor or as an answer to the demands of the popular classes.

Vanilda Paiva states that, even if the growth of instructional networks had been put into practice for the benefit of the rural populations and to favor the technical and professional education of the urban population, the educational strategy had as its principal objective the defense of the social order. Other authors think it is difficult to come to a consensus about what the Estado Novo meant to national life: "Scholars of the subject strongly diverge as to the way the Government began to act and how much the results warranted this action. For some, it dealt a deathblow to the interests of the landowners and the favored the interests of the industrial bourgeoisie. For others, it favored the common people, with an ample social security program and trade unions. For still others, it was the result of a coming together of forces joining new and traditional elite and international capital against the interests of the working class" (Oliveira, 1993, p. 51).

In Paiva's opinion, the Estado Novo period combined objectives of social welfare and economic independence with an antidemocratic politics. A similar analysis could be made of the polemics surrounding workers' education. Some consider that this involved a series of programs designed to elicit favorable opinion for a leader anxious to manipulate the masses. Others recognize the success of the proposals but disqualify them on the grounds that the development of the masses through literacy is "reformism" and identify the "voters" as a mass utilized by the bourgeoisie; others consider that trabalhismo developed an educational and cultural politics aimed at the popular sectors, which oscillated between trying to respond to the demands of the workers and to those of the entrepreneurs. Although the literacy programs had been in great part inspired by the anxiety of local and national leaders to secure more votes, they represented nothing less than a vehicle to grant the vote to hundreds of thousands of excluded citizens. Trabalhismo appears, in this last view, to be a battlefield for ideological hegemony, in which the educative space is full of contradictory positions. The adherence of the working classes to the [Vargas] regime is one of the aspects which most surprises the analysts.

Frei Betto, for whom Vargas's final period constitutes an indelible vestige of childhood, provides us an interesting testimony. In a letter written from prison to his parents and siblings, the priest remembers the day that he turned ten years old. It was the 25th of August, 1954. On the morning of the 24th his father's face looked worried but, hours later, the assiduous reader of Carlos Lacerda, then a liberal, anti-Vargas spokesman who wrote for the Press Tribune, was jubilant. A little while later, he seemed completely stupefied: Vargas had committed suicide. Betto says: "My father was mute like someone who feels obliged to have to enter a new age on top of a cadaver. That year my birthday was simple, almost sad. The tragic had been displayed like a burlesque mask. Vargas was leaving life to enter the history of an epoch in which the Brazilian bourgeoisie huddled in the shadow of a foreign power" (Betto, undated, p. 105).

Pedagogical ideas grew in conditions favored by popular nationalism. Freire's social vocation had the opportunity to transcend itself in a political situation to which he never totally subscribed.

5. THE FORMS OF TRANSCENDENCE

The current founded by Paulo Freire was different from the traditional tendencies of Cristian origin, including that of social Christianism. The text Education as the Practice of Freedom is the beginning of a theoretical alteration that probably culminates in Letters to Guinea-Bissau, a book published many years later. This theoretical alteration revolves around the meanings of the term transcendence, whose inclusion among the principles that orient the curricula of Latin American scholars is tenaciously defended by the Catholic Church.

But Freire learned the concept of transcendence from the work of Emmanuel Mounier, who had already signaled his differences relative to interpretations that only admitted one's movement toward God or within oneself, as Jaspers explained. Mounier believes that such movement cannot remain closed within and considers it legitimate that the transcendent act have as an objective helping others, thus opening to society.

However, in the evangelizing tradition, transcendence justifies the existence of the pedagogical relationship which Freire calls banking. Education and evangelism become identical. The culture requires the educatee to be a "good savage." The culture of the educator must transcend that of the educatee, to be deposited vertically into his/her empty mind. Education is reduced to an irrational,

166

spiritual communication between master and pupil. In his aforementioned study on Freire's pedagogy, Carlos Alberto Torres defends a contrary view: that the transcendentalism of Freirian pedagogy "tends to capture the life of the object and its destiny" and adds that "only in this final level of maximum qualitative consummation can the consciousness act on the phenomenon to transform it since, knowing its direction and tendential legality, it will provoke a historically viable transformation" (1995, p.16).

In Mounier's scheme, the transcendent reality does not exclude the presence of the reality transcended. Freire goes even further: the transcendence is mutual. The educator educates the educatee and the educatee the educator. Without this bipolarity in the cultural transcendence, education would not be possible. The illiterate Brazilian peasant cannot learn unless his/her own culture is the point of departure, so the educator must value it and learn it. Transitivity is not only a quality of the educator's consciousness, but also a possibility for the consciousness of the educatee. In Freirian pedagogy, transitivity is the opportunity that all human beings have to free themselves from the cloister of their social-cultural surroundings and to understand their relationship to society-at-large. In this sense, the transcendence of naiveté through critical thinking has points in common with Marxist positions on consciousness.

In Education as the Practice of Freedom, Freire profoundly connects consciousness and democracy. Although he does this citing Karl Mannheim, the discourse reveals traces of Jacques Maritain's concept of "profane consciousness" (1955). According to Maritain, the "profane consciousness" understands that the movement of the world is not circular, but directed by a certain meaning. However, this goal is not necessarily directed toward progress, which is threatened. A liberal and an antifascist, Maritain maintains that no theory capable of invalidating the entire inheritance of the past will ever exist nor will there be a place for pure reason, unless the historical inheritance grows as a product of human work. For humanity not to "turn to barbarity," the sense of progress must "be felt within history so that the structures of consciousness and the structures of human life move toward better states." Freire conceives consciousness as an occurrence capable of transforming itself and of moving toward freedom.

From Mannheim, Freire recuperates the relation between the education of the masses and the extension of the processes of democratization, as well as the belief that the "state of ignorance" is not limited to illiteracy, but includes the need for critical participation. For Freire, literacy plays a part in this position, drawn from personalism that imagines Man inhabiting the world in order to recreate it. "We were thinking," he says, "of a literacy training which was, in itself, an act of creation capable of unleashing other creative acts" (Freire, 1972, p.123). The point of departure for what Freire will call "naïve consciousness" does not mean absolute ignorance but, rather, the inability to grasp the real connections between occurrences, the data of reality, the phenomena. Naïve people think they can dominate the facts externally and "think they are free to understand them anyway they wish" (Freire, 1972, p.124).

Freire posits the problem of ideology: the ignorant person is not someone who does not know, but someone who establishes mythical causal relationships.

This kind of consciousness he calls "magical": it does not believe it is superior to the facts nor can it dominate its desires, and it recognizes that laws exist outside its own thinking. However, it attributes a superior power to the face value of such facts to which it is submissive.

6. FREIRE AND MARXISM

In his first work, Freire takes the idea of "transitivity" from personalism, with its spiritualist and existentialist charge,. But in Pedagogy of the Oppressed, his thinking is determined by Marxism. The idea of subjectivity is never absent in Marx because, for the German philosopher, a world without people was unthinkable. Marx combated subjectivism and psychologizing, but he did not deny the historical role of subjectivity. People are the product and producers of a reality that turns against them. Thus, to transform the reality that oppresses us is a human task. But, being oppressive, reality acts on oppressors and oppressed alike. The oppressors are dehumanized and it will be up to the oppressed to liberate them as well. To this end, the oppressed have to recuperate the critical consciousness of their oppression, overcoming the state of immersion in which their consciousness resides.

In Pedagogy of the Oppressed, the "consciousness of oppression, critical consciousness", is linked to the dialectical relation between subjectivity and objectivity to which, according to Freire, Marx was referring when he said that real oppression will be greater when the oppressed are conscious of it (Freire, 1975). In this book, the transforming praxis is oriented by the life conditions of the people and distanced from the preoccupation with the transcendent ends of social life and of history. Critical consciousness which, as early as Education as the Practice of Freedom, was conceived as a representation of the empirical reality, understanding its causal and circumstantial connections, will finally have its strategy laid bare in Pedagogy of the Oppressed. Going back to Lukács, in the mid-1960s, Freire warns that the revolutionary party must "explain its action to the masses" not just to give continuity to their revolutionary experiences, but also to consciously activate their succeeding development. According to Freire, Lukács believes Man's "critical insertion" is necessary to transform reality. By decisively incorporating historical materialism, Freire confirms that reality is not pure subjectivity. Concrete reality is limited by determined situations. Consciousness must be conscious of these limits and understand how they relate. But Freire, far from being trapped by mechanicism and thus limiting consciousness to a reflection of the material conditions, lingers on the specificity that it acquires in its dialectical link to these conditions. He uses Lucien Goldman's concepts of "real consciousness" and "possible consciousness" for support. "Possible consciousness" is identified with "untested feasibility" and opposed to "real consciousness" which has to do with "solutions perceived as practicable." And Freire's anti-positivism appears again in all its intensity. The immediately comprehensible facts do not constitute a critical knowledge. This knowledge begins to be built when the complex of contradictions is understood. Continuing and complementing the thought of Pierre Furter (1970), he will defend the position that critical reflection about reality is simultaneously innovative and dialectical.

Linking personalist discourse, Latin American Marxist pedagogy and his readings of Marx, Freire defends the primacy of practice over theory in the transition from "naïve" and "magical" consciousness to "critical consciousness." Theory separated from practice is pure "inoperative verbalism"; practice without theory is "blind verbalism." The primacy of practice over theory should not contribute to relative blindness about the reason behind the facts in which we are immersed. Moreover, "conscientization" consists of action-reflection. The practice is not drained by the revelation of reality, it is also about raising consciousness. 'It is not enough to know the real, it is necessary to transform it,' Marx wrote in his theses on Feuerbach; Freire states that the authenticity of conscientization takes place when the practice of revealing reality constitutes a dynamic and dialectical unity with the practice of transforming reality.

After his passage through Chile, Freire began to concern himself with the uses to which his concept of "conscientization" might be put in different circumstances. He began what he called the "demystification of conscientization." His real error, he stated, was to think that the critical perception of reality was tantamount to its transformation, thereby defusing the political moment (Torres, 1986).

However, in 1985, there would be a new slant:

Yesterday's Paulo Freire, yesterday being situated between the 1950s and the early 1960s, was not clear about something that today's Paulo Freire sees much more clearly. And that is what I call today the politics of education. Or rather, the quality that education has of being political. Because the nature of educative practice is political per se, and that is why it is not really possible to speak of education's political dimension, since it is all politics. That is why today's Paulo Freire – and by 'today' I mean from the end of the 60s to the beginning of the 70s – is clear about social classes. That is also why, for today's Paulo Freire, popular education, in whatever society it occurs, reflects the levels of class struggle in that society." (Torres, 1986, p.38)

Freire clearly stated that education is not a reflection of the relations between classes but, rather, a product of the dialectical relationship between culture and the social means of production. In Freirian theory, subjectivity is not reduced to a reflection of objectivity, but consists of a complex product of human praxis about this materiality.

The classic Freire has nothing to do with reproduction. His reflections are closer to Gramsci's idea of culture than to the reduction of Leninism produced by certain leftists in educational sociology. The idea that education is merely a reflection of the class struggle reduces the role of the politico-pedagogical processes in the transformation of culture and in the construction of critical consciousness for the development of a new ideological bloc.

For Gramsci, in the text "Americanism and Fordism", education is not a direct consequence of the characteristics of class relations from an economic standpoint but, by deriving its meaning from these relationships, education ends up being part of the complex conditions of production, distribution and cultural use the classes make.

When we deal with the complex panorama of Latin America, the relations between education and the social classes exclude the political subjects who, in practice, do not necessarily coincide with them. The leftists again put pressure on Freire. Instead of helping him deepen the multiple connotations of the people-as-subjects (a term used by Freire in his early stages and sternly criticized by his detractors) so that they would acquire class, regional, cultural, linguistic and gender content and be creatively involved in each specific, historical expression of national politics (Laclau, 1977), they forced him to reduce their meaning. They deprived liberation pedagogy of its concrete, victorious and vital expression, the one that it disseminated rapidly in the 1960s, not as a pure expression of one social class but, rather, as the product of a complex of politico-cultural and pedagogical relations among peasants, the petit-bourgeoisie, intellectuals, Catholics, 'personalists', university students and professors in a chaotic political space even if, on the whole, it tended toward popular nationalism. Its character as an instrument for the creation of a new culture was crushed by the obligation to act as a transmission belt of revolutionary theory for the proletariat.

This was a logical conclusion; it comes from considering culture a reflection of structure, from believing in the universality of theory and strategy for social transformation, the inevitability of the appearance of classic socialism, and the superiority of the vanguards of theoreticians when faced with the deficiencies of masses devoid of revolutionary knowledge.

Despite the demands made on him by the Latin-American left, Freire produced original and lasting thought. In the meantime, there is almost nothing left of the traditional Latin American left.

Freire permanently avoided gulags and prisons. Thus, he defends freedom in all pedagogical relations and combats the potential parochialism of pure cultural transmission. Mounier's influence is again present, this time in his citing Nietzsche: "I love all those who take risks, who leap into the whirlwind; I love them with all my heart because they burst through to the other side" (Mounier, 1962, p. 40).

Mounier did not consider people's transcendent desires an agitation but, rather, the negation of the very existence of a closed, isolated, self-sufficient world. They represent continuity and abundance, not repetition. For Jaspers, overcoming one's self is not a project, but a part of growing, surpassing the immediate and attaining a system of values. For Gabriel Marcel, the pressure comes from things that cannot be inventoried; for Malebranche, Man is movement -- always wanting to proceed. Freire chooses the line defended by Mounier. He distinguishes one plus in the educative process which transcends the relationship of educator and educatee, an end-product which is the condition for the possibility of producing a new culture.

7. UTOPIAS AND FREEDOM

Freire was often accused of being an idealist. In his book Pedagogy of the Oppressed, he uses the concept of untested feasibility, interpreted as a future to construct. To grasp untested feasibility implies surmounting a problematic situation through praxis. People do not solve their concrete problems only through their subjectivity.

The search for escape routes from real and imaginary prisons takes us to Freire's childhood, on Encanamento street in the Casa Amarela neighborhood of Recife. The fear of hungry ghosts nourished adult conversations. It was probably his father, Joaquim Temistocles Freire who worked as an officer in the Pernambuco military police force and came from Rio Grande do Norte, who was the one who taught his son that hungry ghosts need darkness or semi-darkness to appear, adopting various shapes.

But the fears began to fade in the mornings and afternoons when Paulo learned to write in the backyard of his house, in the shade of the mango trees, words from his own world and not the adult world, with the earth for a slate and tree branches for chalk. The child's world remained inviolate, but he was taught to enter it and to understand it. Surely, from that time on, Paulo's dreams began to be "historically feasible."

Utopia is linked to conscientization, conscientization implies utopia since, according to Freire, the more aware we are, the more we are able to announce and denounce, since all denouncements are announcements, all conscious criticism is imbued with utopias. Consciousness is both a detachment from reality and a demythologizing.

It can be interpreted that, for Freire, utopia is possible when it is born as a product of the destruction of old phantoms, the capture of the "hungry ghosts" of childhood, by the conscious word. The imagination succeeds in traversing the "limit situations" (Freire, 1977) instead of returning to haunt the prisoner as it smashes into the humid walls of his solitary cell, or against the limits of the naïve consciousness of an illiterate adult or an innocent child. When it is produced as an exchange with other people it is an historic act of transformation, a commitment to the world, the demystification of culture, the birth of politics.

8. THE PEDAGOGICAL RELATIONSHIP OF INTELLECTUALS AND THE PEOPLE

The aforesaid position has a strategic connotation. It influences the characteristics of political formations, denying the thematic imposition of the directors on those they direct, of the master on the pupil, of the intellectual on the people. The word of the oppressed gains political weight.

Doctrine is antagonistic to dialogical education because: "Those who act on people, indoctrinating them to gradually adapt them to a reality which should remain untouched, are dominators. Lamentably, however, whether through vertical programming or banking concepts, revolutionary leaders often fall into this [habit], in their zeal to obtain the adherence of the people to revolutionary action. They approach the peasant or urban masses with projects that may correspond to their

[own] world view, but not to that of the people" (Freire, 1975, pp. 121-122). The Gramscian problematic is developed in its setting, appearing intermittently in the dialogue. The relation between coercion and consensus, the real equilibrium between spontaneity (considered popular wisdom, naïve consciousness) and conscious orientation; the continuity of the culture and its extension to the excluded masses and the negation of its oppressive variant, the creation of a new culture. Gramsci effects a series of transgressions on Lenin's politico-pedagogical concepts. He revalues spontaneity, criticizes politico-pedagogical vanguardism, conceives of popular wisdom as the material with which the intellectual leaders will combine their theory, and lends a decisive weight to the popular word.

Just like Gramsci, [Freire] denounces the persistence of the politico-pedagogical link characteristic of the modern educational system, public instruction. It is a form of oppression which can be incorrectly adopted by those who want to transmit their own idea of the new society. The coincidence between the authors is their reference to how important to the dominant pedagogy is the way in which the politico-pedagogical subject is shaped, in other words, the junctures, which are made between educator and educatee, director and directed. They particularize its political nature.

Forty years ago, in a small village in the Brazilian northeast, a Catholic professor began an experiment. The official version states that he invented a method for rapid literacy learning that bothered some and astonished many. Actually, another way to interpret what happened there exists: it could be said that a discovery essential to the history of the education of oppressed peoples occurred. And a fatal questioning of Latin American liberal positivism as well. It was discovered that the asymmetrical relationship between teacher and student had nothing to do with the nature of education itself. It had been constructed historically. Another discovery was that politics is not an external element of the educative process; education and politics cannot be reduced to subsystems that coincide mutually in the social organism, as functionalism intends them to. Nor is education an inert field reflecting the space where real, material processes are generated. The political element cannot be disassociated from the pedagogical; it is a constituent part, not only reflective of the struggles that occur in other spaces, but acquiring specific connotations of its own. The relation between educator and educatee is a bond heavy with politics and a bloody struggle.

9. EXTENSIONISM OR COMMUNICATION

The pedagogues of liberation were not exempt from permanent oscillations between directivity and non-directivity that also characterize Gramsci's pedagogy. In the Italian case, the problem was solved by letting the relationship be conceived as an expression of the antinomy between coercion and consensus. For Gramsci, the antimony is irresolvable, their balance being one of the problems that bridges all expressions of modern education. Directivity/non-directivity, coercion/consensus, spontaneity/discipline, spontaneity/conscious orientation have a very different significance in Latin America. Drama invades pedagogy when an educator confronts the terrible levels of inequality and frequently renounces the principles of non-directivity after developing health and education [programs] or other efficacious forms of production. Freire (1973) warns of the dangers of extensionism and suggests that the educator should establish a process of communication with the peasants, together finding solutions for their problems. The dimension of the misery in many places in the region does not justify the imposition. Moreover, the great differences between intellectuals and the people frequently generate confusion and now the leftist camp believes that [the people] need culture. Believing this, the idea of conscientization as a process of combined construction of a new culture is disqualified. The universal comes to occupy the space of socio-historical and cultural details and the possibility of the people's involvement in the intellectuals' discourse is nil.

Reacting against the functionalist illuminations, leftist or Christian, a modality of popular education was developed that is characterized by heightened spontaneity and includes elements that recall the old anarchist idea that posits the existence of an instinctive proletarian knowledge, devoid of bourgeois cultural contacts. Numerous experiments were conducted from this perspective in the 1970s and 1980s. Educators were considered inevitable representatives of oppressive power. Their work, increasingly limited by this variant of Freirian theory, ends up stimulating the educatees while the educators abandon their culture and assimilate the culture of the oppressed. Heavy with voluntarism, abstract, and without perspectives, this tendency denies the need for a synthesis between popular knowledge and modern culture. It is worthwhile remembering here the enormous importance that Gramsci placed on the education of the people, based both on humanistic principles and scientific-technical content, in the task of participating in their ideological and cultural emancipation, a condition of their economic, social and political liberation.

Freire demonstrates that the confrontation between dominator and dominated is at the core of the pedagogical relationship and that its specific manifestations at the level of linguistic, thematic, methodological and partisan teaching and learning are highly political. So much so that the relation between educator and educatee is not exempt from a power struggle that has many different facets. The contradictions which form such a linkage can only develop in an uneven way.

Educators and educatees are different, whether they belong to the same social class or the same generation, whether they have grown up in similar or different cultural groupings, whether they share the same mother tongue or have grown up in distinct linguistic universes. Many of these differences are organized according to a logic which turns them into inequalities. But it is the mission of both parties to struggle to distinguish between inequality, which inevitably implies an oppressed and an oppressor, and the differences that compose the material with which the educator and educatees can construct a new culture. Ideological-political-cultural imposition or the negation of differences and the adoption of extreme spontaneity help to reproduce the fragmentation that characterizes Latin American societies.

The relation between the intellectuals-directors-educators and the people or, in other words, the creation of a practical-intellectual administration, is one of the most complex problems in the training trajectory of transforming subjects in Latin America. The obstacles to its creation do not come just from the ideological bloc of the politically and socially dominant. Internal censorship and self-censorship also exist, the gaze which collides with the tree, not being able to distinguish it from the bush or the forest. There is also, especially recently, an enormous fear of freedom.

10. CONCLUSION

Paulo Freire created a pedagogical system, which allows Latin American educators to imagine alternatives to modern education. The system is founded on:
- an interior relationship between politics and education;
- education as the product of a historically and socially instituted relationship and, what is more, a politically mutable one
- the introduction of the concept of dialogical education, which is opposed to banking education, indicating that the educational process does not necessarily lead to the reproduction of the dominant power;
- the concept of dominant education as a result of political and social struggles;
- the concept of educator and educatee as non-essential, non-immutable positions which, moreover, are susceptible to being filled by distinct social subjects;
- the study of the particularities of the political-pedagogical fabric as an object of interest for all democratic pedagogy.

A vast experience developed throughout the whole of Latin America demonstrated that these principles could be the basis of a pedagogy aimed at cultural transformation that refuses instruction and messages of homogenization. In an epoch of such despondency as the one we are passing through, Freirian pedagogy opens up perspectives. Its anti-determinist character and its confidence in the possibility of democracy imbues it with a special interest for those who still dare to advance alternatives to the neo liberal education dominant today.

Translated by Peter Lownds, Los Angeles, March 2003

NOTES

[i] "Trabalhismo" is the political line founded by Getúlio Vargas, who was President of Brazil from 1930 to 1954, the year in which he committed suicide pressured by the North American interests in the Brazilian economy. Vargas founded the *Estado Novo*, a typical Latin American popular nationalism. Vargas founded two political parties, the *Partido Trabalhista Brasileiro* (PTB) -- Brazilian Labor Party – and the *Partido Social Democrático* (PSD) – Social Democratic Party. In 1956, João Goulart, leader of the *Partido Popular Brasileiro* (PPB) – Brazilian Popular Party, was elected Vice President to Juscelino Kubitschek. He assumed the Presidency in September 1961,

after Kubitschek's successor, Janio Quadros' resignation and was deposed on April 1, 1964 by the military coup.

BIBLIOGRAPHY

Betto, Frei (no date). *Cartas da prisão*. São Paulo: Círculo do Livro.

Ezcurra, Ana María (1986). *Doctrina social de la iglesia – Un reformismo antisocialista*. México: Nuevomar.

Freire, Paulo (1972). *La educación como prática de la libertad*. México: Siglo XXI.

Freire, Paulo (1973). *Extensión o comunicación?* México: Siglo XXI

Freire, Paulo (1975). *Pedagogia do Oprimido*. Porto: Edições Afrontamento.

Freire, Paulo (1977). *Fundamentos revolucionarios de pedagogía popular*. Buenos Aires: Editor 904.

Freire, Paulo (1978). *Cartas à Guiné-Bissau – Registro de una experiência em processo*. Lisboa: Moraes Editores.

Freire, Paulo; Betto, Frei (1988). *Esa escuela llamada vida*. Buenos Aires: Legasa.

Fromm, Erich (1962). *Marx y su concepto de hombre*. México: FCE

Furter, Pierre (1970). *Educación y reflexión*. Montevideo: Tierra Nueva.

Gramsci, Antonio (1981). Americanismo y Fordismo. In La alternativa pedagógica. Barcelona: Fontamara.

Laboratorio Educativo: Entrevista a Paulo Freire. *Cuadernos de Educación* (Venezuela), #11, 1974.

Laclau, Ernesto (1977). Hacia una teoría del populismo. In *Política e ideología en la teoría marxista*. México: Siglo XXI.

Maritain, Jacques (1955). *Cristianismo y democracia*. Buenos Aires: Club de Lectores.

Mounier, Emmanuel (1962). *El personalismo*. Buenos Aires: EUDEBA.

Portantiero, Juan Carlos (1977). *Los usos de Gramsci*. México: Pasado y Presente.

Romanelli, Otaíza de Oliveira (1993). *História da educação no Brasil*. Petrópolis: Vozes, 15th edition.

Torres, Carlos Alberto (1995). *Estudios freireanos*. Buenos Aires: Libros de Quirquincho.

Torres, Rosa Maria (1986). *Educación popular: Un encuentro con Paulo Freire*. Quito: CECCA-CEDECO.

ISABEL BOHORQUEZ[i]

UNTESTED FEASIBILITY IN PAULO FREIRE

Behind the profile of a dream

Before I begin to develop my theme, I will take a moment to briefly describe the scene which greets me each day when I come to work. This is neither a casual nor an ornamental description since it positions my discourse within a particle of reality that impels me to seek out and struggle toward the construction of a human and humanizing theory. For this, the choice of Paulo Freire arises as a harmonious and inevitable encounter.

The mothers and the fathers are hurrying up the path to school. It is almost eight o'clock in the morning and numbingly cold but that does not prevent some from pedalling their bicycles faster and getting here on time. Some come on foot, others in old ramshackle autos, only a few have the luxury of good transportation, warm and cozy, to combat the gelid winter gray.

The women will return at midday with their shopping bags on their shoulders, or corn for the chickens, or feeling a bit weary after having cleaned their employers' houses. Some are housewives and do not do outside work, others work at night. Still others have good jobs and think well of themselves.

The men will return at midday in clothes that bespeak their diverse occupations: house-painters, masons, carpenters. Some dress differently, they are on a different path and everyone in the neighborhood knows them.

And the children, the beautiful children, in their white dusters, the girls with wide ribbons or bands in their hair, the boys playing ball before the bell rings, everyone waiting to go to school, to be good people, to progress.

They enter through the wide door which needs a coat of paint. But there are other priorities and that one will have to wait. This old building has educated generations.

I stay to watch these people in the early morning. It is a little ritual that gives meaning to my daily routine. I like watching them say goodbye with kisses and hugs. One last word of advice and a little lunch money, which I know is not a small matter for these parents.

Finally I go in. I never hurry so I can savor this daily testimony that school is a good place to send your kids.

The hope of these people reverberates in me as a challenge.

Even if I wanted to, I could not avoid beginning each day with a dream that education can do something for all these children so that their destiny is not to be cold and to have enough change in their pockets to buy a tasty snack. And even more so for those children who are still on the street, searching for scraps.

C.A. Torres & P. Noguera (Eds.), Social Justice Education for Teachers, 177–189.

From this imperious daily dream comes the need to investigate untested feasibility: a category of analysis that emerges from my consciousness like an existential mandate, an intellectual appetite that wants to understand the physical effect all this has on me.

A MULTIPLICITY OF VIEWS ABOUT A COMPLEX CONCEPT

Grappling with the category of untested feasibility acquaints us with Freire's lucidity and sensitivity, his ability to grasp the postulates and paradigms as well as the demands of his time and puts us in dialogue with his creative capacity to synthesize theories and perspectives which, at first glance, can seem different and even antagonistic.

Many of his critics rejected this open search as alien to any academic expression. Members of one or another ideological faction accused him of syncretism, ingenuousness, and inconsistency to the point of considering him dangerous or an imposter. Orthodox Marxists questioned his democratic position which, to them, was tainted by populism and developmentalism, conservative Christians were bothered by his social and political radicalism and feared his secularizing the Church's salvationist mission, rigid academics did not accept his poetic and eclectic style, while reactionaries of every stripe negated the Freirian vision because of its libertarian and utopian implications.

And this affirmative possibility, committed to real people, hopeful and inspiring, is the problem that interests us.

Our interest in Freire's thought, and especially in his category of untested feasibility, is rooted in the act of examining the impulse, using the term applied by José Eustaquio Romão[ii], that causes social groups, particularly those most dispossessed and dominated, to overcome their "limit situations" by transforming them into "untested feasibility situations." Romão writes: "Finally, it comes down to identifying the impulse that causes men and women to develop the process of civilization, of culture, the movement in search of the human utopia, the Paidéia." And, further on in the same article: "Paulo Freire made a notable contribution to the discussion about the concept of impulse, developing his theory about human beings' consciousness of their own incompleteness as a catalyzing element of dissatisfaction and, dialectically, as a propelling factor in the construction of hope and of utopia, in the tireless search to 'be more.' Among all the beings of the Universe – incomplete, unfinished and inconclusive like us—human beings are unique in their consciousness of their own incompleteness and, because of this, push themselves toward completion, toward plenitude."

Such a category in Freirian thought supposes a vision of the utopic, not 'utopianism' (in the sense that Antonio Monclús[iii] attributes to Thomas Moore), which is postulated as possible solutions with an announced and probable futurity in human occurrence.

Therefore it is necessary to clearly affirm that all societies are set forth as utopias. Even though they differ in the meaning and the way they generate a style of life from these beginnings.

Currently, the whole of planetary society is confronting a decision crucial to its survival. The declared death of ideologies and the primacy of capitalism as an inexorable state of things, the accentuation of inequality and extreme tension in the weft of social groups, especially those most harmed by all this, make it imperative to focus on and step up efforts based on paradigms which reinvent the world and make it more human.

To envision utopias for Latin America, especially in the field of education, requires returning one's gaze to the great tendencies that propelled projects, established systems and created institutions. To attempt to encompass them in a systematic analysis is a task that we will not undertake here, although there are very interesting papers to cite like that of Adriana Puiggrós[iv], who categorizes Latin American pedagogical utopias according to their capitalist, liberal or neoconservative visions, along with the socialist alternative and, as an interdiction, the liberatory pedagogy of Freire which the author considers a proposal that radically confronts the modern pedagogical utopia: "From a different field than Marxist pedagogical critique of modern capitalist education, and [different] as well from bourgeois pedagogical positivity in that it comes from personalist and Christian existentialist roots, it turned against the essence of the dominant pedagogy." (Puiggrós: 1987, 312-313).

APPROACHING THE CONCEPT OF UNTESTED FEASIBILITY

Let us approach the concept of untested feasibility from the Freirian perspective as fundamental to his liberatory pedagogy.

Paulo Freire makes reference to untested feasibility from his earliest writings, he emphasizes it in his Pedagogy of the Oppressed[v] and he continually reprises it up to his final stage. We will say, tentatively, that untested feasibility is that which is presented as a challenge to concretize because never before perceived and something which comes into play as part of the process of conscientization, as a clear indication of the freedom assumed and at risk because it is projected into the world. It is found on the plane of futurity because it is a project aimed toward and it is part of the present because people can align themselves with it to announce or denounce a historical possibility in the making.

Let us see Freire's direct reference in this respect:

"In the last analysis, the themes both contain and are contained in limit-situations; the tasks they imply require limit-acts. When the themes are concealed by the limit-situations and thus are not clearly perceived, the corresponding tasks—people's responses in the form of historical action—can be neither authentically nor critically fulfilled. In this situation, humans are unable to transcend the limit-situations to discover that beyond these situations—and in contradiction to them—lies untested feasibility.

In sum, limit-situations imply the existence of persons who are directly or indirectly served by these situations, and of those who are negated and curbed by them. Once the latter come to perceive these situations as the frontier between being and nothingness, they begin to direct their increasingly critical actions towards achieving the untested feasibility implicit in that perception. On the other hand, those who are served by the present limit-situation regard untested feasibility as a threatening limit situation which must not be allowed to materialize, and act to maintain the status quo." (Pedagogy of the Oppressed, 2000: 102).[vi]

A fundamental point here is to understand the vision that Freire has of human life. He often insisted that people are different than animals in that we surpass our condition of merely adapting to the milieu which we inhabit (for the animal, the world is limited to a supportive role, in other words, a milieu to which one adapts in order to survive). Whereas people, as conditioned beings, historically situated but not determined, can surpass the limits imposed by the here and the now, by yesterday and today. Moreover, their consciousness of themselves and of the world (which is no longer a mere support but a world), makes it possible for them to live in the dialectical relationship between their freedom and their conditioning.

Therefore they can distance themselves so as to be able to see and admire the world and the conditions in which they find themselves (as part of their process of conscientization). Freire says that people surpass their "limit situations" which should not be taken as if they were insuperable barriers, on the other side of which nothing exists. (Freire, 1970: 116). On this point, the author explains that, based on the analysis of Professor Álvaro Vieira Pinto of the ISEB group of his youth, he takes up the problem of the limit situations, divesting it of the original pessimistic vision of Jaspers, because such situations are not an impassable boundary where possibilities end but, rather, the real margin where they can all begin—not the frontier between being and nothingness, but the border between being and being more. This aspect is substantial to understanding the notion of untested feasibility in Freire.

Freire uses the term "generative themes" to describe those which appear in a certain epoch, in a dynamic sense of historical continuity, and which are characterized as being a group of ideas, concepts, hopes, doubts, values, challenges, in dialectic interaction with their opposites. The themes of an epoch are the concrete representation of many of these ideas, values, hopes, etc. and also, according to Freire, obstacles to people's being more. Thus the understanding of these themes implies both the tasks which must be undertaken and the perception of a dialectic relation in play with its opposites.

These themes as a group constitute the thematic universe of the epoch, where people take similarly dialectical and contradictory positions, supporting either the maintenance or the transformation of its structures. Freire says that as the antagonism between the themes increases, a tendency towards mystification, irrationality and sectarianism arises. So reality is emptied of its dynamic and historic sense. This happens when the themes are wrapped in and concealed by "limit situations" which are presented to people as unavoidable determinants. The contrary, liberatory action is to overcome the "limit situations" in which people find themselves reified.

This process of decodifying the themes and releasing their progressive significance as historic tasks aids a process of conscientization that goes from an ingenuous consciousness, submerged, immersed in themes that it is unable to understand as such, to an emergent critical consciousness inserted in the reality being discovered which leads one to think about her/his own condition of existence. On this path, the untested feasibility is brought to light and constructed at the same time.

"Problem-posing education is revolutionary futurity. Hence, it is prophetic (and, as such, hopeful). Hence, it corresponds to the historical nature of humankind. Hence. It affirms women and men as beings who transcend themselves, who move forward and look ahead, for whom immobility represents a fatal threat, for whom looking at the past must only be a means of understanding more clearly what and who they are so that they can more wisely build the future. Hence, it identifies with the movement which engages people as beings aware of their incompletion—an historical movement which has its point of departure, its Subjects and its objective.

The point of departure of the movement lies in the people themselves. But since people do not exist apart from the world, apart from reality, the movement must begin with the human-world relationship. Accordingly, the point of departure must always be with men and women in the 'here and now,' which constitutes the situation within which they are submerged, from which they emerge, and in which they intervene. Only by starting form this situation—which determines their perception of it—can they begin to move. To do this authentically they must perceive their state not as fated and unalterable, but merely as limiting—and therefore challenging." (Pedagogy of the Oppressed, 2000: 84-85)

What is clear from these affirmations is that untested feasibility is a perception and a concretion which corresponds to a process of elucidation of consciousness. It is always on the level of possibility, of opportunity for realization, supposing a shared creative effort on the part of those who intervene.

THE LIFE AND WORK OF PAULO FREIRE AS UNTESTED FEASIBILITY

The first possible justification of the notion of untested feasibility as the anchorage of all Freirian thought has roots in his own life. In how he lived, how his life was a kind of pilgrimage through the world with his ideas and proposals, how he positioned himself in relation to each of his circumstances.

In Letters to Cristina. Reflections on My Life and Work (1994)[vii], a text of great autobiographical value, Freire relates personal experiences with respect to his awakening to the world which reflect what we have just posited:

(...) the difficulties I confronted during my childhood and adolescent years caused in me—rather than an accomodating position before challenges—a curious and hopeful openness toward the world. I never felt inclined to accept reaslity as it was, even when it was still impossible for me to understand the roots of my family's difficulties. I never thought that life was predetermined or that the best thing to do was to accept obstacles as they appeared. On the contrary, even in my very early years I had begun to think that the world needed to be changed, that something wrong with the world could not and should not continue. Perhaps I wanted the world to change because of the negative context in which my family lived. Finding myself immersed in predicaments that did not affect the children around me, I learned to compare my situation with theirs. This led me to conclude that the world needed to be corrected. This active outlook resulted in two significant beliefs:

1. Because I had experienced poverty, I never allowed myself to fall into fatalism; and

2. Because I had been born into a Christian family, I never accepted our precarious situation as an expression of God's wishes. On the contrary, I began to understand that something really wrong with the world needed to be fixed.

Since early on, my position was one of critical optimism. In other words, I held the hope that seldom exists apart from the reverses of fate. (Letters to Cristina, 1996: 13-14)

Freire, with a notable precocity and sensitivity to the reality that, throughout his difficult childhood and adolescence, passed before his eyes, could draw back the veil of pessimistic or 'magical' resignation to open himself to other readings of the world. He soon perceived that many of the vital circumstances that people experience as pain, are due to an injust social order. This perception of the class boundaries is vividly maintained in a personal search which lasted the rest of his life as a kind of response and struggle for those he used to call "existentially exhausted and historically anesthetized" men and women. The difference he soon recognizes between those who suffer such exhaustion and anesthesia and himself is crucial: the former are not conscious of their condition; they assume it [while] submerged in a fatalist vision that the reality of their lives will never change.

"Jaboatão kept offering itself like a new world, one much vaster than the one we had known until then, that of the garden of our house in Recife. A world full of the green of sugarcane, the aroma of its juice, the aroma of the unrefined sugar of its mills. A world full of the squeaking wheels of ox-carts, pulled by gentle animals, maybe more 'fatalist' than gentle, if you know what I mean. The driver whipping Mimo, Pintado and Fandango while he talked to them, trudging slowly onward, ruminating with resigned expressions. But also a world in which the exploitation and the misery of the peasants was being revealed to us in all its daily drama. It is there that the reasons for my radicalism are to be found. (Letters to Cristina, my translation).

We do not intend to go any further in relation to Freire's personal circumstances which really illustrate to what extent this humanist thinker was coherent in his utopian postulates. We simply want to highlight the fact that his life was the reflection of his beliefs. Thus, it is necessary to outline them here as a way of justifying the category under investigation.

The lines of thought that influenced his work are also the reflection of a specific historical era in Brazil and the whole of Latin America in the 1950s and 60s, as well as in the rest of the world. Freire was a man of his era who responded to the problems of his era and of his people.

Torres (2001: 98)[viii] says about Freire's sources that: "(…) his work was founded on hypotheses that reflected the innovative synthesis of the most advanced currents of contemporary philosophical thought, like existentialism, phenomenology, Hegelian dialectic and historical materialism."

Gerhardt (2001:140)[ix] explains that Freire's epistemological theses underwent an evolution that caused him to deepen and radicalize his concepts of the "culture of silence," the relationship between the oppressor and the oppressed, and the process of conscientization, among others, which were synonymous with the revolutionary option. He writes: "The transformations of the epistemological theses also reflect the change of inspirational and bibliographical sources—from Educação como a prática da liberdade (Scheler, Ortega y Gasset, Mannheim, Wright Mills, Whitehead, etc.) to Pedagogia do Oprimido (Marx, Lenin, Mao, Marcuse, etc.) which does not mean that the former had lost importance."

Celso Rui Beisiegel[x] claims something similar: "While in his early works Paulo Freire cited Mannheim, Dewey, Anísio Teixeira, Helio Jaguaribe, Corbusier, Vieira Pinto, Guerreiro Ramos, Zebedei Barbu, Amoroso Lima, Mounier, Bernanos, Jaspers, among others, in Pedagogia do Oprimido we find citations of authors totally ignored in the preceding texts: Hegel, Marx, Engels, Lenin, Fromm, Sartre, Marcuse, Fanon, Memmi, Lukács, Debray, Kossic, Goldman, Althusser, Mao Tse Tung, Fidel Castro, Ernesto Guevara, Camilo Torres...The educator began to travel in a very different theoretical universe."

Coben (2001:87)[xi] asserts that Freire "is an eclectic thinker par excellence. However, his eclecticism is not fortuitous but historically specific and reflects his training as a Catholic intellectual in the period from the mid-1940s until 1964 as well as his ensuing experiences." He goes on to cite de Kadt (1993: 45-50) when the latter, referring to the unity of theory and practice, compares Marxists and radical Catholics: "The Marxists recognize the 'unity of theory and practice'; the radical Catholics share this principle with them, not just as a result of their common roots in Hegelian dialetics, but also as the result of a common concern about existentialist 'commitment.' Freire recognizes influences from a varied gamut of sources, including Aristotle, Hegel and Rousseau, a connection that has been convincingly demonstrated by Taylor."

Up to this point we can observe how the different authors cited coincide. All of them refer to the same philosophical currents and assume that Freire did not adhere to any of them completely but, rather, took from each of them those concepts which supplied him with a viable response for his incessant search to sustain his utopia, and the more responses he found, the more he was transformed by them.

ANTHROPOLOGICAL AND THEOLOGICAL SUPPORT

To think about the world in a Freirian key supposes sharing with him the following points in the theoretical construction of liberatory pedagogy:

That the human being is unfinished, a being under construction. For this reason, she/he seeks completion as the consciousness of her/his incompleteness grows. The internal urgency of this project is a vital element which gives meaning to her/his existence and responds to this search. What is more, as unfinished beings, we are also conditioned (if undetermined) beings. We are programmed to learn, says Freire in a clear allusion to François Jacob[xii]:

"We become capable of imaginatively, curiously, 'stepping back' from ourselves—from the life we lead—and of disposing ourselves to 'know about it.' The moment came when we not only lived, but began to know that we were living—hence it was possible for us to know that we know, and therefore to know that we could do more. What we cannot do, as imaginative, curious beings, is to cease to learn and to seek, to investigate the 'why'of things. We cannot exist without wondering about tomorrow, about what will come, and in favor of what, against what, for whom, against whom it will come. We cannot exist without wondering about how to make 'untested feasibility' concrete which requires that we fight for it.

It is because we are this being—a being of ongoing, curious search, which 'steps back' from itself and from the life it leads—it is because we are this being, given to adventure and the 'passion to know,' for which that freedom becomes indispensable that, constituted in the very struggle for itself, is possible only because, though we are 'programmed,' we are nevertheless not determined. It is because this is 'the way we are' that we live the life of a vocation, a calling, to humanization, and that in dehumanization, which is a concrete fact in history, we live the life of the distortion of the calling—never another human dimension. Neither one, humanization or dehumanization, is sure destiny, given datum, lot, or fate. This is precisely why one is a vocation and the other a distortion of the vocation." (Pedagogy of Hope: 1994, p. 98)

That the human being exists with others, in solidarity and in meeting other people, therefore communication, dialogue is the substance of life, an existential demand. This makes possible [Freire's] pronouncement that people respect the world as a creative act, an act of courage and of liberty.

> (…)However, no one can search for exclusivity individually. This solitary seeking could be translated as 'having more' which is a way of 'being less.' This search should be made with other beings who also seek to 'be more' and in communion with other consciousnesses because, if not, it would make some consciousnesses objects of others. It would reify consciousnesses.

> Jaspers has said: 'I am to the extent that others are as well.'

> Man is not an island. He is communication. Then, there is a close relationship between communion and search. (Education and Change, 1976: 28, translation mine).

> Human existence cannot be silent, nor can it be nourished by false words, but only by true words, with which men and women transform the world. To exist, humanly, is to name the world, to change it. Once named, the world in its turn reappears to the namers as a problem and requires of them a new naming. Human beings are not built in silence, but in word, in work, in action-reflection.

> But while to say the true word—which is work, which is praxis—is to transform the world, saying that word is not the privilege of some few persons, but the right of everyone. Consequently, no one can say a true word alone—nor can she say it for another, in a prescriptive act which robs others of their words. To say the word, referring to the world that has to be transformed, implies people getting together for this transformation. (Pedagogy of the Oppressed, 2000: 88).

That the human beings seek transcendence as the farthest horizon of their consciousness. It is not enough for Freire to know himself, to recognize his individuality and his being among others, with others and for others. This creature perspective, of a created being who seeks its Creator, has a clearly theological origin. And it is situated in how much the meaning of existence is found in a continual search for its fullness in what Freire considers the ontological order of the human condition.

> On the other hand man, and only man, is capable of transcendence. His transcendence increases not only in its 'spiritual'quality, the meaning of which Erich Kahler studies. It is not exclusively the transitivity of his consciousness that allows him to self-objectify and, thus, to recognize different existential orbits, to distinguish the I from the not I. His transcendence, for us, is also based on the root of his finitude, on the consciousness he has of this finitude, of the unfinished being that he is and whose plenitude is found in the union with his Creator. A union that, by its very essence, will never be about domination or domestication, but only ever about liberation. Thus it follows that religion— from the Latin root religare [to relink]—incarnates this transcendental sense of man's relations and must never be an instrument of his alienation. Exactly because he is finite and destitute, man has in this transcendence through love the possibility of returning to his source, which liberates him. In the act of discerning why he exists and not just why he lives, he discovers the meaning of his temporality which begins precisely when, going beyond unidimensional time in a certain way, he understands yesterday, recognizes today and discovers tomorrow." (Education as the practice of freedom, 1969: 29-30, my translation).[xiii]

That the world is a human construction and, consequently, crystallizes an order and some structures that can be transformed. In this way the conditions of life are 'denatured' in that they contain people who are being one way and can be another. This is a crucial problem in the understanding of materiality as an objective context in which the aforesaid process of humanization is developed—not as a polarity but in a dialectic relationship.

> Thus, the dialectical view indicates to us the importance of rejecting as false, for example, a comprehension of awareness as pure reflex of material objectivity, but at the same time the importance of rejecting an understanding of the awareness that would confer upon it a determining power over concrete reality.

In like fashion, the dialectical view indicates to us the incompatibility between it and an inevitable tomorrow, an idea that I have criticized before, in Pedagogy of the Oppressed, and that I now criticize in this essay. The dialectical view is incompatible with the notion that tomorrow is the pure repetition of today, or that tomorrow is something 'predated,' or as I have called it, a given datum, a 'given given.' This 'tamed' or domesticated view of the future, shared by reactionaries and 'revolutionaries' alike—naturally, each in their own way—posits, in the mind of the former, the future as a repetition of the present (which, of course, must undergo 'adverbial' changes), and in the mind of the second, the future as 'inexorable progress.' Both of these views or visions imply a fatalistic 'intelligence' (in the sense of an interpretative 'understanding,' and 'inner reading') of history in which there is no room for authentic hope. (Pedagogy of Hope, 1994: 100-101).

'Can Brazil be repaired?.' I am constantly asked this question and, sometimes, I carry it with me to the shade of this mango tree. Yes, I think it can, as long as we decide to undertake the repairs. No solution is going to simply appear.

It is not by chance that societies are made into this or that, it is not simply fate that they are not taken seriously or become examples of integrity. Societies are not faits accomplis, they are becoming that which we make of them in history, as possibilities. Hence they are our ethical responsibility.

(…) In the understanding of History as possibility, the [concept of] tomorrow is problematic. To make it happen, we need to construct it through the transformation of the [concept of] today. There are possibilities for different 'tomorrows.' The struggle is not as simple as delaying what will happen or assuring its coming; we need to reinvent the world. Education is indispensable in this reinvention. To consider ourselves the subjects and objects of History makes us beings of decision, of rupture. Ethical beings. (In the shade of this mango tree, 1997: 48-50, my translation).

We have not exhausted, by mentioning them, all the sustaining aspects of Freirian theory. We have only alluded to those we consider ineluctable for an understanding of the category of untested feasibility. This is an anthropological vision that is profoundly influenced, principally, by existentialism (the being in construction), phenomenology (the construction of consciousness as intentionality), Marxism (the drama of the economic conditioning of the infrastructure and the ideological conditioning of the superstructure) and the Hegelian dialectic (self-consciousness, which begins as common experience and elevates itself into science)[xiv]—as well as a theological vision of people and the meaning of their existence.

We want, in this manner, to stress that Freire's novelty in respect to the sources on which he based his work, is that he integrated people as individuals, their humanizing process[xv] and their construction of the world in a similarly dialectic relationship. The world is a possibility in permanent construction and so is the person. Even when, with people, we recognize an ontological condition whose negation assumes their 'dehumanization'—the reverse is therefore, also, ontologically possible. Such is the range of Freire's untested feasibility.

We insist on one more aspect: a fundamental problem for phenomenology is the opening of consciousness to the world and the process of knowledge this puts into play. And the very fact of making decisions about one's own existence based on this intentionality which leads the person to detach from the world. In such a way that this mystical process of movement toward something constitutes a primordial motivating force for the educative act.

This influence on comprehending the world and the process of intervening knowledge, takes the form of an explicit manifesto in Freirian theory:

"As women and men, simultaneously reflecting on themselves and on the world, increase the scope of their perception, they begin to direct their observations towards previously inconspicuous phenomena that, while present in what Husserl called 'background awareness[xvi], were not singled out, were not posited on their own account.'

That which had existed objectively but had not been perceived in its deeper implications (if indeed it was perceived at all) begins to 'stand out,' assuming the character of a problem and therefore of challenge. (Here the concept of untested feasibility is born as he expressed it for the first time in this work)[xvii] Thus, men and women begin to single out elements from their 'background awareness' and to reflect upon them. These elements are now objects of their consideration, and, as such, objects of their action and cognition.

(…)Whereas the banking method directly or indirectly reinforces men's fatalistic perception of their situation, the problem-posing method presents this very situation to them as a problem. As the situation becomes the object of their cognition, the naïve or magical peception which produced their fatalism gives way to perception which is able to perceive itself even as it perceives reality, and can thus be critically objective about that reality." (Pedagogy of the Oppressed, 2000: 83, 85).

Finally, we want to take note of the role of the educator in this process. Her necessary commitment, the internal transformation of her very stance, confronting a task that summons her historical 'feasibility.'

If men and women are searchers and their ontological vision is humanization, sooner or later they they may perceive the contradiction in which banking education seeks to maintain them, and then engage themselves in the struggle for their liberation.

But the humanist, revolutionary educator cannot wait for this possibility to materialize. From the outset, her efforts must coincide with those of the students to engage in critical thinking and the quest for mutual humanization. Her efforts must be imbued with a profound trust in people and their creative power. To achieve this, they must be partners of the students in their relations with them. (Pedagogy of the Oppressed, 2000: 75).

Up to this point we have presented untested feasibility in Freire as the spinal axis that justifies the large outlines of his pedagogy—one consonant with his life and his work which synthesizes his historical epoch and the currents of thought which influenced him. To think of people, all people, and the world itself as a great possibility of being and existence is a broad, generous and hopeful idea. It gives meaning to teachers' efforts and puts us on a completely different axis than the one to which we are accustomed. It invades the current scene with vigilant force, in the Freirian way, with a gentle outcry[xviii]. But one which is audible and completely clear.

Even after this affirmation, we are left with many questions. We will only mention two:

One that appears to us as fundamental to the roles of educators, is tied to their training as intellectuals and their commitment to the transformation necessary to confront their historical time and concrete space, to build their own untested feasibility as a risky option for liberation which will allow them to discover themselves as co-creators of the world.

The other question concerns the "simple man" and the reversal of his destiny. His untested feasibility is a personal and communitary expression in a society which pushes him toward a different kind of consciousness—global, planetary, constructed on the basis of a humanizing effort—so as to be able to reinvent a world where all of us can live.

Translated from Spanish by Peter Lownds, Los Angeles, 11/19-11/22/03

NOTES

[i]   The author is a psychologist and teacher from Córdoba, Argentina, licensed in School Administration and Management, currently writing her doctoral dissertation in Educational Sciences. Director of an inner-city school in a neighborbood with high rates of delinquency and social risk, she is a member of Project Angel – dedicated to the preventive care of girls and boys at high risk of sexual exploitation and child prostitution.

[ii]   Romão, José Eustaquio. *Civilização do oprimido*. http://www.paulofreire.org/coprim.htm

[iii]   Monclús, Antonio. *Pedagogía de la contradicción: Paulo Freire*. (Barcelona: Anthropos, 1988). The author develops an important investigation of the work of Freire using utopia as a central category.

[iv]   Puiggrós, Adriana et alii. *Hacia una pedagogia de la imaginación para América Latina*. (Buenos Aires: Contrapunto, 1987).

[v]   Freire, Paulo. *Pedagogia del oprimido*. (Mexico: Siglo XXI, 1970).

[vi]   Freire, Paulo, *Cartas a Cristina. Reflexiones sobre mi vida y mi trabajo*. (Mexico: Siglo XXI, 1996).

[vii]   Gadotti and Torres are well-known Freiran intellectuals who have accompanied his work for many years. Currently both fulfill key functions to assure its continuity. The facts gathered in the biographical work cited are considered highly accurate.

[viii]   Gadotti, Moacir and Torres, Carlos Alberto. *Paulo Freire. Una Biobibliografia*. (Buenos Aires: Siglo XXI, 2001).

[ix]   A Brazilian thinker who systematized Freire's works from the first years of his trajectory and has written various books about it. This citation was extracted from an article on the Internet: Beisiegel, Celso de Rui. *Observaciones sobre la teoría y la práctica en Paulo Freire*. http://www.hottopos.com/mirand 7/observaciones.htm

[x]   Coben, Diana. Gramsci y Freire. *Héroes radicales. Políticas en Educación de adultos*. (Madrid, Miño y Dávila, 2001). She develops her doctoral thesis from a Marxist perspective.

[xi]   See in Freire, Paulo. *Pedagogía de la esperanza. Un reencuentro con la Pedagogía del oprimido.* (Mexico: Siglo XXI, 1993). Also *Cartas a quien pretende enseñar.* (Buenos Aires: Siglo XXI, 1994). And *A la sombra de este árbol.* (Barcelona: El Rouire, 1997).

[xii]   Freire, Paulo. *Educación y Cambio.* (Buenos Aires: Galerna, 1976).

[xiii]   Freire, Paulo. *La Educación como práctica de la libertad.* (Mexico: Siglo XXI, 1969).

[xiv]   Romero Carabajal, Gloria refers to it. *Algunos temas generadores que sustentan el pensamiento de Paulo Freire.* (Mexico, Universidad Iberoamericana, 1983).

[xv]   *Humanization* in the sense that Chardin gives it. See in Theilhard de Chardin, Pierre. *El fenómeno humano.* (Madrid: Taurus, 1965).

[xvi]   Husserl, Edmund. *Notas relativas a una fenomenología pura y una filosofia feneomenológica.* (Mexico: Fondo de Cultura Económica, 1962, p. 79

[xvii]   The commentary is ours.

[xviii]   Freire, Paulo. *El grito manso.* (Buenos Aires: Siglo XXI, 2003).

ANTÓNIO TEODORO[*]

NEW WAYS OF TRANSNATIONAL REGULATION OF EDUCATIONAL POLICIES

Evidences and possibilities

The school system has been crucial in the expansion of literacy. Despite many practical difficulties and different rhythms of development, very early schooling became a global phenomenon which through isomorphism developed in modern world[i]. Like all global phenomena, nowadays' schooling has a local root, despite being a model constructed in a European context and only later gradually universally widespread as the integration of different areas into the capitalist world economy occurred.

The consolidation of the 16th and 17th-centuries school model, rather than that of older learning ways, is the outcome of a long process developed within a complex network of social relationships and changes in representations and normative guidelines related to the world and humanity, as António Nóvoa points out, understandable in a framework where other aspects also emerge, namely (i) the development of a new concept of childhood, (ii) the appearance of a civilisation of mores, (iii) the establishment of a Protestant work ethic and (iv) the implementation of a disciplinary society, which resulted in locking children away in special spaces[ii].

It is in the tutelary shadow of the Church that the school model is shaped and improved over those three centuries deeply influenced by Reformation and Counter-Reformation. But the 18th century, with its deep economic, social and political changes demands important cleavages in the educational area and society's organisation[iii]. In many countries, and through means not always peaceful, the State replaces the Church in education's control and will become the most important agent in the expansion of the school institution.

Throughout the 19th century school becomes a core element in linguistic and cultural homogenisation, of invention of national citizenship, in short, the affirmation of the nation-state. As has been tirelessly stressed by the authors who support the perspective of the modern world system, or the neo-instituationalist conception, school expansion is closely linked to that reality inevitable to the new stage of the economy in the capitalist world, the nation-state.

The ascendant nation-state form itself was fostered by a world political culture emerging from the conflicting dynamics of the world capitalist economy. The nation-state as a mode of political organization involves the formation of citizenship and the conferral of this status on individuals. Citizenship links individuals not merely to the state as a bureaucratic

C.A. Torres & P. Noguera (Eds.), Social Justice Education for Teachers, 191–203.

organization but, more importantly, to the "imagined community" that national states are expected to embody (Anderson 1983). Mass schooling becomes the central set of activities through which the reciprocal links between individuals and nation-states are forged.[iv]

The growing availability of school to all classes and social groups led to the consolidation of models of school organisation and pedagogical organisation able to accommodate an ever growing number of students. With this purpose a grammar schooling[v] has been developing since the 19th century capable of facing the challenge of teaching many as if it were only one[vi].

The school model first developed in Europe will become not just universal but almost the only one possible or even conceivable[vii]. The analysis of how this school model was established and consolidated in the various world regions has become a privileged research field in comparative education. Being a subject of educational sciences which may date back to early 19th century[viii], it was after Second World War II, however, that comparative education underwent a significant development and gained expression within educational sciences.

The appearance of a vast system of international organisations of an intergovernmental nature, both within the United Nations – besides the UN itself other specialised organisations like UNESCO were created in the area of education, science, and culture or the IMF and the World Bank, in the finance and development support – and regarding economic Co-operation within a specific geographic area – OECD is but an example – has given great encouragement to the internationalisation of educational problems[ix]. Devising educational policies, particularly in peripheral (or semi-peripheral) countries within the world system, increasingly depends on legitimisation and technical support of international organisations, which allowed, in the 60s, for rapid spreading of the theories of human capital and educational planning, the hard core of modernisation theories, so fashionable at that time of euphoria, where education became a compulsory instrument of personal self-fulfilment, social progress and economic prosperity[x]. The effort to establish a scientific rationality which permitted the formulation of general laws able to guide the reforming action in the education of each country was at the centre of several initiatives – seminars, conferences, workshops, surveys, studies – conducted by all those international organisations, thus enabling the creation of several networks of contact, financing and exchange of information and knowledge among national political-administrative authorities, social actors, experts and researchers.

The development of these networks relied on the concept of comparative education centred, according to António Nóvoa, around four essential issues: the ideology of progress, a concept of science, the concept of the nation-state and the definition of a comparative methodology. The first aspect ideology of progress, is manifest in the equation education = development, that is, in the notion that the expansion and improvement of educational systems undoubtedly secure socio-economic development. The second aspect, a concept of science is based on the positivist paradigm of social sciences developed from the second half of the 19th century, which accords science – in this case comparative education – the role of establishing general laws on the working of educational systems, thus legitimising the rhetoric of rationalisation of schooling and efficiency of educational policies, considered the core of all reforming action. The third aspect, the concept of the nation-state derives from the assumption of the nation as a privileged community of analysis, which in general leads to studies where attempts are made to underline, above all, the differences and similarities between two or more countries. The fourth and last, the definition of a comparative methodology, acquires its main dimension in the rhetoric of objectivity and quantification, which poses the problem of gathering and analysing data and seldom (or never) that other question, namely the construction itself of data and theoretical framework underlying them[xi].

Perhaps due to its origins, comparative education, in its paradigm which has been generalised by international organisations, has produced very limited knowledge, rather serving as a way for national authorities to legitimise their policies. An instrumental positivism prevails there, leading to what Thomas Popkewitz and Miguel A. Pereyra define as epistemological fallacies of comparative research[xii].

In this perspective I have defended that resorting to the foreign primarily works as an element of legitimisation of options taken at a national level and very little as a serious effort towards the knowledge of the context of other experiences and realities. Conversely, however, constant initiatives, surveys and publications by international organisations can be considered to play a decisive role in regulating national educational policies, by establishing an agenda defining not only the priorities but also the way problems should be equated and solved, which constitutes the establishment of a more or less explicit mandate, depending on how central countries are.

Jurgen Schriewer classifies that kind of diffuse but present, as the semantic construction of world society. Based on Niklas Luhmann's theory on self-reference social systems, Schriewer explains:

A reflective context, limited by political boundaries and/or by linguistic links externalises other reflective contexts which, in turn, refer yet to other contexts, with the result that they represent models and possible stimuli to one another. A network of reciprocal references then emerges from this accumulation of observations among nations. This network acquires its own autonomy, which transmits, confirms and accelerates the planetary universalising of reform representations, models, norms, criteria and options. Such a network becomes an element in the creation of a transnational semantics of pedagogical reform. From the point of view of knowledge sociology, this transnational semantics may be understood as the co-relation of an evolutionary process caused by the dynamics of a functional differentiation in social systems, while it at the same time acts, as semantic construction of world society, on the social structures, transforming them, making them uniform and harmonising them.[xiii]

That relationship between national educational policies and initiatives of technical assistance nature on the part of international organisations, which simultaneously assumes the character of legitimisation and mandate, can well be illustrated through a situation like the one in Portugal, a semi-peripheral country in the European context[xiv], in the period from the end of the World War II to January 1, 1986, when it joined the European Economic Community / European Union (EEC/EU). Privileged relationships with various international organisations with intervention in the educational area can be located in that period, illustrating that dual relationship of legitimisation and mandate: first, with the OECD until 1974; then with UNESCO, in the revolutionary crisis period of 1974-1975; after the normalisation of the revolution, between 1976 and 1978, with the World Bank; and finally again with the OECD, in the period immediately before joining the EEC/EU[xv].

THE NEW FORMS OF TRANSNATIONAL REGULATION IN THE FIELD OF EDUCATIONAL POLICIES, OR A LOW-INTENSITY GLOBALISATION

As a persistent European idea, with its origin going back both to the Promethean concept of growing taming of nature by humans and to the affirmation of an economy-capitalist world with Europe as its centre, the development project rested on two main pillars, the technological transfer and education[xvi]. If the recipients of development, that is the peripheral and semi-peripheral countries, may have had mixed feelings about central countries' promises of technological transfer, overall the pillar of education was unanimously considered the basis for social development and nation building, even when it led to the rejection and impoverishment of local cultures, looked upon as pre-modern and an obstacle to rationalisation of economic development.

The development project started after World War II had the Nation-State as its privileged ground. That project, where modernisation was considered a universal ideal, offered an optimistic perspective for national economic development based on assistance programs of a bi- or multilateral kind, usually conducted by international organisations just established. In this perspective, development initiatives were the outcome of a process where, despite close links between national and international plans, it was the national space that constituted the fundamental political unit when it came to mobilising populations and attaining the modernisation ideal.

Strangely (or nor), that national development project led to a global economic integration, which decisively from the public debt crisis of the 1980s, Philip McMichael's lost decade, moved the development terms from a predominantly national issue to a progressively global one. Development ceased to be a project capable of being conducted within the Nation-State, based on the traditional stimuli to the national market, rather becoming more and more dependant on the world market, led by a global managerialism whose ten commandments are listed in the so-called Washington Consensus (1993): fiscal discipline, priorities in public expense, fiscal reform, financial liberalisation, exchange rates, trade liberalisation, direct foreign investment, privatisation, deregulation and property rights.

Global managerialism refers to the relocation of the power of economic management from nation-states to global institutions. It may not be an absolute relocation, but neither is it a zero-sum game where "global" and "national" are mutually exclusive. Each folds into the other. Most important, national institutions embrace global goals. This is not clearly understood because nation-states still exist and their governments still make policy. It appears to the casual observer that because state exists, national projects must also. In this global context, that is not necessarily the case. Governments are quite often making policy on behalf of the global managers – officials of the multilateral institutions as well as executives of transnational corporation and global bankers.[xvii]

That global development project – globalisation is the generally accepted term – may be understood as something beyond the mere extension of the world system, according to Giddens[xviii], or just the acceleration of the transition age, as Wallerstein[xix] argues. Whatever the meaning, however, that new development project rests on two fundamental pillars, on the one hand a liberalisation strategy and, on the other, the assertion of the competitive advantages axiom, based on a new concept of development, called sustainable, which eventually brings back to the front the neo-classic theory of human capital.

It is not surprising, thus, that Roger Dale argues that the most evident effects of globalisation in educational policies result from the reorganisation of States' priorities in becoming more competitive, namely so as to attract investments of transnational corporations to their countries[xx]. But, he adds, if globalisation can change the parameters and direction of state policies in the educational field, that does not inevitably mean it has to overcome, or even remove, the political peculiarities of the nations (or any sectors). First, because globalisation does not result from a country's imposition on another, possibly supported by the threat of a bilateral military action, but rather, and much more, the consequence of a supranational construction[xxi]. Second, because the consequences in educational policies are indirect, acting through national States, so that the new, distinct rules can be interpreted differently, which usually happens, according to the country's location within the world system. That does not mean, Dale adds, the weakening or dissipation of the power of States already powerful, but rather the strengthening of their capacity to collectively respond to the forces not one of them can, alone, individually control.

As a corollary of the argumentation presented, Dale advances two hypotheses: (a) it is possible to distinguish the effects of globalisation in educational policies from those resulting from the traditional intervention forms by international organisations in the framework of the former developmental model; and (b) the effects of globalisation on national policies are diverse and multifarious, rather than homogeneous and uniform.

In the developmental model, the organisations' technical assistance was (is) actively sought by the national authorities, especially as a way to legitimise internal options; on the other hand, the various differing reports presented by the international organisations constitute(d) a sort of more or less explicit mandate, depending on the countries' centrality. In the globalisation project – and this is the hypothesis advanced in this chapter – the globally structured agenda[xxii] is defined above all having as nerve centre the great international statistic projects and, in particular, the INES[xxiii] project of the Centre for Educational Research and Innovation (CERI) of the OECD. And, in these statistics projects, the selection of the indicators is, surely, the central issue to the fixation from this global agenda.

Due to its impact on educational policies of the central countries (and on many countries located in the semi-periphery of the central areas), the project, developed around the construction and gathering of national educational indicators, assumes a particular relevance. Having as its most visible expression the annual publication of Education at a Glance, this OECD undertaking started as a consequence of a meeting held in Washington, in 1987, through the initiative and invitation of the American Secretary of Education and the OECD Secretariat, attended by representatives of 22 countries as well as several experts and guest observers. The main point of the OECD agenda concerning education was, at the time, quality in education, which acted as a departing issue in the launch of INES project, possibly the most significant and important activity of that international organisation in the whole of the 1990s.

Recognising that the most complex problem was not so much the calculation of valid indicators but, rather, the classification of concepts, the representatives of the OECD member countries and the guest observers examined a series of over 50 possible national indicators, and ended by organising them under four categories: (i) input indicators, ii) output indicators, (iii) process indicators, and (iv) human and financial resources indicators[xxiv].

Putting this project into practice allowed OECD to collect an important database about national educational indicators, which has made the publication of Education at a Glance possible since 1992. In that glance, besides traditional indicators, such as different schooling rates, the various levels of access to education, expenditure on education, teachers' qualifications, a series of new indicators is presented with far-reaching consequences in the formulation of educational policies at a national level[xxv]. Those new indicators are presented by the OECD in a particularly significant way:

> In order to respond to the growing interest of public opinion and authorities, concerning schooling results, over a third of the indicators presented in this edition deal with these results both on a personal level and vis-à-vis the labour market, and with the evaluation of school efficiency. The indicators, based on the first international survey on adult literacy, give an idea of the level of adults' mastering of basic skills and the links between these skills and some characteristics of the educational systems. This issue also includes a complete series of indicators related to the results in Mathematics and Science, covering almost all OECD countries and are based on the Third International Study on Mathematics and Science. On the other hand, the indicators collected in the first survey of the INES project schools contribute to the expansion of the available database related to school efficiency.[xxvi]

But even more significant are the future priorities presented for this project, which constitute a truly global agenda for future or ongoing reforms in several countries' educational systems at this point of century and millennium transition:

> First of all, figures about learning for life and its effects on society and economy are dramatically scarce. As countries can no longer count on the progressive expansion of initial education alone in order to meet the demand for new advanced qualifications, new indicators must help those in charge to improve the basis for learning for life. In order to do that databases must be created on job-based training, continuous and adult education, and on other kinds of learning outside the school. The factors influencing the types of knowledge acquisition along our life are difficult to grasp. Data on adult literacy [...] represent a first step in that direction, as they provide information on the relationship between school curricula and the skills required by adults, and between learning and individual's jobs, whatever the age.

> The evolution of information needs also demands an expansion of the database of results, namely those of students and schools. The sources of information should go beyond the mere analysis of results related to countries by trying to identify the variables influencing those results.[xxvii]

The practical effects of this project are patent in several countries' educational policies at the end of the 1990s, where a similarity is evident regarding the options taken by national governments. But these effects, in the case of central countries, or countries belonging to central regions, are felt above all through the establishment of a global agenda rather than the affirmation of an explicit mandate[xxviii], as, for example, happens in sectors like financial activity, world trade, tourism, mass culture or the media.

We can, then, talk about degrees in the intensity of globalisation. Defining globalisation as "groups of social relationships which translate into the intensification of transnational interactions, be they interstate practices, global capitalist practices or transnational social and cultural practices," Boaventura de Sousa Santos proposes the distinction between high-intensity globalisation for rapid, intense and relatively single-cause globalisation processes, and low-intensity globalisation for slower processes, more diffuse and more ambiguous in their causes, adding:

> The usefulness of this distinction lies in the fact that it makes it possible to clarify unequal power relationships underlying different ways to produce globalisation, which are, therefore, crucial in the concept of globalisation proposed here. Low-intensity globalisation tends to prevail in situations where exchanges are less unequal, that is, where power differences are small (between countries, interests, actors or practices behind the alternative concepts of globalisation). On the contrary, high-intensity globalisation tends to prevail in situations where exchanges are very unequal and power differences are big.[xxix]

In education, the compulsory mediation by national governments in devising their respective policies, usually conditioned by strong internal social movements, makes it possible to argue that we are facing a possible paradigmatic example of low-intensity globalisation.

HEGEMONIC AND COUNTER-HEGEMONIC GLOBALISATIONS: IN SUPPORT OF A PEDAGOGY OF POSSIBILITY IN THE IMPLEMENTATION OF EMANCIPATING POLICIES IN THE EDUCATIONAL FIELD

Stressing the fact that there is no genuine globalisation, as what is generally designated as globalisation is always a successful globalisation of a certain localism, Boaventura de Sousa Santos mentions four ways of producing globalisation, which originate the same number of forms, two of which are predominantly hegemonic, imposing themselves from top to bottom – as is the case with global localism and local globalism – and another two would be predominantly counter-hegemonic, affirming themselves from the bottom up – as are what he call cosmopolitanism and common human heritage[xxx].

Globalisation always presupposes localisation. The main reason why a term is preferred to the other is that "hegemonic scientific discourse [tends to] prefer the history of the world from the winners' perspective"[xxxi]. In his attempt to seek alternatives to hegemonic answers to the crisis of the development theory, Philip McMichael proposes, based on a case study about the Chiapas rebels, the notion of cosmopolitan localism, as a possible way to make a successful connection between the struggle for local rights and the world historic context[xxxii].

> To be sustainable, a global community must situate its constituent community needs within their world-historical context. That means understanding not only how the community has come to be within the context of global processes and relations (such as instituted markets), but also how its members can empower themselves through that context. And that includes ensuring that community empowerment means also empowering the individuals and minorities in those communities. It also means realizing that there are other communities with similar needs precisely because they are woven from similar world-historical threads.[xxxiii]

Contemporary societies are experiencing deep changes – of bifurcation, according to Prigogine – where national space-time has been quietly losing ground since the 1970s in relation to the growing importance of the global and local spaces-times, causing the national social contract crisis, which was the motive behind the development of modern central states as a paradigm of government legitimacy, social and economic welfare, security and collective identity. If globalisation is understood as something beyond the mere continuation of the expansion of the economy-capitalist world, as Giddens insists, or just as the acceleration of the age of transition, as Wallerstein argues, it is important, anyway, to rethink the development project which was at the core of modernity building.

Boaventura de Sousa Santos argues for the need to formulate a new social contract, quite different from the modernity one, more comprehensive, covering "not only humanity and social groups, but also nature"[xxxiv], which involves, in his opinion, a democratic rediscovery of work. In this latter direction goes Alain Touraine when he fights against the idea of the end of work and its replacement with a leisure society since, as he points out, what the last decades have shown is the growing withdrawal of the production society dominated by the market society. As a counterpoint to this opinion, Touraine argues that we are entering a work civilisation where the boundaries between work, leisure and education may become increasingly thin.

> To conclude, we must admit that we have left a production society inspired by the great project of dominate nature, but that is no reason for us to abandon the idea that our society is anything other than a collection of markets and that the actors are anything but consumers, hence behaviour is determined by the mass society. On the contrary, we are witnessing, following a period of really capitalist development, the rebirth of a production society, no longer industry-, but information-based, where technology plays a much more important role than in any past society and where, consequently, work problems, far from becoming secondary, will become more directly crucial that in the industrial society.[xxxv]

A new social contract also implies the transformation of the national sate in what Alain Touraine and Boaventura de Sousa Santos call the newest social movement. Such a proposal stems from the awareness that there exists an erosion of national state sovereignty and of its regulating capacities, since power is assumed to be exerted "within a network in a wider and more conflicting political field," through "a series of organisations and currents," where "the state co-ordination acts as the imagination of the centre"[xxxvi]. By considering that this new political organisation does not have a centre, Boaventura de Sousa Santos then argues that the articulating state – whose institutionalisation still remains to be invented, he adds – should consider itself a newest social movement which stimulates the experimentation of alternative institutional designs which are not confined to representative democracy but rather illustrate what he calls redistributive democracy. The new welfare state, Boaventura de Sousa Santos concludes, is "an experimental state, and it the continuous experimentation with the active participation of citizens that guarantees the welfare sustainability"[xxxvii].

If that new social contract implies a redefinition of the role of the state (and the theories on it), it can also imply the replacement of the contract model itself. Habermas argues that the source of legitimisation of modern juridical orders can only be found in the concept of self-determination: "it is necessary that citizens can at all times conceive of themselves as the actors of the laws they are subjected to as recipients."[xxxviii] This will lead, still according to Habermas to the discussion or deliberation model ending by replacing the contract's – the juridical community is not established by a contract, but rather due to an agreement reached through discussion.

Citizenship constructed on the basis of Habermas's concept of self-determination and without the exclusions of the post-modernity project may become the enzyme in the development of a democratic government concerned with social emancipation.[xxxix] In such a context, the school system may become the core of the affirmation of citizenship in a communication society run in a dialogical way, always bearing in mind, however, that the school is an arena of struggle and compromise which cannot be changed by law or rhetoric, as Paulo Freire used to remind us.

The increased investment in education by national states, though necessary, is not enough for an emancipation policy which regards education as one of the most important empowerment factors, both individually and at the community level. In terms of current debate, marked, on the one hand, by the crumbling of the socialist thought and the conservative thought and, on the other, by the arrogant affirmation of neo-liberalism as the indiscriminate expansion of the market economy, an emancipation policy for education will imply, in the opinion shared with R. Morrow and C. A. Torres, an attitude of resistance to rationalisation of education as hegemonic goal under pretext of increased economic development or, in the Portuguese situation, of the need to overtake the leading runners in European integration.

> In other words, resistance to equity and cultural education topics having been replaced by strategies geared towards the solution of economic demands, apparently more urgent. In this context, the critical education theories were forced to adopt an element of conservation, or even conservatism, in order to defend the most traditional educational functions and goals.[xl]

In these days of paradigmatic transition, the state should become a field of institutional experimentation. Admitting that the school has some characteristics of structural place,[xli] it may argued that it constitutes a public space of institutional experimentation, where the future (and current) generations can be provided with new ways to plan the construction of a fairer world. A world, in Paulo Freire's symbolic words, "rounder, less angular, more humane and in which the great Utopia – Unity in Diversity – can materialise."[xlii]

Perhaps because of that, in the perspective of justice and social equity, it has become not just possible but necessary to adopt an educational agenda concerned with the construction of a democratic education and educational cities built on participation and democracy. Such an agenda, alternative to a so-called rationalisation of educational structures and practices, imposed by the merchandising of the right to education and having in the international comparison of school results evaluation the legitimising referent to its whole action, will certainly have as its core the transformation of the national state into a social movement, engaged in the strengthening of redistributive and participating democracy.

NOTES

* Department of Social and Human Sciences, Universidade Lusófona de Humanidades e Tecnologias, Lisbon.

[i] See, e.g., Francisco O. Ramirez and Marc J. Ventresca, "Building the Institution of Mass Schooling: Isomorphism in the Modern World" (In Bruce Fuller & Richard Rubinson, Eds., *The Political Construction of Education. The State, Scool Expansion and Economic Change*, New York, Westport & London: Praeger, 1992, p. 47-59).

[ii] António Nóvoa, *História da Educação*, unpublished academic paper (Faculdade de Psicologia e Ciências da Educação da Universidade de Lisboa, Lisbon, 1994).

[iii] The greatest is, obviously, the one resulting from the French Revolution, in 1789. On its consequences in the ideological plan, with the emergence of liberalism as ideological glue of economy in the capitalist world and, in the context of power, *the people taking their destiny into their hands*, see, e.g., Immanuel Wallerstein, *After Liberalism* (New York: The New Press, 1995).

[iv] Francisco Ramirez e Marc Ventresca, *op. cit.*, p. 49-50.

[v] See, e.g., David Tyack and Larry Cuban, *Tinkering toward Utopia. A Century of Public School Reform* (Cambridge, MA: Harvard University Press, 1995).

[vi] See, e.g., João Barroso, *Os Liceus. Organização pedagógica e administração, 1836-1960* (Lisbon: Fundação Calouste Gulbenkian/JNICT, 1995).

[vii] António Nóvoa, *Histoire & Comparaison (Essais sur l'Éducation)* (Lisbon: Educa, 1998), p. 52.

[viii] Comparative studies in various scientific areas, particularly in Biology, but also in Law, Linguistics or Pedagogy, experienced a significant development at the beginning of the 19th century. In Pedagogy, the breakthrough in what came to be the area of Comparative Education happened with Marc-Antoine Julien and his *Esquisse et vues préliminaires d'un ouvrage sur léducation comparée*, published in 1817 in Paris.

[ix] See Joel Samoff's seminal article "Institutinalizing International Influence" (in Robert F. Arnove & Carlos Alberto Torres, Eds., *Comparative Education. The Dialectic of the Global and the Local*, Lanham, Boulder, New York & Oxford: Rowman & Littlefield, 1999), p. 51-89.

[x] See Torsten Husén, *L'école en question* (Brussels: Pierre Mardaga, 1979).

[xi] António Nóvoa, "Modèles d'analyse en Éducation Comparée: le cham et la carte", *Les Sciences de l'Éducation - Pour l'Ère Nouvelle*, n.º 2-3 (1995), p. 9-61.

[xii] Thomas S. Popkewitz and Miguel A. Pereyra, "Estudio comparado de las prácticas contemporáneas de reforma de la formación del profesorado en ocho países: configuración de la problemática y construcción de una metodología comparativa", (in Thomas S. Popkewitz, Ed., *Modelos de poder y regulación social en Pedagogia. Crítica comparada de las reformas contemporáneas de la formación del profesorado*, Barcelona: Pomares-Corredor, 1994), p. 15-91.

[xiii] Jürgen Schriewer (1997). L'éducation comparée: mise en perspective historique d'un champ de recherche. *Révue Française de Pédagogie, 121*, p. 23-24.

[xiv] On Portugal's position within the world system, see, among others, Boaventura de Sousa Santos (Ed.), *Portugal, um retrato singular* (Oporto: Afrontamento, 1993). On the educational consequences of that location, see António Teodoro, *A Construção Política da Educação. Estado, Mudança Social e Políticas Educativas no Portugal Contemporâneo* (Oporto: Afrontamento, 2002).

[xv] See my previous paper, A. Teodoro, Educational Policies and New Ways of Governance in a Transnationalization Period, in C. A. Torres & A. Antikainen (eds.), *The International Handbook on the Sociology of Education. An International Assessment of New Research and Theory* (Boulder, Rowman & Littlefield Publishers, 2003), particularly table 9.1, p. 187.

[xvi] Philip McMichael, *Development and Social Change. A Global Perspective* (Thousands Oaks: Pine Forge Press, 1996), p. 241-242.

[xvii] Phiplipp McMichael, *op. cit.*, p. 132.

[xviii] Anthony Giddens, *Beyond Left and Right: The Future of Radical Politics* (Cambridge, UK: Polity Press, 1994).

[xix] Immanuel Wallerstein, "Globalization or the Age of Transition? A Long-Term View of the Trajectory of the World-System" (Fernand Braudel Center, 1999, http://fbc.binghamton.edu/iwtrajws.htm). In this text, Wallerstein assume a violently critical position regarding the globalisation rhetoric: "This discourse is in fact a gigantic misreading of current reality – a deception imposed upon us by powerful groups, and even worse one that we have imposed upon ourselves, often despairingly. It is a discourse that leads us to ignore the real issues before us, and to misunderstand the historical crisis within which we find ourselves. We do indeed stand at a moment a transformation. But this is not that of an already established newly globalized world with clear rules. Rather we are located is an age of transition, transition not

merely of a few backward countries who need to catch up with the spirit of globalization, but a transition in which the entire capitalist world-system will be transformed into something else. The future, far from being inevitable and one to which there is no alternative, is being determinate in this transition that has an extremely uncertain outcome". Though I have taken into account Wallerstein's criticism, in this chapter I have used the concept of globalisation, or, rather, globalisations in the sense proposed by Boaventura de Sousa Santos that we live in a *transitional time*, which he calls *late world system*: "The late world system is formed by three constellations of collective practices: the constellation of interstate practices, the constellation of global capitalist practices and the constellation of transnational social and cultural practices" (Boaventura de Sousa Santos, "Processos de Globalização", in *Globalização: Fatalidade ou Utopia?*. Oporto: Afrontamento, 2001), p. 63.

[xx] Roger Dale (1999), Specifying globalisation effects on national policy: a focus on mechanisms?. *Journal of Educational Policy, 14, (1)*, 1-17.

[xxi] Very interesting the distinction made by Roger Dale between globalisation and *imperialism* or *colonialism*: "This may be an appropriate juncture at which to raise the issue of the difference between globalisation and 'imperialism' or 'colonialism', since it is quite plausible to suggest that the difference between globalisation and imperialism/colonialism is that what once happened only to third world or colonised countries is now happening to the most powerful states, previously the initiators rather than the recipients of external pressures on their national policies" (*Op. cit.*, p. 8).

[xxii] The concept is Roger Dale's (Globalização e Educação: Demonstrando a existência de uma "Cultura Educacional Mundial Comum" ou localizando uma "Agenda Globalmente Estruturada para a Educação"?, *Educação, Sociedade & Culturas, 16*, 2001, pp. 133-169).

[xxiii] Indicators of Educational Systems.

[xxiv] Cf. N. Bottani and H. J. Walberg, À quoi servent les indicateurs internationaux de l'enseignement? In CERI, *L'OCDE et les indicateurs internacionaux de l'enseignement. Un cadre* d'analyse (Paris: OECD/OCDE, 1992), p. 7-13.

[xxv] See, e.g., the two areas privileged by the OECD at the end of the 1990s: assessment of school functioning and external evaluation of learning.

[xxvi] Centre for Educational Research and Innovation [CERI] (1996), *Regards sur l'Éducation. Les indicateurs de l'OCDE*. Paris: OCDE, p. 10.

[xxvii] Idem, *ibidem*, p. 11.

[xxviii] Let it be stressed that this statement only refers to central countries, or those located in central areas. In Third-World countries, as Joel Samoff points out, there exists a true *institutionalisation of international influence* in the most public of public policies, education: "Their mass is truly astounding - thousands of pages, many of them tables, figures, and charts. These externally initiated studies of education in Africa undertaken during the early 1990s are most striking for their similarities, their diversity - of country, of commissioning agency, of specific subject - notwithstanding. With few exceptions, these studies have a common framework, a common approach, and a common methodology. Given their shared starting points, their common findings are not surprising. African education is in crisis. Governments cannot cope. Quality has deteriorated. Funds are misallocated. Management is poor and administration is inefficient. From predominantly Islamic Mauritania in the western Sahara to the mixed cultural, colonial, and political heritage of Mauritius in the Indian Ocean, the recommendations too are similar: Reduce the central government role in providing education. Decentralize. Increase school fees. Expand private schooling. Reduce direct support to students, especially at the tertiary level. Introduce double shifts and multigrade classrooms. Assign high priority to instructional materials. Favor in-service over pre-service teacher education. The shared approach of these studies reflects a medical metaphor. Expatriate-led study teams as visiting clinicians diagnose and then prescribe. The patient (i.e., the country) must be encouraged, perhaps pressured, to swallow the bitter medicine" (*Op. cit.*, p. 51).

[xxix] Boaventura de Sousa Santos, "Os Processos da Globalização" (*op. cit.*, p. 93).

[xxx] See, e.g., Boaventura de Sousa Santos, *Toward a New Common Sense. Law, Science and Politics in the Paradigmatic Transition* (London & New York: Routledge, 1995); and Por uma Concepção Multicultural dos Direitos Humanos (*Revista Crítica de Ciências Sociais, 48*, 1997, 11-32).

[xxxi] Boaventura de Sousa Santos (1997), Por uma Concepção Multicultural dos Direitos Humanos, *Revista Crítica de Ciências Sociais, 48*, p. 15.

xxxii Being another recent event and constituting an important turning point in the understanding of the United Nations' role in the new world order, it would be interesting to conduct a similar case study on the struggle of East Timorese people and the process leading to international recognition of their right to self-determination and independence.

xxxiii Ph. McMichael, *Development and Social Change.*, p. 256-257.

xxxiv Boaventura de Sousa Santos, *Reinventar a Democracia* (Lisbon: Gradiva/Fundação Mário Soares), p. 46.

xxxv Alain Touraine, "Nous entrons dans une civilisation du travail", Comunicação apresentada ao XIV Congresso Mundial de Sociologia, Montréal, 26 Julho - 1 Agosto 1998. [first version, not revised by the author].

xxxvi Boaventura de Sousa Santos, *Reinventar a Democracia*, p. 66.

xxxvii Idem, *ibidem*, p. 67.

xxxviii Jürgen Habermas, *Droit et démocratie. Entre faits et normes* (Paris: Gallimard, 1997), p. 479.

xxxix This concept of enzyme is developed in: Grupo de Lisboa, *Limites à Competição* (Lisbon: Europa-América, 1994).

xl Raymond Allen Morrow and Carlos Alberto Torres, "Jürgen Habermas, Paulo Freire e a Pedagogia Crítica: Novas orientações para a Educação Comparada" (*Educação, Sociedade & Culturas*, n.º 10, 1998), p. 129.

xli The concept of *structural place* was developed by Boaventura de Sousa Santos in *Toward a New Common Sense*: "At the most abstract level, a mode of production of social practice is a set of social relations whose internal contradictions endow it with a specific endogenous dynamic" (*op. cit.*, p. 420).

xlii Paulo Freire, *Política e Educação* (S. Paulo: Cortez), p. 36.

PAULO BLIKSTEIN

TRAVELS IN TROY WITH FREIRE

Technology as an Agent of Emancipation

INTRODUCTION[i]

Oswald de Andrade, in his "Anthropophagic Manifest" of 1928, proclaims that the Brazilian calendar should have been counted from the day in which, accordingly to the legend, anthropophagic natives ate the Sardinha bishop, whose Portuguese vessel was shipwrecked somewhere along the Brazilian coast. Andrade's manifesto, a landmark in Latin American modern literature, expresses poetically what has become a key characteristic of Brazil: cultural and intellectual anthropophagy – the process of appropriation, restructuration, and creative recombination of ideas, theories, products, and processes.

Paulo Freire was a remarkable instance of such anthropophagy. Bringing together existentialism, phenomenology, Marxist and Christian thought, critical pedagogy, and his own experience as educator, he generated a unique body of thought for its radicalism, humanism, literary style and depth.

Trying to understand Freire without comprehending his personal quest is, to say the least, incomplete. It is crucial to understand why Freire struggled so fervently against oppression and advocated emancipation. A visit to the poorer regions of the Northeast of Brazil, where he spent his youth and early career, would probably suffice: the abysmal life conditions and the extraordinarily unfair social structure of such regions are self-explanatory. Indeed, Freire's autobiographical books and essays (Freire, 2001; Freire & Macedo, 1996) reveal a man deeply traumatized by poverty, dehumanization, oppression, and economic exploitation.

Therefore, Freire's language and ideas present so radical a challenge for extant educational systems, that he is more often than not categorized as a utopian. But such an interpretation, by labelling Freirean pedagogy as an impossible dream, only perpetuates the very ills against which Freire was fighting. In fact, from his trenches, Freire was, above all, a man of praxis. His theory was not created in the traditional academic setting as an ivory-tower theoretical exercise, but conceived to change education in real settings. His work with adults at the University of Recife, SESI, Angicos, and numerous other locations and countries resulted in detailed roadmaps for adult educators to implement Freirean learning experiences.

Yet, whereas Freire was driven to impact the real-world, he never denied that "it is one thing to write down concepts in books, but it is another to embody them in praxis" (Freire, 1990). His words ring as true today as they did when he first attempted to put into action his radical educational vision. "Dialogical education" and situating learning within students' lived experience have been vastly influential, but the implementation of these ideas has never been unchallenging (Freire, 1973, 1974, 1992). These difficulties of embodying Paulo Freire in everyday school has led numerous teachers and researchers to categorize him as the proponent of the ideal school which, although desirable, is ultimately unrealizable.

And yet, we submit, the Freirean dream could become a reality. The objective of this chapter is both to demonstrate a "proof of existence" that realizing the Freirean vision is possible even within the underprivileged settings that he was targeting and to reflect on some design principles that may be conducive to realizing his vision. This chapter is a reflection on the implementation of Freire-inspired frameworks, its obstacles and leverage points. I particularly focus on the role of technology in such initiatives, as an emancipatory tool for mobilizing change in schools and empowering students. I posit that the rapid penetration of computers into learning environments constitute an unprecedented opportunity to advance and disseminate a Freirean aesthetic (paraphrasing Valente, 1993) in schools. Digital technologies, such as computers, robotics, digital video, and digital photography, could play a central role in this process: they are protean machines (Papert, 1980) that enable diverse and innovative ways of working, expressing, and building. This chameleonesque adaptivity of computational media, I argue, enables the acknowledgement and embracing of epistemological diversity (Abrahamson, Berland, Shapiro, Unterman, & Wilensky, 2006; Turkle, 1991), engendering an environment in which students, finding their own voice, can concretize their ideas and projects with motivation and engagement.

Emerging from the educational interventions we discuss in this chapter is a design framework for implementing Freirean learning environments. Key to this framework are the following components. First, we identify a community-relevant generative theme. Second, we depart from the community's technological culture and expertise as a basis for introducing new technologies. Third, we deliberately use a mixed-media approach, in which high- and low-tech, on- and off-screen, and high- and low-cost expressive tools coexist for students' production of artifacts. Lastly, we question (or "displace") taken-for-granted school practices and mindsets, even those that are apparently irrelevant to teaching and learning.

I demonstrate this framework with data from a project conducted in 2001 at a public school in São Paulo, located in a low-income community. Focusing on participants' attitudes and usage of digital technologies, I track and analyze their intellectual and emotional engagement, learning trajectories, and the complexity of their projects, which ranged from computer-controlled robots to fiction movies. I conclude that such use of expressive technologies could be a powerful agent of emancipation, à la Paulo Freire, even, and perhaps especially, in economically underserved communities.

FREIRE'S GENERATIVE THEMES

Generative themes constitute perhaps the best-known of Freire's constructs. In The Pedagogy of the Oppressed (1974) and in Teachers as Cultural Workers (1998), Freire explains in detail his method for coding/decoding elements of local cultures toward creating generative themes together with members of these cultures. Two of his key concepts are 'humanization' and concientização (critical consciousness), both of which stress the dichotomy between being immersed in one's reality (only being aware of your own needs) and emerging from this reality (being active in fulfilling those needs). He asserts that learners can go from the "consciousness of the real" to the "consciousness of the possible" as they perceive the "viable new alternatives" beyond the "limiting-situations" (Freire, 1974). In other words, one path to emancipation and humanization[ii] is to perceive oneself as an active agent of change, and the world as a mutable entity – in Freire's poetic prose, "History is the time of possibility and not of determinism [...] The future is not inexorable, the future is problematic." (Freire, 1992, p. 21).

Despite Freire's precision about the genesis and role of his generative themes, multiple interpretations abound. Originally, the themes were cultural or political topics of great concern or importance to learners, which were used in the context of his first experiences in adult education. They served the purpose of generating meaningful discussion amongst learners and educators, as well as identifying generative words. Nevertheless, not infrequently one would find printed textbooks with themes and guides for the teachers to conduct discussions. To propose a theme that purports to address a yet-to-be-determined community's problem trivializes and contradicts the dialogic character of the educational enterprise – it negates the Freirean call to enable a community to participate in taking control over their indigenous needs; It raises the educator to the realm of patron when s/he should be no more than a facilitator of emergent emancipation.

It seems, then, as though disseminating the Freirean vision of 'generative themes' faces the apparent paradox of dictating that which should be negotiated. Indeed, Samuel Perez Garcia warns about the danger of having the generative themes in the agenda of the intellectuals rather than emerging from the learners (García, 2001). Freire himself struggled to maintain the authenticity of the generative themes, in his early projects in Rio Grande do Norte. Freire eventually confronted this form of trivialization of his work by standing up against its manipulation, as Heinz-Peter Gerhardt reports:

> The authors of the textbook [...] chose a political direction with five generative words: people, vote, life, health and bread. Freire opposed himself firmly to teaching ready-made messages for the illiterate. Ready-made messages would produce domesticative effects, either coming from the left or right-wing. Both sides would accept doctrines without criticism, and manipulation would then take place." (Gerhardt, 2000)

It might not be surprising that practitioners have tried to fit Freire's method into known practices, such as the top-down decision of what students should learn (see also Tyack & Cuban (1995) on how schools "change the change before change changes the school"). Yet Freire proposed a far more radical approach, which could only be fully accomplished in immersive contact with the community and the learners. Yet such practice introduces a revolutionary transformation as to who decides what will be learned, as well as who has the authority to sanction such choice.

Note, however, that Freire never proposed that the researcher should refrain from contributing with his/her own themes and ideas (the connecting themes, or temas da dobradiça), but made it clear that the proposition should emerge within a specific context, and embrace themes already identified by the learners as meaningful. Ana Maria de Araújo Freire further confirms the importance of learners' sense of ownership:

> When men and women perceive themselves as makers of culture, we can declare [as] taken […] the first step for them to feel the importance, the need and the possibility to learn reading and writing. They are already literate, politically speaking. (A. M. Freire, 1995)

To be actively engaged in reading and changing the world, one ought to have the necessary tools. The power of language is self-evident: it enables us to voice the problems around us, discuss solutions, interact, debate, and, hopefully, change. One level of perception of viable new alternatives is, thus, through language, reading, writing, discussing. Yet language, a focus of most Freirean projects, is not necessarily the only vehicle of change. Another means is for individuals to design devices, systems, or solutions, using knowledge from science and technology, and then use language to improve these devices through critical interaction with fellow designers. This Vygotskiian notion of learning through communicating as applied to the case of designing personally-meaningful devices has been articulated by another luminary of progressive education: Seymour Papert.

FREIRE MEETS PAPERT

Seymour Papert shares with Paulo Freire an enthusiasm for unleashing the latent learning potential of students by providing environments in which their passions and interests thrive. A mathematician by training, who then worked with Jean Piaget for many years and co-founded the MIT Artificial Intelligence Lab, Papert pioneered the use of digital technologies in education and created the best known computer language for children, LOGO (Papert, 1980). Yet Papert's reasons for advocating the use of computers in education are, perhaps, not what one might expect of a mathematician working at an institution most often associated with achievements in science, technology, and engineering. Far from being technocentric (Papert, 1985), some of his motivations are very similar to Freire's. Papert's theory, Constructionism, builds upon Piaget's Constructivism and claims that the construction of knowledge happens remarkably well when students build and publicly share objects. In Papert's own words,

> "Construction that takes place 'in the head' often happens especially felicitously when it is supported by construction of a more public sort "in the world" – a sand castle or a cake, a Lego house or a corporation, a computer program, a poem, or a theory of the universe. Part of what I mean by 'in the world' is that the product can be shown, discussed, examined, probed, and admired. […] It attaches special importance to the role of constructions in the

world as a support for those in the head, thereby becoming less of a purely mentalist doctrine." (1993, p.142)

Papert advocates technology in schools not as a way to optimize traditional education, but, rather, as an emancipatory set of tools that would put the most powerful construction materials in the hands of children. These protean machines would enable students to design, engineer, and construct, and would cater to a variety of forms of working, expressing, and building. This chameleonesque adaptivity which technology embeds permits the acknowledgement and embracing of different learning styles and epistemologies, engendering a convivial environment in which students can concretize their ideas and projects with intense personal engagement. In a typical Constructionist learning environment, there is rarely a fixed curriculum. Children use technology to build projects, and teachers act as facilitators of the process.

Nevertheless, the Papertian promise of technology has yet to penetrate the educational mainstream. For the most part, schools have adopted computers as tools to empower extant curricular subtexts – i.e., as information devices or teaching machines. But as Freire repeatedly claimed, choosing a curriculum is an intrinsically political act – his analysis of popular literacy booklets revealed how, by means of choice of words, they contained a hidden curriculum of internalizing oppression, making economic exploitation a fact of nature, claiming political participation undesirable, and ignoring the local culture, context, and knowledge (Freire, 1974, 1992).

Similarly, the traditional use of technology in schools contains its own hidden curriculum. It surreptitiously fosters students who are consumers of software and not constructors; adapt to the machine and not reinvent it; and accept the computer as a black box which only specialists can understand, program, or repair. For the most part, these passive uses of technologies include unidirectional access to information (the computer as an electronic library), communicate with other people (the computer as a telephone), and propagate information to others (the computer as a blackboard or newspaper). Not surprisingly, therefore, the new digital technologies are commonly called ICT (Information and Communication Technologies). In sum, a Papertian-cum-Freirean perspective – injecting into a critique of education a subversive political agenda – might position computers, for the most, as commonly recruited by 'the system' to inculcate in future consumers the learned passivity that supports capitalism by perpetuating its inherent iniquities. Yet, the most revolutionary aspect of the computer, at least from a Constructionist perspective (Papert, 1991), is not to use it as an information machine, but as a universal construction environment.

The LOGO programming language was the first attempt in education to demonstrate that the computer is not only an information and communication device, but also an expressive tool for construction and self expression. In the early nineties, Papert's and his disciples at the MIT Media Laboratory extended the powerful ideas of Logo to the physical world by making robotics accessible to children through the Lego Mindstorms kit and the Cricket (Martin, 1993; Resnick, 1991). In the nineties, parallel multi-agent simulation, then only available in advanced research labs, was also made available for young learners (Wilensky & Resnick, 1995, 1999). More recently, new developments are also being made in putting cutting-edge hardware and software in the hands of children to conduct advanced scientific explorations (Blikstein & Wilensky, 2006), create electronic jewellery (Sylvan, 2005), design participatory simulations and games (Wilensky & Stroup, 1999), program videogames (Millner & Resnick, 2005; Sipitakiat, Blikstein, & Cavallo, 2004), create interactive textiles (Buechley, 2006), program virtual robotic systems (Berland & Wilensky, 2006) and explore Environmental Science and Geographical Information Systems (Edelson, 2000).

Therefore, even though at first blush critical pedagogy might appear at odds with technology, what with technology's "imperialistic" connotations, a closer analysis reveals that a Constructionist use of technology is essentially compatible with Freire's emancipation and even Ivan Illich's ferocious criticism (Illich, 1971).

Indeed, Cavallo's pioneering (Cavallo, 2000a) work in rural Thailand attempted to demonstrate this compatibility, suggesting the benefits of conflating indigenous knowledge, innovative learning formulations and digital technologies. Even in remote and neglected regions, he detected a sophisticated culture of building and repurposing internal-combustion engines for use in agriculture, boats, and transportation, which contradicted the widespread assumption that such populations lacked the necessary cognitive foundations to learn about or use modern technologies. Cavallo conducted workshops in which participants were invited to design solutions for salient community problems using digital technologies. His results

> [demonstrate] a significant gain in accomplishment among a population that had not previously exhibited such competence in educational institutions. This work demonstrates how to build on and enhance local knowledge [and] liberate their local knowledge from its specific situated embodiment […] The key point here is that the constructionist use of computational technology leveraged this ability and helped people apply their knowledge to new and varied situations […] The knowledge did not remain limited to the particular technology such as combustion engines, but rather they could use the malleable computer technology as a tool for understanding other domains. (Cavallo, 2000a, p. 780)

Other theorists have also been advancing the discussion about the prospects of indigenous (or local) knowledge (Ladson-Billings, 1995; Lee, 2003; Moll, Amanti, Neff, & González, 1992). If Freire and his disciples are correct, schools should value that kind of knowledge instead of the official curriculum, as a way to simultaneously tap into students' existing representations and make the content relevant to their lives. Yet some degree of knowledge of modern science and technology is important for emancipation. Fortunately, theorists such as Raymond Morrow (this volume) are working on reconciling such contradictory directions into a promising framework (cultural hybridity):

210

"[…] modern science and technology […] remains the necessary authoritative reference point [...] [but] rather than still being tied to a monolithic Cartesian-Newtonian epistemological perspective, academic disciplines have increasingly developed a more plural, inclusive, and contextual understanding of knowledge, one that creates the basis for the kind of authentic dialogue with indigenous knowledge envisioned by Freire. (Morrow, 2005)

The intersection between Freire and Papert, thus, constitutes a fertile and promising ground for research and implementation of innovative learning environments (Cavallo, 2000b). Freire's focus on humanism and Papert's emphasis on the creation of personally meaningful artifacts are highly complementary. I conjecture that constructive, expressive technology makes it possible to further Freire's agenda of emancipation, perhaps as powerfully as with language and literacy. In the next section, I will present case studies of implementations of such environments.

CASE STUDIES

When Fernando José de Almeida, a well-known Brazilian educator, was appointed as Secretary of Education of São Paulo in 2000, hopes for innovation across the school system were high. I was then a graduate student at the Future of Learning group at the MIT Media Laboratory, and we identified an excellent opportunity to collaborate and revisit some of the successful strategies used when Paulo Freire himself was Secretary of Education.

On August 2001, after many months of dialogue, we were set to have a proof-of-concept three-week after-school workshop in the Campos Salles school in Heliópolis, the biggest shantytown in São Paulo. The goal was to show what could be accomplished in a typical public school using technology in a Freirean/Constructionist fashion. The results of this workshop were very positive and enable the conception of a larger project with the Secretary of Education, which encompassed as many as 30 schools throughout São Paulo (Cavallo et al., 2004)[iii]. These subsequent workshops were typically conducted as after-school activities, yet a number of them have ended up as part of regular school work.

This section, which describes the Heliópolis workshop, is structured as a running narrative that follows the succession of implementations, and this narrative is parsed into meaningful episodes, each presenting a design dilemma and each illustrating an emergent design principle. Within this rich narrative hide the details of a design that appeared to work. This is a design that in principle cannot be easily summarized – the very nature of the design is in attention to emergence. These principles will be further discussed in the Discussion section.

THE HELIÓPOLIS WORKSHOP

The Heliópolis workshop was conducted so as to demonstrate what might be accomplished by students with technology in a Freirean-inspired environment. The vision was for students to build projects of their choice, using a wide range of media and technologies: computers, robotics, still pictures, video, and arts materials. In the Freirean spirit, we were to begin by identifying with our participants generative themes that would actuate, motivate, and sustain the project work.

Figure 1 – Two views of the Heliópolis shantytown

In 2001, due to rain shortage and lack of infrastructure investment, Brazil experienced a massive crisis in the electric energy system. Once blackouts became common, the government issued a new law mandating households to save 20% of their energy bill. The everyday life of most Brazilians was deeply altered by the law, and the population was resorting to all sorts of creative solutions to save energy. The crisis, being an everyday concern for all the population, appeared to be a good generative theme for this workshop. I was satisfied that by having identified a theme that was important locally (the energy crisis), students would work on projects close to their reality and interests. I did research on the topic and generated a set of possible ideas, such as building galvanometers, timer devices, waters heaters, energy generators, and robots to control lights. I also wanted to work with our participants on modeling and understanding the energy consumption of a household, trying to identify the critical devices, their energy requirements, and engineering alternative, more energy-efficient devices. Our resources were 13 days of work, Lego robotics kits, sensors, motors, solar panels, video cameras, digital cameras, and arts materials.

On the first day of the workshop, however, everything turned upside-down.

As we met for the first time and I started explaining the theme, I noticed some puzzled faces. Finally, one of participants interrupted me and politely said that the majority of the households in Heliópolis had illegal energy connections (gatos, in Portuguese), and therefore neither energy meters nor bills. It did not make any sense for them to save 20% of energy if they did not even had a meter. My generative theme floundered, but the student went on: with the energy crisis, the utility company became more rigorous with the electricity payments, disconnecting many legally connected households, which could not afford the energy bill anymore. Desperate, they would get themselves an illegal connection. The transformers, being designed to handle the legal number of connected households, were then much more likely to malfunction – causing disastrous fires or power outages. Therefore, the energy crisis for most families was a matter not of saving energy, but of safety and survival. My expectations were thus demolished and with them the grandiose energy-saving projects I had anticipated. Fortunately a whole new range of ideas opened up for the group.

Energy was, indeed, relevant for the students, but in a different way: Students were concerned with safety, but aware that families simply did not have the means to pay the energy bill in case they were to be suddenly made legal. One group, then, set up to create a newspaper and a video-documentary raising awareness about the danger of illegal connections. Their main goal was to teach the population how to make safe, yet illegal, energy connections.

Figure 2 – Students' documentation of the dangerous illegal energy connections, which they hoped to transform through an educational panphlet to teach the population to make safe illegal connections.

This experience underscores the meaning of negotiating in real time and in locus for truly authentic generative themes – such that could not have originated in any textbook; themes that are time- and people-specific. Within the same city, in neighborhoods only a few kilometers away, the consequences of the energy crisis were radically different. Moreover, many of the project-based initiatives I observed in schools across Brazil had themes chosen in advance by teachers who often lived in other parts of town and came from a different socio-economic stratus. Similarly, text books claiming to include useful generative themes are often authored by curriculum designers completely removed from the contexts in which these themes are to be employed. As a result, many project-based teaching interventions enforce upon learners activities that are irrelevant to their interests and culture.

WHO CONTROLS THE EQUIPMENT?

On the first days of the workshop, students acquainted themselves with the new resources and planned their projects. All the students were initially enthralled by the Lego parts, digital cameras, and video cameras. Most students had never touched such equipment, and so I anticipated that the students would find this access to the equipment highly appealing. I was, again, wrong. Even though students seemed excited, some were afraid to use the equipment, and these anxieties were only further stoked by some teachers.

There were historical reasons for such behavior. Access to computers in schools is often regarded as an administrative issue, addressed with strict usage rules and constant supervision. The high cost of the equipment and maintenance (especially in developing countries) amplifies the concern of damaging these machines. As I would later confirm during my fieldwork, in many schools the computer room was even more regimented than regular classrooms. Signs on the walls, firm rules and multiple locks on the doors were just some of the manifestations of it. In some computer labs, students had even to sit on their hands during the initial explanation of the activity, not only for (questionable) reasons of classroom management.

I was not aware of that scenario when the workshop started. My experience in previous workshops taught me that, in such situations, children are overcautious with equipment even without vigilance, and I was willing to take the risk of allowing a completely free access to every tool we had. Therefore, Lego parts, arts materials, electronics materials and my own notebook computer were scattered all over the floor. Two cameras were freely available for students to take pictures or record video. There was no sign-up sheet or strict rules. At first, teachers were very concerned with the system. One of them told me that "We should not leave the equipment loose in the hands of the students [...] they will mess it up, we should have a scheduling mechanism to organize this". Students were also concerned. Before touching any piece of equipment, they would ask about its price. Despite being in awe of all the new artifacts, their concern was clearly associated to the perceptible high cost of the materials. They mentioned, for instance, that their parents would have to work for months to replace a robotics kit or a video camera. Despite the pressure of teachers, I did not implement any controlling mechanism. After a few days, my expectations were confirmed, but teachers were surprised: not only did students self-organize peacefully to share the cameras among the different groups, but also by the end of the workshop nothing was damaged.

During the wrap-up interviews with the participants, I asked students to list their three favorite aspects of the workshop. The results revealed an astonishing figure: 70% mentioned "trust" as their first choice. I followed up by asking students to interpret this finding; the students explained that they felt trusted by me because I let them freely use the equipment, especially my personal notebook which I left on the floor (see Figure 3).

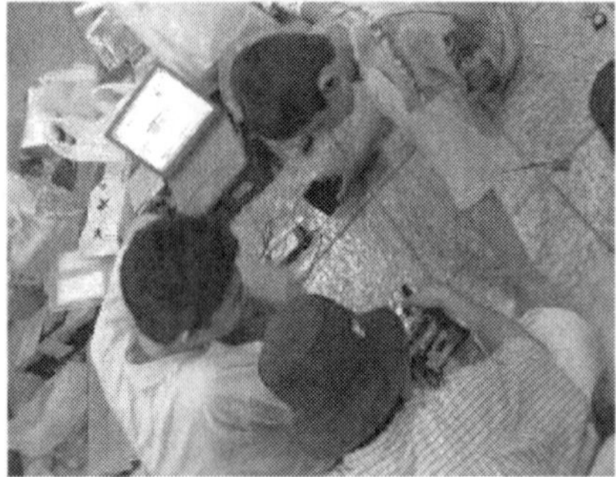

Figure 3 – Students using the facilitator's notebook computer (left), and building on the computer room floor

An apparently expensive computer lying on the floor, available for all to use, turned out to be a meaningful demonstration of trust and, thus, a source of empowerment. The freedom to use the equipment, and in particular the unintentional placement of my notebook on the floor constituted a fundamental displacement from the traditional learning scheme. It was also an example of how an external intervention can both reveal and challenge behaviors taken for granted within a culture. Such a design decision (how to manage access to equipment), which appears to be a minor detail within all the considerations of a teacher or school administrator, turned out to have a major impact on students' affect toward the activity. For an attentive reader of Freire or Foucault (Foucault, 1977), this should not come as a surprise: the manifestations of oppression and power are not necessarily overt. Similarly, manifestations of trust are not always explicit. The unrestricted access to equipment was a design decision, but placing my computer on the floor was a mere accident. While I did not anticipate students to attribute so much importance to that fact, this event is illuminating. There was, after all, a power divide. Used to the rigid computer room rules, children perceived the computer on the floor a message of trust. Repeatedly, as I observed, they had dealt with teachers and administrators who kept Freire only at the discourse level, keeping the praxis very traditional. Dialogical education, requiring the establishment of a true conversation between learner and teacher, cannot survive if discourse and practice are not compatible to the eyes of children.

BUILDING UPON FAMILIAR PRACTICES

Control was not the only issue relevant to the equipment. Students and teachers were very concerned with the equipment's monetary value. The students became uneasy once they learned that the robotics kits were equivalent to one or two months' worth of their families' income, and teachers were shocked to realize that the kit was worth their entire monthly salary. I realized that in such underserved localities, technology is a foreign and rare artifact - an extravagancy consumed by the upper classes. With an average monthly income of just a few hundred dollars, households in Heliopólis did not have computers or sophisticated electronic equipment. In addition, many of the students' parents had lost their jobs to technology. Children were seduced to play with the Lego but were afraid to break it or become attached to objects that would soon be whisked back out of their reach. This sense of foreignness was a barrier for students' engagement. How does one go about introducing technologies in such a challenging context?

While I was still wondering how I might demystify the foreignness of technology and engage students in its exploration, a surprising development took place. While some groups stayed at school working on Lego or making photo-novels, another group started to make a documentary about the illegal energy connections. As a result, we often left the school precincts and went to the community; I visited their houses, small stores, snack places, car repair garages, and the community radio station. By talking and interviewing people, I started to understand that the technological culture in that community had a very particular character. Car mechanics would use all sorts of improvised solutions to keep cars running at a minimum cost. In their homes, people would never discard a broken appliance without trying to fix it in all possible ways. If fixing was impossible, they would repurpose the broken device in creative ways. The community radio station, also, was put together with equipment from different sources, many of which were broken or incompatible and had to be fixed.

In the same sense that David Cavallo identified an "engine culture" in rural Thailand (Cavallo, 2000b), I identified in Heliópolis a repurposing culture. Cavallo's emergent design methodology, which draws heavily on Freire's theory, identifies how indigenous knowledge can be utilized to design technology-enabled learning environments that benefit from familiar practices. Cavallo states that:

> Rather than being deficient, there is tremendous knowledge, experience and expertise indigenous to Thai culture that provides a firm base upon which to build and leverage new knowledge. We believe this to be universal and not merely limited to Thailand (Cavallo, 2000b, p. 201)

Indeed, one of Brazil's most-known cultural practices is the so-called jeitinho brasileiro ("the Brazilian way out"), a practice of creatively solving problems using what is at hand, improvising ideas, instead of waiting for the ideal or formal solution. This implies repurposing, de-, and re-construction of objects as well as customary utilization of recycled and found materials. The repurposing culture was not found exclusively at Heliópolis – nevertheless, due to the harsh economic situation, it was especially apparent there.

The repurposing culture, thus, suggested an appropriate way for introducing technologies to the students. Freire repeatedly warned against romanticized or paternalistic approaches to the local culture, by which the learners are unchallengeable beaux salvages.

> The educator should be immersed in the historic and concrete experience of the students, but never in a paternalistic way by which he starts to speak for them more than truly listening to them. [...] maintaining the oppressed chained to the conditions that were romanticized so that the educator keeps being necessary [...] [or] a romantic hero" (Freire, 1974, p. 59).

Rather than erring, thus, in my role as an educator, I sought ways to mobilize the community's cognitive evolution – to be an agent of change, a catalyst. The challenge of introducing technology as an agent of change for an underserved population was now honed as the challenge of grafting the technology onto the indigenous context of repurposing. The perfect opportunity to use the local repurposing expertise materialized when one of the groups needed one extra Lego motor, yet all the motors were being used in others projects. On the following day, I brought a broken tape recorder to the school and proposed to disassemble it for parts. The group quickly armed itself with screwdrivers and pliers and soon had a perfectly operational motor to use in the project. In addition, they had to build an adapter to make the salvaged motor work with the Lego gears (see Figure 4, right), so, in fact, the task ended up being even more complex than it would have been just using ready-made materials.

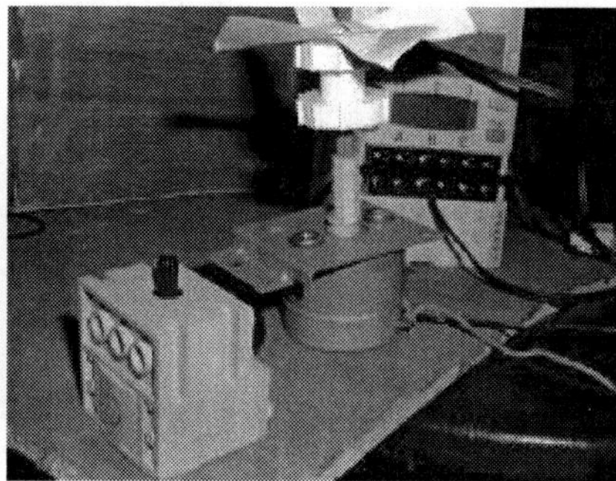

Figure 4 - A student disassembles the tape recorder (left), the expensive Lego motor, and the motor salvaged from the tape recorder (right)

The idea spread quickly, and soon other students were using found materials to build their projects. By the end of our two weeks in Heliópolis, most students had switched to using found/broken electronics materials instead of Lego pieces to build their projects – they appeared more proud assembling project from parts they found by themselves than from ready-made Lego blocks. Indeed, using found materials was more complex a task than using the Lego parts, because the latter were designed to fit perfectly, whereas the former required ingenuity. This practice, thus, enabled students to apply a familiar way of working (the Brazilian jeitinho, the tinkering/repurposing culture) to demystify technology – technology was no longer an expensive foreign tool. In addition, by disassembling electronic devices, students could see inside those previously inscrutable machines, understand how they work, and get exemplars of mechanisms for their own projects, 'glassboxing' the technology behind those devices.

The repurposing-based pedagogical approach to the use of technology was so successful that, for all subsequent workshops, we abandoned Lego altogether as construction material. Participants were invited to bring and disassemble broken and found equipment and materials (sucata, in Portuguese), and integrate them into their projects. Moreover, I provided cheap, customized kits of locally purchased/found electronic and mechanical construction components, and Arnan Sipitakiat developed an open-source robotics interface board, the GoGo Board, which students themselves could assemble (Sipitakiat et al., 2004).

Figure 5 – In later workshops, Lego and commercial materials were abandoned and we used only found/recycled material: Teachers disassembling broken electronics for parts (top left), students scavenging a broken computer monitor (top right), teachers showing "sucata" they are about to dive into (bottom left), and a student solders his own robotics board, the GoGo board, under adult supervision for safety purposes (bottom right)

Introducing found materials was another example of displacement: we departed from familiar ways of working (using and repurposing found materials) but added new elements (robotics, motors, sensors, and computers) significant enough to make people work in new ways, appropriating a new set of tools within their existing practices. In particular, computer technology was a valued technology, inside and outside Heliópolis. Their local practice of repurposing materials, although technically quite sophisticated, was not valued outside their community, being often regarded as a custom of underprivileged populations. By introducing computational technologies based on that existing repurposing culture, not only participants were empowered by the realization that one of their everyday practices was indeed sophisticated and technological, but made their projects, artifacts, and newly learned skills valued by the outside world.

A MICRO-EMERGENT APPROACH

Initially, some students, and especially the girls, were not excited by robotics or computers. Indeed, the relatively lower engagement of girls in technology-related school activities is a common research topic (A. M. Cavallo, 2003; Turkle, 1991). As a facilitator, the girls' reluctance presented me with a dilemma. On one hand, I wanted all students to enjoy a novel learning experience. On the other hand, forcing these reluctant students would violate a crucial principle of the workshop: not forcing upon students a 'technology curriculum', allowing them to choose their own projects and tools.

Freire and Freirean educators faced this dilemma in many occasions. He critiqued the demagogic teacher who renounces his/her role as educator (Freire, 1987) and also the portrayal of learning as a purely entertaining activity, in which students can never feel challenged or frustrated:

> It is important that the child realize, from the beginning, that studying is difficult and demanding, but is pleasant from the beginning. Certain new pedagogies exacerbate the fun, the affectiveness, at the expense of cognition. (Freire, 1993, pp. 89-90)

Rather than elucidating the dilemma, the above quote restates it: how can learning be "pleasant from the beginning" and "difficult and demanding" at the same time? This is, perhaps, the crucial paradox of most Freirean or democratic pedagogies. Between the 'anything-goes' classroom and the traditional scheme, could there be an academically productive and politically legitimate compromise? Richard Gibson notes that

> Freire is only infrequently precise in his theoretical writings about just what it is that a liberating educator is--other than one who offers freedom and rigor-- toward what end? Indeed, his obscurity is frequently noted. [...] Actually, Freire is quite directive. He refers to an 'inductive moment' when 'the liberating educator cannot wait for the students to initiate their own forward progress into an idea or understanding, and the teacher must do it'. (Gibson, 1994)

This dilemma extends well beyond Freire. José Cukier has extensively studied the psychopathologies originating from school (Cukier, 1996), and warns against the demagogical and charismatic educator, who focuses only on the affective link with the students, through seduction, neglecting the educational goal and the content. Paul Zoch argues against the overburdening of teachers for preparing personalized learning experiences, while students "[are] not expected to overcome situations not of [their] liking" (Zoch, 2004, p. 71). Cavallo (2002) reminds that the over-charismatic teacher undermines the autonomy of the learner, as learning becomes associated with being taught by the charismatic as opposed to something that the learner does and controls. Fernando Almeida (2001) describes how school fosters 'split-personalities' in students, by having them learn to assume different personalities all along the day, from the obedient to the outspoken, from the quiet to the participative. Between the two extremes, the traditional authoritarian teacher and the charismatic leader, would there be space for less pathological transactions? Far from providing a definite answer to this question, the multiplicity of expressive tools is an invaluable aide for the educator to find that space. The story of Marisa and Gina[iv], two 6th graders participating in the workshop, is illuminating. They were not excited about robotics, but were very fond of the arts. They wanted to spend the workshop painting, benefiting from the uncommon availability of materials, space, and time. Renata, a 14-year old 8th grader, loved singing and music, but was not particularly found of computers. She also had a particular interest in religion. How does one integrate students' diverse and seemingly "unacademic" passions and interests into the workshop? How does one direct this powerful creative energy toward an educational goal?

One effective tool is Cavallo's applied epistemological anthropology, which consists in "unearthing the meaning learners attribute". In so doing, he states, it is essential that learners build objects of their own interest: the more freedom of expression students experience, the more faithful to their own constitution will the expression be, thus enabling a better design and implement of the learning environments (Cavallo, 2000a). Consequently, these seemingly unacademic passions are not impediments for student learning, but, conversely, wide-open windows into learners' epistemologies, and remarkable opportunities for engagement into 'academic' work, without having to recur to imposing schemes.

Outside of school, students develop talents, passions, ideas and different ways to learn. In a traditional, "single-medium" activity, very common in schools and after-school environments, Marisa and Gina would not have opportunities to engage their arts passion and would most likely disengage from the technology theme. Even more dangerously, we could observe a perverse "stratification" of group work: high-achieving students end up doing the more sophisticated work, and lower achieving students do the menial jobs (Abrahamson & Wilensky, 2005). Therefore, to embrace passion and epistemological pluralism (Turkle, 1991), the environment should offer multiple entry-points and expressive media (Blikstein, 2002). In such mixed-media[v] learning environments (Abrahamson, Blikstein, Lamberty, & Wilensky, 2005) more students are likely to find paths into personally meaningful engagement in group activities.

Consequently, getting to know the students outside of the classroom was all but fundamental. A few days into the workshop, after I perceived this to be a key to its success, I set up to interact with them as much as I could, in the same sense that, in a classical Freirean environment, a researcher should get to know the community's practices and values. We had lunch together several times, took field trips, discussed the projects, or just chatted before and after the workshop sessions. Within the context of the workshop, once students had initially committed themselves to some level of participation, I had some 'license' to contrive situations that were 'contextually authentic'. Departing from my knowledge of the students' interests, I tried to suggest these 'contextually authentic' situations for them to feel valuable to themselves and to the group, generating group and self-esteem.

Thus, my decision about Marisa and Gina was not to direct them immediately toward technological constructions. The two girls were not only allowed but also encouraged to work with art. They first painted a number of pictures that were hung on the lab's walls (see Figure 6). Then they began exploring clay and made small human figures and miniature furniture. Next, they built a cardboard house, painted its walls beautifully, and put all the furniture inside (Figure 6). The girls were extremely happy with their house, and so was everyone else. I still had a concern: their house had nothing technological: no robotics or programming. Those technologies, which could potentially open up many possibilities that conventional material do not allow, were entirely absent from the girls' project. I was tempted to suggest some ideas about how to integrate robotics into the house, but that was concerned lest such a suggestion would come across as a badly disguised imposition. Instead, I occasionally pointed students to other colleagues who were doing potentially synergic projects. There were potential complementarities "in the air," and I wanted students to learn to identify those.

When Marisa and Gina saw some friends using the digital camera to tell stories, they got excited about producing a claymation of the life inside their house. With some help from their friends, they learned how to use the digital camera and the computer software, and worked for hours on this new project.

Figure 6: Marisa poses beside her paintings on the wall (left) and the clay furniture of the toy-house's bedroom (right)

Concurrently, two eighth-graders, Ester and Maria, were searching for an idea for their first robotics projects. They had done some minor constructions, and therefore had some know-how, but were looking for a larger project. I suggested that they look around for ideas, talk to friends, and see what others were doing. Observing that Marisa and Gina had already completed a beautiful house, they asked them to team up to make it a "smart house." Using the robotics kit, for almost a week, the four girls added energy-saving lights, an automatic retractable roof and a temperature controlled ceiling fan for the hot summer days. The fruitful collaboration between the "architect-girls" and the "engineers-girls" is one example of the synergy generated in such environments.

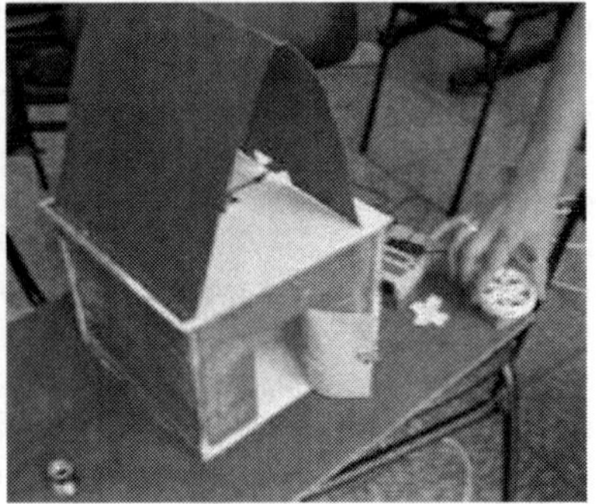

Figure 7 - Marisa and Gina proudly pose with their "low-tech" house (left), which was transformed by Ester and Maria into a smart, high-tech house (right).

Other students exhibited yet different interests and passions. Renata, the 8th grader who loved music and singing, did not know what to build at first. She would spend the day mostly alone, writing poetry. I suggested her to become the disk jockey of the workshop, selecting and playing different CDs everyday. After much resistance, she even agreed to sing for her friends. The shy and artistic Renata was starting to find her place. After a few days, and observing her friends' projects, she felt more secure and decided to build something more concrete. After long conversations with me, during which she revealed a deep religious belief, she decided to undertake the building of the Praying Tower, a complex moving Lego structure that would mimic the movement of the hands of devoted prayers.

Daniela, an 8th-grader, was very shy for the first two days. She would roam across the room observing the work of other groups, but never engaging for more than ten minutes. Realizing that she was not finding a suitable entry point, I suggested she take the video camera and make small TV reports about her colleagues' projects. After just two days in her new job, Daniela's command of the camera was impressive. After a while, though, being a cameraperson who documents other people's work, was not enough for Daniela. She began to plot more ambitious projects, and together with several other students wrote and directed two short documentaries: one about the life of the families who lived near an open-air sewage, and another about the local radio station.

Inspired by Daniela's successful documentary projects, other students, including Marisa and Gina (the "architects" of the smart house), became engrossed in the idea of producing fiction movies. Over the following four days, split into two groups, they wrote and produced two 5-minute movies: one medieval love story about an unhappy king's daughter and her forbidden love ("The Royal Family") and a "vendetta" story of a boyfriend who dared to date two best friends at the same time ("The Spanked Boyfriend").

Figure 8. Two moviemaking projects: students filming "The Royal Family" and producing a documentary about poor families who lived by the open-air sewage.

Yet another synergy involved the moviemaking crew: after a long filming day, these students presented their footage to the rest of the group. Moriz, who had remained at the school, working on his robotics project, saw the big pipes that carried the sewage (see Figure 8, lower right) and devised the idea of generating electrical energy from these currents, which could be used to light up the home. To explore his idea, Moriz built a model consisting of a small generator with a DC motor, plastic, cork, and wood. He attached this model to a capacitor and realized joyfully that the energy could be stored in it, and that, thus, his invention might in fact be viable. Caio, who had spent the previous day experimenting with energy-saving devices, solar panels and capacitors, was thrilled to help him (see Figure 9). Guilherme had yet another idea: to build a car that would automatically avoid flooded areas, which are very common during the rainy season.

Figure 9 - Caio researching solar energy and energy-saving devices, and Guilherme with his flood-safe car.

TEACHER'S INVOLVEMENT OR, "KIDS ARE JUST HAVING FUN."

A theme of our Heliopólis narrative has been that the prefabricated floundered, while the serendipitous prevailed. Our role as educators was not to enforce a precise implementation of a scripted design but to facilitate student interactions with each other and with the available resources and to proffer any counseling we could once students were engaged in their personal projects. Edith Ackermann would say that

> "...wherever 'diversity' reigns, centralized planning, or mere transmission of traditional values won't work. Instead, auto-determination and negotiation – i.e. self-expression and exchanges – are needed". (Ackermann, 2001)

Evidently, this type of approach diverges from the prevailing mindset in most schools, and indeed, this pedagogy generated anxious reactions from some local practitioners. In discussions with them, I identified a number of theories and mental models which blatantly conflicted with the workshop's approach: "You should focus on just one thing," "Children will break the equipment," "Without a specific plan, they will not do anything," "Some students were given the chance to participate and are not working the way we expected them to," and "Kids are just having fun". The epistemological status of the teachers' comments is revealing. It is not only compatible with the traditional school paradigm, but also with the way parents regard school. Cavallo reports that in Thailand parents complained about one workshop that he conducted, saying that the children were only having fun and thus could not possibly be learning (Cavallo, 2000b). The underlying theory of mind is apparently that "playing around" and learning are literally incommensurate. The epistemological belief of the teachers is that there must be concrete goals, plans to get there, and orderly sequences of knowledge construction. The 'conceptual building blocks theory' – that "you cannot learn 'x' without learning 'y' first" was prevalent – and probably reflects a pedagogical legacy of how these teachers were trained and learned what they know.

Despite their initial skepticism, most of those teachers were "converted" by the end of the workshops, particularly Sueli, a Portuguese teacher also responsible for the computer room. On the first days, she would go around inspecting the groups and (literally) pointing her finger at the "lazy" students who were "just going around taking pictures." Some students fought with each other, as a result of the tense climate that had been established by Sueli's behavior. I asked Sueli whether she would sit with students and try and help them in their projects. She told me she knew nothing about robotics and thus did not feel she could possibly be of any assistance. I insisted, and she accepted the challenge, temporarily relinquishing her "supervising" role. Because Sueli did not know anything about robotics, she indeed had to sit with students, but in the capacity of 'learner' rather than 'teacher.' Yet, as the environment and content were equally foreign to students and teacher, Sueli was not embarrassed to admit to students her ignorance on some technical issues. Being in such uncharted territory was a liberating experience for her. Free from the obligation of being the "sage on the stage" or the discipline enforcer, after seven days, Sueli was a different person, spending almost all of her time sitting on the floor helping (and being helped by) students. The computer lab was in complete chaos, with students, computers, cameras and scrap materials scattered all over it – another displacement in and of itself – and Sueli could not be happier.

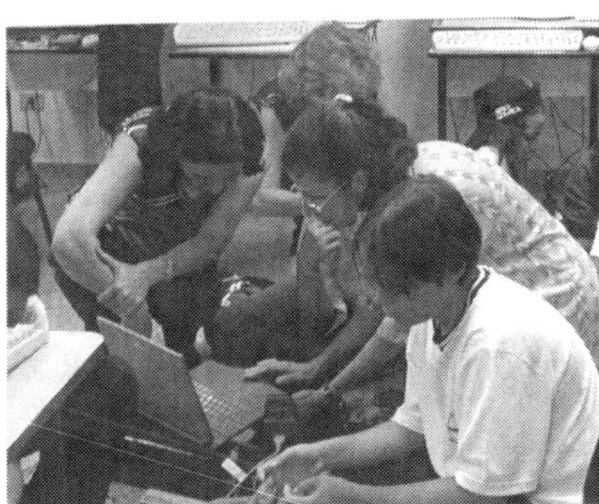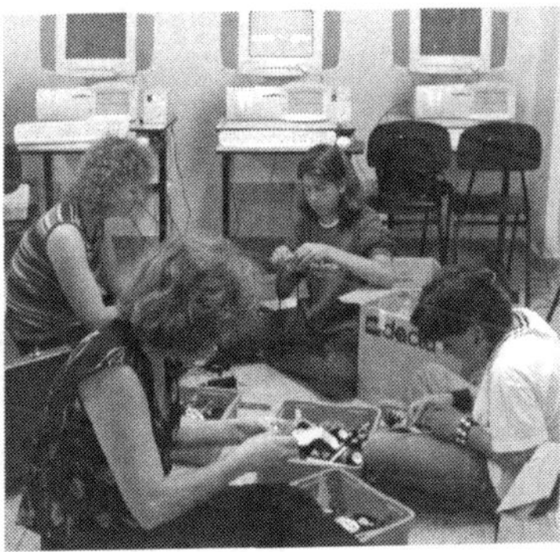

Figure 10 – Sueli (leftmost picture, wearing glasses) and other teachers sitting on the computer lab's floor, helping students in their projects.

Apparently, not only Sueli was pleased with this displacement. In a post-interview, a student of her reported:

> Last year, one boy was playing with a ball, his tennis shoe went off from his foot, and hit a bulb. Everyone that was around went to the Principal office. It was not fair. This time, when we blew the bulbs, the teacher helped us find other ones so that we could keep working.

But students themselves were initially anxious operating in an environment where they lacked precise directions. In their post-interviews, the majority mentioned "being lost" in the beginning:

Gina: In the beginning, I didn't know what to do. I saw a lot of things here, I didn't know where to start. Now, at the end, I have a lot of ideas, but I can't make anything anymore, because it's over… In the beginning I was lost, but then there was the idea of making the house, we put one little thing from here, one little thing from there… even on this last week we had things to do…

Maria: At first I thought I was not going to get familiar with all these instruments… It's so much stuff…. But then I began to like it, and I learned to use all of those things, the photo camera, everything… In the beginning I didn't know what this course was about, I didn't know what I was supposed to do, and then I began to let myself in it more and more… loosing up…

Marisa: In the beginning, I didn't know how to start. I have never worked with Lego, but then, me, Marcelo and Simone, we started to make things, learn, to learn new things…

From my observations and their testimonies, it was apparent that students went through a significant transformation, from being lost to gradually finding their way through the new materials, environment, and methods of working and collaborating. They had never touched a digital camera or built with Lego before, and most did not have a computer at home. Their testimonies do not suggest, as teachers had warned me, that the apparently free environment would generate an irresponsible and inconsequential spirit of childish mischievousness. The environment of the workshop did not inspire an "anything goes" attitude – students' transformation, as they reported, had occurred due to serious work and engagement in a project, and not due to random inconsequential explorations with cameras or Legos.

There were other kinds of transformations -- some very subtle, but no less revealing. Lucio was a relatively shy 7th grader. He built two robotics projects, participated in the documentary about the illegal energy connections and in a fiction movie. One day, he came to the workshop with his mother. He was wearing pleaded pants and a long-sleeve shirt, instead of his customary school uniform (see Figure 11). His mother asked to have a conversation with me – fortunately, she was not pulling him out of the workshop, on the contrary. She told me that her son had become extroverted lately, talking about his school activities, whereas previously he would never discuss school at home. Lucio had asked her to dress him up to come to the workshop, because "it was something very important."

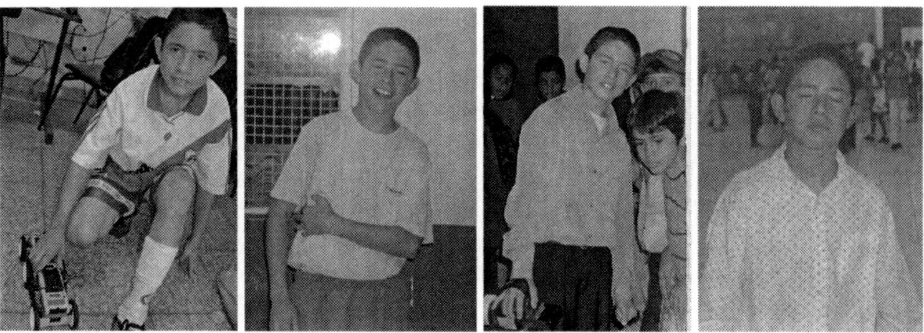

Figure 11 – Lucio before and after: school uniform and t-shirts on the first days (left), pants and shirts thereafter (right)

DISCUSSION

In the previous sections, I presented and discussed selected episodes from a workshop in a public school in São Paulo. Each of these episodes reveals a particular design dilemma that will be discussed in this section. My goal is to demonstrate that school-based implementations of Freirean pedagogy should be interpreted not as curiosities but as viable alternatives to prevalent pedagogy. These are truly enriching experiences, not 'enrichment classes.' School, I argue, could and should be a set of Freirean experiences.

Following, I summarize the main pedagogical strands exemplified in the data.

GENERATIVE THEMES

The choice of 'energy' as the theme at the Heliópolis workshop was an example of how authenticity of generative themes is crucial for the implementation of a Freirean pedagogy. Well-intentioned educators can often be wrong about what matters to a specific community. It is vital to avoid the typical trivialization of local culture, by the way of finding archetypical models and "design" curricula for them. Barbara Rogoff would call this a "boxed" view of culture, which "creates a reality based on these identity categories" (Rogoff, 2003, p.79). Hutchins (1995) argues against the view of culture as a collection of things, which can be listed by someone else, transferred, accumulated. Designers are liable to "box" culture largely because it is difficult to penetrate beneath manifestations of cultural practice. Therefore, building on a superficial view of local culture or introducing prefabricated themes cannot generate the authentic and engaging learning experience which Freire so fervently advocates. At the same time, neither is a blind adherence to the values and customs of the local culture beneficial—we should also identify what is not in the culture —which the educator wishes to introduce.

IS TECHNOLOGY JUST A 'TOOL'?

In the learning stories which I described in this chapter, digital technology was not just a 'tool', but an agent of fundamental displacement, for several reasons:
- 'Chameleonesque adaptivity', or the multiple forms of digital technology: this aspect of computational media enables the acknowledgement and embracing of epistemological diversity, engendering an environment in which students, finding their own voice, can concretize their ideas and projects with motivation and engagement. It enables new, complex, and diverse ways of learning and thinking, both on and off-screen, with familiar and unfamiliar materials, using high and low-tech tools.
- Novel tool for teachers and students: Being a novel artifact for both, technology enabled teachers to step down as the "sage on the stage" and become playful learners again. Students could see their teachers as learners, and learn from their learning strategies.
- Complex projects: Compared to conventional school materials, the projects undertook by students were generally more integrative, diverse, and complex. This complexity, in turn, opens up more possibilities for connection with traditional disciplines. For example, designing sensors or robotics' devices demands extensive research in Physics, Chemistry, and Mathematics.
- Mobility and decentralization: The presence of those technological objects and tools, inherently decentralized, mobile, and sharable, "created a new dynamic that is non-existent in regular classroom, where everything is symbolic, on paper, and there is no opportunity to develop democratic control" (Papert, 2002).
- Multiple entry-points: Technology provides powerful tools for self-expression and multiple entry-points for students with different backgrounds and interests. In an environment which embraced diverse forms of expression and technologies, students would first find themselves comfortable in one particular medium (arts, moviemaking, or robotics) and then transition to other, more challenging media or activities. The role of the facilitator as a matchmaker is critical, identifying potential synergies between projects or people.

Therefore, despite the customary rhetoric, the above list suggests that technology can indeed be a humanizing tool – Pierre Lévy states that "it is the intensive use of tools that constitutes humanity as it is" (Lévy, 1999). Having multiple technologies augments and makes possible inherently humanizing endeavors: creation, expression, and interaction.

MANAGING DIVERSITY

A learner-centered, culturally-aware Freirean aesthetic raises the question of how to manage a classroom in which every student has a different background, as well as diverse interests and talents. Ostensibly, this would entail a significant amount of extra work from the teacher. Our data suggest that such a diversity-sensitive approach may in fact help alleviate the teachers' burden and improve their relationship with students:

– Increasing returns: I have shown that, following an initially laborious and intensive contact with students, through which I became familiar with student ideas, ways of working, passions, and talents, subsequent interactions became much easier. Not only did students become more autonomous and responsible, they learned to teach one another. By allowing students to work on their own ideas, not only could I more effectively understand their epistemology, but unprecedented motivation and engagement were generated. This kind of environment also enables teachers to spend less time as discipline-enforcers.

– Student motivation and engagement: The observations suggest that the lack of strict rules did not generate an "anything goes" or unchallenging environment, in which students would have engaged in activities that are only playful or amusing. In Heliópolis and other workshops, on the contrary, teachers reported being impressed by the number of hours students invested and by students' serious attitude toward the work. In turn, students' reported that they were driven by teachers' 'fair play' and genuine respect.

CONTENT

Should we settle for indigenous local knowledge and deny students the formal knowledge of normative sciences? Aren't these sciences instruments of emancipation? The answer calls for a closer examination of the term "emancipation." Truly emancipatory knowledge has to empower people to forward their own (or their social group's) agendas. A mere internalization of the so called "language of power" (official school content) might give students more mileage in a standardized test or in the job market, but such 'banking' view of content would still be only indirectly connected to actions in these students' world. Consequently, knowledge has no intrinsic value beyond cultural capital, as Bourdieu already discussed in his reproduction theory (Bourdieu & Passeron, 1977). It is not what students are able to do with new knowledge that society typically values, but which social gates the knowledge enables one to cross. Consequently, learning can never be an enjoyable and personally fulfilling goal in and of itself. However, for those students in underprivileged areas in São Paulo, the gates are much less generous, if at all open, and the other side of the gate far more inclement than for middle-class children who, at least, have the prospects of high-paying jobs to retain them in the school system. Ironically, indigenous knowledge is not only valuable in and of itself (Morrow, 2005), but such knowledge can provide valuable avenues into scientific content and powerful ideas (Papert, 1980).

The workshops in São Paulo, indeed, foregrounded multiple links between traditional curriculum and the students' projects, many of which were inspired or guided by indigenous expertise. In order to build his water-avoiding car, Guilherme had to learn about electrical conductivity and even design an experiment with water and different concentrations of kitchen salt – thus reinventing chemistry lab experiments. One could easily imagine this experiment developing into a larger project in a Chemistry class. Caio had to learn about dynamos and capacitors to make his energy-generator for sewage pipes – another sets of topics that could be pursued later in a Physics class. The builders of a trash-recycling truck did extensive research on gearing, transmission, and linear-to-rotational movement conversion – the father of one of them was a car mechanic who was thrilled to help his son in a school project for the first time. Maria and Gina, to build the temperature-controlled fan for their energy-saving house, spent a long time analyzing how a fan generates wind, and how to optimize wind flow. A water-recycling project entailed visits to the local water facility, conversations with the Science teacher, as well as research in Chemistry and Physics. Also, their complex water-tight valves were a highly demanding engineering challenge. The groups that did documentaries, TV reports, and fiction movies had to write scripts, plan interviews, edit their narratives, and learn to express themselves in front of an audience. Within those spontaneous activities, there are endless opportunities to connect students with more traditional school content. If students enjoyed such opportunities along many years, they would eventually engage in most important parts of the traditional academic disciplines. In addition, the more students learn in this fashion, the more they learn about learning itself: students learning to learn is more generative that students only learning content.

CAN TEACHERS 'DO IT'?

The fieldwork suggests that the answer to this crucial question is a loud and clear 'yes'. I worked under inauspicious circumstances: the implementation team was small, most teachers had little or no technological training, most computer labs were not well supported, many materials were not translated into Portuguese, and in many schools basic equipment was lacking. Even under these adverse circumstances, teacher engagement was impressive. After the initial period of adaptation to the new environment, they let themselves become learners again, engaged playfully in projects together with students, and were enthusiastic leaders in subsequent implementations. The fundamental element, as we discussed in previous work (Blikstein, 2002; Cavallo et al., 2004), was to format the professional development of teachers according to the same principles which we wished for them to use with their own students: in our 'teacher training' workshops, practitioners also worked on projects and built working devices to address relevant issues in their community.

GOD IS IN THE DETAILS: IMPACTING THE ECOLOGY OF THE LEARNING ATMOSPHERE

An atmosphere is a useful analogy to reflect about the ecology of learning environments. First, an atmosphere can have micro and macro climates. Second, they emerge out of local interactions. Thirdly, the meta-stability of atmospheres implies that all equilibriums are fragile, and a small variation in one component can set off abrupt systemic change (Blikstein, 2002).

The learning environments described in this chapter, too, manifest a very delicate equilibrium. As scientists are succeeding to explain natural and social behaviors as emergent phenomena (Wilensky, 2001), they realize that the true wonders of nature are in the details - local interactions between discrete elements, fine-tuning, and often overlooked micro-relationships. Dramatic change happens in nature by changing those simple fundamental interactions. For example, in subsequent workshops, teachers tried to deny students the right to choose their projects and team mates, or restrained unilaterally access to equipment. Results were very negative – either students disconnected from the activity, or started to behave as they used to do in a regular class. I observed the same outcome when they tried to stimulate unnecessary competition, over-engineer teamwork, or over-plan activities: even with the same technological tools available, the fragile atmosphere of simultaneous hard work and engaged learning broke down.

I posit that whereas envisioning new pedagogies is about the art of thinking "big," implementing these pedagogies is a science of details. A Freirean pedagogy can only survive if it permeates the mundane. Grand discourses about emancipation are not enough. The most significant part of students' learning experiences resides in the small power struggles, the minute decisions, the microscopic choices of what to teach and what to value, who has voice, who ultimately decides. It is precisely in those apparently insignificant pedagogical and personal transactions that the essence of the atmosphere is constructed.

In this section, I discussed a number of examples of such hidden elements and how they dramatically affect the learning atmosphere. Yet how can my narrative of a specific classroom with specific students possibly be useful to practitioners in their own classrooms? First, it contains examples and design decisions of very typical situations found in 'unscripted' learning environments. Second, this design calls for a more adaptative and flexible approach, in which teachers use their authority to establish democratic rules, and subsequently fade their role as a rule enforcer. Teachers, thus, create a generative space.

CONCLUSION[vi]

This chapter is about expressive technologies for emancipation. I have shown Freirean emancipation is possible, even in schools with scarce resources, but by no means easy. The emergent characteristics of such designs (Cavallo, 2000b) sets these learning environments apart from traditional schooling, and calls for a significant change in teacher education.

Technology is a new kind of Trojan Horse: the educator introduces into the classroom familiar tools, practices and technologies, yet embedded in this familiarity is a potential for affective and conceptual change – a beneficial potential that surreptitiously permeates the classroom atmosphere through a sequence of displacements mediated by the experienced teacher. Students appropriate the Trojan technology as authentic means to liberate themselves from the incarceration of traditional pedagogy. Once deschooled, students shake off the dust and engage in authentic inquiry and construction.

FINAL REMARKS

Paulo Freire frequently referred to himself as the "itinerant of the obvious" (andarilho do óbvio). It might appear peculiar that an educational intervention in a poor fishermen community in a secluded part of Brazil could be so influential to educators all over the world. Almost 50 years later, after television, computers, internet and nanotechnology, here we are, still talking about Angicos.

ACKNOWLEDGEMENTS

First and foremost, I would like to thank all the students, teachers and staff at the Campos Salles school in Heliópolis.

For their support, my thanks to Prof. Roseli de Deus Lopes and her students at the University of São Paulo (especially Alexandra Camargo Alves and Irene Karaguilla Ficheman); Rodrigo Lara Mesquita and his team (Radium Systems/Agência Estado), Arnan Sipitakiat, Prof. Edith Ackermann, Alice Cavallo, Anindita Basu and Jacqueline Karaaslanian (MIT Media Lab), Fernando José de Almeida and his team at the Municipal Secretariat of Education of São Paulo; Ana Maria Albuquerque (for her help during the whole workshop), Adriana Maricato (for coordinating the moviemaking activities), and Flávia Blikstein (for her help during the workshop). Special thanks to my former advisor Dr. David Cavallo (MIT Media Lab), my advisor Prof. Uri Wilensky (Northwestern University), Benjamin Shapiro (Northwestern University) for his reviewing work, and in particular, for his ideas, suggestions, and extensive reviewing work, Prof. Dor Abrahamson (UC Berkeley).

NOTES

[i]   This chapter builds on and further extends my Masters' thesis at the Media Laboratory of the Massachusetts Institute of Technology (MIT), under the supervision of Dr. David Cavallo. More information is available at http://www.blikstein.com/paulo or paulo@blikstein.com.

[ii]   Freire defines humanization as the process of *authentic liberation*, "people's ontological vocation", or becoming more fully human, struggling against oppressive manipulation and control (Freire, 1974)

[iii]   This project, called "The City That We Want", was coordinated by my former advisor, Dr. David Cavallo, and had the collaboration of many partners, such as Profa. Dra. Roseli de Deus Lopes and her team from the University of São Paulo, Rodrigo Lara Mesquita at the Agência Estado, as well as Edith Ackermann, Arnan Sipitakiat and Anindita Basu from the MIT Media Lab.

[iv]   For anonymity, all the names of the children were changed.

[v]   The term 'mixed media' is distinct from 'multimedia,' which has come to mean audiovisual artifacts, such as presentations, interactive CD-ROMs, or websites that are prepared with dedicated computer applications.

[vi]   After Heliópolis, under the direction of Dr. David Cavallo, "The City That We Want" project was extended to 30 schools in 2002 and 2003, reaching more than 3000 students. After 2004, Prof. Renata de Deus Lopes from the University of São Paulo received government funding for another 150 schools. Simultaneously, a non-profit educational foundation (Fundação Bradesco) took the project to its 39 school throughout Brazil.

REFERENCES

Abrahamson, D., Berland, M., Shapiro, B., Unterman, J., & Wilensky, U. (2006). Collaborative Interpretive Argumentation as a Phenomenological-Mathematical Negotiation: A Case of Statistical Analysis of a Computer Simulation of Complex Probability. *For the Learning of Mathematics, 26*(3).

Abrahamson, D., Blikstein, P., Lamberty, K. K., & Wilensky, U. (2005). *Mixed-media learning environments.* In M. Eisenberg & A. Eisenberg (Eds.), *Proceedings of the Fourth International Conference for Interaction Design and Children (IDC 2005).* Boulder, USA.

Abrahamson, D., & Wilensky, U. (2005). *The stratified learning zone: Examining collaborative-learning design in demographically-diverse mathematics classrooms.* In D. Y. White (Chair) & E. H. Gutstein (Discussant), *Equity and diversity studies in mathematics learning and instruction.* Paper presented at the annual meeting of the American Educational Research Association, Montreal, Canada.

Ackermann, E. (2001). Piaget's Constructivism, Papert's Constructionism: What's the difference? Retrieved from http://learning.media.mit.edu/content/publications/EA.Piaget%20_%20Papert.pdf

Almeida, F. J. (1998). Appearances are misleading (As aparências enganam). SEED, pp.73-80, Brasília, Brazil.

Berland, M., & Wilensky, U. (2006). *Constructionist collaborative engineering: Results from an implementation of PVBOT.* Paper presented at the annual meeting of the American Educational Research Association, San Francisco.

Blikstein, P. (2002). *The Trojan Horse as a Trojan Horse: impacting the ecology of the Learning Atmosphere.* Unpublished Masters Thesis, Massachusetts Institute of Technology, Cambridge, USA.

Blikstein, P., & Wilensky, U. (2006). *The Missing Link: A Case Study of Sensing-and-Modeling Toolkits for Constructionist Scientific Investigation.* Proceedings of the Sixth IEEE International Conference on Advanced Learning Technologies (ICALT 2006), Kerkrade, The Netherlands, pp. 980-982.

Bourdieu, P., & Passeron, J. C. (1977). *Reproduction in education, society and culture.* London ; Beverly Hills: Sage Publications.

Buechley, L. (2006). *A Construction Kit for Electronic Textiles.* Paper presented at the IEEE International Symposium on Wearable Computers (ISWC), Montreux, Switzerland.

Cavallo, A. M. (2003). *An investigation into ways that cultural gender roles interfere with the learning of science and engineering.* Paper presented at Eurologo 2003, Porto, Portugal

Cavallo, D. (2000a). Emergent Design and learning environments: Building on indigenous knowledge. *IBM System Journal, 39*(3&4), 768-781.

Cavallo, D. (2000b). Technological Fluency and the Art of Motorcycle Maintenance: Emergent design of learning environments. Unpublished PhD. dissertation. Massachusetts Institute of Technology, Cambridge, USA.

Cavallo, D. (2002). Personal Communication. São Paulo, Brazil.

Cavallo, D., Blikstein, P., Sipitakiat, A., Basu, A., Camargo, A., Lopes, R. D., et al. (2004). *The City that We Want: Generative Themes, Constructionist Technologies and School/Social Change.* Paper presented at the International Workshop on Technology for Education in Developing Countries, Joensuu, Finland.

Cukier, J. (1996). A educação escolar: agente de mudança psíquica positiva ou agente didaticopatogenizante? In N. M. C. Pellanda (Ed.), *Psicanálise hoje: uma revolução do olhar* (pp. 247-284). São Paulo: Vozes.

Edelson, D. (2000). My World GIS. Evanston, USA: PASCO Scientific.

Foucault, M. (1977). *Discipline and punish: the birth of the prison* (1st American ed.). New York: Pantheon Books.

Freire, A. M. (1995). A voz da esposa - A trajetória de Paulo Freire [The Spouse's voice - Paulo Freire's trajectory]. Retrieved 1st September 2005, from http://www.paulofreire.org/esposa.htm

Freire, P. (1973). *Education for critical consciousness* (1st American ed.). New York: Herder and Herder.

Freire, P. (1974). *Pedagogy of the oppressed*. New York: Seabury Press.

Freire, P. (1987). *A Pedagogy for Liberation*. New York: Bergin and Garvey.

Freire, P. (1990). Interview to Carlos Alberto Torres. Retrieved Sept 1st 2005, from http://aurora.icaap.org/talks/freire.html

Freire, P. (1992). *Pedagogia da esperança : um reencontro com a Pedagogia do Oprimido*. São Paulo: Paz e Terra.

Freire, P. (1993). *Pedagogy of the city*. New York: Continuum.

Freire, P. (1998). *Teachers as cultural workers : letters to those who dare teach*. Boulder: Westview Press.

Freire, P. (2001). *The pedagogy of the possible dreams*. São Paulo: UNESP.

Freire, P., & Macedo, D. P. (1996). *Letters to Cristina : reflections on my life and work*. New York: Routledge.

García, S. P. (2001). *Paulo Freire: Educación e Ideologia* (1st ed.). Mexico City: Toma y Lee Editorial.

Gerhardt, H.-P. (2000). Paulo Freire: arqueologia de um pensamento (Paulo Freire: archeology of an idea). Retrieved Sept 1st 2005, from http://www.ppbr.com/ipf/bio/europeia.html

Gibson, R. (1994). *The Promethean Literacy: Paulo Freire's Pedagogy of Reading, Praxis and Liberation*. Unpublished PhD. dissertation, Pennsylvania State University, University Park, USA.

Hutchins, E. (1995). *Cognition in the wild* (2nd ed.). Cambridge: MIT Press.

Illich, I. (1971). *Deschooling society* (1st ed.). New York: Harper & Row.

Ladson-Billings, G. (1995). Toward a theory of culturally relevant pedagogy. *American Education Research Journal, 35*, 465 – 491.

Lee, C. D. (2003). Literacy, Technology and Culture. In G. Hatano & X. Lin (Eds.), *Technology, Culture and Education, Special Issue of Mind, Culture and Activity*.

Lévy, P. (1999). *Cibercultura*. São Paulo: Editora 34.

Martin, F., Resnick, M. (1993). Lego/Logo and electronic bricks: Creating a scienceland for children. In D. L. Ferguson (Ed.), *Advanced educational technologies for mathematics and science*. Berlin, Heidelberg: Springer-Verlag.

Millner, A., & Resnick, M. (2005). *Tools for Creating Custom Physical Computer Interfaces*. Paper presented at the Interaction Design for Children Conference (IDC 2005).

Moll, L. C., Amanti, C., Neff, D., & González, N. (1992). Funds of knowledge for teaching: Using a qualitative approach to connect homes and classrooms. *Theory into Practice, 31*(2), 132-141.

Morrow, R. A. (in press). Paulo Freire, Indigenous Knowledge and Eurocentric Critiques of Development. In C. A. Torres & Noguera, P. (Eds.), *Paulo Freire: Education and the Possible Dream*.

Papert, S. (1980). *Mindstorms : children, computers, and powerful ideas*. New York: Basic Books.

Papert, S. (1985). Computer Criticism vs. Technocentric Thinking. *MIT Logo 85 Theoretical Papers*, 22-30.

Papert, S. (1991). Situating Constructionism. In S. Papert & I. Harel (Eds.), *Constructionism*. Cambridge, MA: MIT Press.

Papert, S. (1993). *The children's machine: rethinking school in the age of the computer*. New York: BasicBooks.

Papert, S. (2002). Personal Communication, Cambridge, USA.

Resnick, M., Ocko, S., Papert, S. (1991). Lego/Logo: Learning through and about design. In I. Harel, Papert, S. (Ed.), *Constructionism*. Norwood: Ablex.

Rogoff, B. (2003). *The cultural nature of human development*. New York: Oxford University Press.

Sipitakiat, A., Blikstein, P., & Cavallo, D. P. (2004). *GoGo Board: Augmenting Programmable Bricks for Economically Challenged Audiences*. Paper presented at the International Conference of the Learning Sciences, Los Angeles, USA.

Sylvan, E. (2005). *Integrating Aesthetic, Engineering, and Scientific Understanding in a Hands-on Design Activity*. Paper presented at the Interaction Design for Children Conference (IDC 2005), Boulder, USA.

Turkle, S., Papert, S. (1991). Epistemological Pluralism and Revaluation of the Concrete. In I. Harel & S. Papert (Eds.), *Constructionism* (pp. 161-192). Norwood: Ablex Publishing Co.

Tyack, D., & Cuban, L. (1995). *Tinkering towards utopia: a century of public school reform* (7th ed.). Cambridge: Harvard University Press.

Valente, J. A. (1993). Por quê o computador na educação. In J. A. Valente (Ed.), *Computadores e Conhecimento: Repensando a Educação* (pp. 24-44). Campinas: Unicamp.

Wilensky, U. (2001). *Modeling Nature's Emergent Patterns with Multi-Agent Languages*. Paper presented at Eurologo 2001, Linz, Austria.

Wilensky, U., & Resnick, M. (1995). *New Thinking for New Sciences: Constructionist Approaches for Exploring Complexity*. Paper presented at the Presented at the annual conference of the American Educational Research Association, San Francisco, USA.

Wilensky, U., & Resnick, M. (1999). Thinking in levels: A dynamic systems approach to making sense of the world. *Journal of Science Education and Technology, 8*(1), 3-18.

Wilensky, U., & Stroup, W. (1999). *Learning Through Participatory Simulations: Network-Based Design for Systems Learning in Classrooms*. Paper presented at the Computer Supported Collaborative Learning Conference (CSCL 1999), Palo Alto, USA.

Zoch, P. (2004). *Doomed to fail: The Built-In Defects of American Education*. Chicago: National Book Network.